Refugees and forced displacement

Refugees and forced displacement: International security, human vulnerability, and the state

Edward Newman and Joanne van Selm, editors

United Nations University Press

TOKYO · NEW YORK · PARIS

United Nations University Press
The United Nations University, 53-70, Jingumae 5-chome,
Shibuya-ku, Tokyo 150-8925, Japan
Tel: +81-3-3499-2811   Fax: +81-3-3406-7345
E-mail: sales@hq.unu.edu (general enquiries): press@hq.unu.edu
http://www.unu.edu

United Nations University Office in North America
2 United Nations Plaza, Room DC2-2062, New York, NY 10017, USA
Tel: +1-212-963-6387   Fax: +1-212-371-9454
E-mail: unuona@ony.unu.edu

United Nations University Press is the publishing division of the United Nations University.

Cover design by Joyce C. Weston
Cover art "Refuge" by Debra Clem

Printed in Hong Kong

UNUP-1086
ISBN 92-808-1086-3

Library of Congress Cataloging-in-Publication Data

Refugees and forced displacement : international security, human vulnerability, and the state / Edward Newman and Joanne van Selm, editors.
    p. cm.
Includes bibliographical references and index.
   ISBN 92-808-1086-3
   1. Refugees. 2. Forced migration. 3. Security, International. 4. Refugees—Legal status, laws, etc. I. Newman, Edward, 1970– II. Selm, Joanne van.
JV6346.R4 R45 2003
341.4′86—dc21   2003006856

Contents

Foreword

A multitude of internal conflicts and resulting massive human displacement brought the linkages between international and national security and refugee protection to the foreground once again in the 1990s. This turbulent decade was reminiscent of the inter-war period, which, amongst other things, led to the establishment of the first UN High Commissioner for Refugees (UNHCR). Immediately after the Second World War, the protection and solutions for millions of displaced people necessitated another paradigm shift, namely the creation of an international and global refugee regime at whose centre are the 1951 Convention Relating to the Status of Refugees and its 1967 Protocol. The UNHCR has been given the task of upholding this refugee regime. The past decade brought forward the need for another paradigm shift in order to prevent and respond effectively to the multitude of internal conflicts as well as to the new types of threats emanating from the realities of a globalizing world. This time around, a shift is required in our understanding of security.

Increasingly, emphasis is placed on the primary responsibility of states to protect their nationals as the fundamental and ultimate function of sovereignty. State security should no longer be narrowly interpreted in terms of protecting territory against external threats, but must also include the protection of citizens. The focus should, therefore, be on ensuring the safety of people, or human security. As events since 11 September 2001 have demonstrated, the fight against terrorism requires a strong sense of national security, but this should be complemented by human security. Protection against critical and pervasive threats is at the centre of human security and should be linked to a strategy that empowers people. In many respects, the protection and empowerment of people are mutually reinforcing strategies. Security should also be interpreted in a broad sense. It is not limited to protection against war, conflict, or serious human rights violations, but also extends to protection from serious economic deprivation. Without access to adequate food, shelter, health, and other necessities, the value of legal protection is limited, and vice versa.

This book puts forward a broader understanding of national security and makes an important contribution towards understanding and addressing forced displacement in a comprehensive manner. The discussions are provocative and some authors draw attention to the potential weaknesses of the human security approach. This debate is important as there appears to be consensus that a reappraisal of the current refugee regime is needed in order to deal effectively with the nexus between displacement and security and between displacement and development, and with external and internal movements of people. For too long the study of refugee issues has been seen as an isolated and often secondary challenge. It should now be analysed within a much broader context, with the needs and rights of people at the centre rather than on the periphery. This book represents a substantial input into this developing debate.

Sadako Ogata
United Nations High Commissioner for Refugees, 1991–2000

Part I

Political, security, and normative perspectives

1

Refugees, international security, and human vulnerability: Introduction and survey

Edward Newman

Your humanitarian work is used, or rather abused, as a substitute for political action to address the root causes of mass displacement. You have become part of a "containment strategy", by which this world's more fortunate and powerful countries seek to keep the problems of the poorer at arm's length. How else can one explain the disparity between the relatively generous funding for relief efforts in countries close to the frontiers of the prosperous world, and the much more parsimonious effort made for those who suffer in remoter parts of the world such as Asia or Africa? And how else can one explain the contrast between the generosity which poor countries are expected to show, when hundreds of thousands of refugees pour across their frontiers, and the precautions taken to ensure that as few asylum seekers as possible ever reach the shores of rich countries?[1]

Refugees, human displacement, and international politics

Migration, whether voluntary or forced, has always been a characteristic of individual and collective human behaviour. Refugee flows and human displacement have, *ad infinitum*, been a feature, and consequence, of conflict within and between societies. It is questionable whether there have been qualitative changes in patterns of forced displacement over the past century despite the popular perception of refugee flows and human displacement as phenomena that have seen marked upturns in recent years. Nevertheless, one key change in the twentieth century was the move by governments towards regulating migration, in particular immigration, and towards defining those who were to be granted the special status of refugees. This change is fundamentally linked to the subject of this volume: the question of how governments regulate immigration and define categories of immigrants has, over time, led people to view migration as an issue related to the security both of the state and of existing citizens and legal residents. Simultaneously, there has been an evolution of security analysis that can shed new light and renewed attention upon the importance of refugees and human displacement in international relations and security. There have also been changes in the nature of the state, in socio-economic organization within states and at the international level, and in demography that indicate particular patterns – or at least explanations – of contemporary forced migration. This volume examines the phenomena of refugees and human displacement in the context of these background themes, which can be classified broadly as socio-economic and conflict related.

In terms of socio-economic factors, the explanatory variables of migration are well known. The international economic environment is broadly characterized by globalization and neo-liberal orthodoxy. Many scholars have asserted that changes in economic organization and the reduction of state capacity have contributed to poverty and inequality, and that this is an underlying explanatory cause of migration.[2] In the developing world, traditional social support mechanisms have been eroded by the modernization of economic production. In many societies, localized high population density, in conjunction with environmental degradation and resource shortages, has rendered areas untenable for human support. Urbanization, coupled with changes in social and economic organization that have reduced the viability of rural lifestyles, has encouraged the movement of people into unsustainable urban lifestyles. All have been offered as underlying explanations for migration, sometimes with a linear increase – increases of inequality and poverty in the world directly relating to the numbers of people seeking more prosperous and stable lives in other countries. More visibly and more demonstrably, violent conflict and persecution are key explanatory variables for refugee flows and displacement within and across borders.[3] Ethnic and civil conflict, state building, state collapse and failure, and government persecution are all inherently violent and lead directly to mass forced migration.

The broader context for migration flows is often identified as being a consequence of globalization, technological progress, and interdependence: easier and cheaper transportation across greater distances, a greater awareness of better opportunities "elsewhere," a reduction of physical boundaries to movement in some regions of the world.

All of these factors help to explain refugee flows, displacement, and migration (both forced and voluntary). However, this volume is not premised upon the idea of a fundamentally changed environment or unique modern conditions that have brought about qualitatively new patterns of migration. We do not primarily seek to explain why, where, or how refugee flows or displacements occur; we rather address the nexus between security concerns and migratory flows in looking at how societies do and could deal with the consequences of migration. In doing so, we find that the legal, political/normative, institutional, and conceptual frameworks through which the international community addresses refugee and displacement issues are inadequate in the context of contemporary conflict and international relations.

The starting point for this is based upon the following propositions:

1. Refugees are in various contexts both a cause and a consequence of conflict. As such, the management of refugee movements and the protection of displaced people should be an integral – not peripheral – part of conflict settlement and peace-building within communities and an integral element of regional security. Human displacement itself is a major factor in national and international instability, requiring policy responses that recognize this and a model of security that is broad and multifaceted. Many conflicts have involved the displacement of population groups as a motive and weapon of conflict. Refugee flows and displacement are in turn central to "post-conflict" reconstruction and peace-building. In Bosnia–Herzegovina, Georgia (Abkhazia), Angola, Rwanda, Congo, Palestine/Israel, and numerous other places in the world, displaced populations have been the critical element in continuing conflict and instability, the obstruction of peace processes, and the undermining of attempts at economic development. Refugee flows are demonstrably a source of international – mainly regional – conflict through causing instability in neighbouring countries, triggering intervention, and sometimes providing a basis for warrior refugee communities within camps that can form the source of insurgency, resistance, and terrorist movements.

2. International legal instruments do not perfectly reflect the contemporary reality of displacement or of protection and asylum needs. However, the tools of protection established in these legal instruments are not as deficient as their application by contemporary governments leads one to believe. When the existing international refugee regimes were established, the political images of refugees and asylum needs – and obligations – were quite different from those of today. The global refugee regime – based on the Convention Relating to the Status of Refugees of 1951 and its 1967 Protocol, and the Office of the UN High Commissioner for Refugees (UNHCR) – was initially a temporary arrangement established in a Cold War context that centred on a Western concern to assist people seeking refuge from communist

countries.[4] Although the regime has displayed an admirable adaptation to evolving demands, expanding its remit temporally and spatially, it operates under great practical, conceptual, and legal strain. The definition of a refugee is a person who, "owing to well-founded fear of being persecuted for reasons of race, religion, nationality, membership in a particular social group, or political opinion, is outside the country of his nationality [or of habitual residence], and is unable to or, owing to such fear, is unwilling to avail himself of the protection of that country" (1951 Convention Relating to the Status of Refugees, Article 1(2)). Mass displacement owing to generalized violence and conflict or civil war, or war-related conditions such as famine and homelessness, has strained the application of this definition. So has the visibility in developed countries of people not ideologically or racially welcome. Economic migrants further blur the definitions; there are often not clear distinctions. The legal rights of refugees – as refugees and also as humans with human rights – are often demonstrably unfulfilled or violated. Other times these rights are unclear or not defined. There are significant discrepancies in terms of the granting of asylum, international protection, and assistance in different regions and in the conditions for refugees and displaced populations. Opportunities and assistance to refugees and displaced people are in large part a reflection of politics, geostrategic interests, and fickle international donor and media priorities.

3. The refugee definition cited above includes an important criterion that excludes a great many of the world's displaced persons. In order to fall within the realm of the protection of the international refugee regime, such persons must have crossed the border of their country of nationality or habitual residence and be in another country. On some occasions, the United Nations has designated UNHCR or another UN agency to lead efforts to offer assistance to internally displaced persons (IDPs). On rare occasions, the international community has intervened militarily or politically in a civil war situation on behalf of IDPs. For the most part, however, the principle of state sovereignty, which requires the consent of the state involved to any assistance for its own displaced citizens, has prevented these people from either receiving aid or being granted adequate protection. Progress has certainly been made in recent years, but this remains a glaring problem in the face of human suffering. Indeed, in the security discourse, internally displaced people often represent the starkest example of a tension between human security and legal and political constructions such as state sovereignty.

4. The institution of asylum is under grave threat. Many politicians governing states see refugees and asylum seekers in negative terms, as

a threat to social cohesion or employment, or even as posing a threat of insurgency and terrorism. Since the terrorist attacks against the United States on 11 September 2001, this latter concern has been exacerbated. In both developing and developed countries, governments have for some time been constructing legal and physical barriers against the influx of asylum seekers or those displaced by war. "Safe countries" of origin, whose citizens are in effect precluded from asylum, visa regulations, carrier sanctions, shifting the burden of assessing and processing claims to adjoining territories, physical closing of borders, detention of asylum seekers, and withdrawal of welfare support have all been employed to interdict and deter asylum seekers.[5] The image of economic migrants and "bogus asylum seekers" overwhelming Western societies is a regular characteristic of media reporting on refugee issues and political debate. The reality is that developing countries shoulder the social and economic strain of the vast majority of asylum seekers and people displaced through conflict and state failure. This imbalance must be recognized and acknowledged. In the developed and developing world alike, the reality is that violations of international refugee and human rights law occur on a vast scale. There has been a "shift from the protection *of* asylum seekers to protection *from* them."[6] Some commentators and politicians have hinted that the 1951 Convention was a "Cold War" document that is not appropriate for the contemporary era.

5. The orthodox definition of international security – premised on the military defence of territory – puts human displacement and refugees at the periphery of politics. This is wrong for two reasons. First, as this volume will demonstrate, human displacement is both a cause and a consequence of conflict within and between societies. Second, normative and political developments in the post–Cold War world have reached a point where international security no longer automatically or solely privileges the state above all other agents as the referent object of security. At the turn of the century, individuals and communities are increasingly central in security thinking – legally, ethically, and politically. "Human security" is a key component of this evolving security discourse. It is a normative, ethical movement and it also rests on self-interested empirical reasoning. It is normative in the sense that it argues that there is an ethical responsibility to reorient security around the individual in a redistributive sense, in the context of changes in political community and the emergence of transnational norms relating to human rights. Those who have the capacity to extend security to people perilously lacking it have a basic human obligation to do so. Human security also rests upon empirical reasoning regarding the foundations of stability within and between states.

Attitudes and institutions that privilege "high politics" above disease, human rights, hunger, or illiteracy are embedded in international relations and foreign policy decision-making. This is not to presume that human security is necessarily in conflict with state sovereignty; the state, as an aggregation of capacity and resources, remains the central provider of security in ideal circumstances. It does, however, suggest that international security traditionally defined – territorial integrity – does not necessarily correlate with human security, and that an overemphasis upon statist security can be to the detriment of human welfare needs. Traditional conceptions of state security are a necessary but not sufficient condition of human welfare. The citizens of states that are "secure" according to the traditional concept of security can be perilously insecure to a degree that demands a reappraisal of the concept. Human security is a reorientation to redress this asymmetry of attention.[7] Human security therefore regards human displacement as a pressing issue not only because it has repercussions on other essential constructions – such as state borders and economic development – but because individuals and people collectively have rights that must be upheld even when they do not fit squarely with the "high politics" agenda of conventional international security.

6. Much of the discussion relating to human displacement and refugees is on a policy level, drawing upon security studies, international law, and international relations theory. Most of this analysis is aimed at addressing the challenges in the context of existing processes, institutions, and vocabularies.[8] However, there may be a need to step outside or challenge the existing rules of the game if that is what is necessary to realize that refugees have the same rights as anyone else and need to be centralized in international security policy. The normative and ethical framework for analysing the refugee debate must be examined anew. Many of the "givens" – constructions such as state sovereignty, international security, citizenship, identity, and international law – may require a fundamental reappraisal. Normative moral theory allows such a questioning. It brings into question all of our assumptions regarding "security": it questions what should be the focus of security, both within societies and internationally; it challenges the distinction between "high" and "low" politics, and the privileging of the former at the expense of the latter, especially in the context of the prevailing "national security" paradigm; it questions the institutions and policies with which we invest our security; it questions the idea that people living within different political communities are not entitled to the same rights and opportunities as we are.[9]

7. The distinction between different types of migrants – including asylum seekers, economic migrants, and those displaced by war and in need of

temporary protection – is often clearer in theory than in reality. The blurring of the distinction in legal, political, and semantic terms works against the rights of asylum seekers and displaced people, and is being exploited by actors who prefer more restrictive policies. Definitions, norms, and terminologies require careful, positive reassessment.

8. The normative framework within which we consider our moral obligations regarding refugees, displacement, and asylum must be reappraised in the context of solidarist ideas of global community and human security. In a sense this owes a lot to the liberal and cosmopolitan traditions of political thought. Thus, in recent years the individual has been accorded greater prominence in international governance and codes of conduct. This is reflected in the emergence of norms and institutions, in both a regional and global context, that embrace issues ranging from development, criminal and humanitarian law, human rights, humanitarian intervention, economics, to democracy. Yet the exclusionary institution of sovereignty is still paramount. And in political discourse the notion of "insiders" and "outsiders" is still the underlying assumption. In the interplay of liberal and statist thought, there are obvious tensions and contradictions that need to be deconstructed and worked out. In most countries, solidarist sentiment in the face of deprivation and grave human suffering is an established part of political and public discourse. Yet restrictive policies are increasingly a part of Western national and international policy and legal infrastructure. Why is there such a mismatch between solidarist human sentiment and legal/political institutions?

9. Many of the challenges from refugees, and the challenges posed by societies and governments to refugee protection, have been exacerbated by the events of 11 September 2001. This has taken a number of forms. First, the terrorist attacks and the ensuing "war on terror" reinforced our understanding of the connections between human displacement and international security. It became clear that the origins of the unchecked fundamentalist Taliban, and their links to al-Qaida, lay in the long-term refugee camps of Pakistan.[10] Dispossessed, aggrieved, and rootless populations are a potential breeding ground for radical political movements and terrorism inside and across borders. "Permanent" refugee camps can give rise to enmity among the displaced and provide a source of insurgency and instability elsewhere, especially when those people, often not receiving the attention of a government or international organization, are preyed upon by people with evil intent and the means to sway followers and carry out their destructive plans. Second, the terrorist attacks have accelerated the move towards more restrictive asylum and refugee policies. After the terrorist attacks, refugee movements and asylum seekers

have been regarded by some with a heightened wariness as sources of instability and even potential sources of terrorism. Despite the empirical weakness of any claimed connection between asylum and terrorism, this perspective has provided a pretext for some political leaders (especially of the right) to exploit the "threat" of terrorism for political gains and further tighten asylum policies. In the United States, the most affected immigrant group in terms of admissions policies has been resettled refugees. The refugee admission quota was set at a ceiling of 70,000 for 2002. Only some 30,000 were admitted as the programme stalled with new security controls in place, both in verifying the identity of refugees and in terms of permissions for officers of the Immigration and Naturalization Service to travel in order to carry out status determination procedures. Although concerns have arisen about the possibility that terrorists could enter Western states disguised as asylum seekers, little has been done to establish greater controls over other immigrant groups, including foreign students (although that was the immigration category most used by the September the 11th hijackers). In other words, the most vulnerable group – refugees – have been the target of the greatest number of new controls, although they were already the most scrutinized arrivals.

UNHCR, the European Commission, and others have pointed out that the concern that terrorists will use the asylum channel is unfounded for a number of reasons. As the Commission has noted, the stringent procedures that accompany the process of applying for asylum in European states (as well as in the United States, Canada, Australia, and other states) mean that a terrorist would not find that route palatable. Secondly, the 1951 Convention contains clauses that exclude certain individuals from refugee status. These include people about whom there is "serious reason for considering that" they have committed crimes against humanity, serious non-political crimes, and crimes against the principles of the United Nations (Article 1F). What is lacking is a genuine commitment by states to apply these clauses seriously and appropriately and to develop the ways and means to deal with those individuals who are excluded from refugee status but who cannot be returned to their country of origin because they would be in danger there (their return would then constitute *refoulement*) and who may even not be admissible for trial in the country that has rejected their asylum claim.[11]

Connected with this, the prominence of terrorism in the security mindset of many governments is resulting in an increased tendency to "profile" immigrants, naturalized citizens, asylum seekers, and refugees, thus increasing the implicit discrimination and explicit exclusion that have characterized asylum policies since the end of the Cold War.

People of Arab origin and Muslims are particularly vulnerable to discrimination. There have been concerns that anti-terrorist and security legislation privileges anti-terrorist concerns over the rights of genuine asylum seekers. UNHCR has expressed concern that "bona-fide asylum seekers may be victimized as a result of public prejudice and unduly restrictive legislation or administrative measures."[12] The UNHCR's concerns cover racism and xenophobia; the tendency to link asylum seekers and refugees to crime and terrorism; restricted admission and access to refugee status determination; exclusion based on religion, ethnicity, nationality, or political affiliation; deteriorating treatment of asylum seekers; withdrawal of refugee status; deportation and extradition; and increasing obstacles to resettlement. It is important to note that restrictive and discriminatory asylum policies are not confined to "Western" or European states.[13]

The evolving security discourse and refugees

International security has traditionally been defined, ultimately, as the military defence of territory. The context is traditionally seen as an anarchic state system whose chief characteristic is a perennial competition for security based upon (primarily military) power. In international relations theory, this is "structural realism": although unit-level changes may occur inside states, the system remains a self-help, anarchic, hierarchical arena that conditions or even determines the behaviour and attitudes of the units.[14] National security therefore is the imperative of defending territory against, and deterring, "external" military threats. A sense of "security dilemma" – for example during the Cold War – provides a pretext for the extremes of the narrow national security paradigm. Mainstream structural realism is a systemic, structure-dominant school. Therefore, developments such as democratization within states, the growing multiplicity of transnational actors, economic interdependence, and the growth and thickening of international institutionalization are viewed as not changing the basic nature of the system: "the structure of international politics is not transformed by changes internal to states, however widespread the changes may be."[15] Interests, identities, and the need for relative gains are determined by structure. Agency is secondary.

In the context of this structural realist analytical security framework, refugees are almost invisible: they are an inevitable and peripheral consequence – although not a cause – of conflict, insecurity, and instability. The realist model focuses mainly on conflict amongst states and the structural determinants of conflict in a state-centric environment. Accordingly, human displacement is seen as part of a "humanitarian" agenda issue, a spillover, but substantively separate, from the security agenda. Furthermore, refugees were to a large extent simply part of the ideological and political game of the Cold War. Those within Europe were protected by the strategic use of the 1951 Convention. Only in 1967 did developed states expand the refugee regime to cover those arriving from Africa, Asia, and Latin America, fleeing conflicts induced by the Cold War in those regions too. During many major conflicts in which refugees were a result of the battles, refugees' well-being was assured or presumed owing to their links to one or other "side": the flow of Vietnamese refugees was managed through international agreements, relieving the pressure on South-East Asian states because the burden of the protection of the anti-communist refugees was shouldered by the anti-communist Western states. The issue of refugeehood was subsumed in the ideological issues relating to conflict more broadly.

Patterns of refugee flows

The "realist" view of conflict prevailed during the Cold War and this has helped to give rise to a common and spurious assumption that patterns of conflict have changed, when in fact it is rather the way in which we analyse conflict that has changed. According to this assumption, trends in modern conflict, which reflect a high level of civil war and state collapse, have resulted in a proportionately high rate of victimization and human displacement amongst non-combatants. The conclusion of the Carnegie Commission on Preventing Deadly Conflict echoed a widely accepted belief:

These internal conflicts commonly are fought with conventional weapons and rely on strategies of ethnic expulsion and annihilation. More civilians are killed than soldiers (by one estimate at the rate of about nine to one), and belligerents use strategies and tactics that deliberately target women, children, the poor, and the weak.... In some wars today, 90 percent of those killed in conflict are non-combatants, compared with less than 15 percent when the century began. In Rwanda alone, approximately 40 percent of the population has been killed or displaced since 1994.[16]

The UNHCR's *State of the World's Refugees* report follows a similar line. It suggests that there have been "changing dynamics of displacement"[17] and describes "the changing nature of conflict."[18] It observes the "devastating civilian toll of *recent* wars," stating that "in the post–Cold War period, civil wars and communal conflicts have involved wide-scale, deliberate targeting of civilian populations."[19] Again, amongst many academics, a common theme is that "the global dynamics of flight and refuge are changing" in the context of the "changing nature of conflict."[20] The data presented by the UNHCR appear at first to support this.

In fact these patterns, trends, and departures are partly the construction of researchers, international civil servants, and politicians – albeit well intentioned. In many cases, this constructed reality is a response to the perception that states in and of themselves have felt threatened by migration and displacement: it is a pandering to the discourse that states and governments seemed to want.[21] Clearly, civilian victimization and human displacement – both within and across borders – are a cruel characteristic of contemporary conflict. However, it is important to clarify whether these represent a genuine departure or change from the past (say, the Cold War) or are simply fluctuations owing to specific incidents of conflict. The UNHCR states that "[r]efugee movements are no longer side effects of conflict, but in many cases are central to the objectives and tactics of war."[22] It observes that the brutality of "contemporary" civil conflict includes gender-specific violence, rape, mass murder, the use of child soldiers, and the spread of terror through conspicuous atrocities.[23] But it is questionable whether there has been a dramatic qualitative increase in these activities in a linear manner that would point to an obvious changing dynamic of refugee flows or displacement.

Clearly, historical, technological, and socio-economic changes have had an impact on societies in many different ways. The nature and impact of conflict have changed in line with this. In the post-war era, for example, a number of historical forces and processes have influenced trends and patterns of refugees, displacement, and migration – both legal and illegal. The Second World War left some 40 million people in Europe outside the borders of their homeland. Decolonization and the wars of independence, proxy Cold War conflicts, state collapse, globalization, the end of the Cold War, and the so-called "resurgence" of identity politics have all had an impact. A common device is to make a comparison between contemporary post–Cold War conflict – which involves a relatively high level of civil conflict and state failure, resulting in civilian victimization and deliberate and consequential displacement – and "earlier times," such as the turn of the twentieth century, when it is asserted that warfare was primarily between states and fought by soldiers. This is the implication of the Carnegie Report conclusions. But it is far from clear that there is a genuine departure or change from the past historically. Human displacement has always been central to the objectives and tactics of certain types of war.

Certainly it is possible to identify conflicts (such as the First World War) that may indicate a high combatant-to-civilian victim ratio when compared with a civil war (such as Bosnia or Rwanda) at the end of the twentieth century. But it would be misleading to deduce from this that the patterns of conflict and civilian victimization have changed in a linear fashion. The First World War was hardly a typical conflict and, around the same time as the battle of the Somme, large-scale civilian victimization and displacement were occurring elsewhere – the Armenian "genocide," for example. One could make a similar point regarding the post-war context. The UNHCR statistics suggest a fairly steady, exponential increase in refugees and internally displaced persons, especially after 1990, which is in line with the common image of a resurgence of domestic conflict in the immediate post–Cold War era. Yet this may well be accounted for by two alternative explanations: a lack of reliable data over time, and the increased *visibility* of human displacement and civilian victimization. Moreover, the manner in which these phenomena have become increasingly international issues, and thus "of concern" to UNHCR and, by extension, to "the international community," has often obscured the fact that they have always occurred, to varying degrees.

The seemingly international nature of displacement is itself fuelled by two phenomena that may lead people to think there are more refugees. First, as is often noted, viable transportation links between the region of origin of refugees and places in which they might seek protection have made mobility more likely. Second, through television, people in the developed world see displacement and suffering as they occur. Television cameras were in Macedonia to see how Kosovars became trapped in no-man's land when protection was not forthcoming beyond the immediate region in March and April 1999.[24]

If one considers the post-war era, and even with a lack of reliable data, one can intuitively reason that displacement and civilian victimization have not shown a clear direction or pattern as a proportion of all victims of conflict. Indeed, contrary to much contemporary thinking, one could even argue that conflict has become more limited in terms of its civilian death toll and impact upon displacement since the end of the Cold War. The post-colonial conflicts in Africa (for example, Angola, Mozambique, Congo, Nigeria–Biafra, Rwanda, Burundi), Asia (for example, India, Pakistan, Bangladesh, Sri Lanka, Vietnam, Indonesia, Cambodia), and the Middle East resulted in huge numbers of displaced persons, both within and across boundaries. Similarly, in Latin America (for example, Nicaragua, Colombia, Guatemala, El Salvador, Argentina, and Chile) conflicts or uprisings resulted in displacements and civilian victimization that were markedly worse than those in the post–Cold War era. In addition, although not traditionally considered as situations of "conflict," Russia and China experienced upheavals that resulted in the death or displacement of many millions of people. Afghanistan, too, saw displacement on a scale during the Cold War that dwarfed what occurred since, until late 2001.

Even in the case of "inter-state" war, where the presumption of many analysts has been that the proportion of civilian to combatant victims is lower than in intra-state war, and displacement is accordingly less, history tells a different story. In Germany's advance across the Soviet Union starting in June 1941 – Operation Barbarossa – the number of displaced civilians was astronomical. The civilian toll of the conflict between Japan and its Asian neighbours during the Second World War is also well known. One hardly need mention the expulsion and extermination of millions of European Jews during the Second World War. It is simply not empirically verifiable to state, in a definitive and linear sense, that "[t]he number of refugees, those crossing international borders, is declining while the number of IDPs, those displaced within borders, is increasing dramatically."[25] At the same time, given the absence of reliable data, it is also difficult to refute such a claim conclusively.

Refugees and human security

Human security is the latest turn in the evolving security discourse. Defining human security is conceptually and practically troublesome, but a broad definition may be as follows:

Human security is concerned with the protection of people from critical and life-threatening dangers, regardless of whether the threats are rooted in anthropogenic activities or natural events, whether they lie within or outside states, and whether they are direct or structural. It is "human-centered" in that its principal focus is on people both as individuals and as communal groups. It is "security oriented" in that the focus is on freedom from fear, danger and threat.[26]

In other words, contemporary security, if it is to be relevant to changing conditions and needs, must focus on the individual or people collectively. This does not exclude the importance of traditional ideas of security, but it does suggest that it may be more effective to reorient the provision of security around people – wherever the threat comes from.

Traditional conceptions of state security – based on the military defence of territory – are an important but not a sufficient condition of human welfare. Human security has at its heart a multidisciplinary and comprehensive approach to *critical* welfare issues and questions of survival. Challenges and solutions are seen not as phenomena that can be addressed in isolation from each other, but as being interconnected, and even sometimes interdependent. Human security must be approached in an inclusive and holistic manner – not only examining the symptoms or manifestations of human insecurity, but also seeking to produce recommendations that address root causes.

Does the concept of human security bring new insights or new analytical rigour to the study of refugees and human displacement? Can refugees and the states that seek to manage the impact of refugee flows and guarantee the protection of refugees ultimately benefit from it? To answer positively, one could argue that human security thinking can highlight the plight of refugees, attract more resources, and push the issue higher up the policy agenda. Refugees suffer through being displaced and they suffer while being displaced. Even in resettlement or return, they experience particular vulnerabilities. Their needs are not adequately met through the conventional "high politics" security mindset. Therefore, it could be argued, human security offers a reorientation of security that embraces both the ethical and humanitarian requirements and the practical needs of contemporary security. A negative response to the question might suggest that the concept of human security is itself analytically weak – in fact not a concept at all – in addition to being overly broad. Moreover, in terms of forced migration and human displacement, as some of the authors in this book indicate, there is a danger that, by "securitizing" refugees, a pretext is provided for states to interdict and deter them even more. The result can be an even greater deterioration in the rights of refugees and a heightened sense of vulnerability.

The legal rights of refugees, institutional responses and support mechanisms, must be reoriented within a framework of a broader definition of security in the contemporary interdependent era. The ethical framework regarding refugees, displacement, and asylum – our moral responsibilities beyond borders – must be reconsidered in light of the emergence of solidarist ideas of global community and human security. This book seeks to make a contribution to this debate. An overarching objective is to suggest strategies through which legal, political/normative, and institutional frameworks can genuinely confront these challenges rather than simply putting a "cap" on the situation and developing policies that keep refugees "out of our backyard."

Outline of the volume

Part I deals with a broad range of political, security, and normative perspectives. Gil Loescher ("Refugees as Grounds for International Action") demonstrates that refugee flows should and must be seen as a pressing security challenge. In recent years, traditional notions of security and sovereignty have been challenged, placing refugee issues much higher on the international agenda and creating the need for international action. This has become more pronounced since the terrorist attacks of 11 September 2001. Refugee movements have increasingly come to be seen as a cause of instability; refugees are viewed not only as people in need of protection and assistance but also as potential threats to national security and even as a potential source of armed terror. Although international responses to humanitarian crises remain more often than not reactive, self-interested, and based on ad hoc initiatives, there is growing international awareness of the linkage between human rights abuses, forcible displacement of civilian populations, and local, regional, and international security. Humanitarian measures alone are seldom enough to deal with refugee problems. A wide range of actions – an intervention continuum – must therefore be considered and evaluated to avert large-scale refugee crises. Sustained political and diplomatic initiatives, development assistance, human rights monitoring, and the strengthening of civil societies through the building of democratic institutions are all measures that, if initiated early and given sufficient economic resources and political support, can prevent the outbreak of violence and the mass displacement of populations. However, where armed hostilities have already broken out within a country and are accompanied by widespread violations of human rights, "hard" forms of intervention, including military action, may be necessary to bring such violations to a halt. Acting early to avert refugee crises can be demanding, but it is considerably less expensive than dealing with the fallout of a full-blown and protracted crisis. The imposition of refugees on other states, as a threat to peace and security, falls under Chapter VII of the UN Charter and therefore legitimizes enforcement action not subject to the limits of purely humanitarian action.

With the increasing recognition of the link between refugee flows and national, regional, and international security, international intervention related to refugee flows has in fact become more frequent since the end of the Cold War. Such intervention, in other words, is not only increasingly justifiable but actually happening. However, Loescher accepts the difficulties of achieving widespread international agreement on the use of force to resolve refugee problems. He therefore suggests that some steps are needed in the short term to deal with the problems associated with mass forcible displacements of people. At a minimum, these include the establishment of an international rapid reaction capacity along with credible safe haven policies to respond to refugee emergencies, and the promotion and building of civil society infrastructure and human rights monitoring in local communities in conflict. Currently, the United Nations, and the international system more generally, are not well equipped to deal with human rights violations and state-building responsibilities.

Until the capacity of the UN human rights regime is fully developed, non-governmental organizations (especially human rights NGOs) will have to assume a larger share of responsibility for ensuring the protection of forcibly displaced people. In countries where central government itself is weak or non-existent and therefore unable to protect its citizens, the key issue will be not only how to bring together contending groups but how to build institutions of governance.

Gary G. Troeller ("Refugees and Human Displacement in Contemporary International Relations: Reconciling State and Individual Sovereignty") provides the social and political context for refugees and human displacement. He situates the challenge in the context of different and sometimes competing forces and norms, including globalization, secessionism and fragmentation, communal violence, and ideas of good governance and individual sovereignty. These involve four conflicting concepts: state sovereignty, the right to national self-determination, democracy, and respect for human rights. Glaring inequalities in wealth between industrialized and poorer countries as a result of pervasive market forces; armed conflict; and state persecution – these are all inherent in the contemporary international political system. In turn, forced displacement and refugees are a defining characteristic of the post–Cold War era and contemporary international relations. Troeller observes that refugees, long regarded as a peripheral issue or a matter of discretionary charitable concern to policy makers, now figure prominently on the international policy agenda. Liberal internationalists argue that, in the name of basic values, something must be done to address this issue. Even realists, largely driven by concern for national interests acknowledge that the sheer numbers involved can constitute a threat to regional security. Along with the impact of a globalizing economy, the refugee issue has forced many academics and policy makers to recognize that the basic unit of analysis in international relations – the state – is no longer wholly adequate as an explanatory or predictive tool and, by extension, traditional conceptions of dealing with security issues are inadequate in an increasingly post-Westphalian world. Within these broad underlying themes, Troeller focuses on the causes of forced displacement and the legal and normative framework of refugee protection. The chapter then moves to developments in the post–Cold War period and current challenges confronting the Office of the United Nations High Commissioner for Refugees, not least in the aftermath of September 11. It is argued that there is an increasingly solid basis for action that would significantly mitigate if not resolve the refugee issue if the political will can be marshalled.

Joanne van Selm ("Refugee Protection Policies and Security Issues") considers the differing policy approaches to refugee protection practised in developed states, posing the following questions: Can different or particular security concerns and "national interests" explain divergences and patterns in refugee protection policy approaches in developed states? Can broader conceptions of security, which go beyond military and state-centric dimensions, positively impact upon refugee protection? These questions are of particular relevance for a volume that seeks to examine a range of issues and debates relating to refugees and displaced people in modern conflict. The question of how refugee protection policy operates, differs, and converges around the globe is of major importance.

Three types of refugee protection policy approach are described in this chapter: distinct but linked refugee and immigration approaches; refugee protection subsumed by immigration concerns; and asylum processing as immigration control. The characterization of each approach refers to global security concerns, national interest concerns in the sense of safety and security issues, and the link to immigration policies in order to include societal and human security concerns. The themes of "control" and "management" are pervasive. The examples of each type are the United States, Australia, and the European Union. Van Selm uses this framework to explore the central issues of refugee policies and restrictions: resettlement, temporary protection, asylum and detention, offshore processing, and the link between security and asylum in different regional and national settings. She finds divergent, particularistic goals of national immigration and refugee protection policies underlying some of the most significant differences between the policy approaches in different settings. The US focus on selection and citizenship is in part a reflection of the way in which national interest informs the "recruitment" process, as is the use of detention for spontaneous arrivals. Australia's use of resettlement places for unauthorized boat arrivals and of mandatory detention can be explained by its security concerns. Concerns about border security might make it logical to treat those breaching it as (potential) criminals, even if such a practice is indefensible by most other standards. Using the existing quota makes some sense in terms of maintaining the public image of control – the numbers do not increase in spite of the spontaneous arrivals.

Astri Suhrke ("Human Security and the Protection of Refugees") considers the merits and limitations of examining refugee challenges and solutions in the context of the evolving – and contested – security discourse. In particular, she focuses on the broadening of security studies from a traditional military and state-centred model to the concepts of "societal security" and "human security," and she raises a number of core questions. What are the implications and impact of this discourse upon academic and policy discussions? What are the implications of placing the discourse on migrants and refugees in a security context, or what is often called its "securitization"? Is it useful to reconceptualize refugee issues in terms of "human security," as some suggest?

From both a normative and an analytical perspective, Suhrke argues that the term "human security" is not useful for examining the needs of individual groups that, on some critical dimensions of belonging, stand apart from the community in which they find themselves. Applying a "security" perspective to examine the needs of "outsiders" and their relationship to the community typically involves assumptions of antagonistic relations and non-tradable interests. In other words, the negative effects often assumed to follow the "securitization" of the discourse on refugee movements that was associated with "societal security" in the 1990s are likely to occur even when the adjective is "human" rather than "societal." If the aim is to build a normative and policy-oriented model that places the interests of the displaced populations at the centre, a better starting point is "vulnerability." The concept lends itself to methodological and empirical elaboration, and does not evoke the same conflictual connotations as "security."

Mervyn Frost ("Thinking Ethically about Refugees: A Case for the Transformation of Global Governance") argues that refugee issues must be understood as essentially ethical problems and not merely technical, legal, political, or administrative challenges. On this basis, he sets out a particular approach to the ethical problems presented to us by migrants. The strength of this mode of analysis is that it allows us to see the changes that are taking place in our global practices from within which we make our judgements about how, from an ethical point of view, we ought to treat migrants of all kinds. The analysis he offers is radical in that it shows how the language we use about international ethics, especially the language of universal human rights, indicates how aspects of domestic and international law are now in need of reform. A crucial feature of his argument is that our own constitution as free people depends on our treating migrants ethically. Frost situates his argument in constitutive communitarian thought, which holds that we are constituted as the actors we are within social practices, not simply by merit of our birth. All practices contain a range of different kinds of rules which specify, *inter alia*, who may participate, how to participate, what participants should aim at, what will count as success in that practice (and what as failure), what the consequences of rule breaking are, what punishments are authorized, to mention but a few. A particularly difficult kind of ethical dilemma confronts us when, as participants in good standing in more than one social practice simultaneously (and we are all constituted in this way), we find that what is required of us by the ethic embedded in one of these practices is contradicted by what is required of us by the ethic embedded in one or more of the other practices. It is these kinds of predicament that Frost applies to refugee issues. In response, he demonstrates that we must become *ethical constructivists*.

If we are to capitalize upon a deepening understanding of refugees and displacement in international security, a systematic grasp of the causes and consequences of these phenomena is essential. Susanne Schmeidl ("The Early Warning of Forced Migration: State or Human Security?") argues that a central part of this is early warning of conflicts and refugee migration as a way to avoid human suffering as well as to decrease the financial burden on the international community. As Schmeidl observes, although almost everyone accepts the logic and utility of a reliable system of early warning, there are methodological difficulties in constructing such a system. There are also political sensitivities. In methodological terms, the challenge is to generate a set of propositions that have general explanatory relevance during times of crisis for the purposes of forewarning of displacement and refugee flows. In a sense, this gets to the heart of one of the central problems of social science: at one level every conflict or social phenomenon is unique and therefore it is difficult to construct predictive indicators; at the same time, patterns emerge upon which flexible contingencies can be prepared. Political sensitivities concern "interference" in internal affairs in terms of monitoring indicators and in terms of publicly warning of imminent catastrophe. Political dangers also exist: early warning analysis can be used to head off incoming displacement in times of crisis, including the closing of borders. Early warning may not necessarily be congruent with the human rights or needs of displaced people.

Part II examines the dynamics of displacement, return, and resettlement. Erin Mooney ("Towards a Protection Regime for Internally Displaced Persons") addresses the challenge of internally displaced persons. Some 25 million people are displaced within the borders of their own country as a result of armed conflict, internal strife, and serious violations of human rights. Essentially, they are "internal refugees" – people who would be considered refugees were they to cross an international border. For most purposes they have the same needs as refugees – protection from violence, housing, sustenance, education, health care, employment – but, having not crossed a border, they do not benefit from the same system of international protection and assistance. International action on behalf of the displaced is ad hoc and therefore not assured. Responsibility for providing protection and assistance to internally displaced persons rests with their government. However, governments are often unable or unwilling to meet these obligations fully, sometimes even deliberately displacing populations or denying them their rights. There is thus a pressing need to bridge the institutional, legal, and policy gap that has so often hampered effective responses to the protection and assistance of internally displaced persons. Concretely, an international regime for protecting internally displaced persons worldwide would need to consist of international standards, institutional apparatus, and operational strategies integrated into a coherent and cohesive system of response. Mooney's chapter examines the extent to which normative, institutional, and strategic frameworks are in place for protecting internally displaced persons and identifies steps that are necessary to further their development and, taken collectively, that of a comprehensive and effective protection regime.

Mooney concludes that the international community is better equipped today to address the protection needs of the internally displaced than it was 10 years ago when the issue was first placed on the international agenda. A normative framework has been developed with the formulation of the Guiding Principles on Internal Displacement, which spell out the rights of the internally displaced and the obligations of states, insurgent forces, and international actors towards them. Institutional arrangements, though by no means fully defined or dependable in ensuring international protection and assistance for internally displaced persons worldwide, nonetheless have been tested and are being strengthened. Protection is finally now recognized as a priority concern, and an international protection regime for internally displaced persons has begun to take shape. Even so, it is argued that, to constitute a comprehensive regime, the three separate components of standards, institutional mechanisms, and strategies of protection, once firmly in place, must collectively amount to a cohesive and consistent system of effective response. Mooney suggests that the Guiding Principles on Internal Displacement, which not only are the culmination of efforts to develop a normative framework but also have acted as a catalyst in the development of more effective institutional arrangements and the design of protection strategies, are already proving to be an important unifying thread. Beyond simply consolidating and clarifying the norms of special importance to internally displaced persons and thereby laying down the legal foundation of protection, the Principles are serving as a tool for building an entire protection regime for internally displaced persons.

Khalid Koser ("Reconciling Control and Compassion? Human Smuggling and the Right to Asylum") explores an area that is under-studied and often misunderstood: the link between human smuggling and asylum. The assumption amongst most national decision makers, the public, and the media is that human smuggling is characterized by the illegal transportation of economic migrants. However, there is growing evidence that a significant proportion of asylum seekers rely on smugglers to enter industrialized nations. At the same time, smuggling clearly can and often does expose them to vulnerability. On the one hand, advocates are concerned that successfully stamping out smuggling would deprive many people of the possibility of seeking asylum in the industrialized nations, but on the other hand they can hardly be seen to support a system that exploits asylum seekers. At least partly as a result of this quandary, asylum advocates – including the UNHCR – have been surprisingly reticent in the human smuggling debate, and legislation by states to stop smuggling has advanced more or less unchallenged, despite its implications for asylum seekers. As a result, some advocates have begun to lament that the debate has already been lost, and that asylum in industrialized nations may be doomed. Koser accepts (and supports) greater measures to combat human smuggling, which can only become more stringent after the terrorist attacks of 11 September 2001. At the same time, he argues that human smuggling cannot be stopped unless asylum is centralized in the policy framework. In other words, the rise of human smuggling on political agendas actually presents a fairly unusual opportunity for state security and the individual security of asylum seekers to be combined – for control and compassion to be reconciled. The role of asylum advocates, it is suggested, should be to suggest realistic asylum policies that might operate in tandem with anti-smuggling policies.

B. S. Chimni ("Post-Conflict Peace-Building and the Return of Refugees: Concepts, Practices, and Institutions") embraces an underlying theme of the book: repatriation has come to be seen by the international community and the UNHCR as *the* solution to the global refugee problem. Local integration and resettlement in third countries have been de-emphasized, applicable to less than 1 per cent of the world's refugees. Therefore, he argues, the current focus is on early return, often without satisfactory knowledge of the sustainability of return, or the needs of reintegration, or of the conditions that are necessary for long-term development. There is an absence of any systematic theoretical and legal framework for so-called "peace-building" strategies or a critical and integral understanding of the problems that characterize "post-conflict" societies or of refugees who return to them. The result is an array of measures that have rarely been arrived at in consultation with refugees and returnees, and that are often coercive or work at cross purposes with each other. They have been assembled in the matrix of a neo-liberal vision which, among other things, does not focus on the international causes of internal conflicts and excludes the possibility of building a participatory "post-conflict" state. Chimni argues that the basic problem with the policies relating to the return of refugees to "post-conflict" societies and their reintegration is the poverty of the epistemology deployed to identify suitable measures that will go to promote "sustainable return." He concludes that the United Nations system is trying virtually to (re)produce a sustainable society and state without addressing the international causes of structural violence, and that is destined to failure.

Patricia Weiss Fagen ("The Long-Term Challenges of Reconstruction and Reintegration: Case-Studies of Haiti and Bosnia–Herzegovina") also explores the challenges of reintegration, learning from the experiences of two cases. She observes that donors and operational agencies put great emphasis on establishing the foundations of good governance, security, civil society organizations, and economic development as quickly as possible, i.e. during the emergency phase and even during actual conflict. In practice, however, the "massive intervention and quick fix" approaches typical of humanitarian emergencies rarely yield durable results. The disappointing performance of international assistance during emergencies underscores the prevalent lack of coordination, duplication of efforts, fragmented programmes, and expenditures that are too large to be absorbed locally that so often characterize these situations. Considering two very different countries, Fagen illustrates how international actors invested major resources during the early phase of their involvement, but impeded the achievement of the very results they sought by failing to plan comprehensively and by reducing resources too quickly. The cases of Haiti and Bosnia–Herzegovina – far from the least successful examples of international humanitarian interventions – illustrate a limited understanding of, or preparation for, the challenges of long-term transition periods. Donors and agencies proposed to lay the foundations for political, social, and economic objectives (which require a decade or more to achieve under favourable conditions) on the basis of planning, funding, and mandates that change from year to year. Even where there are indications that international interventions are producing favourable results, the supporting agencies have found themselves unable to capitalize on this success owing to arbitrarily determined phase-out projections. Continued funding for fundamental changes was still programmed according to unrealistic indicators that are supposed to establish year-to-year progress, although in nearly all cases improvements in one area are accompanied by – or cause – regressions in another. Finally, donor fatigue sets in when it is perceived that an emergency has been managed, but well before the desired durable changes can reasonably be expected.

In terms of Bosnia, Fagen concludes that international resources could have been used to greater effect in addressing post-conflict peace-building and return. Establishing citizen security should have been among the first objectives. Despite the fact that humanitarian assistance was plentiful at first, the international community could not induce refugees and displaced minority populations to attempt to reclaim their homes in areas hostile to their ethnic group. In both Bosnia and Haiti, which are still in the midst of the transition from war to peace, international agencies have been cutting back operations and donors reducing support, despite the fact that the specific needs for which international assistance was initially mobilized are still high, and before national institutions and capacities to meet these needs have been established.

In some respects the needs of refugees are essentially gender neutral – something that is reflected in the main institutions, laws, and organizations that manage and address refugee and displacement issues. Yet approximately 75–80 per cent of the displaced are women and children. Women suffer differently during conflict and displacement and have particular needs. The experience of flight and displacement has different implications for male and female members of a population. The human rights dimensions leading to flight are also gendered. Although women may experience the same human rights deprivations as men, human rights violations often take different forms for women and men because of their perceived gender roles.

Julie Mertus ("Sovereignty, Gender, and Displacement") argues that refugee issues reflect the socially constructed roles of women *and* men in society, and that displacement itself is gendered and influenced by real and perceived roles, responsibilities, constraints, opportunities, and needs of men and women in society. The existence of an uprooted and imperilled population should be filtered through a "gender lens," to include root human rights violations and other causes of flight, the type of violence and other rights violations encountered during flight and in temporary encampments, and the consideration of permanent solutions for resettlement or return. At the same time, the mechanisms for both the delivery of humanitarian aid and the protection and resettlement or return of uprooted and imperilled people should account for the gender dimensions of their work. Mertus argues that the gendered process of displacement occurs within the context of shifting and competing sovereignties described throughout her chapter. She thus considers two interrelated variables: the gender dimensions of displacement and changing approaches to sovereignty. Each dimension has important consequences for displaced populations.

Mertus demonstrates that there has been progress in recognizing gendered needs, but that four sets of roadblocks remain: (i) a gap between policies adopted at headquarters and their implementation in the field; (ii) a continued failure to address the needs of uprooted populations who remain internally displaced; (iii) the continued inability of those who suffer gender-based persecution to obtain asylum; and (iv) the failure of gender programmes to address the position of men.

Part III considers international actors and institutions, broadly defined, that play a role in the refugee and displacement debates. Gregor Noll ("Securitizing Sovereignty? States, Refugees, and the Regionalization of International Law") addresses the quandaries and difficulties confronting refugee law in a world of sovereign states. In principle, international law should guarantee both state sovereignty and individual sovereignty. The existence and autonomy of a state are secured by the obligation incumbent on other states to respect its territorial integrity and the prohibition on intervening in domestic affairs. At the individual level, internationally guaranteed human rights serve comparable functions: they secure a minimum of autonomy and even preserve an "exit" option, because each individual retains a right to leave any country, including his or her own. In the area of forced displacement, this ostensible harmony has never existed in practice. The "right to seek and enjoy asylum" laid down in Article 14 of the 1948 Universal Declaration of Human Rights has largely remained an unfulfilled privilege for refugees, mainly because it was designed to insulate states granting asylum from reproaches by countries of origin rather than to protect individuals.

The lack of entry rights also stems from the 1951 Refugee Convention. Although it launched an abstract refugee definition and a basic norm of non-return (the prohibition of *refoulement*), it fails to address the crucial question of access to an asylum state in an effective and unequivocal manner. To be protected by the Convention, the refugee needs to make contact with the territory of a potential asylum state. This is the Achilles heel of the international refugee regime: states may block access to their territory, and thus avoid situations in which persons in need of protection could invoke the provisions of the 1951 Refugee Convention or other protective norms of international human rights law.

Noll suggests that the dynamics behind recent developments in refugee and migration law can be condensed to an interplay between three factors: the number of refugees on state territory, the level of rights accorded to them, and the degree of solidarity between states in protecting them. Although there is a minimum level of rights in international law that states cannot undercut, international solidarity in refugee reception is largely absent, so host countries make every effort to reduce the number of refugees by systematically outlawing refugee migration and by blocking all possible avenues of access. These limitative dynamics take many expressions, and affect the internal domain, the transit routes, and also the countries or regions of origin. A marked feature of these limitative dynamics is that they undercut both individual sovereignty and the sovereignty of other states. Destination states in the North are constantly redesigning their asylum systems in order to remove incentives for protection seekers. They legislate on new reasons to reject claims and they attempt to make the return of rejected cases more efficient. This puts the protective provisions of international law under increasing pressure and challenges the principle of non-discrimination in a number of areas. Destination states in the North also attempt to control the travel routes of protection seekers and to cut them off by administrative measures such as visa requirements, sanctions against carriers transporting aliens without documents, and externalized forms of border control. Such policies affect the exercise of the human right to leave any country. Attempts to control refugee migration may even go so far as to comprise military intervention. But intervention may also take milder forms than the use of force. Transit states as well as countries of origin are increasingly coming under pressure to police their territory or their seaways in order to block refugee migration.

Noll argues that the language of "human security" is unhelpful and merely colludes in the losses for individual sovereignty that contemporary refugee policies entail. He considers the range of national responses to refugee flows, from outright rejection of protective obligations (*insulation*) via refugee reception (*palliation* of human rights violations) to enforcement action in the country of crisis (*intervention*). Isolation, palliation, and intervention raise different questions of international law, and the objective is to demarcate the boundaries.

The international norms, institutions, and laws that govern the management of refugees and their rights are clearly a central objective of refugee policies and analysis. They provide a policy focus for most of the discussion of the volume, and almost all the chapters individually address the institutional and legal dimensions of their respective subjects, including recommendations for improvements. William Maley ("A New Tower of Babel? Reappraising the Architecture of Refugee Protection") focuses specifically on the international institutional mechanisms of refugee protection and identifies the most pressing concerns that confront them.

As a starting point, Maley observes that the definition of refugees has become problematic. The 1951 Convention definition – a person who, "owing to well-founded fear of being persecuted for reasons of race, religion, nationality, membership in a particular social group, or political opinion, is outside the country of his nationality and is unable or, owing to such fear, is unwilling to avail himself of the protection of that country" – does not match the volume and nature of displaced peoples in need of sustenance, shelter, and care when events drive them en masse from their homes, whether they cross a border or not. This is more an issue of refugee relief. The kinds of response demanded vary considerably, and so does the disposition of the international community to respond appropriately: relief is calculated to keep refugees at arm's length from Western populations. There is no shortage of actors in the field to provide aid to refugees. But too often they occupy a dysfunctional Tower of Babel, metaphorically speaking languages that their fellows cannot understand. And the refugees whom they aim to help are the immediate victims of their operational and organizational weaknesses. It is therefore worth while to explore how things might be done better. Maley examines the ways in which refugee assistance has been shaped by the contours of the international system and by the characteristics of international organizations. He discusses specific problems of refugee assistance, drawing for examples on developments from the post–Cold War period. He then considers past proposals to reform refugee mechanisms, and offers suggestions for institutional reorganization to overcome some of the most troubling problems that beset the present regime for refugee protection. A theme that runs through the chapter is that *all* refugee assistance has political implications, and that to believe in a "pure" humanitarianism divorced from politics is profoundly naive.

A central question in international relations in recent years is the extent to which the media have a substantive/decisive impact upon "outcomes" at different policy levels. In terms of the politics of refugees and displacement, a number of questions are of interest to this volume. The impact of the media on public discussion relating to refugees and on public perceptions of asylum seekers/refugees; the nature of media imagery, terminology, metaphor, and choice of coverage; the impact of the media on national policies towards asylum and refugees; government control of the media and of information going to the media; and the impact of the media on donor behaviour – these are all important subjects for analysis. Peter Mares ("Distance Makes the Heart Grow Fonder: Media Images of Refugees and Asylum Seekers") looks at the way the media in the developed world portray refugees and asylum seekers, especially in Australia. He argues that the level of concern and empathy expressed in the media for the plight of refugees and asylum seekers is in inverse relation to their proximity to the place where any given report appears. Viewed from a distance, displaced people are often portrayed as helpless victims of circumstance, deserving of compassion and assistance. This imagery changes dramatically when refugees and asylum seekers make their way to the developed world to seek protection under the 1951 Convention. Refugees and asylum seekers who display this level of agency suddenly shed the veneer of innocence and become a threat to the order and security of the receiving state. They are transformed from passive objects of compassion into untrustworthy actors who provoke a sense of fear. Mares claims that this results, in part, from a lack of political courage among authority figures in developed nations, and sometimes from political expediency. He also argues that humanitarian agencies are themselves at times responsible for promoting unrealistic and unsustainable images of refugees that ill prepare developed nation audiences for coping with the complexity of the unauthorized movement of people in the contemporary world.

Finally, Mark Raper explores the comparative advantages that NGOs bring to the refugee issue in "Changing Roles of NGOs in Refugee Assistance." He describes how NGOs offer an effective avenue for interpreting and addressing the needs of the millions of needy people, and argues that their comparative advantage is based on their independence (which often enables them to gain early access to affected populations), their flexibility and mobility, their capacity to collaborate with many other actors, and their credibility. His chapter is written from the perspective of an NGO practitioner and considers the various roles of the private sector in the humanitarian field, the relationships between NGOs, governments, and international organizations, and the practical, professional, and even ethical challenges posed to NGOs by the new contexts. He demonstrates the range of tasks relating to both local and international NGOs – including advocacy and protection, monitoring human rights standards, cooperating with other service agencies, and assisting in return, reintegration, and reconstruction. In doing so he recounts the challenges that NGOs face, including the difficulties of gaining access in times of emergency, issues of safety, and the dilemmas of cooperating with different types of actors in the field.

In conclusion, Raper argues that the success of NGOs often comes from their flexibility and capacity to innovate in response to needs, as well as from their ability to form alliances among themselves but also with other interest groups such as ethnic associations, workers, students, and religious groups. In serving forcibly displaced people, NGOs' roles differ from those of governments and international organizations, yet they provide a needed complement to them. While acknowledging the painful factors that give rise to the NGOs, we can give thanks that they are growing, acknowledge their focus on the human and ethical aspects, and welcome the initiatives for service and cooperation that they represent.

Notes

1. Address by United Nations Secretary-General Kofi Annan, delivered to the fifty-first session of the Executive Committee of the High Commissioner for Refugees, Palais des Nations, Geneva, 2 October 2000. Press Release SG/SM/7570, 2 October 2000.
2. See Saskia Sassen, *Globalization and Its Discontents: Essays on the New Mobility of People and Money*, New York: New Press, 1999; Stephen Castles and Mark J. Miller, *The Age of Migration*, 2nd edn, New York: Guilford Press, 1998.

 3. See Aristide Zolberg, Astri Suhrke, and Sergio Aguayo, *Escape from Violence: Conflict and the Refugee Crisis in the Developing World*, Oxford: Oxford University Press, 1989.
 4. UNHCR, *The State of the World's Refugees: Fifty Years of Humanitarian Action*, Oxford: Oxford University Press, 2000, chap. 1.
 5. See Joanne van Selm, "Access to Procedures: 'Safe Third Countries', 'Safe Countries of Origin' and 'Time Limits'," paper commissioned for the UNHCR's Global Consultations, at www.unhcr.ch (2001).
 6. Emek M. Ucarer, "Managing Asylum and European Integration: Expanding Spheres of Exclusion?" *International Studies Perspectives*, vol. 2, no. 3, 2001, p. 289.
 7. Edward Newman, "Human Security and Constructivism," *International Studies Perspectives*, vol. 2, no. 3, 2001.
 8. See, for example, Guy S. Goodwin-Gill, *The Refugee in International Law*, Oxford: Oxford University Press, 1996; Gil Loescher, *Beyond Charity: International Cooperation and the Global Refugee Crisis*, Oxford: Oxford University Press, 1994; Joanne van Selm, *Refugee Protection in Europe: Lessons of the Yugoslav Crisis*, The Hague: Kluwer Law International, 1998.
 9. Hans van Ginkel and Edward Newman, "In Quest of 'Human Security'," *Japan Review of International Affairs*, vol. 14, no. 1, Spring 2000.
10. See, for example, Peter Bergen, *Holy War Inc.*, New York: Free Press, 2001.
11. See Commission of the European Communities, "Commission Working Document: The Relationship between Safeguarding Internal Security and Complying with International Protection Obligations and Instruments," Brussels, 5 December 2001, COM (2001) 743 final; "Farewell, Londonistan?" *The Economist*, 31 January 2002; "September 11: Has Anything Changed?" *Forced Migration Review*, June 2002. ·
12. UNHCR, "Ten Refugee Protection Concerns in the Aftermath of Sept. 11," Press Release, Geneva, 23 October 2001.
13. Amnesty International, "The Arab Convention for the Suppression of Terrorism: A Serious Threat to Human Rights," London, January 2002.
14. Kenneth Waltz, "Structural Realism after the Cold War," *International Security*, vol. 25, no. 1, 2000.
15. Ibid., p. 10.
16. *Carnegie Commission on Preventing Deadly Conflict, Preventing Deadly Conflict, Final Report*, Washington DC: Carnegie Commission on Preventing Deadly Conflict, 1997, pp. xvii and 11.
17. UNHCR, *The State of the World's Refugees*, chap. 11.
18. Ibid., pp. 276–280.
19. Ibid., p. 277, emphasis added.
20. Albrecht Schnabel, "Preventing the Plight of Refugees," *Peace Review*, vol. 13, no. 1, 2001, p. 109.
21. See, for example, James C. Hathaway, *Reconceiving International Refugee Law*, Dordrecht: Martinus Nijhof, 1997.
22. UNHCR, *The State of the World's Refugees*, p. 282.
23. Ibid., pp. 277–280.
24. See Joanne van Selm, ed., *Kosovo's Refugees in the European Union*, London: Continuum, 2000, and Joanne van Selm, "Perceptions of Kosovo's Refugees," in Mary Buckley and Sally Cummings, eds., *Kosovo: Perceptions of War and Its Aftermath*, London: Continuum, 2001.
25. Schnabel, "Preventing the Plight of Refugees," p. 109.
26. UNU working definition, 2001.

2

Refugees as grounds for international action

Gil Loescher

One of the greatest challenges confronting the international community is to link the task of refugee protection and human security to the broader defence of human rights. During recent years, traditional notions of security and sovereignty have been challenged, placing refugee issues much higher on the international agenda and creating new opportunities for international action. In the wake of the terrorist attacks in the United States and the global war against terrorism after 11 September 2001, refugee movements have increasingly come to be seen as an issue of instability. Refugees are viewed not only as people in need of protection and assistance but also as potential threats to national security and even as a potential source of armed terror. Although international responses to humanitarian crises remain more often than not reactive, self-interested, and based on ad hoc initiatives, there is growing international awareness of the linkage between human rights abuses, forcible displacement of civilian populations, and local, regional, and international security.[1] Forcible displacement is a major factor in conflict and the continuation of conflict, requiring policy responses that recognize this.

The sobering experiences with interventions in protracted humanitarian and security crises during the past decade underscore the fact that humanitarian measures alone are seldom enough to deal with refugee problems. A wide range of actions, most of them far short of military action, can be taken to avert large-scale refugee crises. An intervention continuum now exists, ranging from the use of "good offices," diplomacy,

31

and "shaming" of states to the employment of sanctions and the use of military force. Sustained political and diplomatic initiatives, development assistance, human rights monitoring, and the strengthening of civil society through the building of democratic institutions are all measures that, if initiated early and given sufficient economic resources and political support, would help prevent the outbreak of violence and the mass displacement of populations. International humanitarian agencies, such as the United Nations High Commissioner for Refugees (UNHCR), promote the concept of "soft intervention" to prevent situations from degenerating into violent conflicts. However, where armed hostilities have already broken out within a country and are accompanied by widespread violations of human rights, "hard" forms of intervention, including military action, may be necessary to bring such violations to a halt.

Acting early to avert refugee crises can be demanding, but it is considerably less expensive than dealing with the fallout of a full-blown and protracted crisis.[2] What we have seen in recent years has not been an attempt to stop or prevent genocide and refugee movements by full-scale use of force. Rather, international action has on most occasions attempted to limit these crises and to provide relief after the damage has been done. It does not make sense for the international community to continue to pour resources into emergency relief and post-crisis rehabilitation and to neglect basic causes that produce terrible upheavals and mass displacements.

The thesis of this chapter is that governments cannot afford to ignore the brutalities of civil and communal conflicts and the human rights abuses that not only uproot entire communities but also cause deep-seated popular resentments and alienation and create the breeding grounds for radical political movements and terrorism. Such events engage the national security interests of states, particularly when internal conflicts result in wider regional wars and when the spillover of refugees destabilizes neighbouring countries. A large-scale movement of people across national borders, under duress, internationalizes what might otherwise be a purely domestic issue of conflict. The chapter argues that this is becoming a norm, in theory and in practice, which is increasingly accepted as grounds for international action, including armed intervention, against the state within which the refugee flow is generated.

Refugee movements and local, regional, and international security

Before taking up these arguments, however, it is important to appreciate the burden that contemporary refugee flows typically impose on receiving states. The reality of this burden has forced a growing recognition of the way refugee issues link the internal and external realms. As Stanley Hoffmann has said, "there is no way of isolating oneself from the effects of gross [human rights] violations abroad: they breed refugees, exiles, and dissidents who come knocking at our doors – and we must choose between bolting the doors, thus increasing misery and violence outside, and opening them, at some cost to our own well being."[3] The impact of a refugee flow on countries of refuge can be measured in direct and indirect economic costs, in negative social and cultural consequences, in threats to security both internally and externally, and in its broader effect on the fabric of global stability.[4]

Western donor countries, through the international refugee regime, bear a portion of the financial cost for refugee relief and assistance. But this is only part of the picture. As the numbers of asylum seekers in Western countries has increased, so have the total costs of procedures to determine refugee status and of the assistance provided to asylum seekers. By one estimate, that expense among developed countries reached US$10 billion in 2000,[5] an amount roughly 10 times the worldwide expenditure of the UNHCR for that year.

Although the perception of the threat and costs that refugees pose to host societies is frequently exaggerated or manipulated,[6] there are many instances of the security of recipient governments and communities being threatened in a fundamental way by mass in-migration. Some 90 per cent of the world's refugees are sheltered in the world's poorest states, where declining economies, chronic unemployment, and shortage of land and other resources cause growing resistance and open hostility to refugees. Thus the cost of hosting refugees falls disproportionately on nations least able to afford such strain; the presence of large impoverished refugee populations further strains resources and perpetuates the poverty of the host nation. Sudden and large-scale refugee influxes can endanger social and economic stability and security, particularly in countries already experiencing economic underdevelopment, unstable political systems, and ethnic or other social cleavages. The impact of refugees on the environment in already marginal areas can be devastating. When they compete for jobs, refugees drive wages down, and when they compete for scarce goods they create inflation. They require social services beyond those provided by international agencies, putting further strain on domestic structures that may already have been inadequate. To make matters worse, international relief efforts normally focus on refugees rather than on members of the local host population. With recent shortfalls in donor funding, the UNHCR has had to cut back on supporting integrated and area-based assistance programmes that had previously provided assistance to local populations as well as to refugees. These developments have served to increase local resentment of refugees, to exacerbate competition for the few resources available, and to reinforce the perception that refugees receive preferential treatment from the international community.

Refugee movements often threaten inter-communal harmony and undermine major societal values by altering the ethnic, cultural, religious, and linguistic composition of host populations. In countries with racial, ethnic, religious, or other tensions – that is, most countries – a refugee influx can place great strain on the system. Mass influxes can endanger social and economic stability, particularly in countries where ethnic rivalries may be virulent, where the central government is weak and consensus on the legitimacy of the political system is lacking, and where essential resources are limited. A large influx of refugees with ties to a particular domestic group can upset the internal balance and even threaten the existing system, as occurred when huge numbers of Albanian Kosovars fled into neighbouring Macedonia, threatening the host society's finely tuned ethnic composition. Universally, societies fear that uncontrolled migration may swamp their existing cultural identity. Refugees typically seek to preserve their own cultural heritage and national identity in line with their aspiration eventually to return to their homeland, thus complicating their integration into the host society.

Security concerns for the host state, particularly for less developed states, begin with the question of whether it can physically control the refugee population. At the local level, refugees are frequently associated with problems such as crime, banditry, prostitution, alcoholism, and drugs. In many instances, host countries do not have the capacity or willingness to maintain law and order in the remote areas where the largest numbers of refugees are often to be found. Refugees become the scapegoat for many of the host country's ills, and governments and opposition groups are prone to use the refugees' presence to encourage nationalistic and xenophobic sentiments.

Refugees are a security risk for some host states in more direct ways as well. Refugees frequently become a political force in their host country, influencing its policies and particularly its relationship with the country of origin. Refugee communities may align themselves with opposition parties and use this leverage as pressure on ruling governments to advance their own interests. Refugees can be "warehoused" in refugee camps for years, even decades. Without hope and despairing of the future, some refugees turn to violence and become easy recruits for terrorist networks. Armed militia and criminal elements often take refuge in refugee camps and use them for recuperation and to recruit and to mobilize for ongoing conflicts in their countries of origin. Raids and guerrilla activity across the border may drag the host state into an existing conflict, and in fact this may be the deliberate strategy of armed exile groups. The offer of sanctuary to refugees may in itself invite military retaliation; in response to real or perceived threats of "refugee warrior communities," refugee camps have increasingly become military targets. In some cases host states have themselves armed or helped to arm refugee fighting groups as a weapon against the country of origin, but then found themselves unable to control the consequences of having done so. This occurred in the Great Lakes region of Africa, resulting in the destabilization of the entire region in the late 1990s.

More often, mass expulsions are used by the sending country deliberately to destabilize or embarrass strategic or political adversaries and to undermine regional stability. As Hoffmann notes, "states can easily export mischief, so to speak, by dumping refugees or economic migrants on neighbors."[7] In such circumstances, expulsions are seriously destabilizing to receiving countries and in some cases are analogous to military invasions. Clearly, when refugees are being used as a weapon, the target state is within its rights in invoking the right of self-defence.[8]

Despite the fact that the bulk of the world's refugees remain in the developing world, the industrialized states feel increasingly threatened by the influx of refugee flows. This is in part a result of the fact that asylum seekers are no longer limited to neighbouring states. "Jet age" refugees now appear on the doorstep of distant nations. This comes, of course, on top of a steep rise in the number of illegal immigrants to the West from the developing world and Eastern Europe, many of whom use migrant smuggling and trafficking organizations to reach the West. This has resulted in a widespread perception among Western governments and their publics that they have lost control of their borders and that refugees and immigrants pose a threat to the national identity of host societies.[9] This trend has been exacerbated by the war against terrorism since September 2001. In an effort to toughen their immigration laws to prevent terrorists from entering their territories, European Union and North American governments rushed through measures that threatened to sacrifice the right to seek asylum.[10]

In Europe, the gulf between the cultural background of contemporary refugee groups and that of Europeans causes special concern. There are serious reservations about the ability of these groups to assimilate and about the willingness of Western publics to tolerate aliens in their midst. These feelings, reinforced by racial and religious prejudices, pose difficult social and political problems for European governments. Xenophobic and racist attitudes are obvious among some segments of these populations, and racist attacks are increasing in every country hosting immigrant minorities. Islamic groups are particularly targeted, especially since the September 11 incidents. Anti-immigrant and anti-refugee feelings and backlash are being exploited not only by extreme right-wing parties but also by mainstream political parties throughout Europe. As a consequence, ethnic profiling and detention of members of Islamic groups and other minorities, including immigrants and asylum seekers, have increased dramatically in Western Europe and North America.

Finally, the security implications of refugee movements extend to refugees themselves in other regions as well. In Africa, for example, harassment and mistreatment of refugees and forced repatriation have become common practices. With the international neglect of many of that continent's refugee populations, and in the absence of international assistance to support local integration programmes, most African governments have adopted policies that force refugees to live in confined camps.[11] Life in refugee camps has become increasingly dangerous. Not only are refugee camps and settlements frequently the target of direct military attacks, but refugees in these areas are also affected by a variety of other threats to their physical security. These include rape and armed robbery, forced military conscription, arbitrary arrest and imprisonment, violence between refugees and members of the local population, fighting between different groups within the same refugee community, domestic and sexual violence, and armed confrontations between refugees of different nationalities.[12]

Refugee flows as threats to peace under Chapter VII of the UN Charter

In recent years, refugee movements have played a historically unprecedented role in international politics and have repeatedly been at the centre of a rapid succession of international crises, from the Kurdish uprising in northern Iraq in 1991 to the mass exoduses from Kosovo and East Timor in 1999. Refugee movements have frequently been cited by states and international organizations as a basis for action regarding both civil and international conflicts.

There has been increasing recognition that massive refugee flows do in fact constitute a threat to international peace and security, and that they therefore invoke the enforcement powers of the United Nations. As a threat to peace and security, the imposition of refugees on other states falls under Chapter VII of the UN Charter and therefore legitimizes enforcement action not subject to the limits of purely humanitarian action. This link has been recognized for at least the past 15 years. As early as 1986, the report of a Group of Governmental Experts on International Cooperation to Avert New Flows of Refugees recognized the "great political, economic and social burdens [of massive flows of refugees] upon the international community as a whole, with dire effects on developing countries, particularly those with limited resources of their own."[13] Accordingly, it recommended intervention by the international community through the good offices of the Secretary-General, refugee prevention actions by appropriate UN bodies (including the Security Council), and better use of aid programmes to deter massive displacements. The report was subsequently endorsed by the UN General Assembly, which explicitly defined such flows as a threat to peace and security, thus opening the door to action by the Security Council under Chapter VII several years later. It should be pointed out that Article 2(7) of the UN Charter, protecting the domestic jurisdiction of member states, specifically exempts from this protection enforcement actions taken under Chapter VII. In short, a country that forces its people to flee or takes actions that compel them to leave in a manner that threatens regional peace and security has in effect internationalized its internal affairs, and provides a cogent justification for policy makers elsewhere to act directly upon the source of the threat.

This argument was also made over six decades ago by James G. McDonald, the League of Nations High Commissioner for Refugees, when he resigned in frustration at the lack of international action to halt the persecution in Germany, which was causing refugee flows to neighbouring countries. In his dramatic letter of resignation of 27 December 1935, McDonald wrote that "it will not be enough to continue the activities on behalf of those who flee from the Reich. Efforts must be made to remove or mitigate the causes which create German refugees." Such efforts, declared McDonald, fell under the League's authority to deal with any matter affecting the peace of the world, since "the protection of the individual from racial or religious intolerance is a vital condition of international peace and security."[14] The argument is also made by contemporary analysts of refugee issues: "When there is aggression by a state against its own minority such that the domestic issue becomes an international one and is perceived to threaten peace and security because the minority begin a mass flight, then defensive military intervention is justified."[15] Others point out that, if refugee flows constitute an "internationally wrongful act" or "international crime" under the principles of state responsibility, this is also a violation of the Charter and therefore responses to it are not intervention in a state's domestic affairs.[16]

These arguments are accompanied by changing conceptions of "threats" and "security" in inter-state relations. Certain internal acts and policies – especially those triggering mass expulsions or refugee movements – are increasingly regarded as threats to others, particularly by their neighbours. From this perspective, grievous human rights abuses are not an internal matter when neighbouring states must bear the cost of repression by having refugees forced on them. In recent years the Security Council itself has taken an increasingly inclusive view of "threats to peace" where actual hostilities remained limited largely to the territory of a single state.[17] The UN Security Council's Summit Declaration of 1992 included "nonmilitary sources of instability in the economic, social, humanitarian and ecological fields" as threats to international peace and security, while specifying "election monitoring, human rights verification, and the repatriation of refugees" as "integral parts of the Security Council's efforts to maintain international peace and security."[18] As Rosemarie Rogers and Emily Copeland note, "these expanded notions of what constitute threats to international or national security have important implications for the issue of forced migration: they make it easier to classify forced migration flows or the presence of forced migrants in a host country as security threats."[19]

This new thinking ties in with changing ideas of national sovereignty.[20] Although sovereignty is still regarded as a cornerstone of the international political and legal system, domestic matters previously shielded from outside interference have become open to comment and action. Since the most elementary justification for the modern state is its ability to provide reasonable security for its citizens, states that force these same citizens to flee call into question the very basis of their sovereignty. There is notably greater revulsion on the part of the international community toward using "sovereignty" to shield gross patterns of persecution, and notably less hesitation in employing pre-emptive, as opposed to reactive, approaches to such problems. Finally, there is the question of whether "sovereignty" is a consideration at all in the increasingly frequent case of "failed states" or "crises of authority" when there is no generally recognized government exercising effective authority over a state's territory. In such cases, the absence of an invitation by the targeted state is hardly determinant; what we need are reasonable criteria for determining when a state ceases to be a state, transferring to the international community not only the right but also the duty to intervene.

Intervening in refugee-producing situations on the basis of a threat to peace and security, rather than on a purely humanitarian basis, also changes some of the considerations and conditions in execution. "Proportionality" would remain a condition, as in any sanctioned use of force, but the calculus would proceed on a different basis. Intervention would be aimed not just at the immediate relief of victims, but also at rectifying the conditions that comprise a continuing threat to the peace of other states. Obviously such an "enforcement" mission could require broader changes, including in the extreme case removal of the offending government.

Secondly, the "disinterest" often specified for humanitarian interventions is not possible, since intervention to prevent refugee flows is justified precisely *because of* the impact on other states. The fact that this is a case of states acting in their own interest is in fact one reason to hope that such actions will be more effective than some actions have been in the past. This leaves the issue of how interveners can be prevented from exploiting such situations for particular gains unrelated to refugee flows. The obvious answer would be to require multilateral legitimization and execution as much as possible; in a crude sense, "interest" would provide the motive power for such justified interventions, while multilateral mechanisms would provide the steering and control.

Intervention in practice

In addition to the increasing recognition of the link between refugee flows and national, regional, and international security, international intervention related to refugee flows has in fact become more frequent in state declaration and practice since the end of the Cold War. Such intervention, in other words, is not only increasingly justifiable but actually happening. Generally, it was widely accepted during the Cold War that the use of force to save victims of massive human rights abuses was a violation of the UN Charter, which restricts the right of states to use force to purposes of self-defence. However, even during the Cold War, unilateral military interventions were carried out without the collective legitimization of the UN Security Council or other international bodies. India's intervention in East Pakistan (Bangladesh) in 1971, Vietnam's invasion of Cambodia to topple the Khmer Rouge in 1978, and Tanzania's intervention in Uganda in 1979 to overthrow Idi Amin were three cases where "hideous repression within the target state, and consequent huge refugee flows, would have seemed to provide a ready-made justification for [intervention]."[21] Yet, in none of these cases did the intervening states try to invoke the doctrine of humanitarian intervention.

During the post–Cold War era of the 1990s, international intervention as a response to refugee flows quietly, albeit haltingly, became a de facto norm in state declaration and practice. In a number of post–Cold War crises, refugees came to serve as an index of internal disorder and as *prima facie* evidence of the violation of human rights and humanitarian standards. No other issue, perhaps, provided such a clear and unassailable link between humanitarian concerns and legitimate international security issues. As a result, the Security Council, under pressure from Western governments and their publics, increasingly authorized interventions for the enforcement of global humanitarian norms under Chapter VII of the UN Charter. Mass movements of people in northern Iraq,

Liberia, and Haiti, to list but a few examples, consequently set precedents for international, regional, and unilateral intervention in the internal affairs of states.[22]

Although there developed a growing international awareness of the links between human rights abuses, forcible displacement of civilian populations, and local, regional, and international security, international responses to human rights and refugee crises remained generally reactive, self-interested, and based on ad hoc initiatives. There was no guarantee that states would intervene in situations where it was desperately needed, as in Rwanda in 1994. Bruised by their failure to restore stability in Somalia, the world's major governments and the United Nations chose to do nothing in the face of wanton mass killings in Rwanda. The major lesson drawn from the Somalia operation, particularly by the United States, was that the interventions of the early 1990s had overextended the United Nations and that in the future interventions should be much more limited and essentially restricted to the most strategically important areas of the world. In Rwanda, the real problems over intervention were not legal and conceptual. Rather those states with the capacity to intervene chose not to put their soldiers' lives at risk in a country of which their electorates knew little. As Kofi Annan acknowledged in his annual report to the UN General Assembly in 1999: "the failure to intervene was driven more by the reluctance of Member States to pay the human and other costs of intervention, and by doubts that the use of force would be successful, than by concerns about sovereignty."[23] Similar concerns prevented Western governments from committing sufficient ground forces to Bosnia with an enforcement mission to defend the so-called "safe areas," including Srebrenica. Indeed, no Western government intervened to defend human rights in the 1990s unless it was confident that the risk of casualties to its soldiers was almost zero. Even in Afghanistan following the attacks on New York and Washington, DC, the United States avoided a large-scale ground invasion that would risk incurring high numbers of American casualties, in favour of a relatively risk-free massive air campaign to root out al-Qaida and to overthrow the Taliban regime.

By the end of the 1990s, it was also true that few governments were prepared to support intervention in the absence of express Security Council authorization.[24] In Kosovo, the North Atlantic Treaty Organisation (NATO) went to war because important security interests were perceived to be at stake, including the credibility of the Western military alliance, and the use of air power meant that almost no soldiers' lives would be at risk. Whereas the United States and its NATO allies justified intervention in Kosovo and Serbia on the grounds that morality should trump legality in exceptional situations where governments commit massive human rights violations within their borders, other states strongly opposed the claim that NATO's action was lawful. Fearful that states might lose their claim to protection under the principle of non-intervention and concerned that humanitarian claims on the part of the West constituted a cover for the pursuit of selfish interests, Russia, China, and India, among others, argued that intervention without UN Security Council authority jeopardized the foundations of international order and contravened UN Charter principles of sovereignty and non-intervention. There was concern that, without the restraint of the Security Council veto, the principle of non-intervention would be softened and the international community would be on a "slippery slope" leading to a dramatic increase in inter-state use of force in the form of interventions to resolve internal conflicts.[25] Moreover, NATO's intervention in Kosovo was widely criticized for undermining the humanitarian objectives of the intervention. Rather than preventing a humanitarian disaster, NATO's air campaign accelerated Serb ethnic cleansing and led to the deaths of thousands of Kosovar Albanians. The escalation of the initial air campaign resulted in the bombing of a range of civilian facilities that were claimed to constitute legitimate military targets, causing further loss of life among civilian bystanders. Thus, the Kosovo operation underlined the fundamental problem of what to do when the permanent members of the UN Security Council are divided and how to reconcile conflicting UN Charter principles of sovereignty, non-intervention, and the protection of human rights. Above all, Kosovo demonstrated the lack of enthusiasm among many states for legitimizing interventions not authorized by the UN Security Council.

Despite growing acceptance of the links between refugee movements, human security, and intervention, the attachment to the principle of state sovereignty remains strong, especially among several of the most powerful Western states, and others such as Russia, China, India, Iran, and many developing and non-aligned states. There exists significant objection to the "right" to intervene and to the use of force to resolve human security problems, including refugee crises. Moreover, the major powers, including the United States, have been highly selective about whether and to what extent to get involved in security crises and humanitarian emergencies. State perceptions of the probability of success and considerations about costs remain significant barriers to the use of intervention. Last, but not least, the veto and voting procedure in the UN Security Council represent a strong restraint against a dramatic increase in intervention. Consequently, it seems likely that intervention on human rights grounds, even when there is a clear link to security, will continue to be a highly contested issue among states. At a minimum, it seems intervention will be considered legitimate only when it operates with the authorization of the Security Council.

The terror attacks in the United States and the US-led attacks against Afghanistan laid the groundwork for a series of interventions in the so-called global war against terror. The overthrow of the Taliban regime in Afghanistan was the first stage in a worldwide campaign against countries that allegedly harbour terrorist networks, including Iraq, Somalia, Yemen, Sudan, North Korea, the Philippines, Indonesia, and Iran. Although the United States was able to hold together a shaky but workable international coalition in its war against Afghanistan, the US–British intervention was not without controversy. A significant proportion of the world's population, particularly the Islamic world, considered the military intervention illegitimate. The possible extension of the armed war against terrorism to Iraq and beyond will even more severely test the US-led coalition, not only in the Middle East and other Islamic countries but also among its allies in Western Europe.

Unfortunately but almost predictably, the fight against terrorism has endangered the rights of refugees and migrants around the world. Most governments, including those in Europe and North America, have introduced stringent new anti-terrorist laws or have given new life to old laws once used to suppress peaceful dissent and other civil and political liberties. Asylum seekers and refugees in particular have been associated with the terrorist threat. In order to address their vulnerabilities to terrorism, governments have further tightened their immigration systems and visa regimes. Consequently, the prospects for refugee protection have declined precipitously since September 2001. Not only are refugees likely to become pawns in a geopolitical struggle in which they are redefined as agents of insecurity and terrorism, but new interventions in the Middle East or East Africa are likely to trigger yet more mass refugee flows.

Need for new and different responses

Despite the dangers inherent in the new geopolitics of anti-terrorism, there may be greater compatibility between protecting refugees and enforcing human rights, protecting security interests, and promoting international order than is the current perception of most governments today. Refugee movements demonstrate the close relationship between gross human rights violations within states and threats to regional security and stability. The connection between human rights violations and refugee movements is not simply an accidental one in which humanitarian intervention is fortuitously justified by the presence of refugees. The link is organic, in that "refugees are human rights violations made visible," in the words of a former US Coordinator of Refugee Affairs.[26]

Refugee movements are perhaps the clearest example of the principle that "once the consequences of a policy enacted for domestic purposes become external, the policy itself is open to international comment and action, with proclamations of 'sovereign rights' being no defense against outside interference."[27] As summarized in the words of Myron Weiner, "A country that forces its citizens to leave or creates conditions which induce them to leave has internationalized its internal actions.... If a people violate the boundaries of a neighboring country, then they and their government should expect others to intervene in their internal affairs."[28]

Ignoring this linkage in an age of globalization will simply lead to greater isolation and deprivation, which can breed anger, frustration, and terrorism among other things and pose yet new threats to regional and international security and order. Political realism demands that higher priority be given to combating human rights violations because of their propensity to cause regional and international instability and hence refugee movements. This will require incorporating, in current re-evaluations of state security doctrine, greater international attention to human rights violations. It is also the case that, if states remain indifferent to the plight of the world's refugees, the social and political fibre of their own societies will suffer. The way states deal with refugees speaks volumes about their human rights health and their tolerance for ethnic and racial minorities.

This chapter has argued that the imposition of refugees on other states falls under Chapter VII of the UN Charter and therefore legitimizes enforcement action not subject to the limits of purely humanitarian intervention. However, the history of the past decade has been that it is not always easy to get widespread international agreement on the use of force to resolve refugee problems. Therefore, some steps are needed in the short term to deal with the problems associated with mass forcible displacements of people. At a minimum, these include the establishment of an international rapid reaction capacity, along with credible safe haven policies to respond to refugee emergencies and the promotion and building of civil society infrastructure and human rights monitoring in local communities in conflict.

There is an urgent need for the United Nations to create effective enforcement machinery for stopping genocide and mass murder leading to mass refugee outflows. The establishment of a UN rapid reaction force composed of volunteers to be sent to crises at short notice or of multilateral brigades to be dedicated to the United Nations for intervention purposes is an essential component of a more effective future international response. Similarly, future effectiveness in dealing with internal crises leading to refugee outflows will depend on the way the European Union develops its Common Foreign and Security Policy. The

December 1999 EU Summit in Helsinki declared the establishment by 2003 of a rapid reaction capability comprising some 60,000 military forces which could be used to respond to such crises. The Helsinki Summit also foresaw the strengthening of the capacity for deploying civilian crisis management facilities, including civilian police and legal, judicial, and prison systems in post-conflict situations.

Even with new machinery available for intervention, there will still be the need to find ways to convince member states of the Security Council, especially the permanent members, that there should be restrictions on the use of the veto in exceptional cases where genocide and mass killings occur. A key question for the future will be whether it is possible to achieve consensus on situations in which it would be permissible for intervening states to override the power of the veto.

Currently, the United Nations, and the international system more generally, are not well equipped to deal with human rights violations and state-building responsibilities.[29] If the international community hopes to respond more effectively to the global problem of refugees and internal displacement, it must also strengthen the United Nations' capacity to monitor developments in human rights issues and to intercede on behalf of forced migrants. Governments must guarantee a meaningful funding base to the specialized human rights bodies of the United Nations and withdraw the financial and political constraints on human rights action.

The creation of the Office of the UN High Commissioner for Human Rights (UNHCHR) in 1993 brought a higher profile to human rights within the UN system and enhanced the monitoring of protection concerns in major crises.[30] There has also been an increase in the presence of the UN Human Rights Office staff in the field and increased activities by special rapporteurs appointed by the UN Human Rights Commission to document human rights violations in certain countries and to report back to the Commission. A key to strengthening the UN capacity to monitor human rights in the future is enhancing its capacity to undertake a protection role in the field. Nevertheless, as in the past, major weaknesses continue to exist in the UN human rights system. Countries can and often do obstruct any new initiatives by refusing entry to human rights officials and monitors. The Office is still handicapped by significant lack of resources.[31] And, despite considerable improvements, interagency coordination and the institutional division of labour regarding human rights within the United Nations remain problematic.

Until the capacity of the UN human rights regime is fully developed, non-governmental organizations (NGOs), especially human rights NGOs, will have to assume a larger share of responsibility for ensuring the protection of forcibly displaced people.[32] Protection of refugees and other displaced people requires a readiness on the part of human rights agencies to act on observed human rights abuses. In order to accomplish this, human rights NGOs need to establish a continuous presence in regions experiencing conflict.[33] NGOs provide a basis for consciousness-raising regarding humanitarian norms and democratic principles within regions, and they could enable local organizations to assume responsibility for monitoring, intervening, and managing humanitarian programmes without major external involvement. Human rights organizations, such as Human Rights Watch and Amnesty International, fill some of this gap. Yet most of these organizations have their headquarters in the West, where their constituency base and funding are the strongest. There is an urgent need to support NGO efforts to train and place independent human rights monitors in regions where they can provide liaison with local organizations interested in the problem, and to assess the protection needs of refugees, asylum seekers, and the internally displaced. These Refugee Watch organizations could record and publicize human rights violations without jeopardizing operational relief agency services. UN agencies could also contribute to this development through programmes aimed at strengthening the capacity of NGOs to work in the human rights field.

Relief NGOs, likewise, have an essential protection role to play. Many NGOs today are far more willing and able to address protection issues than they have been in the past. Their presence in most civil war situations makes them important sources of information, which is crucial for human rights monitoring, early warning of conflicts and refugee crises, and preventive diplomacy. Humanitarian organizations that operate in conflict situations should institutionalize procedures to manage and report information on human rights abuses by their own personnel in the field. Efforts should also be made to improve both the channels of communication and the readiness to act on human rights information at high political levels. At a minimum, NGOs, with the assistance of UN agencies, should train their staff regarding human rights principles and protection techniques to be used in the field.

Moreover, because NGOs have a central role in securing access to the civilian victims of conflicts and are often in close contact with both governments and opposition movements, they can play a significant part in conflict resolution. As a result of working with disenfranchised populations, NGOs are also often able to gain an understanding of the underlying tensions causing the conflict. Such information is crucial to conflict resolution processes, particularly in societies where ongoing human rights violations have become part of the spectrum of issues to be resolved in any comprehensive settlement. The presence of NGOs within communities at war and their ability to move among civilian populations and armed forces are characteristics not shared by UN agencies and donor governments. Thus, NGOs are well placed to engage in a new comprehensive form of humanitarian action, encompassing assistance and protection, mediation, and conflict resolution.[34]

In countries where central government itself is weak or non-existent and therefore unable to protect its citizens, the key issue will be not only how to bring together contending groups but how to build institutions of governance. In the Middle East, East and West Africa, and South Asia, where most of the world's most protracted refugee populations exist, there are few, if any, NGOs to monitor governments' treatment of refugees or human rights behaviour generally. Most governments in these regions also lack the legal and institutional capacity to promote refugee protection. In such situations, economic development and social stability are inseparable. Rehabilitative relief and development activities must be accompanied by support for civil society[35] in order to be effective. Sustainable progress can be achieved only if built on a strong civil foundation that allows the gains made to be consolidated throughout society. Without this foundation, relief and development activities will constitute a one-time consumption of resources that will result in little long-term change. The development of civil society is also related to the avoidance of violence. Violent political conflict and political extremism generally can be avoided only in a context in which the citizenry is able to participate meaningfully in the political decisions that affect their lives by holding the persons and institutions that exercise power over them accountable for their actions.[36] Finally, local communities need to be encouraged to develop their own religious, cultural, and institutional means to ensure security. In the future, there will have to be a growing focus on cooperation at the international and local levels, particularly in achieving peace and greater security, without which there will be a risk of a resurgence of conflict.[37]

Refugees are both a cause and a consequence of regional and global instability and conflict and directly engage the interests of states all over the world. The flight of refugees is the most clear-cut expression of the spillover effects of domestic instability and violence onto other states and into neighbouring regions. More active intervention by the international community is in the long-term interest of all governments – stability and growth depend generally on controlling disruptive forced migrations. Moreover, the global refugee problem is not going to disappear soon; in fact, as we have seen in the dramatic global developments since 11 September 2001, it is assuming new dimensions that require new and different responses.

Notes

1. This chapter draws in part on earlier work by Alan Dowty and Gil Loescher, "Refugee Flows as Grounds for International Action," *International Security*, vol. 21, no. 1, Summer 1996, pp. 43–71.

2. See Carnegie Commission on Preventing Deadly Conflict, *Preventing Deadly Conflict*, Washington DC: Carnegie Corporation of New York, 1997.

3. Stanley Hoffman, *Duties beyond Borders: On the Limits and Possibilities of Ethical International Politics*, Syracuse, NY: Syracuse University Press, 1981, p. 111.

4. Gil Loescher, *Refugee Movements and International Security*, London: IISS, 1992.

5. Marilyn Achiron, "A Timeless Treaty under Attack," *Refugees*, vol. 2, no. 123, 2001, p. 20.

6. Facts and reasoned argument often take a back seat when migration is discussed. When discussing the perceived "threats" posed by refugees and migrants, it is important to stress that these individuals also make positive contributions to receiving societies. According to some studies, for example, the effects of migration flows on receiving countries in the West are likely to be an overall net economic gain, with the possibility of a slight increase in unemployment and a slight downward pressure on wages. Even in developing countries, refugees are not always a burden on their local hosts; they may make a positive contribution to the economy in the areas where they settle. Refugees are survivors and often arrive in their new countries with skills, education, work practices, and personal resourcefulness that can have a highly positive impact on economic growth. When substantial international assistance is available, roads, schools, health centres, and agricultural extension services are established, benefiting both refugees and local communities. Unfortunately, these examples are often the exception rather than the norm, as current practice forces refugees to live in camps and to rely on the distribution of food and health supplies rather than encouraging them to contribute to their hosts' economies.

7. Stanley Hoffman, "Sovereignty and Ethics of Intervention," lecture at the Joan B. Kroc Institute for International Peace Studies, University of Notre Dame, USA, 24 January 1995.

8. Myron Weiner, ed., *International Migration and Security*, Boulder, CO: Westview Press, 1993, pp. 8–9, and Leon Gordenker, *Refugees in International Politics*, New York: Columbia University Press, 1987, pp. 188–189.

9. For a discussion and debate about the impact of refugee and migration flows on national identity and societal security, see O. Wæver, B. Buzan, M. Kelstrup, and P. Lemaitre, eds., *Identity, Migration and the New Security Agenda in Europe*, London: Pinter, 1993; B. Buzan, *People, States and Fear: An Agenda for International Security Studies in the Post–Cold War Era*, Hemel Hempstead: Harvester-Wheatsheaf, 1991; B. Buzan, O. Wæver, and D. DeWilde, eds., *Security: A New Framework for Analysis*, London: Lynne Rienner, 1998; and Joanne van Selm, ed., *Kosovo Refugees in the European Union*, London: Pinter, 2000. See also chapter 5 in this volume by Astri Suhrke.

10. See Human Rights Watch, *World Report 2002*, New York: Human Rights Watch, 2002, pp. 628–644.

11. For discussion of these security threats to the person in Africa, see Jeff Crisp, "Africa's Refugees: Patterns, Problems and Policy Challenges," *New Issues in Refugee Research*, Geneva: UNHCR, Working Paper no. 28, August 2000.

12. Human Rights Watch has issued numerous reports about threats to the physical security of refugees in Africa and about the deteriorating conditions in refugee camps.

13. UN Doc. A/41/324, 13 May 1986; see the analysis in Luke Lee, "Toward a World without Refugees: The United Nations Group of Governmental Experts on International Cooperation to Avert New Flows of Refugees," *British Yearbook of International Law*, vol. 57 (London: H. Frowde), 1986, pp. 317–336.

14. League document C.13, M.12, 1936, annex, quoted by Gervase Coles, in Gil Loescher and Laila Monahan, eds., *Refugees and International Relations*, Oxford: Clarendon Press, 1989, pp. 409–410.

15. Howard Adelman, "The Ethics of Humanitarian Intervention: The Case of Kurdish Refugees," *Public Affairs Quarterly*, vol. 6, no. 1, January 1992, p. 75.

16. Lee, "Toward a World without Refugees," p. 332.

17. Lori Fisler Damrosch, "Changing Conceptions of Intervention in International Law," in Laura W. Reed and Carl Kaysen, eds., *Emerging Norms of Justified Intervention*, Cambridge, MA: American Academy of Arts and Sciences, 1993, p. 100ff.

18. *UN Security Council Summit Declaration*, New York: United Nations, 1992.

19. Rosemarie Rogers and Emily Copeland, *Forced Migration: Policy Issues in the Post–Cold War Period*, Medford, MA: Fletcher School of Law and Diplomacy, Tufts University, 1993, p. 12.

20. For background, see Lori Fisler Damrosch, ed., *Enforcing Restraint: Collective Intervention in Internal Conflicts*, New York: Council on Foreign Relations Press, 1993; Nigel Rodley, ed., *To Loose the Band of Wickedness: International Intervention in the Defence of Human Rights*, London: Brasseys, 1992; and Christopher Greenwood, "Is There a Right of Humanitarian Intervention?" *The World Today*, vol. 49, no. 2, February 1993, pp. 34–40.

21. Adam Roberts, "Humanitarian War: Military Intervention and Human Rights," *International Affairs*, vol. 69, no. 3, July 1993, p. 434.

22. For a discussion of these cases as well as for the Cold War period, see Nicholas J. Wheeler, *Saving Strangers: Humanitarian Intervention in International Society*, Oxford: Oxford University Press, 2000.

23. Kofi Annan, *Preventing War and Disaster: A Growing Global Challenge*, New York: United Nations, 1999, p. 21.

24. For a discussion of the intervention in Kosovo, see Nicholas J. Wheeler, "Humanitarian Intervention after Kosovo: Emergent Norm, Moral Duty or the Coming Anarchy?" *International Affairs*, vol. 77, no. 1, Winter 2001, pp. 113–128.

25. Annie Julie Semb, "The New Practice of UN Authorized Interventions: A Slippery Slope of Forcible Interference?" *Journal of Peace Research*, vol. 37, no. 4, July 2000, pp. 469–488.

26. Jonathan Moore, "Refugees and Foreign Policy: Immediate Needs and Durable Solutions," lecture at Harvard University, USA, 6 April 1987.

27. John Chipman, "The Future of Strategic Studies: Beyond Even Grand Strategy," *Survival*, vol. 34, no. 1, Spring 1992, p. 112.

28. Weiner, *International Migration and Security*, pp. 25–26.

29. For further discussion, see Gil Loescher, *The UNHCR and World Politics: A Perilous Path*, Oxford: Oxford University Press, 2001.

30. As part of a UN-wide effort to give a higher priority to the integration of human rights into the various activities and programmes of the United Nations, the High Commissioner is now a member of the four executive committees that orchestrate the United Nations' work in humanitarian affairs, peace and security, economic and social affairs, and development.

31. According to *The Financial Times*, 20 March 2001, the Office of the UNHCHR had a regular budget of US$21–22 million, or 2 per cent of the UN budget during 2000. Vol-

REFUGEES AS GROUNDS FOR INTERNATIONAL ACTION 49

untary contributions from governments raised another US$44 million, but the agency's activities need to be funded regularly out of the core UN budget.

32. For background see Elizabeth Ferris, "The Role of Non-Governmental Organizations in the International Refugee Regime," in Niklaus Steiner, Gil Loescher, and Mark Gibney, eds., *UNHCR and the Protection of Refugees and Human Rights* (forthcoming).

33. Diane Paul, *Beyond Monitoring and Reporting: The Field-Level Protection of Civilians under Threat*, New York: Jacob Blaustein Institute for the Advancement of Human Rights and the Center for the Study of Societies in Crisis, 2000, and Mark Frohardt, Diane Paul, and Larry Minear, *Protecting Human Rights: The Challenge to Humanitarian Organizations*, Providence, RI: Watson Institute for International Studies, Occasional Paper no. 35, 1999.

34. Kimberly Maynard, *Healing Communities in Conflict: International Assistance in Complex Emergencies*, New York: Columbia University Press, 1999.

35. "Civil society" refers to non-state community-based groups, such as religious associations, advocacy groups focusing on human rights, democracy, or the environment, civic associations, business and professional associations, labour unions, women's groups, cooperatives, academic institutions, and student groups.

36. Jochen Hippler, *The Democratisation of Disempowerment: The Problem of Democracy in the Third World*, London: Pluto Press, 1995, and Marc Howard Ross, *The Management of Conflict: Interpretations and Interests in Comparative Perspective*, New Haven, CT: Yale University Press, 1993.

37. Paul Richards, *Fighting for the Rain Forest: War, Youth and Resources in Sierra Leone*, Oxford: James Currey, 1996. Richards makes a number of suggestions regarding the mobilization of local institutions and means to deal with conflict, including "smart relief," more creative use of the local radio, and greater involvement of local communities in analysing why conflicts occur and how they can be prevented.

3

Refugees and human displacement in contemporary international relations: Reconciling state and individual sovereignty

Gary G. Troeller

In the contemporary era, the forces of globalization at one level, and those of ethnic conflict, nationalist secessionism, and communal violence at another, characterize the patterns of instability in many parts of the world. The concepts of good governance, civil society, the protection of human rights/security, individual sovereignty, and humanitarian intervention are gaining currency in policy discourse. The prominence these concepts enjoy, at least rhetorically, is tied in no small way to two related but distinct phenomena: migratory movements and the forced displacement of peoples. The former is related to glaring inequalities in wealth between industrialized and poorer countries and the impact of market forces. The latter is directly related to massive human displacement as a consequence of armed conflict, persecution, and widespread human rights abuse.

The phenomenon of forced displacement – through violent conflict or structural deprivation – has resulted in refugees becoming a defining characteristic of the post–Cold War era and contemporary international relations. Refugees, long regarded as a peripheral issue or a matter of discretionary charitable concern to policy makers, now figure prominently on the international policy agenda. Liberal internationalists argue that, in the name of humanitarian principles, something must be done to address both the root causes and the manifestations of this issue. Realists, largely driven by concerns of national interests and the opinion that conflict is a natural feature of international politics, also acknowledge that the sheer numbers involved often constitute a threat to regional security and at times to wider international security. Along with the impact of a globalizing economy, the refugee issue has forced many academics and policy makers to recognize that the basic unit of analysis in international relations – the state – is no longer wholly adequate as an explanatory or predictive tool and, by extension, traditional conceptions of dealing with security issues are inadequate in an increasingly post-Westphalian world.

The chapter first focuses on the causes of forced displacement and the legal and normative framework of refugee protection. The chapter then moves to developments in the post–Cold War period and current challenges confronting the Office of the United Nations High Commissioner for Refugees (UNHCR), not least in the aftermath of the terrorist attacks in the United States of 11 September 2001. It is argued that there is an increasingly solid basis for action that would significantly mitigate, if not resolve, the refugee issue if the political will can be marshalled.

World disorder: Concepts in conflict

Greed, ideological differences, and religious tensions have always played a role in human displacement. However, to understand the genesis of forced displacement, the continuing inability of the "international community" to deal with this problem coherently and consistently, and the likelihood of future displacements, it is useful to look at the four underlying principles of world order, most of which are enshrined in the UN Charter and all of which, as Stanley Hoffman has observed, "are flawed and in conflict with one another."[1] These principles are state sovereignty, the right to national self-determination, democracy (based on constitutional government), and respect for human rights. Although limits of space preclude a full discussion of these principles, the contradictions rather than complementarity of these concepts can briefly be outlined as follows.

The UN Charter enjoins its members, under the principle of state sovereignty, to respect the territorial integrity of other state members. Yet the concept has little relevance in a rapidly globalizing economy given the nexus of financial, industrial, and commercial relations that consistently breach traditional notions of state sovereignty. However, the principle does tend to shield smaller states from more overt forms of imperialist or military aggression, which explains why the Group of 77, among others state actors, so fiercely uphold this principle. Unfortunately, it also provides some states with a legal barrier behind which they can carry out atrocities against their own citizens.

The second principle is that of the right to national self-determination. From the late nineteenth century, liberals from Mazzini to Woodrow Wilson believed that a world of sovereign nation-states, each having achieved its destiny of obtaining a state of its own, would live in harmony. Yet no one has ever adequately defined what the national or the "national self" is. Moreover, if one takes the concepts of ethnicity and language as the principal determinants of what constitutes a nation, there are an estimated 5,000 nations and 6,000 distinct languages in the world.[2] The possibilities for further challenges to state sovereignty and international order in terms of an exponential increase in state formation may be imagined.

To counteract the potential divisiveness of nation-states, Wilsonian liberals proposed a third principle, that of constitutional democracy, on the Kantian assumption that democracies, with their respect for citizens' rights and rational discussion, would not resort to war. However the UN Charter, unlike the European Union, does not require that all UN members be democracies. In essence, sovereignty and self-determination have more legitimacy than self-government. In terms of governance, as a counterbalance to sovereignty the Charter mentions the fourth principle: respect for human rights and fundamental freedoms via international cooperation. In terms of world order, the gulf between domestic affairs and inter-state relations remains distinct.

The tension between principles is further compounded by the fact that not all democracies are liberal in nature or respect individual and minority rights. Indeed, not a few democracies are democratic in name only, if not Jacobin in nature, allowing nothing to stand in the way of the majority or dominant ethnic group. In many new democracies, voting blocs are largely reflections of ethnic constituencies. In countries lacking a long democratic tradition, the absence of developed mediating institutions means that elections tend to follow ethnic lines. Even liberal democracies may reserve rights and benefits for nationals, and deny other fundamental rights to foreigners and immigrants. In light of these realities it is understandable that the fourth principle, universal human rights, which would protect people irrespective of which regime they lived under, has gained prominence over recent decades. Given the countervailing tendencies of these basic principles of international order it will be clear that it is difficult for most states to pursue all four simultaneously.

The normative and legal framework of refugee protection

Isaiah Berlin called the twentieth century that "dreadful century"[3] when an estimated 100 million persons died in armed conflict and an additional 170 million perished as a consequence of political violence. Reliable statistics on refugee numbers over the past 100 years do not exist. However, if figures were available they would no doubt be as compelling as the numbers of fatalities from armed conflict or political violence. In the aftermath of the Second World War the United Nations was established to promote world peace. At roughly the same time, impelled by the horrors of the Holocaust, the human rights movement not only gathered momentum but shifted emphasis from a less than auspicious record in protecting minority rights in the 1930s and 1940s to a focus on individual human rights. Between 1948 and the present, 24 international human rights instruments have been established and one, the Convention Against Slavery, reaffirmed.[4]

These international instruments include the benchmark Universal Declaration of Human Rights, which addresses many rights crucial to refugee protection such as the right to life, liberty, and security of the person; the right not to be subjected to cruel, inhuman, or degrading treatment; the right to freedom of movement and the right to leave and return to one's country; the right not to be subjected to arbitrary arrest, detention, or exile; and the right to nationality. The 1951 Convention Relating to the Status of Refugees was the first in a series of human rights treaties that transcribed the ideals of the Universal Declaration into legally binding obligations. The legal link between human rights and refugee protection is found in Article 14 of the Universal Declaration, which affirms the "right to seek and enjoy in other countries asylum from persecution."

The 1951 Convention remains the most specific and comprehensive treaty for any vulnerable group and sets out a "bill of rights" for refugees, the paramount right being the prohibition of *refoulement*, or return of asylum seekers at borders. The 1951 Convention has been ratified by approximately two-thirds of the member states of the United Nations. Although the Convention provides an impressive array of rights for refugees, it does not define, *inter alia*, "persecution" or proper levels of reception of refugees and asylum seekers. Standards in this connection are, however, developed in three other legal instruments known collectively as "the UN Bill of Rights": the Universal Declaration, the 1966 International Covenant on Civil and Political Rights, and the 1966 International Covenant on Economic, Social and Cultural Rights. Particular categories of refugees and displaced peoples receive specific attention in such treaties as the 1979 UN Convention on the Elimination of All Forms of Discrimination Against Women and the 1989 Convention on the Rights of the Child (CRC). In the CRC, the principle of the "best interests of the child" has special meaning for displaced children, as the norm runs through all procedures and decisions concerning a child irrespective of migration status. Other important instruments are the 1984

Convention Against Torture and Other Cruel, Inhuman or Degrading Treatment or Punishment and the 1950 European Convention for the Protection of Human Rights.[5]

While the Cold War forestalled much progress on the human rights front in a practical sense, given the absence of firm enforcement mechanisms for the overwhelming majority of instruments, the advance of the human rights movement did represent a significant development in the formation of an ethical counterweight to power-based national interest reinforced by emphasis on state sovereignty. Moreover, during the Cold War the 1951 Convention, supplemented by regional instruments such as the Organization of African Unity Convention on Refugees in Africa and the Cartegena Declaration in Latin America, which address displacement as a result of generalized violence or breakdown in public order, enabled some 35 million refugees to be granted asylum and ultimately to return home in safety and dignity or to find a new home in other countries.

Despite the resilience of the refugee protection regime since its inception in the early days of the Cold War, there have been worrying developments, particularly since the mid-1980s, which threaten the 3,500-year-old tradition of asylum and call into question the applicability of the international protection framework. A number of reasons can be suggested. An increasing number of non-European asylum seekers from all over the world were arriving directly in Europe. These newcomers – Iranians, Iraqis, Turks, and Sri Lankans, among others – did not conform to the Cold War stereotype of refugees. Unlike the massive, organized resettlement of Indo-Chinese in the 1970s and 1980s, these movements were spontaneous. They resulted from a series of internal conflicts and human rights violations in Asia, Africa, Latin America, and the Middle East.[6]

This phenomenon coincided with the economic recession of the 1980s. Precipitated by the oil crisis of the early 1970s, this severely reduced Europe's need for migrant labour. The increase in asylum seekers was further driven by easier access to air travel and by the spread of television and video to even the most remote parts of the world, where images of the good life in the industrialized world accentuated the chasm between rich and poor. In the absence of migration possibilities, a certain percentage of persons seeking better economic and social conditions entered the asylum channel. The change in the Cold War European mould of asylum seeker and the phenomenon of mixed flows of peoples seeking asylum, including economic migrants, tended to blur the distinction between legitimate asylum seekers and those seeking better opportunities and led to a sentiment that the overwhelming majority of asylum seekers were "bogus."

Between 1983 and 1989 the number of asylum seekers in Western

Europe increased from 70,000 to 200,000.[7] The asylum determination mechanisms of West European governments were increasingly strained and the annual cost of determining status and providing social benefits soared. According to one estimate, the combined cost of administering the asylum process and providing benefits to asylum seekers in the 13 major industrialized countries increased from approximately US$500 million in 1983 to US$7 billion in 1990.[8] By 1992, asylum applications in Europe peaked at some 700,000, with the disintegration of Yugoslavia. During this period, in addition to genuine asylum seekers, many poor residents of former communist states in Europe, particularly Romanians and Bulgarians exercising their new-found freedom of movement, entered the asylum channel looking for better opportunities.[9]

Post–Cold War balance sheet and humanitarian response

With the end of the Cold War there was a short-lived optimism that the triumph of liberal democracy and market forces would lead to a new era characterized by peace and stability. There was also an outburst of renewed faith in the United Nations, and optimism was further exemplified by Boutros Ghali's *Agenda for Peace* in 1992. Between 1988 and 1994, 21 new peace-keeping or peace-building operations were mounted, compared with 13 UN peace-keeping operations during the previous 40 years. This optimism gave further impetus to the human rights movement. However, as is well known, hopes for a New World Order quickly faded with the upsurge in what are popularly described as ethnic conflicts and the related phenomenon of nationalist secession movements. The increase in intra-state conflict also led to massive forced displacement and further pressures on asylum countries.

Since the end of the Cold War, over 50 states have undergone major transformations, approximately 100 armed conflicts have been fought, over 4 million persons have died as a result of armed conflict or political violence,[10] and the UNHCR has seen the number of persons under its care rise from 15 million in 1990 to over 27 million in 1995. The magnitude of the latter figure is better appreciated when one considers that in 1970 the UNHCR was responsible for 2 million refugees. Although civilians have always suffered in conflicts, there is a difference between the nature of warfare at the beginning of the twentieth century and contemporary conflicts. At the turn of the twentieth century, civilians accounted for approximately 5 per cent of casualties in armed conflicts. In contemporary conflicts, 90 per cent of the casualties are civilian.[11] Those fortunate enough to survive are refugees. The processes of national self-determination, democratization, and new state formation, the last usually involving the breakup of existing states, normally entail violence. Since the fall of the Berlin Wall, 30 new states have gained independence, bringing the membership of the United Nations from 159 in 1989 to its current level of 189. These countervailing forces, coupled with the related phenomenon of ethnic and communal strife, account for much of the conflict and forced displacement of peoples that has been the hallmark of the post–Cold War period.

Unfortunately, the inclination of the major players to resort to UN-sponsored peace-keeping and peace-building missions has receded with the perceived failure of the United Nations to handle Somalia and former Yugloslavia satisfactorily. At the end of the twentieth century, peace-enforcement missions were being conducted by regional groups (US-led force in Haiti, the Military Observer Group of the Economic Community of West African States (ECOMOG) in West Africa, and the North Atlantic Treaty Organisation (NATO) in Kosovo). NATO's intervention in Kosovo under the banner of "humanitarian intervention" continues to be debated, in terms of strategy, tactics, and deployment without Security Council authorization. Simultaneously, its actions have intensified discussions on the issue of a "just war," the unacceptability of gross human rights violations – including forced human displacement – carried out behind the shield of sovereignty, and the importance of respecting minority rights.

The human rights movement has gathered renewed force over the past decade. Moreover, there is an incontestable increase in public awareness regarding the moral imperative "to do something" to assist people beyond borders. There is a vibrant discussion of multilateral intervention (humanitarian intervention properly understood), defined as a comprehensive approach to intervention sanctioned by the United Nations, whether to prevent outright hostilities or, at least in post-conflict situations, to avoid a recurrence of the same problems, via the timely involvement of humanitarian, financial, development institutions, non-governmental organizations (NGOs), and international troop or police contingents, as appropriate. However, it is far from clear if this emerging norm is or will be translated into practice. The likelihood is that such interventions will continue to be selective in application, at least for the foreseeable future. Some conflicts attract more attention than others. The absence of timely and effective action to stem gross human rights violations in Africa, particularly in Rwanda and Sierra Leone, where terrible atrocities have been committed, is a prime example. Kosovo and East Timor offer more recent examples of the same trend. Memories of ineffective intervention in Somalia and Bosnia have reinforced those realists in policy-making circles who characterize such interventions as "foreign policy as social work."[12] In the absence of an overarching foreign policy framework and the political will to develop and apply mechanisms to resolve intra-state conflict, multilateral intervention, involving both political will and the requisite deployment of force if necessary, is likely to be timely and relatively effective only when there is a convergence of political interests of the key players involved, as was demonstrated in Iraq in 1991.

As a result of the tumult that has characterized the political landscape during the past decade, the 1990s saw a major transformation in UNHCR's operations. From a reactive, exile-oriented, and refugee-specific approach, the UNHCR adopted a proactive, homeland-oriented, and holistic approach – proactive in the sense that the Office is more involved in activities aimed at preventing human rights abuses and situations that give rise to forced displacement; homeland-oriented because the UNHCR has increasingly emphasized not only the duties of asylum countries but also the responsibilities of countries of origin; holistic because the organization has endeavoured to pursue a more comprehensive, long-term approach to the problem of forced displacement that emphasizes the needs of not only refugees but also internally displaced, returnees, asylum seekers, stateless persons, and others of concern. The organization has also stressed the nexus between relief, rehabilitation, reconstruction, and development, especially in post-conflict situations in order to prevent secondary exoduses.[13]

The UNHCR has forged links with peace-keeping units, vastly expanded its assistance activities and operations in conflict zones, and strengthened its role as the lead coordinating agency in emergency operations, and is currently present in over 120 countries. It has also deepened its links with development institutions, including the World Bank and the United Nations Development Programme (UNDP), as well as expanded the network of NGOs and human rights bodies with which it cooperates, *inter alia*, to address the issue of the continuum ranging from relief to post-conflict reconstruction. The Office has also become more involved with the internally displaced. Although the organization's expertise has been sharpened as a result of its involvement in, and lessons learned from, its major emergency operations Iraq, former Yugoslavia, the Great Lakes region, and Kosovo, the UNHCR is hampered in carrying out its mandate owing to perennial funding problems and limited staff resources.

Given the unwillingness of concerned powers to undertake multilateral political intervention to prevent or resolve armed conflicts at an early stage, the international community is likely to continue to rely on the UNHCR and related agencies to fill the breach via classical humanitarian assistance. Rather than taking a more comprehensive approach to resolving the causes leading to forced displacement, unarmed relief workers will be left to deal with the consequences. The involvement of the UNHCR in providing international legal protection to those who have lost state protection is necessary; no other UN agency or NGO can do this. It is not, however, sufficient. In other words, the UNHCR cannot provide physical protection in open conflict situations or single-handedly resolve such conflicts. Although non-political, the UNHCR does not work in a political vacuum. People flee not by accident but for reasons of persecution or generalized armed conflict. The issues that caused flight must be addressed in a comprehensive manner and this, given the dimensions of forced displacement, requires multilateral action. Humanitarian, political, and security problems and their solutions are linked.

Unfortunately, many governments, rich and poor alike, do not share this view. The proliferation of conflict in the post–Cold War era, related media coverage, and the numbers of people fleeing human rights violations as well as poverty have caused many countries to perceive the pressure of emigration, and by extension asylum seekers, from distant and not so distant lands as a direct threat to their own identity.

Refugee protection at a crossroads

During the Cold War, refugees were largely perceived as the direct or indirect result of the East–West standoff. Refugees figured prominently in foreign policy considerations of the United States and many of its allies and thus enjoyed strategic importance in the context of great power rivalry. Hence industrialized countries were predisposed to accept asylum applications. This predisposition ended with the fall of the Berlin Wall, the dissolution of the Soviet Union, and the upsurge in asylum applications, particularly in Western Europe. Although the majority of the world's refugees still reside in poor third world countries, the previously warm welcome that industrialized countries showed to the asylum seeker has decidedly cooled. Today the emphasis is on migration control rather than asylum rights. The new defensiveness has resulted in the development of large-scale refugee flows such as those from former Yugoslavia and Kosovo being handled through temporary protection regimes and attempts at "burden-sharing." Additionally, many European Union (EU) governments have introduced restrictive measures based on three resolutions approved in London in 1992 by EU ministers responsible for immigration. These measures defined "manifestly unfounded" asylum applications, host (or safe) third countries that asylum seekers had transited and to which they can be returned, and countries where there is generally no risk of persecution. These procedures were aimed at accelerating the assessment of asylum claims and expediting refugee returns.

The resolutions are not binding, but they have been applied in EU member states and further afield.[14]

These measures have been reinforced by other policies established to combat mixed flows of refugees and illegal immigrants trying to access Europe, entangling both groups in the same migration control net. These non-arrival policies range from carrier sanctions – fines for airlines transporting improperly documented asylum seekers – through extended visa requirements, to outposting immigration officers to intercept prospective asylum seekers without proper documentation to prevent them from reaching their destination. With channels for legal entry increasingly blocked off – not least in the absence of an EU immigration policy – asylum seekers as well as economic migrants have turned to smugglers and traffickers, which has not instilled public confidence in the integrity of asylum seekers. The debate around asylum has become polarized, and alarmists, whether in political parties or in the media, have resorted to xenophobic and at times racist rhetoric to advance their own agenda.

Against this background, the 1951 Convention has come under attack. A large number of countries apply the refugee definition restrictively, for example in their reluctance to recognize persons fleeing from generalized conflicts or non-state agents of persecution as Convention refugees. As a result, the percentage of persons recognized under the 1951 Convention has dropped, with many given lesser status, such as humanitarian or "B" status or special leave to remain. Frustrated by their inability to control illegal immigration, and mistakenly perceiving the Convention as a migration tool, several countries have resorted to drastic approaches. For example, the strategy proposal under the 1998 Austrian EU presidency called for a defence line around Europe to secure the continent from asylum seekers and immigrants as well as for the amendment or replacement of the Convention altogether. Similar calls for reopening the Convention or scrapping it altogether have been voiced in policy circles in other European countries and Australia.

There has been a counter-argument. The heads of state and government of the European Union, meeting in 1999 in Tampere, Finland, under the Finnish EU presidency, reaffirmed the rights of individuals to seek asylum, placing asylum rights ahead of migration controls and outlining a number of guarantees for those in need of protection in or access to the European Union "based on the full and inclusive application" of the 1951 Convention. The Tampere Conclusions included reference to a comprehensive approach to migration and political, development, and human rights issues in countries of origin and transit.[15] It remains to be seen, however, the degree to which "the spirit of Tampere" will be translated into appropriate EU-wide asylum legislation.

Given repeated criticisms from various quarters that the 1951 Convention is no longer relevant and should be re-examined if not replaced, in 2000 the UNHCR decided to launch the Global Consultations process with the dual purpose of reaffirming the enduring integrity of the treaty and revitalizing the international refugee protection regime. The Consultations process involves governments, academics, and NGOs along with UNHCR officials. It examines legal issues pertaining to differing interpretations of the refugee definition under the Convention, for example with regard to "non-state agents of persecution," gender-based persecution, and safe countries. Additionally, the Global Consultations look at practical issues on which the Convention is silent, such as mass flight situations, burden-sharing, and temporary protection. The goal of this process, which was concluded in mid-2002, was to reach common agreement on many issues that have been the subject of debate as well as common practice, to publish the results of deliberations on key issues as a guide to refugee status determination, and to set an Agenda for Protection. The centrepiece of the Global Consultations was the first ever meeting of states party to the Convention on 12 December 2001 in Geneva, where more than 150 countries were represented and over 70 ministers attended. Another goal was to reach agreement on a more effective monitoring system regarding the implementation of the Convention. The challenges inherent in sustaining the international protection regime have of course been made more difficult by the events of 11 September 2001, which have heightened feelings of insecurity among the general public and governments alike, and reinforced the trend towards more immigration control and restrictive practices regarding "foreigners" at the expense of asylum rights.

The way forward

In a particularly courageous speech to the General Assembly on 20 September 1999, UN Secretary-General Kofi Annan spoke of rights beyond borders, of "individual sovereignty," and of the human rights and fundamental freedoms of each individual under the UN Charter, further challenging the old consensus based on the Treaty of Westphalia. The Secretary-General said that traditional definitions of national interest must be broadened in the new millennium to embrace common goals and values, recognizing that in an increasingly interdependent world the collective interest *is* the national interest. He has also underscored the problem of the readiness to intervene in some areas of conflict while "limiting ourselves to humanitarian palliatives in other crises that ought to shame us into action."[16]

Against this background can we argue that the normative, legal, institutional, and political framework through which we address human rights, refugees, and conflict remains inadequate to the task? Although the political consensus is still evolving and institutional mechanisms are still problematic, it should be clear that the growing body of human rights norms and laws referred to above provides an increasingly solid basis for action. Examples are the recent establishment of war crimes tribunals for the former Yugoslavia and Rwanda and the establishment of an International Criminal Court. The arrests of the former president of Chile, Augusto Pinochet, and of Slobodan Milosevic of Yugoslavia and the extradition of Milosevic to The Hague to appear before the War Crimes Tribunal also mark a watershed in this context, as does the conviction of three Serb soldiers for rape as a war crime. Moreover Canada, Japan, and Norway have mainstreamed human security in their foreign policies.

As Alan Dowty, Gil Loescher, and others have pointed out, international customary law has been advancing in the direction of humanitarian intervention, particularly in situations leading to transborder forced displacement of peoples, based on the common dictum of *sic utere tuo ut alienum non laedes* ("use your own property in such a manner as not to injure that of another"). They cite Oppenheim, who states that this maxim "is applicable to relations of States no less than to those of individuals" and is one "of those general principles of law recognized by civilized States which [the International Court of Justice] is bound to apply by virtue of Article 38 of its Statute."[17]

Along with these developments, the United Nations has invoked Chapter VII of the Charter in situations of massive forced displacement even if the displacement was primarily internal, as the United Nations characterized the dissolution of Somalia in the early 1990s. This was the first time the United Nations intervened in the domestic affairs of a member state when that "state did not pose a military threat to its neighbours." The United Nations also intervened without the consent of the state concerned. Under Security Council Resolution 751 of 24 April 1993, the United Nations justified its interventon in Somalia on the basis of "the magnitude of human suffering," which constituted a threat to international peace and security. The other major precedent for intervention was under Resolution 688 of 5 April 1991, when the United Nations invoked Chapter VII to intervene in Iraq to preserve international peace and security given the magnitude of the Kurdish exodus into neighbouring Turkey; it subsequently deployed forces inside northern Iraq to protect the Kurdish minority from its own central government.[18]

Although other problems exist in international relations, by now it is commonly acknowledged that the core problem in terms of conflict is what Leslie Gelb, President of the US Council on Foreign Relations, has called uncivil civil wars, which threaten the tenuous stability of many newer states and even chip away at the cohesion of many long-functioning states. In addition to the actual or potential traditional transborder security implications of such conflicts, they also represent a grave threat to fundamental freedoms and human rights, or essential human security, as evidenced by the forced displacement of peoples.

Without wishing to underplay the complexities of intra-state conflict and the reluctance of many states and most of the orthodox community of realists involved in policy formulation to come to grips with the fact that we have already entered a post-Westphalian period, it should be noted that much of the modus operandi to deal with conflict resolution and human rights abuses already exists. It is a question of whether we wish to use the tools at hand and to develop new ones as necessary. It must also be acknowledged that any effective approach will entail a further erosion of sovereignty, which has long since failed to live up to its absolute pretensions in the context of interdependence and globalization.

Although a number of authors have advanced blueprints for models and measures for containing conflict, one of the most interesting and comprehensive recent exercises in this area has been the Carnegie Commission on Preventing Deadly Conflict. The Commission's final report, published in 1997, set out an interesting array of preventive measures – grouped under operational prevention, strategies in the face of crisis, and structural measures – to deal with the root causes of conflicts, which, contrary to the assumptions of realists, the Commission found neither inevitable nor insoluble. These tools, in brief, involve not only early warning mechanisms – which, although disparate, already exist but continue to go unheeded – but much stronger multilateral responses involving political, military, economic, and humanitarian intervention, including adequately equipped, standing rapid deployment peace-keeping and peace-making forces (already foreseen under the Charter in 1945 but never established) numbering 5,000–10,000 troops. The Danes and the Dutch have already offered to make such a force available to the United Nations. The Brahimi Report[19] outlines what should be done to invigorate UN peace-keeping capacity in the wake of the Kosovo crisis, and the European Union is pursuing the establishment of a 60,000-strong rapid reaction force. Rather than creating a new agency or agencies for dealing with the internally displaced and humanitarian response, which some have called for, increasing cooperation between key UN agencies involved in the existing inter-agency group on humanitarian response under the auspices of the Office for the Coordination of Humanitarian Affairs should be sufficient to meet new challenges.

For those realists who argue either that such conflicts cannot be stopped or that it would be too costly to do so, it is worth mentioning that Major-General Romeo Dallaire, the Canadian UN commander in Kigali,

Rwanda, in 1994, has said that, had he been provided with a mechanized, well-trained, and rapidly deployed force of 5,000 at the outset of the hostilities, much of the slaughter that culminated in up to 800,000 deaths within a three-month period could have been averted. (An independent panel of senior military officers generally agreed with him.) As to the argument that the costs of such an operation would have been too high, three years of humanitarian intervention cost the international community US$2 billion. It has been estimated that preventive intervention would have cost a third of that sum.[20]

The foregoing measures would have to be complemented by active regional institutions, the assistance of a variety of non-state actors, and above all courageous and clear-sighted leadership at the national and international level that is not captive to cheap "quick-fix" or early exit strategies, which should belong to a bygone era. The reasons behind many conflicts are complex and thus require a sustained and multifaceted approach, not least in combating poverty through mini-Marshall plans and putting an end to discriminatory practices.

Education is key element in any attempt to promote tolerance and prevent widespread violence. Most specialists in the field of ethnic conflict, although acknowledging the force of ethnically based identity, do not subscribe to the thesis that ethnic conflict is inevitable or that some parts of the world are condemned to chaos. The evils of this type of conflict are embedded in the minds of individuals, not in their genes, religion, or race. Historical prejudices can be addressed through education. Measures can be taken to avoid situations developing that enable demagogues to exploit ancient animosities, demonize groups, and orchestrate atrocities. In the "information age" it should be possible to use positive information to counter negative information, distorted histories, or the perceptions some groups have of other groups. A culture of prevention must be created, and its ethos and message must be mainstreamed into the curriculum of schools and religious institutions, supported by the media, and reinforced by the United Nations and other regional and international organizations so as to become part of the global heritage. In an increasingly interdependent world with instant information, we no longer have the negative luxury of denial or averting our eyes, let alone maintaining that what happens in a far away country, about whose people we know little, does not concern us.

Given the often countervailing tendencies of sovereignty, the right to national self-determination, and protection of human rights, the Carnegie Commission recommends that "as a fundamental principle, claims by national or ethnic communities or national groups should not be pursued by force. The effort to help to avert deadly conflict is thus a matter not only of humanitarian obligation but also of enlightened self-interest."[21]

Focusing on individual sovereignty and human security in the new millennium

The pattern of civil conflict and state fragmentation that characterized the last decade of the twentieth century is likely to continue into the new millennium. The growing number of weak or failed states resulting from civil conflict is perhaps symptomatic of the contemporary international system. Although a norm for humanitarian intervention has been evolving over the past decade, in the 1990s such actions were at best ad hoc, selective, and belated. Given the proliferation of states and the processes involved, the issue of forced displacement of peoples owing to human rights violations and conflict is likely to acquire even more political resonance in future. As the Carnegie Commission's report demonstrates, the blueprints and many of the tools necessary to address this challenge are already available. It is a question of the political will to establish a new regime to mobilize action. One positive element of the assault on the Westphalian system may be the gradual acceptance by the international community that human security or individual sovereignty – defined, at the very minimum, as security from forced displacement as a result of conflict, persecution, and gross violations of human rights – should take precedence over the traditional emphasis on state sovereignty.

Recognition of the overriding value of human security coupled with the political will to act upon rather than turn away from the problems leading to forced displacement would be a fitting tribute to the recently celebrated fiftieth anniversaries of the Universal Declaration of Human Rights and the 1951 Convention Relating to the Status of Refugees. It would also be an affirmation that recent history need not repeat itself.

Notes

1. S. Hoffman, "Delusions of World Order," *New York Review of Books*, 9 April 1992, p. 37. Many of the points made in this section have been developed by Hoffman.
2. W. Welsh, "Domestic Politics and Ethnic Conflict," in M. E. Brown, ed., *Ethnic Conflict and International Security*, Princeton, NJ: Princeton University Press, 1993, p. 45, and D. P. Moynihan, *Pandaemonium Ethnicity in International Politics*, Oxford: Oxford University Press, 1993, p. 89.
3. N. Gordels, "Two Concepts of Nationalism. An Interview with Isaiah Berlin," *New York Review of Books*, 21 November 1991, p. 19.
4. Carnegie Commission on Preventing Deadly Conflict, *Preventing Deadly Conflict, Final Report*, Washington DC: Carnegie Commission on Preventing Deadly Conflict, 1997, p. 11.
5. Brian Gorlick, "Human Rights and Refugees: Enhancing Protection through International Law," *Nordic Journal of International Law*, vol. 69, 2000, pp. 119–122. See also Dennis McNamara, "Linkages between Human Rights, Values and Refugees," Sympo-

sium commemorating the 50th Anniversary of the Universal Declaration of Human Rights, Chulalonkorn University, Bangkok, 25 May 1998.

6. UNHCR, *The State of the World's Refugees: Fifty Years of Humanitarian Action*, Oxford: Oxford University Press, 2000, pp. 156–157.

7. Ibid., p. 156.

8. Ibid., p. 158.

9. Ibid.

10. Carnegie Commission, *Preventing Deadly Conflict*, p. 3.

11. The figure on civilian casualties at the turn of the twentieth century is taken from UNDP, *Human Rights Development Report, 1998*, Oxford: Oxford University Press, 1998, p. 35. The figure on armed conflicts since the end of the Cold War is mentioned in J. T. Matthews, "Power Shift," *Foreign Affairs*, January/February 1997, p. 51. The percentage of civilian casualties in contemporary conflicts is cited in G. Loescher, *Beyond Charity: International Cooperation and the Global Refugee Crisis*, New York: Oxford University Press, 1993, p. 13.

12. Parts of this section draw on my "Refugees, Human Rights and the Issue of Human Security," in E. Newman and Oliver Richmond, eds., *The UN and Human Security*, London: Palgrave/Macmillan, 2001.

13. UNHCR, *The State of the World's Refugees*, p. 4.

14. Ibid., p. 159.

15. For a further discussion of asylum restrictions briefly outlined here, see UNHCR, *The State of the World's Refugees*, pp. 158–183.

16. Jim Hoaglund, "It's Time to Re-think the Old Notion of Sovereignty," *International Herald Tribune*, 28 October 1999, p. 8.

17. R. Y. Jennings, "Some International Law Aspects of the Refugee Question," *British Year Book of International Law*, vol. 20, 1939, p. 112; L. Oppenheim, *International Law, vol. 1, Peace*, 8th edn., edited by H. Lauterpacht, London: Longman, Green and Co., 1955, pp. 346–347; see also Ian Brownlie, *Principles of Public International Law*, 3rd edn., Oxford: Oxford University Press, 1979, pp. 443–445; and Guy S. Goodwin-Gill, *The Refugee in International Law*, Oxford: Oxford University Press, 1983, p. 228. Cited in Alan Dowty and Gil Loescher, "Refugee Flows: Internationalization of Human Rights Violations," paper presented at a Joint Conference of the International Studies Association and the Japanese Association of International Relations on "Globalism, Regionalism and Nationalism and Asia in Search of the 21st Century," Makuhari, Japan, 20–22 September 1996, p. 13.

18. Dowty and Loescher, "Refugee Flows," pp. 22–24.

19. *The Report of the Panel on United Nations Peace Operations*, UN Doc. A/55/305-S/2000/809, 21 August 2000.

20. Carnegie Commission, *Preventing Deadly Conflict*, pp. 5 and 6.

21. Ibid., p. xxv.

4

Refugee protection policies and security issues

Joanne van Selm

The purpose of this chapter is to consider the differing policy approaches to refugee protection practised in developed states, posing the following questions:

- Can different or particular security concerns and "national interests" explain divergences and patterns in refugee protection policy approaches in developed states?
- Can broader conceptions of security, which go beyond military and state-centric dimensions, positively impact upon refugee protection?

These questions are of particular relevance in the context of a volume that seeks to examine a range of issues and debates relating to refugees and displaced people in modern conflict. The question of how refugee protection policy operates, differs, and converges around the globe is of major importance. It would be useful to extend this discussion globally but, to be concise, the focus is on developed states that in principle base their systems of government on similar fundamentals and have signed up to similar international agreements related to refugee protection and human rights.

The universal legal basis to refugee status, on which the policies of refugee protection rest, is widely understood as relating not to those displaced by conflict but to those with an individual persecution-related need, based on discrimination, and a related right to receive protection outside their country of origin. Remarkably few of the displaced persons of recent years have been deemed to fall within the realm of the internationally agreed legal determination of refugee status. However, many people have received some form of protection and assistance from governments and organizations implementing policies that take the protection of the displaced beyond the protection of those determined to qualify for refugee status.

Three types of refugee protection policy approach will be described:
1. distinct but linked refugee and immigration approaches;
2. refugee protection subsumed by immigration concerns;
3. asylum processing as immigration control.

The characterization of each approach will refer to global security concerns, national interest concerns in the sense of safety and security issues, and the link to immigration policies in order to include societal and human security concerns. The themes of "control" and "management" will be pervasive. The examples of each type are the United States, Australia, and the European Union. In each case the role of national interest and security concerns (societal, national, global, and human) in the creation and implementation of the approach will be assessed. Roughly equivalent issues will be compared, including resettlement, temporary protection, and restrictions and deterrents.

Distinct but linked refugee and immigration approaches: The United States

The United States operates an immigration system that permits the legal entry of a whole spectrum of economic migrants, asylum seekers, and resettled refugees. In spite of the range of legal entry and residence categories, there is also a significant level of illegal migration to the United States. In this section, four facets of the US approach to asylum and refugee immigration will be described: the resettlement programme; Temporary Protected Status; the use of detention in the asylum system; and the use made of the US facility in Cuba's Guantanamo Bay, and interdiction on the high seas. It will be shown that asylum and refugee issues in the United States are part of its overall immigration approach, with distinct channels in effect for those seeking, or recognized as needing, protection and those seeking opportunities with economic or lifestyle gains as a major incentive. This demonstration will serve to explain the roles that national interest and security concerns play in the development of US refugee protection policies.

Resettlement

The Refugee Act of 1980 provided for a legal and humanitarian rationale to the US resettlement programme, replacing the Cold War political rationale that previously prevailed.[1] However, the literature on the implementation of this refugee resettlement programme makes it clear that what is legal and humanitarian is in essence everything for which the United States sees itself standing. Newland notes that the details of this new rationale were not made explicit in 1980, or thereafter, leaving the resettlement programme hanging on the remnants of the Cold War agenda and thus open to interpretation:

As immigration and refugee policy move up on the political agenda, such programs are no longer of interest only to their advocates. In an atmosphere in which all federal spending – and particularly any that smacks of "foreign aid" or "welfare" – is subject to scrutiny, advocates must be prepared to make the case for specific programs in the context of a coherent refugee policy that serves the national purpose.[2]

Part of the overall policy strategy in offering resettlement is to stimulate other states, including states neighbouring the country of origin, to offer first asylum to those in need of protection. However, this strategy can backfire in situations where the United States decides that resettlement of a given group of refugees is not in its interest: if there is no promise of resettlement, then why offer first asylum, is the question posed by poorer states.[3]

The definition of a refugee in the 1951 Convention and 1967 Protocol Relating to the Status of Refugees specifies that the person under consideration be outside his or her country of origin.[4] Indeed, being outside the country of origin is the feature that distinguishes a refugee from an internally displaced person. The United States is a signatory to the 1967 Protocol (but not the 1951 Convention). Yet an interesting feature of the resettlement programme is that for its purposes a *refugee* is defined as "[a]n alien outside the United States who is unable or unwilling to return to his or her country of nationality because of persecution or a well-founded fear of persecution" on the same five grounds of persecution mentioned as in the Refugee Convention. "Persons within their country of nationality may be treated as refugees, provided that the President, after consultation with Congress, declares that they are of special humanitarian concern to the United States."[5] In other words, whereas the Convention definition is used, for example, by European states to apply only to those within their own borders, in the context of US refugee resettlement, the "refugee" must be outside United States, and may even be in his or her country of origin. The United States also assesses asylum claims made by people arriving spontaneously. Those people may be defined as refugees at the end of positive processing, although they are commonly referred to as *asylees*. Those being resettled arrive as refugees.

A ceiling is put on refugee resettlement each year. Since the mid-1990s it has been at or around the 90,000 mark. A variety of criteria are used to assess which of the world's 20 million plus refugees will be among the 90,000. US interests are one criterion: will the resettlement assist a friendly state, or make a strong statement about a particular foe? Family ties are also used: does the individual have family members already in the United States? In this way, immigration considerations are employed in deciding which of the great many people in need of protection might be resettled. These criteria may even force out other people with stronger protection needs.

Resettled refugees enter a programme of assistance under the Office of Refugee Resettlement (ORR); this has a significant focus on employment, again showing the link to immigration considerations. Resettled refugees are eligible for adjustment to lawful permanent residence status (Green Card immigrant) after one year of residence in the United States, and are exempt from the worldwide annual limitations linked to the granting of Green Cards.

For the purposes of this comparative chapter, it is interesting and useful to note that, when almost 1 million Kosovars were displaced during the NATO intervention in their republic in 1999, the United States, after hesitation and consideration of a plan to evacuate some of the refugees to Guantanamo Bay for short-term protection, granted access for 20,000 Kosovars under the resettlement programme – as refugees – with status and the opportunity to adjust to permanent legal residence after one year. This is in marked contrast to the temporary status offered by Australia and European states to those fleeing exactly the same circumstances (see below).

The US resettlement programme is used to give a strong level of management, or the appearance thereof, to the arrival and situation of refugees in the United States. The United States has considerable power to choose which of the world's refugees become refugees in the United States, even if it is only selecting some 80,000 to 90,000 out of 20 million annually. The mere fact of such selection is linked not only to domestic policy concerns about the acceptability of certain groups of refugees or the appeal to public sympathies, but also to foreign policy concerns expressed in terms of national interest in supporting allied states.

Domestic policy concerns caused the (short-term) cessation of the resettlement programme in the wake of the terrorist attacks of 11 September 2001. Advocates in the United States strongly opposed this closure, stating that those resettled as refugees have consistently undergone far more stringent background checks than any other immigrant to the United States. As refugee law includes the possibility of exclusion from refugee status of those who commit a range of crimes, the tools are available to ensure that the resettlement programme could function in the interest of the United States' domestic and foreign policy by maintaining the humanitarian profile of the country. However, the immediate domestic fear in the face of terrorism seemed to override those concerns – the programme was shut down, nominally owing to the tardiness of the administrative branch in renewing the programme, as is necessary each year in September.

Temporary Protected Status

Temporary Protected Status (TPS) is used to grant immigration status to nationals of designated countries. The countries designated are those to which people cannot return because of safety concerns, such as an ongoing armed conflict or a natural disaster. As such, TPS is not a matter, strictly speaking, of refugee protection; indeed its function is to regularize the status of people who were already in the United States prior to the announcement date of the TPS programme related to a particular state. Those people were most likely to have been illegally in the country to that point. TPS is in effect an amnesty, with time limits. The feature of TPS that responds to state security concerns is that, in regularizing status for a limited period of time, the government grants employment authorization for the same period in the strong belief (confirmed in past cases) that, while legally employed, people with TPS either remit significant amounts of their earnings or save them to invest in the country of origin and its reconstruction at a later point. These remittances are many times the amount of development or reconstruction assistance that the United States gives to the country of origin. In addition, the grant of TPS can forge a stronger bond between the United States and the country of origin of those gaining status in this way. Indeed, in cases of natural disasters, such as the after-effects of earthquakes or floods, the announcement of TPS being granted to nationals may be made by the US administration and the government of the country of origin in a joint news conference.

Asylum and detention

The imprisonment of arriving asylum seekers is a practice that grew dramatically in the United States in the 1980s, and was reinforced by the provisions of the 1996 Illegal Immigration and Immigrant Law.[6] People who arrive in the United States without valid travel documents (a valid passport and visa, where a visa is necessary) and make an asylum claim are put into "expedited removals." This means they are detained until such time as an asylum officer of the Immigration and Naturalization

Service (INS) or an immigration judge has determined that there is "a credible fear of persecution" and thus a strong chance that the individual in question would be eligible for asylum. If there is such a credible fear, and the person has friends, family, or community ties in the United States, then he or she should be paroled. However, many cases have been documented by non-governmental organizations (NGOs) of asylum seekers being detained for months or years in prisons, jails, and detention facilities.[7] Detention conditions are frequently described as "inhuman," with concerns raised about the health and well-being of the asylum seekers who are detained. Often people are detained on the authority of local INS staff. There appears to be some sort of "enforcement culture" in the INS at its local levels that causes staff to practise detention in a way that inspires concern at the national level.[8]

The practice of detaining asylum seekers in effect merges those spontaneously seeking asylum in the United States with all other immigrants who enter the country irregularly and without the documentation specified as necessary for legal entry. Once in detention, asylum seekers face a barrage of measures that cut them off from many of their basic rights, including access to legal counsel and other visitors, means of communication, and access to the support of NGOs and other care-givers.[9]

NGOs suggest that one source of inspiration for the 1996 Act, which mandated detention for asylum seekers in the expedited removal process, was the media and popular attention given to the fact that one of the people charged with the 1993 World Trade Center bombing had entered the country as an asylum seeker. For many people, the words "asylum seeker" and "terrorist" became linked, and they would be further linked by suspicion following the attacks using hijacked planes as weapons against the World Trade Center and the Pentagon in September 2001. In the latter situation, none of the 19 suicide-hijackers entered the United States as asylum seekers; in fact at least 13 of the 19 had entered with legal visas issued by US consular staff. However, detention on the basis of immigration irregularities was used relatively arbitrarily in the first month following that attack to detain hundreds of people while concerns about further acts of terrorism ran high.

The practice of detention criminalizes spontaneously arriving asylum seekers in general, especially as they are often detained in regular jail facilities. In terms of characterizing refugee policy practices within the parameters of state and individual sovereignty or security, this means that state choice about who is a refugee (through the resettlement programme) is prioritized over individual choice in seeking protection in a country that for many around the world symbolizes opportunity and freedom.

Offshore processing

In September 1981, the United States and the Republic of Haiti reached an agreement that allowed the US Coast Guard to interdict boatloads of Haitians seeking to enter the United States, take them aboard Coast Guard cutters, and return them to Haiti. Over the next 10 years, a system was developed whereby the INS would carry out immigration interviews, to ascertain the presence of any protection need, while the Haitians were still on board the cutters. The notion of offshore processing was thus born.[10]

In November 1991, faced with increasing departures following the military-led coup in Haiti that ousted President Jean-Bertrand Aristide, the US government sought a way to allow screened out Haitians to leave the cutters without entering the United States. The solution was to open the US Naval Station at Guantanamo Bay, Cuba, and establish tent camps there to house the migrants. A screening programme was also set up at the base, with officers of the newly established Asylum Corps carrying out interviews to test the extent of "credible fear." Of 34,000 Haitians interviewed as part of the screening programme, some 10,000 established credible fear and were transferred to the US mainland to have their asylum claims processed. According to reports, the Asylum Corps, stimulated by the INS leadership and deflecting political pressure, sought to apply the asylum regulations evenly, fairly, and efficiently, even if that meant that screen-in rates would go as high as 85 per cent. In the end, however, political pressure and the fear of increasing numbers won the day, and the programme ended in May 1992.[11]

In 1994, the use of Guantanamo Bay as an offshore processing station and out-of-country holding area was resurrected as some 20,000 Haitians and 30,000 Cubans left their countries in small boats. By keeping them in Guantanamo and insisting in August 1994 that all must return to their home country, the Clinton administration intended to discourage both Cubans and Haitians from arriving in southern Florida to request asylum. By mid-November, following the US interventions on their island, most Haitians had left Guantanamo. Some of the Cubans appeared to want to leave, but US lawyers in Florida had sued the federal government to prevent their return to Cuba until they were advised fully of their rights.[12] Additional places were made available under the quota of Cubans eligible for permanent immigrant visas to allow children in Guantanamo, whether unaccompanied or with families, to move to the United States, in defiance of a ban on going directly from Guantanamo to the United States. By May 1995 there were still 22,000 Cubans in Guantanamo.[13] On 2 May it was announced that, after two months of secret talks with Castro's representatives, the Clinton administration would permit the admission of these people to the United States, but that any Cubans attempting to arrive in the United States in future would be returned to Cuba.[14]

In 1999, some 4,782 migrants were interdicted at sea, an increase of 24 per cent over the previous year. Of these, 1,619 were Cubans (the largest group), up from 421 in 1997 and 903 in 1998.[15] The second-largest group were Chinese at 1,092, up from 200 in 1997 and in 1998, followed by Haitians at 1,039, slightly fewer than in 1998.[16] The Chinese interdicted at sea were initially detained in Guam but, as facilities reached capacity levels, they were diverted to Tinian, part of the Commonwealth of Northern Mariana Islands, a move that seemed to bring about a reduction in attempted arrivals in Guam (where US immigration laws apply).[17] The US Committee for Refugees expressed concern that asylum seekers interdicted at sea were not being given full access to asylum procedures, which they would have if they reached the mainland or another area where US laws apply, such as Guam. Those whose claims were processed on board ship, in Guantanamo, or in Tinian were not being granted the same rights as people whose attempt to make a sea landing proved more successful.

The United States' initial response to Macedonia's calls for assistance in protecting Kosovars in 1999 was to suggest participation in a humanitarian evacuation programme by transferring some 20,000 Kosovars to Guantanamo Bay, where they would remain "temporarily" prior to returning to Kosovo or being processed for entry to the United States. This plan was met with concern by a range of NGOs and policy analysts in Washington DC. The fear that "the prison-like atmosphere at Guantanamo Naval Base could only exacerbate the trauma and suffering of the Kosovar refugees, who should be placed in a hospitable environment and not in conditions of confinement," was expressed.[18] The US Committee for Refugees suggested that the refugees themselves were not indicating a desire to leave the region, so transfer to Albania, which was offered (and also took place), was more appropriate than evacuation.[19] Martin suggested that, on the surface, TPS was most appropriate for Kosovars.[20] In the event, the US government turned to its traditional manner of transferring refugees from a country of first asylum to its shores, and included the Kosovars in its resettlement programme.

The United States conducts its refugee protection policy within the framework of a wide and developed immigration policy. At almost every step, national security concerns and state sovereignty play a role in the US approach to immigration yet, on certain occasions, humanitarian principles seem either to overcome those concerns or to become one with them. Thus the INS managed for a brief period to beat off state concerns about the numbers of Haitians who would gain access in 1991–1992; advocates managed to convince government that Guantanamo was not the solution for Kosovars; and Temporary Protected Status grants immigration rights in situations of humanitarian need. Those security concerns certainly influence the model; the question is, do they explain it? Or is the US system to be explained by the culture of a nation of immigrants and immigration? And if the latter, how does that culture relate to the national security interests that same nation expresses?

Refugee protection subsumed in immigration: Australia

Australia's immigration system has traditionally been a rather "controlled" system, in the sense that the vast majority of immigrants and refugees have arrived with prior authorization for their immigration. Immigrants have been recruited on a skills basis; refugees have been selected according to the intensity of the danger of their situation and their existing connections to Australia and Australians. Two major challenges to this orderly system have both brought about policy changes in the way immigration to Australia has been conceptualized and authorized, including with respect to resettlement and detention. The first challenge came with the crisis over Vietnamese boat people in 1975. The second is an ongoing challenge at the time of writing, as boats are again a primary form of transport for people fleeing a range of conflicts and crises and using the services of smugglers to reach what they think will be a safe shore.

Burnt boats

Viviani explains that:

The story of Australia's policy towards the entry of Indochinese has elements of both pride and shame, of fair treatment alongside bias and arbitrary dealing with the lives of families and individuals, of bureaucratic ineptitude and probity and of ministerial stupidity and inspiration. Overall ministers and senior officials have not served the Australian people as well as they should have in this area of policy and administration and the costs of their failure have been largely borne by Indochinese in Australia.[21]

The White Australia policy had been officially abolished in 1973 so, officially at least, the discriminatory restrictions on non-European immigration were gone. However, many in Australia constructed an Asian "threat" out of the arrival of the Indo-Chinese, a "threat" picture that endures decades later. The "threat" lay in the spontaneous arrivals of the Indo-Chinese in small boats from 1978 onwards, challenging Australia's sovereignty and border control. "With hindsight, it is now clear that Australia managed this first small but significant peaceful challenge to its sovereignty successfully," says Viviani. "The key to this success was to agree to a relatively generous resettlement program from Southeast Asian refugee camps."[22] The "orderly departure programme" from Vietnam and countries of first asylum increased in scope as more people were leaving the country in the late 1980s, and only in 1991/1992 did the figures drop significantly. Australia's asylum seeker statistics fell from 22,100 in fiscal year 1991 (July to June) to 6,100 in 1992 (January to December).[23]

This "release" from the first major challenge coincided with a change in the global political situation, which would give rise to the second challenge. As the Cold War ended, international migration flows changed. Australia's response to the changes, which included increases in refugee numbers worldwide and in the number of people willing and able to become economic migrants, was to reduce "its total migration numbers to historically low levels and radically tighten its entry controls over the period 1989 to 1994."[24] In spite of those reduced immigration numbers, the allocation for refugees and humanitarian entry remained roughly what it had been over previous years: some 13,000 per year. Entry criteria tightened in the country, but the resettlement places for offshore processing remained intact. Viviani cites two new factors in government rhetoric that could account for the policy change, which developed "a culture of control, deterrence and detention for boat arrivals." The first was the problem of what to do about the status of the significant number of Chinese still in Australia after the 1989 Tiananmen Square massacre, and the second was "the apparent conviction of immigration ministers and their advisors from 1989 that a new 'flood' of boats to Australia from Asia was imminent and somehow to be 'deterred'."[25] That fear started to come true in the late 1990s, and really crystallized in 2001. However, following Viviani's line of argument, it could be convincingly stated that the Australian government's so-called pre-emptive policies actually caused this prophesy to become self-fulfilling.

More boats

The Australian government reported that 4,174 people arrived without authorization on 75 boats in fiscal year 1999/2000, compared with 920 people on 42 boats in 1998/1999 – an increase of 354 per cent.[26] A number of the "resettlement" places are reserved for "onshore" visas; that is, they are used not to resettle people but to grant status to people who have already arrived in Australia. In February 2000, the Immigration Minister, Philip Ruddock, increased the proportion of "onshore" places and ordered a freeze on the processing of offshore refugee visas. This means that only about half the 12,000 places are available for "offshore" humanitarian visa processing, i.e. for what the rest of the world understands as resettlement. One senator said in response to this resettlement freeze that it would "just encourage asylum seekers to try and enter illegally."[27]

Perhaps the major dramatic incident representing the second challenge to Australia's refugee protection policy came in August 2001, when the Norwegian-registered ship M.V. *Tampa* answered distress calls and an Australian request to rescue 438 people from a sinking ship. The people were asylum seekers, on what they thought was the final leg of their journey being smuggled via Indonesia to Australia. Many of them were said to be Afghans. The long stand-off between Australia and Indonesia also involved Norway, the UN High Commissioner for Refugees (UNHCR) as a mediator, and New Zealand, East Timor, and Nauru as states that offered to help. The Australian Department of Foreign Affairs and Trade issued an overview of Australia's immigration record to the media. According to that information, since 1948 some 5.7 million people had migrated to Australia, including, since 1945, 590,000 people under refugee and humanitarian programmes. In 2000–2001, 80,610 people were granted non-humanitarian migration visas to Australia, and 13,733 people were granted humanitarian visas, 7,992 of them being offshore grantees.

This last statistic indicates the management issue in the refugee protection policy that is central to this chapter: Australia hopes to control its refugee protection by selecting all of its refugees itself, offshore. The pride in this means of control is reflected in the following statement:

Australia is one of only nine countries in the world that operates a dedicated offshore humanitarian resettlement program every year. Of the nine, Australia is one of the three most generous. On a per capita basis, Australia is second only to Canada.[28]

In fact, the big picture is somewhat different from this snapshot.

To settle or to resettle?

The second challenge to Australia's orderly system was highlighted by the *Tampa* and two further incidents. On 7 October 2001, H.M.A.S. *Adelaide* fired shots at a boat carrying asylum seekers that was approaching Christmas Island. The Australian government issued pictures accompanying claims that parents threw their children from the boat into the sea in an attempt to force entry to Australia. On 19 October 2001, 421 asylum seekers drowned when their overcrowded ship travelling to Australia from Indonesia capsized. This challenge has seen Australia limit the use of its resettlement places by reserving them increasingly for people who have landed in Australia. In the political handling of this situation it is striking that those arriving spontaneously are often referred to as "queue jumpers," meaning that by arriving under their own steam people are avoiding the queues of the resettlement programme. Meanwhile, an incident in late October 2001 illustrated that those who have been waiting are becoming increasingly impatient as the places made available for their resettlement reduce. In this incident, some 100 asylum seekers who had been awaiting resettlement from Indonesia protested their plight at the UNHCR offices in Jakarta, and were forcibly evicted by Indonesian police.[29] When announcing the resettlement freeze in February 2000, the Immigration Minister had said:

It is grossly unfair to people who are refugees outside Australia in the most vulnerable situations, that their places may be taken by people in Australia who may be able to establish claims.... I'm very upset about it, I don't like it, but it's the only way in which we can *ensure the system will function effectively.*[30]

In effect this change means that the immigration of refugees, and in particular the decision as to which of the world's 20 million refugees find protection in Australia, is, in the name of efficiency, taken out of the Australian government's and the UNHCR's hands, and placed into the hands of the would-be asylum seekers and the smugglers they pay.

In trying to ensure effective functioning of the system, the changes involved a switch in numbers, not an increase. In 1999–2000 there were 12,000 places on the resettlement programme, plus 800 from the previous fiscal year. The split in this number started the year as 10,000 offshore and 2,000 onshore, but was later shifted to 8,000 and 4,000, respectively. Of the 8,000 offshore places, 4,000 were for the refugee category (using the Convention definition); 3,100 for the "special humanitarian program" – people found to have suffered discrimination amounting to a gross abuse of human rights, with strong support from an Australian citizen, resident, or community group; and 900 for the "special assistance" category – people with close links to Australia but not meeting the criteria of other categories.[31]

In 2000, Australia received 19,404 applications for asylum (1.14 asylum applicants per 1,000 head of population).[32] This was more than double the number of applications made in 1999 (9,500), which was 0.56 per 1,000 head of population.[33] The use of the resettlement places as a quota for asylum applicants within Australia does not necessarily have a causal relationship with the numbers of people seeking refuge by using whatever means possible to arrive at Australia's shores: the relative prices charged by smugglers; the intensity of conflicts in countries with as easy access to Australia as to other potential protecting states; publicity of Australia as a result of the 2000 Sydney Olympics; and increasing restrictions in other parts of the world might all have a bearing on the numbers. The fact remains that, in the face of those increasing numbers, Australia has chosen to realign a resettlement programme that had been targeted at offshore processing, in order to give more places to onshore applicants. (Resettled refugees are defined as applying outside their country of origin, in which they fear persecution, and outside Australia, to which they seek to be resettled. Onshore applicants need to arrive in an unauthorized fashion and seek asylum on arrival, according to the official definitions.) The impression, at least, is one of encouraging unauthorized arrivals, yet the other side of the coin is the search for deterrents to those same potential asylum seekers.

Detention

One of the deterrent measures is the mandatory detention of all spontaneous arrivals in Australia, who, whether or not they make a claim to asylum and protection, are considered as illegal immigrants if they have arrived without advance authorization (which is most usually the case for those arriving by boat, as well as for some arriving by air).[34] This policy is defended as being the only way to ensure that people do not disappear into society. The mandatory detention system has given rise to much criticism, from the United Nations (not only UNHCR but also the Human Rights Commission), NGOs and other advocates, and segments of the Australian media.[35] The Human Rights and Equal Opportunity Commission, in its report of an inquiry into the detention of asylum seekers, points out that such detention contravenes international human rights law in many cases. However, it recommends that detention could be used for a limited range of purposes, which must be clearly set out in law, and when such detention is for a minimal period. The purposes mentioned include: to verify identity, to determine elements on which the claim to refugee status and protection is based, and to protect national security or public order.[36]

Immigration Minister Ruddock has defended the system of detention as being part of a potent message to smugglers: through detention people are in full view of the authorities and could be deported if their claim to asylum is found to be unfounded.[37] This highlights part of the political dilemma in dealing with spontaneously arriving asylum claimants: if you let all of them stay, there is no point in having a determination procedure; but, if you force some to go, you will always make mistakes. And, in the process of controlling the movement of those who you may want to deport, you inevitably curtail the freedom of those who deserve protection and assistance, at least for the period of time during which you are establishing the difference.

Not all asylum seekers are detained: those who arrive lawfully in Australia and are found to indeed be in need of protection may be granted a Protection Visa, permitting permanent residence.[38] Since 20 October 1999, people who arrive unlawfully and are found to have a protection need (and who will in the meantime have been detained) are eligible for a Temporary Protection Visa (TPV), which provides protection for three years in the first instance. The TPV is granted to those found to be refugees, and although it grants rights to employment, benefits including health care and counselling, and the possibility to apply for permanent protection after 30 months, it denies the rights that those granted a permanent visa have to family reunification, to return if they leave Australia (i.e. to a travel document, which is a fundamental part of the 1951 Convention Relating to the Status of Refugees), and for access to the mainstream welfare system that goes beyond basic health-care needs.[39]

The Australian government's so-called "Pacific solution" is another element of deterrence to the arrival of asylum seekers by boat. This involves agreements with, for example, Nauru and Papua New Guinea that people intercepted at sea be transferred to those islands and their asylum claims processed there, in return for significant payment. Papua New Guinea was to receive A$1 million for the first 216 asylum seekers received in this way. Those whose claims are accepted will be resettled – though that could take some time.[40]

Temporary protection

Australia created a new Temporary Safe Haven visa during the Kosovo crisis of 1999, permitting those seeking short-term protection from conflicts to apply and reside temporarily in Australia. Applicants signed a declaration stating that they understood and agreed to the Australian government's offer of temporary safe haven and would leave when the government required that they do so.[41] This category has, to date, been used for Kosovars and East Timorese. When the time came, in the government's view, for a return to Kosovo in summer 1999, several hundred of the 4,000 people concerned filed law suits and, through legal and political pressure, managed to remain in Australia for several more months. Some were granted longer temporary permits to remain, but others were deported by the government and some were encouraged to leave through sponsorship by the existing Albanian community in Australia and through measures ensuring the possibility of a return to Australia should their situation prove to be unsafe in Kosovo.[42]

The Australian system demonstrates a strong state interest in controlling immigration. Security concerns about the number of arrivals have led the government to choose to use the existing programme in an effort to confirm its control of the situation as a whole. It is, however, questionable whether the departure from an orderly arrival programme has been positive for either state or individual security – even if it may give the individuals concerned more autonomy in actively seeking asylum rather than quite passively remaining in line. This positive "spin," however, cannot outweigh the clear dangers associated with the use of smugglers and hazardous crossings in overcrowded boats. Rather than obvious security concerns influencing refugee protection policy in the Australian case, it seems that the perception of an insecure border, demonstrated by the arrival of boats, has driven policy changes over the years. This concern can certainly explain the changes in policies; the bigger question for Australia is whether that is a genuine security concern, or some kind of phantom that could be better managed in other ways.

Asylum processing as immigration control: The European Union

In European states, migration generally, and asylum in particular, are high on the public political agenda. A range of explanations could be given for this. Displacement-inducing crises took place on the continent of Europe during the 1990s (particularly in former Yugoslavia) and such crises may not be over. With media attention on smuggling, the appearance of a lack of control is amplified daily. What is more, asylum and immigration policies generally are prominent in the European integration debate. As the 15 member states of the European Union seek further integration in their management of migration, it becomes more apparent to policy makers and public alike that they have very different policies, based on their development within particular cultures, societies, and political systems.[43]

Asylum as virtually the only means of immigration:
A changing story?

The European asylum debate of the 1990s was characterized by governmental rhetoric about how people are abusing the asylum system. However, it could be argued that governments have themselves abused the asylum channel, or at least used it for purposes for which it was not designed, because it has become the sole means of legal entry for all would-be immigrants without skills and an employment visa, close family ties, or a university place. Alongside asylum seekers, many economic migrants have had to claim asylum in order to enter a country in which they firmly believe they will secure a better life for themselves than would ever be possible in their country of origin.

With the changing economic circumstances of the end of the 1990s and, no less importantly, the changing perception of the demographic circumstances in Europe, this abuse of the asylum system looked likely to come to an end. Such an end to the ways of the previous decade would surely be in the interests of states, of their populations, and of economic migrants and refugees. The European Commission issued a Communication on an immigration policy for the European Union.[44] The Swiss government established the Bern Initiative, discussing migration management in an intergovernmental setting, involving countries of origin as well as the European and other Western states. However, all of these initiatives may be, at least temporarily, damaged by the events of September and October 2001.

Linking security and asylum

At the end of the Cold War, EU states were fearful of massive displacements from Eastern Europe, now unchecked by the severe restrictions of communist exit controls. The images of hundreds of thousands of East Germans heading through Hungary and Czechoslovakia towards borders with Austria and West Germany – the visible indication that the communist hold on the East was breaking – fuelled fears that millions of people might try to seek opportunities they had been denied over the previous decades by moving to Western Europe. If they did so at a time when the communist grip was truly weakened, and the likelihood of persecution and human rights abuses less than during those previous decades, then West European states would be less likely to find those people fulfilling the criteria set for refugee protection.

In the event, the movement of persons who might have sought asylum was more limited than feared. However, the fear itself had set in motion concerns about insecurity from the East other than the traditional nuclear and other weaponry-based security concerns. Whereas weapon-based concerns of home populations could be met by an increase in a country's defensive and potentially aggressive arsenal, and the occasional flexing of muscles through speeches as well as military exercises, it was more difficult to counter the fears raised by the spectre of massive immigration. The only way was to increase restrictions on admission and the potential for integration of immigrants and asylum seekers. European governments needed to show they were in control, just as they had needed to show they were in control of the military situation in decades gone by. However, all the models of rational actors, standard operating procedures, and other foreign and security policy thinking tools were based on state actors. All the models of understanding perceptions and bureaucratic politics were likewise based on groups of individuals, in their roles as politicians, civil servants, and military officers, thinking about their state interests and acting accordingly in response to any policy shifts. Although potential migrants and asylum seekers may be perfectly rational actors (there is nothing irrational in seeking either safety or opportunity), they are a different kind of diverse actor from those governments are used to dealing with. What is more, the notion that immigrant arrivals are a challenge to security is also more complex and controversial than the notion that the arrival of an exploding bomb would challenge security. In particular, some of those arriving would be seeking refuge from armed conflicts: their security having been threatened in a "traditional" sense, it would appear difficult to make their very presence on West European territory appear credible as a threat.

The Balkan crises

As the ministers of the European Community sought through inter-governmental agreements to restrict admission to their territories and to bring asylum and immigration issues onto the integration agenda more formally, conflict broke out on the periphery of the Community, causing the displacement of hundreds of thousands of people and calling into question the increasing restrictions. For example, among the restrictions were visa requirements. As conflict in the Balkans worsened through 1992, West European states one by one placed visa requirements on citizens of the Federal Republic of Yugoslavia, Slovenia, Croatia, and Bosnia–Herzegovina. With embassies in Sarajevo closing, those people who most needed to escape conflict and even individual persecution were theoretically to head to Zagreb, Belgrade, or Ljubljana to collect a visa in a passport in order to be legally permitted to enter a West European state. Such entry restrictions should not, according to the letter and spirit of the 1951 Convention, affect a claim to refugee status. However, the symbolism is the important feature for this chapter: in order to give the appearance of control over the immigration aspects of the displacements from former Yugoslavia, West European governments increased the bureaucratic measure nominally required for entry to their territory, at the expense of the fear and anguish that any attempt to acquire such documentation must have brought.

Temporary protection

As the exodus from Bosnia–Herzegovina became, in 1992/1993, a large-scale influx to European Union member states (particularly Germany and the Netherlands) and other European states (Austria, Sweden, and Switzerland), European governments generally sought two regional approaches to add to their "protection portfolio": "temporary protection" and "burden-sharing." These two elements have become inextricably linked for most European policy makers, even if descriptions of what the two approaches mean vary enormously.

The creation of temporary protection policies by European governments was not novel. Temporary stay in a country of first asylum prior to resettlement had been practised in Europe previously: Hungarians in 1956 had been protected for up to nine months in Austria and Yugoslavia before moving on as regular immigrants to settle and work in other European (and Western) states. Europe had also been the final destination of Vietnamese who had first been temporarily offered asylum on condition of burden-sharing resettlement in Malaysia, Thailand, and other South-East Asian states. The 1990s however saw a new twist in temporary protection. This form of temporary protection was an alternative to asylum and generally premised on the understanding that the "exit strategy" would be return rather than resettlement, and certainly rather than the longer-term residence that the future ultimately held for many Bosnians in spite of the reluctance of their hosts.

Likewise, the notion of burden-sharing took on new twists. In the past, burden-sharing had been the term used to describe how richer, more distant, developed states shouldered some of the financial responsibility for protection in poorer, neighbouring states and often resettled refugees, offering them a durable solution to their lack of protection. In the 1990s, European burden-sharing came to mean distributing the protection responsibility between a group of cooperating developed states within one continent.

The use of temporary protection approaches for Bosnians fleeing civil war and ethnic cleansing came about because of the complexities and conjunctures of timing, law, and politics. In the late 1980s and early 1990s, Western Europe had been limiting access to the protection of asylum, because the numbers of people arriving to claim refugee status had been increasing. Restrictions such as visa imposition, carrier sanctions, and strict interpretation of the Geneva Convention definition

(Article 1A) were being developed in response. Strict application and interpretation of the Convention definition were the reason given for needing to create alternative protection modes for those fleeing a conflict. The definition describes individuals whose fear of persecution is deemed to be well founded. Large numbers of people fleeing generalized violence were generally understood by governments not to be in fear of persecution as individuals but to be in fear of the consequences of war as a group. The UNHCR, mandated to promote the protection of refugees, saw its major donors reluctant to grant Convention status but apparently willing to permit limited numbers of people to reside on their territory for the duration of the conflict, with fewer rights than they would have had if recognized as refugees. The UNHCR thus acquiesced and agreed that temporary protection was a feasible path to take.

In spite of the process of policy harmonization undertaken formally since 1993 in the European Union, no common practice or policy of temporary protection was developed. Different approaches came into being, suited to each state's asylum systems. The European Commission attempted to find agreement to a common approach in the 1990s, but failed, largely because it did not take on the "solidarity" issue in the way the big states (either for sharing the responsibility or against it) desired.[45] In May 2000 the Commission submitted a proposal for a directive.[46] Unlike previous approaches, this proposal treats temporary protection as a prelude to asylum or as an interim measure, not as an independent protective tool. It also deals only with mass influx cases and is thus tailored to conflict situations, rather than dealing with individual cases of humanitarian need, which should rather be dealt with using the 1951 Convention or forms of supplementary protection that are not time specific.

The May 2000 proposal came after the exodus from Kosovo prior to, during, and after the NATO bombardments of March–June 1999. Whereas temporary protection for Bosnians had been anything but temporary in most cases, for a great many Kosovars their stay in EU states was temporary. However, they in effect received a form of double temporary protection: initial short-term refuge in a neighbouring state (Macedonia) followed by what might be called temporary resettlement to the EU states and others under the Humanitarian Evacuation Programme (HEP). Addressing security concerns in a country of first asylum, Macedonia, the HEP could be described as a version of the type of burden-sharing seen in the Indo-Chinese case, except that resettlement was not *resettlement* in the "traditional" understanding of the word for the European states involved, because it was intended to be temporary (unlike resettlement to the United States). To that extent, this was a new departure in policy terms, which may or may not be replicable in future, depending on variables over which protecting states might have little or no control.

Protect at a distance? The High Level Working Group plans

In December 1998, the European Council, following a Dutch initiative, created a High Level Working Group on Asylum and Migration Policies. Many facets of this development have drawn criticism – as well as positive reactions. One area of criticism is the understanding on the part of NGOs in particular that an aim of this group will be to develop and promote the notion of "reception in the region." This spectre concerns NGOs because it would be a further means of limiting access to protection and asylum within the European Union. The approach would involve the EU states establishing refugee camps and processing or determination centres in countries neighbouring a state experiencing a massive exodus. This might challenge the sovereignty of the states in which the camps are located, and might also at least constrain if not violate the rights of the refugees. (Refugees would be able to seek asylum in countries other than their own and enjoy protection by a state other than their own, only the state in which they seek asylum and the state protecting them may not be the same state.) However, this state primacy is the key facet that distinguishes this notion from the establishment of camp facilities by the UNHCR over the past five decades. The concern if states take on this role is that they may be rather more selective, on the basis of domestic and foreign policy interests, about which states and crises they become involved in, and how much they spend on providing protection and assistance in different situations and locations.

Reception in the region was first put into its "frightening new clothes" in Europe in a 1994 paper written by the Dutch Secretary of State for Justice, Aad Kosto. In the context of the Bosnian crisis it did not become policy. However, in the Kosovo displacement crisis, a reception in the region approach was put into practice as various EU states established camps in both Albania and Macedonia. They seemed to vie with each other for the luxuriousness of facilities, the exact opposite of the approach to asylum and protection within the EU states, where the goal is to be more austere than the neighbours. These national camps gave focal points for leading politicians to visit "our refugees in our camps" far from home but to play to the concerns of the home audience, shocked by images of real refugees, who are just like us, on Europe's doorstep.[47]

Reception in the region might imply that the state establishing a camp takes on duties with regard to resettlement, or, on the other hand, it might open an avenue permitting it to avoid resettlement by providing a "safe flight alternative." In Albania in 1999, many Kosovar refugees received protection in camps established, equipped, and managed by EU member states and, in the short period during which those people really could not possibly return home, this first asylum was deemed sufficient. There is speculation that, had the crisis continued for much longer, many of the refugees would have sought means to leave Albania and travel to EU member states, whether organized by those states or using the services of smugglers. In the latter case, it is not clear from a policy perspective whether EU states would have granted even temporary protection or have sought to return people to their own camps in the region.

Asylum is the form of immigration open to the majority of would-be immigrants to the European Union, and so it appears to be abused, not only by migrants who do not really seek or need protection but also by states that have sought first to limit immigration to asylum only, and then to limit asylum, even for those in need, when people continue to arrive on their territory. State abuse of the refugee status system is also potentially present in the temporary protection regime, although this type of protection could perform a mediating role in some mass influx or mass exodus situations to ensure protection for the majority without the burden on individuals and states of lengthy individual procedures in the first instance.[48] The real abuse of the refugee system in the use of temporary protection comes about if individuals are left with relative uncertainty for too long. The European models demonstrate little in the way of control or management of arrivals, but a strong desire to apply controlling measures after arrival has taken place. The security concerns in Europe that have influenced the rhetoric around the refugee protection system have been myriad, including the concern about armed, violent conflict spilling across the continent and the so-called "societal security" concerns of the impact of immigration on cultures and identities. Although these security concerns can certainly be said to have influenced the form protection policies have taken, it is difficult to assess whether they provide a full explanation, particularly as other policy options may better address the needs and concerns that states in Europe express.

Diverging policies/converging goals? Conclusions and policy options

The questions posed at the start of this chapter were:
• Can different or particular security concerns and "national interests" explain divergences and patterns in refugee protection policy approaches in developed states?
• Can broader conceptions of security, which go beyond military and state-centric dimensions, positively impact upon refugee protection?

In the United States, national interest plays a strong role in refugee protection policies. Australia has two major security concerns: the challenge posed by the breaching of its borders by uninvited boat arrivals and the challenge to its identity. The EU states have security concerns about the number of arrivals and about refugee integration within the social security offered by welfare states.

These divergent, particularistic goals of national immigration and refugee protection policies underlie some of the most significant differences between the policy approaches. The US focus on selection and citizenship is in part a reflection of the way in which national interest informs the "recruitment" process, as is the use of detention for spontaneous arrivals – people who choose the United States rather than being chosen, if they do not make positive asylum requests. Australia's use of resettlement places for unauthorized boat arrivals and of mandatory detention can both be explained by its security concerns. Concerns about border security might make it logical to treat those breaching it as (potential) criminals, even if such a practice is indefensible by most other standards. Using the existing quota makes some sense in terms of maintaining the public image of control: the numbers do not increase in spite of the spontaneous arrivals. Yet the rhetoric about queues and about spontaneous arrivals leapfrogging the world's persecuted, who are imagined to be patiently waiting in line, exposes management flaws in the policy. European concerns about numbers and the protection of society explain the restrictive use of admission criteria and the limitation of immigration to asylum and family unity – both of which reflect the fundamental understanding of Europe as the cradle of human rights.

Different but similar

Scratch deeper, however, and the goals of refugee protection policy seem more similar than these divergent and particular interests and concerns indicate. All the states considered here seek both to lay claim to human rights as the basis for their refugee protection approach, and to guarantee the fundamental rights and freedoms of their existing citizens, including knowing who any newcomers may be – or at least that they are people who "belong." In addition, the governments of the states assessed seek a mode of societal "harmony" and inclusion.

Academics and NGOs often express concern about many of the policy initiatives undertaken by the states studied here. These concerns stem from a distinctly human-rights-based, normative assessment of the policies, which are considered to be counter to human rights in many cases simply because they are pro-sovereignty. Governments' refugee protection policies in principle call on refugee law and human rights instruments for backing but assess the situation of refugees from the point of view of how the state can live comfortably with the protection of some newcomers who manifest a need for the legal protection that refugee status brings, i.e. individuals who otherwise would not be protected in the state system. The United States and Australia have tended to view this protection as being long term, and so refugee protection leads to citizenship. European governments have tended rather to see refugee protection as something that is needed in the short term but not in the long term, because the situation in a country of origin is bound to change sometime.

A model for improved human-rights-based protection for refugees does not have to be universal in nature. Some use the notion of universal human rights to imply that there can or should be a universal model of protection. This ignores the types of particular and differing security concerns that states seek to address while attempting to achieve a mode of protection that upholds human rights. Although all states claim sovereignty, their form of sovereignty and the implications of their sovereign relationship with their populations may be at the root of differing refugee protection policies, even if those policies would all seek to satisfy universal human rights claims.

Cooperation

States share certain global-level concerns and can often understand each other's particular security concerns, so long as they do not conflict with their own. The policy reactions of states to globally similar security concerns may differ for historical, cultural, and societal reasons. However, such common concerns may lead states to cooperate more closely on the nature of refugee protection approaches. In addition, states are clearly looking to each other for transferable lessons, and using the same or similar terminology to mean different things (for example, temporary protection).

Control or management?

The three examples of refugee protection policy set out in this chapter have a common element – "control." This is the essence of the struggle between state security and human vulnerability: the state wishes to remain in control but its power to control is challenged because concerns about human vulnerabilities have resulted in instruments intended to uphold the individual's security – in the form of human rights and other humanitarian protections.

International agreements on who is recognized as a refugee and the level of rights attached to that status seek to clarify this issue for states as much as for the individual. In order to protect people who cannot avail themselves of the protection of their country of origin, another state needs to be assigned to the individual, at least in the short term. Otherwise, those individuals without "state belonging" will not be protected in the state system, because the state system, in so far as it organizes individuals into groups, is concerned to attach each individual to a state that will represent and protect him or her. International refugee law is thus not only protecting individuals but also protecting the integrity of the state system. As human rights issues have risen in prominence, the question of whether a person is a refugee or not, and how they should be protected, has become characterized as a battle between the state and the individual, rather than a compromise between states to ensure all or most individuals "fit" somewhere. The language of "control" has taken a front-line role – whereas "management" was the original issue and, in fact, "management" is what is required. "Control" implies that the state can determine whether or not individuals arrive at its borders, and the fact that they are present therefore makes the state seem lacking somehow. "Management" implies rather that the state acknowledges that there is a situation with which it must deal to the generally mutual satisfaction of the various actors that depend on it to do so.

A change in ideology, from control to management, would be one policy course that could be taken by the states discussed.

In order to manage refugee protection, developed states could go back to some of the basics: if individuals are within a state's borders and reasonably cannot go back to the state to which they belong because that state will persecute rather than protect them, or because that state is dysfunctional or unable to protect them owing to a conflict, then the state within whose borders the individuals are present has to decide whether or not to give those individuals its protection. Granting protection is not the same as just letting a person stay. Deciding to grant protection is a matter of managing the crisis of an individual who claims not to have any other protection. The management of the case is the concern of the state for two reasons. First, if no other state is protecting that individual, then one basic element of the international state system is failing, and the state in which the person actually is cannot turn to any other state to take responsibility for that person should the need arise. Secondly, if there are individuals within the state with whom other members of the state's society must interact, they need a basis on which to judge who those people are and what their political, cultural, and societal role is. So the individual in need does not issue the only call to management; the entire state system and the existing population do likewise. How the management takes place is another matter – the fact that the state must manage the protection of refugees is clear.

Besides replacing the control ideology with a management ideology, states should look to cooperation, which means not coerced policy change in other states but mutual understanding of how protection can best be managed for all involved.

In determining how to manage, it has been demonstrated that the different states have divergent political, cultural, and social bases to their "management styles." These do not need to converge to enhance refugee protection in the interests of states, societies, and individuals. Currently the centrality of "control ideology" means that states look to each other for policy ideas that will help them be more restrictive. A "management ideology" would imply that states learn from each other what could be creatively adapted tools to better organize their refugee protection process, and to better understand each other so as not to mismanage by imposing unrealistic demands, or demands that are not based in reality, on each other. Cooperation on refugee protection policies need not mean that a single approach becomes the only way in which protection can be managed; it means developing policies that are non-competitive and that respond to the global security needs involved in protecting refugees – including not only human rights protection but also protection of and understanding in the state system. Policies that involve requesting other states to take on the protection of refugees – for example, because the refugee is in that state *en route* from the state of origin to the state in which protection is requested (the "safe third country" concept) – could be part of a well-managed protection approach if the states involved really understand each other's approaches to protection and as long as the individual's fundamental rights, including the right to non-*refoulement* (non-return to a situation of danger), are guaranteed. There is no need to try to deny the specific security concerns of national interests or to unify policy in order to make refugee protection a more managed sphere of activity in a world that sovereign states can never fully control.

Notes

1. Kathleen Newland, *US Refugee Policy: Dilemmas and Directions*, Washington DC: Carnegie Endowment for International Peace, 1995, p. 10.
2. Ibid., p. 11.
3. Ibid., p. 13.
4. Article 1A.
5. Immigration and Naturalization Service (INS), www.ins.usdoj.gov/graphics/aboutins/statistics/statyrbook96/chapter2.pdf.
6. Lawyers Committee for Human Rights, *Refugees behind Bars: The Imprisonment*

   of Asylum-Seekers in the Wake of the 1996 Immigration Act, August 1999, at
   www.lchr.org/refugee/behindbars.htm.
7. Ibid.
8. Amnesty International USA, *Rights for All: Detention of Asylum Seekers*, at
   www.amnesty-usa.org/rightsforall/asylum/ins/ins-01.html.
9. Ibid.
10. INS, "This Month in Immigration History: November 1991," at www.ins.usdoj.gov/
    graphics/aboutins/history/nov91.htm.
11. Susan Beck, "Cast Away: How the INS Tried to Save the Haitians and How Bush
    Administration Hardline Policies Prevailed," *The American Lawyer*, October 1992,
    pp. 54–59.
12. "Cuban and Haitian Refugees," *Migration News*, vol. 1, no. 12, December 1994.
13. "Early Intervention to Prevent Mass Emigration," *Migration News*, vol. 2, no. 5, May
    1995.
14. "Guantanamo Cubans to Enter the US," *Migration News*, vol. 2, no. 6, June 1995.
15. US Committee for Refugees (USCR), "Country Report: United States," at
    www.refugees.org/world/countryrpt/amer_carib/us.htm.
16. Ibid.
17. Ibid.
18. United States Conference of Catholic Bishops, Migration and Refugee Services,
    "Statement on the Kosovo Refugee Crisis: Statement of Most Reverend Nicholas A.
    DiMarzio, Auxiliary Bishop of Newark, New Jersey, Chairman, Committee on Migra-
    tion National Conference of Catholic Bishops," 6 April 1999, at www.ncbuscc.org/
    comm/archives/99-079a.htm.
19. US Committee for Refugees, "For Kosovar Refugees, Guantanamo Is Not the
    Answer," press release, 9 April 1999, at www.refugees.org/news/press_releases/1999/
    040999.htm.
20. Susan Martin, "Humanitarian Refugees in the United States," at www.unikonstanz.de/
    FuF/ueberfak/fzaa/german/veranstaltungen.../mpf6_martin.htm.
21. Nancy Viviani, *The Indochinese in Australia 1975–1995: From Burnt Boats to Barbecues*,
    Melbourne: Oxford University Press, Australia, 1996, p. 6.
22. Ibid., p. 8.
23. UK Home Office at www.ind.homeoffice.gov.uk/default.asp?PageId=1170.
24. Viviani, *The Indochinese in Australia*, p. 18.
25. Ibid., p. 19.
26. USCR, "Country Reports: Australia, 2001," at www.refugees.org/world/countryrpt/
    easia_pacific/2001/Australia.htm.
27. Australian Democrats Senator Andrew Bartlett, cited in ibid.
28. Australian Department of Foreign Affairs and Trade, "Australia's Immigration Record
    – Background Information," at www.dfat.gov.au/media/tampa_immi_bg.html (undated).
29. "Desperate Asylum Seekers Clash with Indonesian Police," *Guardian Online*, 30 Octo-
    ber 2001.
30. Cited in USCR, "Country Reports: Australia, 2001," emphasis added.
31. USCR, "Country Reports: Australia, 2001."
32. UNHCR statistics at www.unhcr.ch/.
33. In 1999 the number of asylum seekers per 1,000 head of population was comparable to
    that in France and Finland. The Netherlands, with a similar population size to Australia
    but far greater population density, had 2.5 asylum seekers per 1,000 head of population.
    See www.ind.homeoffice.gov.uk/default.asp?PageId=1170.
34. In chapter 15 in this volume, Mares notes that two-thirds of all asylum applicants arrive
    lawfully in Australia.

35. See, for example, Human Rights and Equal Opportunity Commission, *Those Who've Come across the Seas*, Report of the Commission's inquiry into the detention of unauthorized arrivals in Australia, May 1998.
36. Ibid., p. vii.
37. Philip Ruddock, "Rebuttal of Four Corners Program, Legislative Provisions Restore Integrity to Refugees Convention," Media Release 118/2001, at www.minister.immi. gov.au/media_releases/media01/r01118.htm.
38. Fact Sheet 42, "Assistance for Asylum Seekers in Australia," at www.immi.gov. au/facts/42assist.htm.
39. Fact Sheet 63, "Temporary Protection Visas," at www.immi.gov.au/facts/63visas.htm.
40. K. Taylor, "PNG to Take 800 More Asylum Seekers," *The Age*, 18 January 2002, and other articles at www.theage.com.au/issues/immigration/index.html.
41. Fact Sheet 62, "Operation Safe Haven – Kosovars and East Timorese," at www.immi. gov.au/facts/62haven.htm.
42. "Australia: All Kosovars to Go," 15 July 1999; "Australia: Kosovars Resist Return," 6 April 2000; "Australia: Kosovars Get Return Reprieve," 7 April 2000; "Australia: Kosovars Refuse to Return," 10 April 2000; "Australia: Kosovars Agree to Go," 12 April 2000; "Australia: Kosovars Offered 'Special Programme'," 13 April 2000; "Australia: Kosovars Ordered to Leave," 14 April 2000; "Australia: Kosovars Flown Home," 17 April 2000; "Australia Deports 12 Kosovar Refugees," 23 August 2000 – all in UNHCR, *Refugees Daily*.
43. *Journal of Refugee Studies*, vol. 13, no. 1, 2000, Special Issue on EU states.
44. Commission of the European Communities, *Communication from the Commission to the Council and the European Parliament on a Community Immigration Policy*, COM (2000) 757, Brussels, 22 November 2000.
45. Commission of the European Communities, *Proposal to the Council for a Joint Action Based on Article K3(2)(b) of the Treaty on European Union Concerning Temporary Protection of Displaced Persons*, COM (97) 93 final [97/0081 (CNS)], Brussels, 5 March 1997.
46. Commission of the European Communities, *Proposal for a Council Directive on Minimum Standards for Giving Temporary Protection in the Event of a Mass Influx of Displaced Persons and on Measures Promoting a Balance of Efforts between Member States in Receiving Such Persons and Bearing the Consequences Thereof*, COM (2000) 303 final [2000/0127 (CNS)], Brussels, 24 May 2000.
47. See *Forced Migration Review*, vol. 5, August 1999.
48. See Joanne van Selm-Thorburn, *Refugee Protection in Europe: Lessons of the Yugoslav Crisis*, Dordrecht: Martinus Nijhoff, 1998.

5

Human security and the protection of refugees

Astri Suhrke

This chapter examines recent definitions of "security" in relation to issues of refugee policy. In particular, it focuses on the concepts of "societal security" and "human security," and considers a number of questions. What are the circumstances of their appearance in academic and policy discussions? What are the implications of placing the discourse on migrants and refugees in a security context, or what is often called its "securitization"? Is it useful to reconceptualize refugee issues in terms of "human security," as some suggest? In the concluding section, I will propose that, if the underlying normative purpose of refugee studies is to generate knowledge to enhance protection and assistance for refugees, then the concept of "vulnerability" is more suitable than "security," and this applies to the term "human security" as well.

Security as a contested concept

As Barry Buzan has convincingly argued, "security," like "justice," is an essentially contested concept.[1] Although contemporary observers generally agree that the analytical core of the term includes protection of central values and basic means of survival, there is much less agreement on the substantive meaning in concrete cases. Whose security is at stake? What are the dimensions of security? Definitions and invocations of security tend to vary according to ideological orientations and policy agendas. The term "national security" has been used to defend or promote a range of particularistic interests. Terms such as "environmental security" are a means of placing the environment towards the top of the policy agenda. The security of individuals – "human security" – has been counterposed to the traditional concept of the security of states.

The normative loading of the word "security" reflects its origins in state practice. As Booth has noted, "[e]ver since the time of Thomas Hobbes, but in reality earlier, security has been the primary obligation of governments. To place an item on the security agenda is therefore to raise its profile."[2] Conventionally, security was defined in terms of the national security of states, and this remains a principal usage. The so-called *traditionalists* additionally define security in military terms. This was the prevailing paradigm during the Cold War and is central to the neo-realist school of international relations. By contrast, a much broader *non-traditional* usage subsequently developed to include non-military aspects of security (environmental, societal, and economic).

The non-traditional rethinking started in the 1980s under pressure of a changing policy agenda – especially on environmental issues – but accelerated dramatically with the end of the Cold War.[3] In the early 1990s, the so-called Copenhagen school added another dimension by systematically exploring "societal security."[4] Analytically speaking, the rethinking in security studies – or what Krause and Williams call "critical security studies" – took place along two axes.[5] "The wideners" expanded the concept to include economic, environmental, and society security, but typically in relation to human collectivities that were organized in states. "The deepeners" defined security in terms of other referent objects: individuals ("human" security), particular groups (women), or all-encompassing collectivities ("global").[6] In the scholarly community, "deepening" has been a weak tendency relative to "widening," in terms of both the attention commanded, published output, and, possibly, analytical refinement.[7]

The new orientations reflected changes in the international system, which downgraded the traditional importance of military security of the Western states. At the same time, structural changes in the international system – the collapse of the Soviet empire, "failing" states in the developing world, and resurgent ethnic conflict – generated new insecurities. Globalization reinforced non-military pressures on established state practice and economies.

At the same time, numerous institutional and group interests that wanted to call attention to their agenda and justify institutional budgets reached for the "security" label. With the end of the Cold War, the term was no longer monopolized by the military establishments and could circulate freely. "Security" became a widely used category for promoting a range of policy issues. As one analyst argued, "If we are serious about human rights, economic development, the lot of women ... then we must simply accept the problems of an expanded [security] agenda."[8]

The rethinking took place in both policy and academic circles, but above all in the powerful Northern states. Not only were they directly and favourably affected by the changing military security in a post–Cold War world, they also possessed more resources to assess the implications. Scholarly paradigms were adjusted, reflecting both the sensitivity of scholars to a changing reality and their dependence on the political establishment in the industrialized North for research funding. A key initiative in this regard was a large MacArthur Foundation programme in the early 1990s to encourage scholarly thinking about "new security" issues. The Woodrow Wilson Center in Washington DC initiated a large, multi-year project on Environment and Security. Other examples abound.

Societal security

The concept of "society security" was most systematically examined by a group of European scholars working with the Centre for Peace and Conflict Resolution in Copenhagen (COPRI), one of the four Nordic peace research institutes. The project resulted in a 1993 book that was regarded as path-breaking within the security studies community of scholars.[9] Simultaneously, it can be seen as an initiative by scholars associated with the peace research tradition to "mainstream" their work by exploring non-military and non-offensive implications of "security."[10]

The Copenhagen school, as it came to be called, defined societal security in relation to the protection of core values in the identity of a human collectivity, in the contemporary world usually organized within states, but analytically and historically also relevant to other trans-generational human collectivities (religious communities, non-national ethnic groups). The modern prototype of such collective identity is nationalism.

Identity in this sense can be threatened from various directions (or what the authors call "sectors"): militarily through conquest and occupation, economically by domination or deprivation of resources, environmentally by damage to an environment that is the critical carrier of social identity, as well as from the society itself. The principal external threats to identity from the societal sector are migration, cultural infusions, or cultural "imperialism."

As the authors note, the pairing "migration and threat" has strong negative ideological connotations. They conclude:

The closeness to fascist ideology is troubling: is it therefore inadvisable to raise this agenda of societal security? Isn't there a risk that the result is to legitimise xenophobic and nationalist reactions against foreigners or against integration – "We are just defending our societal security!" This could be a risk, but it seems to us a risk we have to take. This danger has to be offset against the necessity to use the concept of societal security to try to understand what is actually happening: the social construction of societal insecurity.[11]

Some scholars and activists engaged in support of refugees argue that the risk in fact materialized. The "securitization" of the policy debate on refugee and migration movements in the 1990s, they claim, served to reinforce the restrictive asylum tendencies in Europe during that decade, and manifested themselves during the Kosovo refugee crisis as well.[12] This may be so. On the other hand, it is clear that asylum restrictions in Europe originated in a much broader set of political, social, and economic dynamics, some of which were in evidence already in the second half of the 1970s.[13]

What, then, can be said about the concept "societal security" in terms of its analytical clarity and policy implications? It is a normatively loaded term that evokes at least two main associations: "peace and security" and "threat and security." Both reflect the traditional connotations of the usage related to the state and the military. Although at first glance quite different, the two pairings become more similar if we interpret the first, not unreasonably, to suggest that peace is a result of security obtained through defence against threats of various kinds. Thus, security almost inescapably becomes part of a bundle of semiotics to which belong "enemy," "threat," and "we/they" as well. In relation to issues of social identity, this connotation is problematic because it associates change with threat and insecurity, ignoring the elementary fact that changes in social identity – even core values – can equally be experienced as growth and enrichment.

The concept has analytical weaknesses as well. It does not permit easy distinction between subcultures within a collectivity. What is the identity that is to be safeguarded in the name of "societal security"? Whose identity? Nor is the connection between identity and security self-evident. How much change to what values/identities is required for "societal security" to be threatened? Arguably, social identity changes that are gradual and part of an interactive process are not likely to be viewed as serious threats, if threats at all, even if they nibble away at what may be considered core values. Imposed, abrupt, and involuntary change will rightly be viewed as much more threatening. When such change is imposed by force, and in addition jeopardizes the basic means of survival of the community in question, we are clearly operating within a common sense understanding of security threats. This understanding is in line with the prevailing social science use, as Buzan has noted.[14]

Contemporary migration and refugee movements have infrequently been of a magnitude, speed, or nature to constitute a security threat in this sense. Migration, moreover, is only one among several exogenous and endogenous factors that affect and transform social identities, particularly in the present age of technological globalization. The visible nature of newly arrived refugees and migrations nevertheless makes them likely scapegoats for resentment over more invisible sources of change and felt insecurities.

There are some cases where migration or refugee movements have such severe impacts on the host state that – if the security paradigm is to be retained – they can reasonably be said to threaten both societal and other elements of security. In the past half-century, this has involved mass refugee movements whose impact reflects the sheer weight of numbers as well as certain strategic characteristics. By their numbers, they can severely distort the local economy and destroy the environment (the sudden movement of a quarter of a million Rwandan refugees into Tanzania after the genocide in 1994). Their ethnic or political characteristics may disturb delicate internal balances (Kosovo-Albanians in Macedonia in 1999). When they arrive with armed contingents that continue to fight on the host territory ("refugee warriors"), they invite retaliation and thus export the conflict from where they came (Rwandan refugees in Zaire/ Democratic Republic of the Congo from 1994). In all cases, it should be noted, "identity" or "societal security" was not the most critical issue in the conflicts that ensued in the receiving area. Even when expressed in terms of "identity" or ethnic conflict, the underlying contestation concerned control over economic and political power.

Other types of migratory movements can threaten the core values as well as the basic means of survival of the host community. Small groups of technologically backward indigenous peoples are typically vulnerable to in-migration from economically more advanced groups, especially if migration takes place within the country and the migrants are supported or resettled by the state in a particular area. "Societal security" in this situation would be that of the indigenous subgroup. The resultant migration-*cum*-conflict dynamic is familiar from the tribal hill areas of South Asia and, most recently, the outer islands of Indonesia (Dyaks). As Myron Weiner has demonstrated, migration in such situations threatens the identity, the economy, the social cohesion, and, in the end, the very collective existence of the community in the receiving area.[15]

These situations are far removed from the conditions of the stable and strong industrialized societies that formed the backdrop and central reference point for the Copenhagen school's explorations of societal security. Indeed, the first empirical test of the concept was in relation to external migration into European states.[16] Nevertheless, the nature of "migratory threat" situations elsewhere, and in very different circumstances, suggests why refugee movements may generate considerable fear and encourage "securitization" of the policy discourse even in regions where they are not likely to constitute a security risk in any meaningful sense of the word.

As the above examples indicate, one critical ingredient in a migratory threat situation is the unwillingness or inability of the state in the receiving area to close off or otherwise condition the inflow. This may be the case when weak or non-functioning states are faced with a mass inflow of refugees, or when migration takes place within one jurisdiction and state power sides with the migrants against weaker and fewer peoples forming a distinct subnationality in the receiving area. In both cases, the people in the receiving area are unable to control the inflow. The same issue of control is inherent in all refugee situations. Although states generally reserve the right to control in-migration as the prerogative of a sovereign, they are under considerable international pressure to admit (or at least not *refouler*) refugees regardless of numbers and ethno-political nature. Most states at present have undertaken an international legal obligation, in effect, to waive considerable control when it comes to the admission of refugees. In practice, few do so. If they were to abide seriously by their obligations, one can easily envisage claimants arriving in very considerable numbers, especially in the industrialized and prosperous Northern states. Whether this would constitute a threat to "societal security" would depend upon the particulars of the case, but the possibility that this might happen has led these states to take firm measures to reassert control.

This helps explain why governments in Europe and North America increasingly have restricted access to seek asylum. It likewise explains the high profile of refugee matters and their "securitization" by states (as well as by right-wing groups, who ideologically and sociologically are attracted to the principle of control). Finally, it explains why, given the considerable ability and willingness of most industrialized states to control the intake of peoples, migration and refugee movements hardly constitute a threat to their "societal security" in these states. This reality likewise reduces the relevance of "societal security" as a concept for analysing the impact of refugees and migration into "first world" states, though it may be more useful elsewhere.

Human security

Whereas "societal security" was launched as a concept to examine the impact of migration on the receiving areas, "human security" would at first glance seem a useful framework for examining the needs of the migrants themselves, especially forced migrants such as refugees. As van Selm argues, human security can be seen as

a link with societal security, a useful alternative to it, or even a contradiction of it. If those supporting human security seek to protect vulnerable individuals, and those offering the understanding of societal security seek the support of identity, even at the expense of vulnerable individuals (or indeed while making some individuals more vulnerable), then there are obvious areas for further reflection.[17]

As the concept "human security" has evolved in the last decade, it has at least two distinct meanings:

1. *A broad, nearly encompassing concept that links a wide range of developmental and physical security dimensions.* The distinguishing characteristic is that it is the individual – not the state or society – whose security is to be enhanced. This is the early usage promoted by the United Nations Development Programme (UNDP) and, in a separate discourse, by scholars of the "critical security studies" school.[18]
2. *A specific policy agenda promoted by a network of states or international organizations.* One network was initiated by Canada and Norway in the mid-1990s and had by the end of the decade become semi-institutionalized. The agenda prominently included issues such as a ban on land mines, prohibition of child soldiers, control of small arms, and promotion of the International Criminal Court. The issues were deliberately put under a "human security" umbrella. Another policy issue frequently associated with "human security," and promoted by a diverse coalition of international organizations, UN agencies, and non-governmental organizations, is post-crisis reconstruction and "peace-building."

The idea of "human security" was extracted from a stock of ideas that had become increasingly salient towards the end of the twentieth century. Humanitarian ideals had become a principal normative reference for states and organizations to clarify their own obligations and the responsibility of others. An "embedded humanitarianism" could be discerned, similar to the notion of "embedded liberalism" that analysts used to characterize the Western world after 1945.[19] In both cases, the term "embedded" suggests that the norms are diffuse, often permitting non-articulated compromises, yet generally understood in a consensual way and invested with legitimating power.

As a social construct, the term "human security" permits many inter-pretations, and those promoting it are still struggling to formulate an authoritative and consensual definition. The concept has some roots in the central principle of international humanitarian law – that is, to civi-lize warfare and aid its victims. In the modern European tradition, rights and duties in this regard were first codified in the late nineteenth century, and have since been progressively elaborated in international humani-tarian law and by the Red Cross movement. "Human security" can be seen as a distillation of the central objective in this body of law: to save lives and reduce the suffering of individuals during armed conflict.

A more immediate origin of the term is found in the 1994 UNDP annual report. "Human security" appears here as part of a vision for a "people-oriented economic development." The starting point is poverty rather than war, but "human security" promises an escape from both.[20] The UNDP report examines "human security" in relation to "human development," drawing on notions of justice that appeared in the devel-opment literature in the early 1970s. At that time, "human development" served as a counterpoint to economistic and growth-oriented concepts of development, where the objective was to produce material goods and humans were viewed mainly as inputs of labour. Critics argued that development must be assessed in terms of its implications for people (hence the emphasis on basic human needs, equity, and non-exploitative growth). Equally, the development process must be determined by pop-ular participation and autonomous definition of needs and wants (so that "thirst" is not defined as "the need for a Coke," as Ivan Illich wrote in his classic 1970 essay). During the second half of the 1970s, this criticism branched in two main directions: a "small is beautiful" perspective, and a more theoretically rigorous neo-Marxist criticism of neo-classical para-digms. By the late 1990s, only the non-Marxist tradition of "human development" had survived. It was in part a rather woolly notion of "human-centred development";[21] in part quasi-quantitative, especially as developed with UNDP's human development indicators. The common core was an emphasis on equity and the need to reduce the number of losers in the development process.

The major contribution of the 1994 UNDP report to this literature was its attempt to define human security and human development and to sort out their relationship. The result, however, was confusingly circular. "Human security" was presented both as an end-state of affairs – "safety from such chronic threats as hunger, disease and repression" – and as a process in the sense of "protection from sudden and hurtful disruptions in the patterns of daily life." As an end-state, human security was further broken down with respect to sectors such as employment, health, educa-tion, and the environment. Human security was seen as essential for human development; without minimal stability and security in daily life, there could be no development – human or otherwise. But the obverse was true as well. Long-term development that improves social and economic life would produce human security, the report concluded. In this reasoning, there is no difference between human development and human security, or between the process and the end-state.

Yet the main purpose of the agency was hardly to make an analytical breakthrough but to place UNDP concerns about poverty at the centre of the public policy debate. By "securitizing" its concerns, the agency succeeded at least in the sense that it is still widely credited with inventing the term.

A similar dynamic explains the policy initiative taken by the Canadian and Norwegian governments in the late 1990s. Both states had a humanitarian tradition in foreign policy, and both were either in, or trying to get into, the UN Security Council. Seeking to express a policy vision that elevated humanitarian issues to "high politics," both governments seized on "human security" as a useful label. In due course, it became an umbrella for a collection of worthwhile specific issues (for example, the ban on land mines and child soldiers, the promotion of the International Criminal Court) around which an informal coalition of states formed. As Keith Krause has shown, the idea was mainly promoted by the national security sections in the respective foreign ministries of the sponsors.[22] Consequently – and in contrast to the UNDP orientation – the concept was now operationalized to focus on issues of security and law, not development. In an authoritative policy definition, however, the Canadian government incorporated both physical and economic dimensions; the main point was that the individual, and not the state, was the referent object. In the words of Foreign Minister Lloyd Axworthy,

[i]n essence, human security means safety for people from both violent and non-violent threats. It is a condition or state of being characterized by freedom from pervasive threats to people's rights, their safety or even their lives.... From a foreign policy perspective, human security is perhaps best understood as a shift in perspective or orientation. It is an alternative way of seeing the world, taking people as its point of reference, rather than focusing exclusively on the security of territory or governments.[23]

From an analytical perspective, the definition seems too inclusive to be useful. From a policy perspective, the assessment would be more mixed. The concept might help to mobilize support and influence agendas, although it leaves the most difficult and central questions open: *Who* is going to provide the security? *What* are the limits of humanitarian intervention? *How* is security to be provided and, specifically, how can assistance or sanctions be operationalized so as to minimize rather than increase human suffering? When objectives conflict, *which* interests are to be served – those of states or those of the individual beneficiaries? How will conflicting interests be mediated when the security interests of individual beneficiaries conflict, or individual and group security interests are incompatible?

The United Nations High Commissioner for Refugees (UNHCR) was this time not among the conceptual entrepreneurs; yet, when prodded, the agency recognized the agenda-setting value of the term. In May 1999, the High Commissioner, Sadako Ogata, was invited to deliver the keynote address at the second meeting of the Canadian–Norwegian-sponsored "human security" coalition of states. It was the first time the High Commissioner systematically sought to relate the concept to refugees.

At the 1999 meeting, the High Commissioner did not precisely define "human security" in relation to refugees beyond noting that "[r]efugees are doubly insecure: they flee because they are afraid; and in fleeing they start a precarious existence."[24] She proceeded to emphasize two types of situations and related policy needs that must be addressed in order to improve the human security of potential or actual refugees:

(a) prevention of conflict and peace-building to protect and assist internally displaced persons (IDPs) and refugees in areas of conflict; states and organizations should form strategic partnerships with UNHCR for this purpose;

(b) filling "the gap" between relief and development in the aftermath of a violent conflict so that returning refugees and IDPs could more readily be integrated and not risk repeated displacement.

Both were high-priority items on the UNHCR's agenda. The High Commissioner evidently used the occasion to wrap them in a symbol that would enhance their acceptance to the audience of states present. The High Commissioner had earlier taken the lead in seeking new institutional and financial measures to fill "the gap," to this end initiating what came to be know as the Brookings process and forging a relationship with the World Bank. As for conflict prevention and "peace-building," the UNHCR's experience in the Balkans and the Great Lakes region of Central Africa in the 1990s had made the High Commissioner an outspoken advocate of political action that could make intervention in humanitarian crises more effective. A humanitarian agency, she emphasized, could be no substitute for a political response, although sometimes it was cast in this role. The frequent references to the Balkan operations in Mrs. Ogata's speech underscored the point.

The High Commissioner did not flag two issues that one might have expected as natural under the human security umbrella. There was only a passing reference to the security of refugees in camps (for example in

Eastern Zaire since 1994). The subject was apparently subsumed under the "ladder of security" concept developed in the UNHCR in the 1990s to address physical security problems in refugee camps. More remarkably, perhaps, there was no reference to asylum. As the traditional and legal cornerstone of protection, and as a core dimension of the UNHCR's mandate, asylum might be expected to figure centrally in a policy-oriented definition of human security that focused on aid to refugees.

The reasons asylum was not linked to human security probably reflect the overall changes in the UNHCR's approach to refugees in the 1990s, including the changing balance between assistance and protection, the restrictions on traditional asylum imposed by most states, particularly in the industrialized North, and the consequent shift to preventive and interventionist measures.[25] Moreover, from a protection perspective, it was not clear that invoking an imprecise policy term would significantly add to the security provided by the extant and much more precise legal texts on asylum and refugee rights.

Human security and human vulnerability

Policy concepts whose purpose is to mobilize public support and influence political agendas may not require a coherent core or clear boundaries. But these requirements do apply to an analytical exercise because the very purpose of such a definition is to sort cases, setting one category apart from the rest. Does "human security" have this potential?

Little serious effort has been made so far to develop the concept analytically. Although Krause has pioneered serious work, his approach, by seeking to explain which factors contributed to the discourse and whether it has affected practice, is not phenomenological but historical and institutional.[26] My own attempts to explore the concept as an analytical tool had recourse to the concept of "vulnerability," by defining human security as reduced vulnerability.[27] However, because vulnerability was not independently defined, the result was tautological: human security was in effect defined as the opposite of human insecurity. Different shortcomings are evident in the work by Booth.[28] The inherent difficulty, it seems, is the level of analysis: the individual. Although a definition could be founded on an objective element of physical survival, non-derogable human rights, and protection of core identity, there is a large element of subjective judgement in what is required for human security. Since "the individual preferences of all people could not possibly be taken into account," as Tarry argues, "human security" becomes too inclusive to be analytically useful.[29]

In sum, "human security," like "national security," must remain an essentially contested concept. It has normative and policy uses but does not lend itself to a delimitation whose precise boundaries command general agreement. What, then, are the implications for linking it to the study of, and response to, refugees?

First, for organizations and individuals concerned with aiding refugees, invoking the emotionally loaded concept may have an agenda-setting and mobilizing effect. On the other hand, if the term "societal security" has served to "securitize" the discourse on refugees – with all the negative implications noted above – the term "human security" might well have the same effect. Although the adjective differs, the noun remains and is likely to generate the familiar connotations of "threat," "enemy," and "we/they." At best, the term will be at war with itself, as Robert E. Robertson has noted in another connection, with "human" connoting the needs of the individual and "security" carrying the heavy baggage of the interests of state and society.[30]

"Security" also has another dimension. Under conditions of scarce resources and an international system organized into nation-states, the benefit claims by some individuals will in some measure affect claims by other individuals. The cost of trade-offs is reduced under conditions of growth, but only a very few goods (pure public goods) are truly indivisible and non-exhaustible. Regulating the constant trade-offs between and among claims is what the political process is all about. Moving the discourse to the realm of "security" changes the language in a way that makes trade-offs more difficult. With claims and counter-claims phrased in terms of security, trading benefits and forging compromises become more difficult. Who is willing to trade off his/her security?

If applied to refugees, "securitization" from "human security" thus is likely to generate the same non-productive and conflict-laden dialogue as "societal security," with threat, enemy, we/they, and no compromise as staple terms. In so far as scholarly paradigms matter at all – which critics of the Copenhagen school suggest – then human security is not likely to encourage a discourse that facilitates protection and assistance.

What are the alternatives? First, from a policy perspective, the critical elements of what might be subsumed under the "human security" label are already incorporated in a legally binding international convention. The 1951 Convention Relating to the Status of Refugees recognizes certain rights of asylum seekers and refugees, although it also permits signatory states some leeway. For refugee advocacy purposes, the 1951 Convention and related body of human rights law seem a more suitable weapon of choice than fuzzy and potentially negative symbols like "human security."

From an analytical point of view, the term "human security" may be useful in encouraging dispassionate scholarship to examine the relationship between the security of refugees (as defined) and that of the host community. Barry Buzan argues in *People, States and Fear* that, when it comes to ideologically contested concepts, social scientists can make a better contribution by clarifying the contradictions and dilemmas that these concepts entail than by articulating ideal-normative models.[31] He tries to sort out the dilemmas posed by security as understood on three levels: the individual, the nation, and the international system. A similar exercise involving only the first two levels, and focusing on refugees and the (host) nation (including subgroups), could be carried out. Indeed, much of what constitutes the empirical field of refugee studies does this in bits and pieces by examining the needs and demands of refugees, how these impact on recipient communities and in which sectors, and how host state policies affect the protection and assistance of refugees. At present, this knowledge is fragmented and particularistic. Greater efforts could be made to aggregate and generalize.

If normative, policy-oriented models that focus on the needs and rights of refugees were to be constructed, the concept of vulnerability would arguably serve as a more appropriate foundation stone than "human security." The term is beneficiary oriented and does not generate the negative we/they or "threat images" that "security" does. It is already widely used and operationalized in the international policy community serving refugees, displaced persons, and other individuals in need of assistance. The major UN agencies with humanitarian programmes have working definitions, guidebooks, and at times fairly elaborate models for identifying vulnerable groups and individuals in their respective mandate sectors. Thus, the World Food Programme has been standardizing methods for assessing vulnerability in relation to food security (based on estimated crops, market availability of food, and social coping mechanisms, etc., as against calorie intake requirements). UNICEF (the UN Children's Fund) has a set of guidelines to identify vulnerable groups (for example child soldiers) and appropriate standards of support to reduce vulnerability (in health and education). The UNHCR has defined vulnerable groups in relation to its repatriation programme[32] and to resettlement[33] and for camp support. Typically, groups such as unaccompanied children and the elderly, the handicapped and chronically ill, women-at-risk, torture cases, and single heads of household are, in various contexts, assumed to be vulnerable. Sorting out common concepts and underlying characteristics of "vulnerability" as operationalized by aid agencies could be one element in such a normative model.

Normative model-building could also draw upon the conceptual and methodological work done by national and international authorities in estimating vulnerability to natural disasters and climate change. Thus, the Intergovernmental Panel on Climate Change assessed the vulnerability of 10 geographic regions in relation to potential effects of climate change. "Vulnerability" is defined as "the extent to which climate change may damage or harm a system: it is a function of both sensitivity to climate and the ability to adapt to new conditions."[34] In the United States, the Environmental Protection Agency and various national authorities have similar working definitions for vulnerability, whether it is the "susceptibility [of the environment] to degradation or damage"[35] or community vulnerability to coastal hazards (which includes location, use of critical facilities, and mitigating opportunities).[36]

Equivalent vulnerability of particular groups, such as refugees, would then consider potential damaging effects from the social and physical environment, as against mitigating factors (such as coping strategies and access to social, political, and economic resources). In other words, it is a model that lends itself to conceptual elaboration as well as empirical application. Although beneficiary centred and oriented towards the protection and assistance of refugees, the model does not call up passive, dependence responses – and top–down strategies by the aid actors – because a critical element of the model is the various ways in which the beneficiaries themselves can contribute to the mitigating factors that reduce vulnerability.

Conclusions

The term "security" has conventionally been associated with the interests of collectivities (states and societies) or aspects of social existence that affect collectivities (such as the environment). Efforts have recently been made to develop the competing concept of "human security." So far, these efforts have been made by governments or international agencies seeking to promote policy issues of particular concern. The scholarly community has made efforts to explore the analytical dimensions of the concept in ways that could make it useful in a social science context, especially in relation to forced migration.

From both a normative and an analytical perspective, it is argued here that the term "human security" is not useful for examining the needs of individual groups that, on some critical dimensions of belonging, stand apart from the community in which they find themselves (refugees and other displaced persons). Applying a "security" perspective to examine the needs of "outsiders" and their relationship to the community typically involves assumptions of antagonistic relations and non-tradable interests. In other words, the negative effects often assumed to follow the "securitization" of the discourse on refugee movements that was associated with "societal security" in the 1990s are likely to occur even when the adjective is "human" rather than "societal."

If the aim is to build a normative and policy-oriented model that places the interests of the displaced populations at the centre, a better starting point is "vulnerability." The concept lends itself to methodological and empirical elaboration, and does not evoke the same conflictual connotations as "security." The concept has been developed into rather sophisticated models in related areas (climate change and natural disasters), and has already been operationalized by most of the aid agencies working for displaced persons. The function of a normative model of vulnerability for displaced persons would be to extract from these concepts and practices relevant elements and aggregate them into a set of more formalized relationships that would have general applicability to the population in question.

Notes

1. Barry Buzan, *People, States and Fear. An Agenda for International Security Studies in the Post–Cold War Era*, 2nd edn, New York: Harvester Wheatsheaf, 1991.
2. K. Booth, *A Security Regime in Southern Africa: Theoretical Considerations*, Working Paper Series 30, Centre for Southern African Studies, University of the Western Cape, 1994, p. 3.
3. Thomas Homer-Dixon, "Environmental Scarcities and Violent Conflict," *International Security*, vol. 18, no. 1, 1994; Joseph S. Nye Jr. and Sean M. Lynn-Jones, "International Security Studies," *International Security*, vol. 12, no. 4, 1988; Jessica Tuchman Mathews, "Redefining Security," *Foreign Affairs*, vol. 68, no. 2, 1989; Richard Ullman, "Redefining Security," *International Security*, vol. 8, no. 1, 1989.
4. Buzan, *People, States and Fear*; Ole Wæver et al., *Identity, Migration and the New Security Agenda in Europe*, New York: St. Martin's Press, 1993; Barry Buzan, Ole Wæver, and Jaap de Wilde, *Security. A New Framework for Analysis*, Boulder, CO: Lynne Rienner, 1998.
5. Keith Krause and Michael C. Williams, eds., *Critical Security Studies*, Minneapolis: University of Minnesota Press, 1997.
6. Krause and Williams, *Critical Security Studies*; Michael T. Klare and Daniel C. Thomas, eds., *World Security: Challenges for a New Century*, New York: St. Martin's Press, 1994.
7. Sarah Tarry, "'Deepening' and 'Widening': An Analysis of Security Definitions in the 1990s," paper, University of Calgary, 1999, at www.stratnet.ucalgary.ca/journal/1999/article3.html.
8. Booth, *A Security Regime in Southern Africa*, p. 3.
9. Wæver et al., *Identity, Migration and the New Security Agenda in Europe*.
10. Buzan, *People, States and Fear*.
11. Wæver et al., *Identity, Migration and the New Security Agenda in Europe*, pp. 188–189.
12. Joanne van Selm, ed., *Kosovo's Refugees in the European Union*, London: Pinter, 2000.
13. Daniele Joly and Robin Cohen, eds., *Reluctant Hosts: Europe and Its Refugees*, Aldershot: Avebury, 1989; Daniele Joly, *Haven or Hell? Asylum Policies and Refugees in Europe*, London: Macmillan, 1996; Charles Keely and Sharon S. Russell, "Responses of

Industrial Countries to Asylum-seekers, Refugees and Migrants," *Journal of International Affairs*, vol. 47, no. 2, 1994.

14. Buzan, *People, States and Fear*, pp. 16–17.
15. Myron Weiner, ed., *International Migration and Security*, Boulder, CO: Westview Press, 1993.
16. Wæver et al., *Identity, Migration and the New Security Agenda in Europe*.
17. Van Selm, *Kosovo's Refugees in the European Union*, p. 207.
18. Keith Krause, "Une approche critique de la sécurité humaine," paper, Institut universitaire de hautes études internationales, Geneva, September 2000.
19. John G. Ruggie, "International Regimes, Transactions and Change: Embedded Liberalism in the Postwar Economic Order," in Stephen D. Krasner, ed., *International Regimes*, Ithaca, NY: Cornell University Press, 1983.
20. UNDP, *Human Development Report*, New York, 1994.
21. Majid Rahnema, ed., *The Post-Development Reader*, London: Zed Books, 1997.
22. Krause, "Une approche critique de la sécurité humaine."
23. DEFAIT, "Human Security: Safety for People in a Changing World," Department of Foreign Affairs and International Trade, Ottawa, 1999.
24. UNHCR, "Human Security: A Refugee Perspective," speech by Sadako Ogata, Bergen, Norway, 19 May 1999, p. 2.
25. Astri Suhrke and Kathleen Newland, "UNHCR: Uphill into the Future," *International Migration Review*, vol. 35, no. 1, Spring 2001, pp. 284–302.
26. Krause, "Une approche critique de la sécurité humaine."
27. Astri Suhrke, "Human Security and the Interests of States," *Security Dialogue*, vol. 30, no. 3, 1999.
28. Booth, *A Security Regime in Southern Africa*.
29. Tarry, "'Deepening' and 'Widening': An Analysis of Security Definitions in the 1990s," p. 8.
30. Cited in Audrey R. Chapman, "A 'Violations Approach' for Monitoring the International Covenant on Economic, Social and Cultural Rights," *Human Rights Quarterly*, vol. 18, no. 1, 1996, p. 1.
31. Buzan, *People, States and Fear*.
32. UNHCR, *Handbook on Voluntary Repatriation*, Geneva, 1966.
33. UNHCR Executive Committee, *Conclusions XLII*, 1991.
34. Intergovernmental Panel on Climate Change, *IPCC Special Report on the Regional Impacts of Climate Change. An Assessment of Vulnerability*, at www.grida.no/climate/ipcc/regional.
35. Environmental Protection Agency, *Terms of the Environment*, 2000, at www.epa.gov.
36. National Oceanic & Atmospheric Administration Coastal Services Center, *Community Vulnerability Assessment Tool*, 1999, at www.csc.noaa.gov.

6

Thinking ethically about refugees: A case for the transformation of global governance

Mervyn Frost

Everyone who is a participant in the practices of contemporary global politics faces a set of problems concerned with migrants of one kind or another and these are at base ethical problems. In the category of "migrant" I include political refugees and illegal economic migrants. The ethical problems presented to us are becoming more pressing by the day. In this chapter I wish to do three things. First, I shall make the case that the problems must be understood as essentially ethical and that in some profound sense we are missing the point if we continue to see the problems presented by migrants as merely technical, legal, political, or administrative. In this opening section I shall also argue that it would be wrong to see them as problems that are well understood as arising from clashes between rival religious, cultural, or national groups. Second, I shall present the outline of what I take to be a particularly useful way of understanding the ethical problems presented to us by migrants and refugees. The particular strength of this mode of analysis is that it allows us to see the changes that are taking place in our global practices from within which we make our judgements about how, from an ethical point of view, we ought to treat migrants of all kinds. Third, I shall endeavour to spell out what the implications of this analysis are for those who are concerned with the question "What ought to be done about the problems presented to us by migrants and refugees as we experience them in the contemporary world?" The analysis offered is radical in that it shows how the language we use about international ethics, especially the language of universal human rights, indicates how aspects of domestic and international law are now in need of reform. A crucial feature of the argument is that our own constitution as free people depends on our treating migrants ethically.

In what ways are the problems presented to us by migrants fundamentally ethical problems? First, we can identify some problems concerning refugees that are clearly not ethical. Some such problems are merely *technical*. For example, after the discovery in London of stowaways on the Eurostar train that links England with France, the management of Eurostar together with the British police could explore mechanisms for preventing this happening in future. Suggestions might include better fencing around the points of embarkation, installing better electronic surveillance equipment on the trains and at the stations, and so on. The problem being faced is clearly a technical one: how best to prevent people stowing away on the Eurostar trains. We can easily think of many other technical problems related to illegal migrants, such as finding ways to process asylum applications more quickly, or setting up suitable reception centres for asylum seekers.

There is another kind of problem that arises with regard to migrants of one kind or another. These we might call *political* problems. A good example occurred in Dover in the United Kingdom, where the local residents raised objections to the number of asylum seekers who were being allowed entry to Dover after registering their claim to asylum status with the Port Authorities. The residents of Dover claimed that the asylum seekers who arrived in Dover society often committed crimes, that they posed a threat to the fabric of society, and that they were a drain on the resources of the local social services. What defines the actions of the Dover residents as "political" is that they were seeking to bring pressure to bear on local and central government to tighten the rules governing the entry of refugees into Britain. Politics is defined here as what is done by people with a view to changing the basic rules of association under which they live. This seems to accord well with how we normally use the word "politics."[1]

Sometimes migrants are seen as posing an *economic* problem to the people of a given state. For example, the view is often heard in South Africa that illegal migrants from Mozambique are a threat to the economic well-being of South African citizens in that they are seeking to "steal" the jobs that properly belong to South African citizens. This theft of jobs is also often presented as having the effect of depressing the pay of South African workers because the Mozambicans are prepared to work for far lower wages than are currently being paid to South African workers.

A fourth way of portraying the problem posed by migrants and refugees is to present them as posing a threat to the *culture* of the society into which they are moving. Thus, for example, large-scale migrations are portrayed as threatening the traditional ways of life of the British, the French, the Swiss, the Germans, and so on.

Yet another way of presenting the migrant problem is to claim that they form some kind of *religious* threat to the target society. Thus an influx of Islamic people into a Christian society would be construed as a major threat to the religious integrity of that society. This is the "swamping" argument sometimes heard from within, for example, portions of the former Yugoslavia.

None of these ways of understanding the problems posed by migrants presents the problem as an ethical one. In all the cases outlined above the actors concerned understand the problem to be of a practical nature. This, of course, is not to deny that those making the judgements mentioned above might acknowledge that their portrayal of the situation stems from strongly held ethical beliefs. Thus, for example, the residents of Dover might report that they have a right as British citizens not to have their society invaded by foreigners with a tendency towards crime; the South Africans might say they have a right not to have "their" jobs stolen by Mozambicans; the Christians would say they have a right not to be swamped by Islamic believers, and so on. Notwithstanding the ethical foundations of their judgements, in all the cases I have described the problem for the people concerned is a practical one – what has to be solved is a set of practical problems. Reduced to its simplest, the problem is "How (by what means) can we control the influx of migrants in order to protect our town, state, economy, culture, or religion?"

When the problem posed by migrants is represented in the ways I have spelled out above, then we can expect lawyers to engage in exercises of comparative law to seek out better ways of controlling migrancy; sociologists and political scientists to strive for better understandings of the underlying causes of migratory phenomena so that they might inform policy makers of the best ways to control them; economists to investigate the influence of migrant labour on local markets; cultural theorists to investigate the ways in which migrants either do or do not contribute to the enriching or weakening of specific cultures, and so on. International relations scholars who approach the migrancy problem as a practical one will be interested in the impact of mass migration on the global balance of power and its implications for international security. With such problems in mind, they might set out to explore the efficacy of different devices designed to produce early warning of destabilizing mass migrations.

All of the above are examples of *problem-solving* approaches to migrancy. In each case some actor (or set of actors) is confronting the problems posed by migrants. In seeking to understand these, the actors in question might launch research programmes to gather information about the patterns, causes, and consequences of migration. They might set up comparative studies to compare and contrast different approaches to the problem. What would be missing from all these approaches to migrancy is any sense that migrants present us with ethical dilemmas, which call into question our very conception of who we are – that the phenomenon of migrancy presents us with a set of questions that, once confronted, might precipitate within us a reflective process that could end in our own ethical transformation or reconstruction.

Constitutive theory and its understanding of ethical dilemmas

In order to make it clear just how migrants present us with problems of ethical transformation, this section will outline an approach to ethics that I have called constitutive theory.[2] There are six central components of this theory.

First, we are constituted as the actors we are within social practices. Our status as an actor of this or that kind is not simply given to us at birth. We learn what is involved in being an actor within social practice. Examples of practices include family life, sports games, religions, and states. A practice consists of people following a certain set of rules (often referred to as the rules of the game). These may be articulated or tacit. One knows what is involved in rule-following once one knows what is involved in getting a particular act right and, conversely, what is involved in making a mistake. By learning how to follow the rules that constitute any given practice, individual men and women are constituted as actors/ players/participants in that practice. Thus, by learning to follow the rules of chess, one is constituted as a chess player; by learning to follow the rules of soccer, one is constituted as a soccer player; and, by learning to follow the rules constitutive of a democratic state, one is constituted as a citizen of such a state, and so on.

Second, we are all constituted as actors in any number of different practices. We are constituted as participants in families, markets, church groups, political parties, universities, sports clubs, and states simultaneously. It is not possible to envisage or consider one's identity without reference to a range of social practices.

Third, all practices contain a range of different kinds of rules that specify, *inter alia*, who may participate, how to participate, what participants should aim at, what will count as success in that practice (and what as failure), what the consequences of rule-breaking are, and what punishments are authorized, to mention but a few.

Fourth, all practices have embedded in them what might be termed an ethic. These are the values that are fundamental to that practice, such that, were participants to renounce a commitment to these, they would no longer be taken as serious participants in that practice. They would, as it were, be excommunicated from that practice, and this point is central to constitutive theory. Consider the example of an international organization such as the United Nations. The states that participate in this organization sign up to the Charter, which has an embedded ethic within it. A central component of this is the value of peace and security. Were a state systematically and rigorously to say and do things that indicated it was diametrically opposed to peace and security, a point might be reached at which the other participants would no longer consider the state in question to be a *bona fide* participant in this practice. This is not to deny that on many issues the participants in the United Nations might well argue back and forth about what precisely the embedded ethic of the United Nations is, but in broad outline they know what the parameters of such a debate are. To drive the point home, consider an example taken from sport – such as soccer, cricket, netball, or hockey. A component of the ethic internal to each of these is that players are engaged in a game whose purpose is to win. If some player systematically played in such a way as to secure a loss for his/her side, then at some point he or she would no longer be consider a *bona fide* player of that game. To recapitulate this point: all practices are underpinned by some value or values the consistent flouting of which would result in the person in question having his or her status as a participant in that practice withdrawn. In constitutive theory I call the values that are fundamental to a given practice in this way *ethical* values. It is important to note that participants within a given practice might have vigorous disagreements amongst themselves about the precise interpretation that ought to be put on the ethical values of that practice. For example, within the practice we know as the European Union participants may engage in intense debate about the precise interpretation to be accorded the idea of sovereignty, which is one of the values that is ethically fundamental for all those who are participants in that practice. There are similar ethical disputes among the members of the United Nations about the exact interpretation to be put on the value "national self-determination" and on many other values that are ethically foundational for the United Nations.

Fifth, and this is the most important point for this chapter, a particularly difficult kind of ethical dilemma confronts us when we, as participants in good standing in more than one social practice simultaneously (and we are all constituted in this way), find that what is required of us by the ethic embedded in one of these practices is contradicted by what is required of us by the ethic embedded in one or more of the other practices. Those who are both shareholders in a multinational corporation and fervent members of a nationalist movement provide a good example of this. The contradiction strikes them when they find that what is ethically required of them in the one (moving capital offshore) comes to contradict in a fundamental way what is ethically required of them in the other (protecting the interest of the nation by curtailing the movement of capital).[3]

What causes such predicaments to arise? Several different possibilities are worthy of mention here. At the heart of them all, though, is the phenomenon of change. Practices are not static. Games change (from soccer to rugby); institutions develop and are modified to accommodate new circumstances. Sometimes with the passing of time internal contradictions emerge (Karl Marx developed a whole theory of social change based on this insight). Economic practices, such as the practice of capitalism, might start small within specific towns, cities, and states, but with time they slide over boundaries into uncharted territory. Scientific practices lead to the making of discoveries that lead to changes in the practice of science itself. Extraneous factors influence the way practices grow or wither. Here I have in mind epidemics (the Black Death, Aids, polio, and turberculosis, to mention but a few) or disasters such as volcanic eruptions, earthquakes, global warming, global cooling, and many others.

Sixth, when we find ourselves participants in practices whose ethical foundations are at odds with one another, we have no option but to become what might be termed *ethical constructivists*. We need to do this in order to achieve some ethical coherence in our lives. Consider those I mentioned above who want to be both good capitalists (as shareholders in multinational corporations) and staunch nationalists. How might such people cope with their simultaneous participation in these two contradictory practices? The following options seem to exhaust the possibilities. A first option might be to give up being a player in global capitalism. A second option would be to cease participation in the nationalist practice. The third and most likely option is to engage in an exercise of reinterpretation (which might lead to a reconstruction) of one or both of the practices, such that the contradiction between the ethics embedded in them is dissolved. This might be done, for example, by arguing that nationalism does not require economic protectionism and isolationism, or by showing that capitalism in one country is a viable proposition.[4]

I call this striving for a fit between the ethics of practices that have apparently become contradictory *ethical constructivism*. In this striving, actors reinterpret practices. In certain circumstances, the reinterpretation leads to the transformation of the practice(s) in question. This, in turn, may then lead to the transformation of the actors who are participants in these practices.

A central contention of this chapter is that, with regard to our global practices (and particularly as these relate to questions concerning all forms of international migration), we are currently in the middle of just such a transformation. A new global practice has emerged that appears to be contradicting core elements of the old order. The ethical discomfort caused by this apparent contradiction has given rise to a stream of journal articles, books, conferences, and so on, about the place of economic migrants, asylum seekers, and refugees in the new international order within which we find ourselves. Before I can meaningfully spell out the key features of the transformation that we are going through, I need to sketch briefly the old order that is being transformed.

The traditional order

What, from an ethical point of view, is owed to migrants across state boundaries has traditionally been understood from the point of view of sovereign states in the society of sovereign states. International law as embodied in, for example, the 1951 Convention Relating to the Status of Refugees states that in certain circumstances states have an obligation to grant asylum to those who have a well-founded fear of being persecuted for reasons of race, religion, nationality, membership of a particular social group, or political opinion. The law is about the obligation on states, not about the rights of individual asylum seekers.[5] The Convention must be understood as creating an exception to the general rule that states have the power inherent in their sovereignty to forbid the entrance of aliens to their territories.[6]

It seems reasonable to assume that the ethical theory that underlies this set of legal arrangements must be more or less as follows. The core social arrangement within which people are constituted as international actors is the system of sovereign states. We as individuals are constructed as international actors as members (citizens) of sovereign states. The members of the society of sovereign states make arrangements (often through treaties) to regulate the movement of people across state boundaries, whether as tourists, scholars, diplomats, business people, economic migrants, refugees, or asylum seekers. The final authority (the sovereign authority) to set up international law regulating such movement rests with individual states within the society of sovereign states. Underlying this line of thought is the guiding idea that in general people will spend their lives in the state within which they were first constituted as citizens and that the authority governing their movement across state borders lies with governments of states.

In general, movements of individuals across state boundaries will be temporary, as is the case with tourism, educational travel, business travel, diplomacy, and so on. If, exceptionally, individuals seek to move away from their state of origin with a view to becoming citizens of another state, they will require the permission of the state to which they wish to emigrate. From time to time though, in the aftermath of war or when a particular state has an especially harsh government, people might flee from their home state to another in order to seek refuge from persecution. In order to cope with such circumstances, the society of states has, over time, created a body of international law.

This international law was made on the premise that the need for refuge would arise only in exceptional circumstances – when people are forced to flee their home state as a result of some great threat. The underlying metaphor, which is built into the very language here, is that of seeking refuge from a storm. In this case the refuge sought is from an exceptional harm that might befall the refugees in their home state. For those who think along these lines, the two key questions are: What is to count as a harm of sufficient severity to warrant a state's being obligated to open its door to such aliens? And, once states have given refuge to aliens, what kind of treatment are they bound to give them?

It seems to me that a lot of what is written by lawyers, journalists, and academics about international migrants (be they refugees fleeing a war, asylum seekers fleeing persecution, or common-or-garden economic migrants) still proceeds from this traditional mindset, which is dominated by notions of sovereignty. In what follows I suggest that this fails to take into account the emergence of a new global practice that threatens to upset our traditional ways of thinking. This suggests that it is no longer purely a matter for the discretion of individual states to decide who should be allowed to move where across state boundaries.

The ethical challenge posed by migrants in contemporary world politics

We are now in a position to indicate just how refugees, migrants, economic migrants, and asylum seekers present us with ethical problems as opposed to merely practical ones. I propose that we are in an ethical predicament with regard to refugees (and with regard to other kinds of migrants) just because we are constituted as who we are in two global practices whose internal ethics appear to be pulling us in contradictory directions. This contradiction is made manifest when we come face to face with the problem of migration. When we confront the migrants we are no longer quite sure who we are. This calls for elaboration.

Global civil society

In the first of these practices, people such as me and the majority of you who are reading this, together with a truly vast number of people beyond this group, consider ourselves to be the holders of certain fundamental human rights. I have often argued that most adult, sane members of humankind consider themselves to have certain fundamental human rights. But, for my present purposes, nothing turns on whether or not I can prove that. I am happy simply to stipulate that the argument I am about to put forward is addressed to those who do consider themselves to be rights holders.

The current attention being accorded to migrants of all kinds (asylum seekers, illegal economic migrants, refugees from civil wars, the women and children being moved about by human traffickers, and so on) does not arise as a result of a more or less standard practical problem that has suddenly grown in size and scale. To speak metaphorically, it is not as if a small hole in a fence has suddenly become a large one, causing people to call for the repairperson to come urgently. For, objectively speaking, although there have been dramatic increases in the number of international migrants and of internally displaced people in war-ravaged states, the scope and scale of the migrations are certainly not calamitous. The numbers of people who recently arrived in France off a boat grounded on the southern coast, or the influx of stowaway migrants to Britain from the Balkans, or the flow of Kurdish people into Italy are not by any stretch of the imagination large enough to pose a serious physical threat to the states in question. There is also little evidence to support the "this is a trickle which will soon turn to a flood" thesis. No West European state is in the grips of a physical pandemic of migration which is about to overwhelm it.

The sound and fury around the issue of migrants stem from a far deeper unease. Our, essentially correct, perception is that the migrants at the borders are not marauding hordes at the gates, but are people who, in terms of the ethical dictates of our own practices, the practices within which we are constituted as who we are, have ethical claims that they may legitimately make on us. We who are settled, and who prosper within the states to which the migrants seek to come, are constituted as the actors we value ourselves to be within practices that require that we recognize the migrants at the border as more than vermin to be eradicated. We must recognize the people at the border as people who, with us, are participants in certain global practices. These global practices give us the ethical standing that we value at a fundamental level.

In referring to "we" I am talking then to all those people worldwide who belong to states that profess a commitment to human rights; to all those people in all those states that have signed up to the UN Declaration of Human Rights; to all those people who are committed to international law, which now has many human rights conventions built into it; to all those people who belong to non-governmental organizations with a concern for human rights abuses worldwide; and to all those people who read the liberal press as it writes of human rights abuses wherever they occur. I am also addressing all those who are participants in the global market and who believe that in participating in this they are using some or all of the following fundamental rights: the right to make contracts, the right to own property, the right to form associations for mutual profit, the right to buy and sell, the right to invest, the right to move about seeking new markets, and so on. Most certainly I am addressing the governments of the states of the European Union and other European democracies who, on an ongoing basis, profess their commitments to human rights.

Let me call the formation of people who make rights claims for themselves, and who recognize rights claims coming from others, *global civil society*. In so far as the members of this society recognize the rights claims they make upon one another, they form a practice. It does not matter that most of the claims they make upon one another are claims that are defensive vis-à-vis others; these claims still indicate the common commitment of these actors to a set of rules. The rights claims I am talking of here are the rights often referred to as first-generation negative liberties, such as the right to safety of the person, freedom of speech, freedom of conscience, freedom of movement, assembly, and contract, together with the right to own private property. Members of this society differ amongst themselves about what rights ought to be included on the list, but the details of these disputes are not important for the general argument being made here. Of course, many of those who make first-generation rights claims upon one another also make second-generation rights claims. For my present purposes I am not concerned about these latter claims, for these depend on the prior existence of a political entity of some kind with the power to tax and redistribute. We can conceive of civil society independently of such polities.

What are the major features of this global civil society? We can say quite a lot about its general form. Our knowledge of its form comes from the way we, who participate in it, speak. The logic of the language we use in global civil society suggests that it is a society without borders. We claim rights for ourselves and recognize them in other human beings who meet the necessary criteria, wherever they happen to be. We do not, for example, specify that people have rights only when they are in one or another particular territory. We do not say that someone loses his or her rights because she or he has left the territory of Britain.

A second major feature of global civil society is that it is a society without government; it is a society of individuals. To use the technical term, it is an anarchy.

A third feature is that it is a society without a selection committee to vet new applications for membership. People enter into global civil society simply by learning how to make rights claims and recognize claims made by others. They become members by learning how to participate in civil society, in much the same way as people learn to participate in the practice of speaking English simply by learning how to do the language. They learn by doing. They do not have to go through any screening process.

The fourth feature of global civil society is that it is a society with a set of non-intervention rules built around individuals. These specify that each individual in civil society is to be accorded a domain by the other members of that society such that within it he or she is free to make the final choice about certain matters. Thus, for example, a member of civil society with the right to freedom of speech is accorded the final say on whether to speak or not. We may say that others do not have a right to intervene in that person's decision about whether to speak.

Let us call the members of global civil society civilians. Civilians are the participants in global civil society who have a domain of freedom protected by an elaborate set of non-intervention rules. This is simply another way of saying that civilians have rights.[7]

Given that the activity of claiming rights against one another must be understood as taking place within a social practice, and given that all social practices have embedded in them an ethic of one kind or another, we may at this point ask "What is the ethic embedded in global civil society?" The somewhat general but nevertheless accurate answer, it seems to me, is that it is an ethic that specifies that human autonomy is a fundamental value. Civil society preserves this value through its set of constitutive rules, which enable individual men and women to order their lives as they see fit, subject only to the restriction that they respect other people's rights. In a full discussion of this topic, I would at this point have to elaborate on the core notion of "autonomy" and to spell out the set of rights necessary for its achievement. This is not the place for that.

How are we to understand the place of migrants and refugees within the context of global civil society? The answer seems clear. In civil society, civilians are free to move about, migrate, or seek refuge, wherever they wish, subject only to the constraint that they not abuse the rights of their fellow civilians. Thus, from the point of view of civil society, a civilian living in Dover, when considering how to react to a civilian arriving from another region of civil society, such as Turkey, ought to respect the right of the Turkish civilian to move freely about global civil society.

Until such time as civilians (from wherever they may come) commit an offence against the rights of their fellow civilians, no bar should be put on their free movement through global civil society, which is borderless.

Civilians might have a number of reasons for wanting to move about the world. They might be in search of friendship, love, worship with others, sporting opportunities, profit-making opportunities, or the chance to participate in educational institutions. In global civil society, which of these a person wishes to do, and where he or she wishes to do them, would be a matter solely for his or her discretion. The final pattern of legitimate relationships in civil society at any one time would be determined by the million and one choices by members of global civil society making use of their basic rights while respecting the rights of others.

It is crucial to note that the claims we make as civilians, and the claims we recognize other civilians as making, do not depend at all on our being members of this or that state, or their being subordinate to this or that legal system. Furthermore, the rights claims we make, and the claims we recognize others as making, do not depend for their validity on our having the machinery to enforce these rights. Thus, for example, when people in quasi-states in Africa claim that authoritarian governments are infringing their rights, we recognize their claim whether or not they are in a position to enforce them. Of course, in many places around the world rights holders make use of the machinery that states possess to secure their civil society rights. But the *validity* of a specific rights claim does not depend on the claimant's ability to show that the claim is located in an existing and effective legal system. In our modern world, the language of civil society is becoming ubiquitous. More and more people are speaking the language of rights, and it seems fair to say that the society, which is global in its reach, is becoming as it were "thicker."

In this chapter, with its focus on refugees and migrants of all kinds, my central conclusion is that *as civilians* we are obliged to regard all other civilians as having a fundamental right to freedom of movement. From this perspective, all people who arrive in this place where we live – whether they arrive by boat, as stowaways in trains, as smuggled cargo in lorries, by swimming across rivers, or by climbing fences – need to be regarded, in the first place, as civilians making use of their right to freedom of movement. They must be regarded as innocent of wrongdoing unless they are found to have infringed the rights of their fellow civilians. In our day-to-day lives, many of us often make use of our civilian rights in less dramatic ways than the ones I have just described. We travel about, both locally and further afield, as tourists, as members of sports clubs seeking out other sportsmen and women to play with, as students seeking interesting institutions at which to study, in search of jobs, in search of markets, and so on.

In this section, I wish to stress that migrants pose no particularly difficult ethical problems for us *when seen from the position of global civil society*. Their behaviour is a quite unproblematic provided that they do not engage in rights-abusing activity. Problems do arise, however, when we take into account that we are not only participants in global civil society, but also simultaneously participants in the society of democratic and democratizing states.

The global society of democratic and democratizing states

The practice I refer to as the society of democratic and democratizing states includes all states that are already functioning democracies and many other states that declare themselves to be on the road to democracy. Within this second global society, we are constituted as citizens; that is, we recognize one another as the holders of comprehensive sets of citizenship rights. The citizenship rights we grant one another include the right to stand for office, the right to vote in regular elections, the right to hold our governments to account, the right to information about government policy, the right to form political parties, and the right to form pressure groups to lobby our parliaments. These are but a few of the citizenship rights we establish for ourselves within the practice of democratic and democratizing states.

A major feature of this practice, of course, is that it consists of a set of states with determinate borders. A constitutive rule of the practice is the rule referring to the right of states to non-intervention in their domestic affairs, which are considered to fall in the private domain of the state concerned. The states in the system consider themselves to be sovereign. This is a complex term, but one aspect of its meaning is that it grants to states the right to control who may cross their borders.

Strikingly, in this practice, citizens consider themselves to be justified in doing whatever they think necessary in pursuit of the national interest of their state. Their governments are specifically tasked with promoting the interest of the state.

What is the ethic embedded in this practice of democratic and democratizing states? It is, as with civil society, one that values the notion of individual autonomy. In this case, though, there are two different actors whose autonomy has to be constituted and preserved within the practice. First, states themselves are constituted as actors in such a way as to guarantee them a measure of legal autonomy within the international community of states. Second, the autonomy of the states reflects the autonomy of the individual citizens who comprise them. The form of recognition that citizens give one another in democratic states is such that they recognize one another as beings who are entitled to participate in the processes of self-government in an autonomous state. In states that are not yet fully autonomous, this is their aspiration. For the members of this practice this status is of very great value indeed. To be denied it would be to be denied a fundamentally valuable form of autonomy. People in polities that are less than fully autonomous, such as colonies, are from our point of view (that is, from the point of view of those of us who value democratic citizenship) deprived of this fundamental value.

For the purposes of this chapter it is important to understand why states take themselves to have the right to police their borders. First, a state is at least a social arrangement within which citizens cooperate with one another for mutual advantage. They cooperate in order to provide for one another's security, to provide certain welfare services for one another, and to establish a stable framework of law between them within which they can conduct their daily transactions. In order to operate such a system of cooperation, states and the citizens within them need to know precisely who are the citizens within their state. Furthermore, they need to know the full geographical extent of their cooperative system. In short, they need to know who is inside the state and who is beyond it. Just as it would not be possible to run a household without knowing who its members are, so too it is not possible to run a state without knowing who belongs to it. Second, the very notion of a self-governing polity suggests that those within it know who belongs to the self-governing unit in question. This requires that the insiders can distinguish themselves from the outsiders – participants need to know who the "we" is that forms the self-governing community. Third, in order to be fully autonomous, a self-governing social formation must have control over the fundamental question of who is to be a member of the self-governing whole. Without this knowledge, it would not be possible to specify the unit that is to be self-governing.

It is important to notice that, besides the internal dimensions of autonomy discussed above, there is also an important external dimension. The autonomy enjoyed by citizens in a democratic state depends on their state being recognized as an autonomous state by other autonomous democratic states; otherwise, the value of autonomy is not realized. For example, the so-called independent "states" that were created by the apartheid government in South Africa, because they were not recognized as autonomous states by the rest of the international community of states, did not provide the citizens of those "states" with full autonomy. Thus the value of citizenship is not purely *internal* to a single state; it must be realized in the wider practice of democratic states as well. It has an *external* dimension.

On the relationship between global civil society and the global society of democratic and democratizing states

Many millions of people around the world are participants in both global civil society and the society of democratic and democratizing states. In the former they/we are constituted as civilians and in the latter they/we constitute one another as citizens. The existence and the membership of these social practices are both verified by the things we say and the claims that we make about ourselves and against others.

Since we are simultaneously constituted as actors in both of these practices, the obvious question to ask at this point is: Do these practices complement one another or are they mutually antagonistic? Another way of putting this question is to ask: Do these practices cohere with one with another? A third formulation would be: Can we participate in both without landing ourselves in difficult contradictions?

One famous answer to this set of questions is provided by G. W. F. Hegel, who presented citizenship as a status that complements and enriches the ethical standing we enjoy in civil society and that overcomes some of the problems encountered in it.[8] To be confined solely to the status we enjoy as civilians in civil society would not be an attractive option. In civil society, although we accord one another a measure of autonomy through certain forms of mutual recognition, we also, by doing this, establish a society with some very negative features. For example, in civil society we experience our fellow rights holders as competitors. On many issues, if we do not win the advantage, our fellow rights holders will do so (and they will do so at our cost). Thus, if I win the lucrative contract, you may lose it; if I gain a friend, it may be that you do not; if I win someone's hand in love, you may lose it; and so on. All this would make for an alienated society. It would be a society without a sense of community. Furthermore, it would be a society with grossly uneven power relationships. Through the passage of time and after many different transactions between rights holders, a pattern of holdings would emerge that would secure power for some and the lack of it for others. The most dramatic proof of this is to be found in the global market as it exists today.

Once we supplement participation in global civil society with participation in a democratic state, we remedy some of these shortcomings experienced in civil society. Most importantly, we gain a sense of community. As citizens, we recognize one another as equal co-participants in a self-governing polity. Where the operation of civil society necessarily produces a set of uneven power relationships, as citizens in a democratic state we are well placed to enact legislation that remedies what we might take to be unjust distributions of power and resources. Where transactions in civil society often seem to be zero sum, many transactions within democratic states are clearly positive sum.

A crucial point to notice here is that the values that are realized in citizen-to-citizen relationships depend on citizens also enjoying the rights of civilians at the same time. In other words, the kinds of freedoms we constitute for one another when we recognize one another as citizens depend on the prior recognition we give to one another as civilians – as rights holders in civil society. It is not possible to make sense of the notion of citizenship if one does not assume that citizens also have a full set of first-generation civilian rights. The citizenship rights to stand for office, to vote in elections, to hold governments to account, and to participate in political parties would hardly be meaningful if those who held them did not also have the standard civilian rights to freedom of speech, freedom of assembly, freedom of conscience, and all the other first-generation rights. In the former Soviet Union, an attempt was made to confer citizenship rights on people, while at the same time denying to them the normal set of civilian rights. The net result was that their citizenship rights turned out to be worthless.

In most well-established democracies there is no stark tension between the status people have in civil society as rights holders and their status as citizens within the democratic state. This is because the democratic state overtly protects the basic civil society rights of its citizens. This protection is often built into the constitution in the form of a Bill of Fundamental Rights and Freedoms.

Although within a particular state there may be no overt tension between being a rights holder in civil society and being a citizen in the democratic state, great problems appear when we think of civil society as a global practice. Civil society (the practice within which we recognize one another as rights holders) is now no longer merely or primarily an intra-state practice, but is global in reach. The language we use makes it quite clear that our respect for other people as rights holders does not stop at the frontiers of our own state. We regard the society of rights holders as stretching far beyond the borders of our immediate states. The implications of this extension of the scope of global civil society are profound.

If we examine civil society and the society of democratic and democratizing states as global practices, then there indeed now appears to be a major contradiction facing those, like us, who would participate in both practices simultaneously. On the face of the matter, civil society requires us to respect other people's basic rights no matter where they happen to be, whereas the society of democratic and democratizing states allows us to put the interests of our own state above the rights protected by civil society. It seems to be a matter for the discretion of each state to decide who it may admit into the territory of that state and who it wishes to keep out. If this is indeed so, it clearly follows that, if the border of any particular state is sealed against a certain category of person (Blacks, Whites, Islamic people, Jewish people, etc.), then the people thus excluded may rightly claim that they are being denied, at the least, their civilian right to freedom of movement. For the people who are denied this right, the practice of democratic states will be experienced not as a supplement to their civil society rights but as an erosion of those rights. For example, civilians who arrive at the port of Dover on the border of the United Kingdom, and who are denied entry, will experience that denial as an infringement of their civilian rights. Had the state system not existed, they would have been free to move into this portion of global civil society (the portion currently occupied by the state of the United Kingdom), provided, of course, that they did not infringe the rights of their fellow civilians.

Is there a way in which those of us who take ourselves to be both civilians in civil society and citizens in the society of democratic states can avoid this apparent contradiction? There are several options that we can rule out forthwith.

One negative option would be to renounce our commitment to the human rights practice – we could abandon our participation in civil society. We could do this by simply asserting that we no longer regard ourselves as rights holders in a global and borderless practice of rights holders. Instead, we might acknowledge rights claims only from those in a territorially defined civil society, one whose borders coincided with those of the state within which we live.

While acknowledging the civilian rights of those who live within our state, we might suggest that people who make rights claims in far-flung places ought to be interpreted as expressing their wish that their local state would somehow establish rights in their area. On this view, civil society would be something that states construct. Individual human rights would have to be understood as deriving from the authority of the state. Were this option taken, we would have to reform our language quite drastically. We would have to cease all talk of people beyond the borders of our states as having, with us, a set of fundamental human rights that is valid in all places. Instead, we would have to make claims such as, "In the USA, people have fundamental human rights, but not in Armenia, Afghanistan and Albania."

Another negative option would be to renounce our commitment to the system of sovereign democratic states. We might start expressing misgivings about the moral values established within the Westphalian state system and set about arguing in favour of alternative political arrangements.

We see something like this taking place in the work of Andrew Linklater and David Held, who mount a sustained attack on the way in which international relations theorists have been preoccupied with the state-centric model of international relations.[9] They put the case for an alternative set of political arrangements, which has been referred to as "neo-medievalist" or alternatively "post-Westphalian." Opting for this course of action would require us to give up the form of autonomy we currently enjoy through our participation as citizens in sovereign democratic states within the system of democratic and democraticizing states.

There is, however, a third way in which we can be both civilians and citizens in the modern world without falling into contradiction and hypocrisy. This involves interpreting global civil society as a practice in which participation is a precondition for the successful establishment of citizenship in the higher-order practice known as the society of democratic and democratizing states. On this view, states that seek to establish autonomy for their citizens through a process of democratic citizenship must respect and nurture the whole, borderless, global practice of civil society, not merely the portion that falls within the territory of their specific state. *In short, we can reconcile civilianship with citizenship by making it clear that only states that respect and nurture the rights civilians have in global civil society can establish full freedom for their citizens.* This implies that absolutist, authoritarian, or tyrannical states, although they may have some measure of power, do not have full legitimacy in the eyes of the other states in the system of democratic and democratizing states. They will gain that legitimacy only by adopting policies internally and externally that uphold the individual rights constituted for civilians in global civil society.

Were we to adopt this understanding of the ethical relationship between these two global practices, we would be required to reformulate the way we talk about migrants and refugees quite drastically.

The line of reasoning outlined above would suggest that civilians have a right to move about global civil society freely. In the ethical structure I have sketched, the initial ethical assumption about all migrants must be that they, like us, are rights holders in global civil society. They hold the full set of first-generation rights that we do. The most important of these, for the purposes of the present argument, is that they have a right to freedom of movement. Making use of this civilian right to move about the world is a legitimate activity. Thus, when we come to contemplate what, from an ethical point of view, would be a justifiable piece of legislation specifying who should be permitted to enter a state and who should be kept out, the default position must be that all rights holders in global civil society have a right to freedom of movement. Thus, in general, from an ethical point of view, it would be wrong to prohibit migrants from entering the territory of any given state. People who arrive at the border of a sovereign state have a right, as civilians, to cross it. Only in special cases would a government be justified in passing legislation to stop them. What special cases might be pertinent here?[10]

The obvious answer is that, where there is good reason to suppose that a given migrant has infringed the rights of civilians or intends to do so, this might be reason to deny him or her access. The onus of proof, though, ought to be on the government concerned not on the individual civilian.

To argue from the language of rights, which we use ever more frequently, that the default position is one that permits civilians free movement about global civil society is not to suggest that civilians have a right to become citizens in any state of their choice. For citizenship requires a relationship of mutual recognition between a whole group of citizens who together form a democratic state. Civilian X might express a wish to become a UK citizen, but whether or not he/she may depends on whether British citizens wish to confer this status on him or her. Civilians who enter into a portion of global civil society covered by a democratic state, such as the United Kingdom, normally first establish themselves as rights-respecting members of civil society before subsequently applying for citizenship within that state. So full membership of a democratic state achieved through the conferring of citizenship is not a question that has to be settled by border control.

At this point it is important to remember that, on the argument I am presenting, the status we achieve as civilians in global civil society is not an ideal ethical status. It has severe drawbacks that are overcome only when we civilians constitute ourselves as citizens through a process of mutual recognition within sovereign democratic states within a system of sovereign democratic states. The moral authority of a state to establish democratic citizenship (and its authority to determine who are to be citizens and who not) depends crucially on the recognition granted to it by the practice of democratic states as a whole. For example, the freedom that citizens enjoy in a democracy such as the United Kingdom depends on the recognition that the United Kingdom receives from the other states in the society of democratic and democratizing states. The practice seen as a global practice of states is justified as an improvement on civil society only in so far as it succeeds in establishing effective democratic citizenship for all civilians everywhere. Ethical policies at this level have to take into consideration that the value achieved by citizenship requires the establishment of a global practice of democratic states. Citizenship is not a value that can be unilaterally established by a single state. We are all under an ethical imperative to seek to promote civilians to full citizenship. In what state this constitution should take place is of course a matter for argument and negotiation. Acts of co-constitution must be voluntary. It would seem obvious that those who have become embedded in a particular part of civil society should seek to be constituted as citizens in that part of global civil society.

If my ethical argument on this point is convincing, it has an interesting implication for how we ought to think of refugees, *strictu sensu*. Those who arrive at the borders of our democratic states because they fear persecution in their own state, or have been driven from their own state because of its collapse, are, of course, civilians. They are rights holders with a right to move about global civil society seeking their fortunes, each in his or her own way. But these people are from an ethical point of view more than this. They are also people who are being denied, for one reason or another, citizenship in their own states. We ought to think of such people with the following in mind. Our own standing as citizens depends on our being recognized by other free people, by other citizens. If these others are suddenly denied citizenship in their own states (because of state collapse or tyranny, for example), then they can no longer give us the recognition we need for our own freedom. For this reason we have an interest in securing for them active and effective citizenship. If there is nothing we can do to restore democracy to their own state, then we ought to secure for them at least temporary active citizenship in our state. It is important to note that such people are not merely an ethical problem for the state at whose borders they have arrived; they pose an ethical problem for the system of democratic states as a whole.

With the above in mind we can then see that the legislation aimed at regulating the inflow of refugees should be informed primarily by a consideration of what can be done to secure full and effective citizenship for these applicants. Many complicated solutions might be suggested here. One possible ethical policy would be to provide temporary accommodation within the target state plus international manoeuvres to secure the reconstruction of the state from which the refugees came so that they might enjoy effective citizenship there.

On the view I have put forward in this chapter, there are two points to stress above all. First, migrants (from tourists to asylum seekers) have civilian rights to move about civil society, which we must remember is global and has no borders. Any legislation that tries to prevent migrants of any kind from crossing state borders to move about the portion of civil society located within a particular state must be presumed unethical until it is proven that there is good reason to suggest that these particular migrants would not respect the constraints of civil society – in other words, would not respect the human rights of their fellow civilians. Second, migrants who have had their citizenship eroded in their home state (or whose citizenship rights in a democracy have never been established) ought to be seen not as supplicants deserving charity but as people whom we need to establish as citizens in democratic free states in order to secure our own freedom. Our own standing as free people depends on our receiving recognition from others who are similarly free. We therefore need to make policies that will best achieve this goal.

Notes

1. We say that suffragettes were engaged in politics when they sought to change the law that specified who would have the franchise; we say that colonial people engaged in politics when they sought to have the rules defining the relationship between centre and periphery changed; and so on. Readers can test this against freely chosen examples of their own choice.
2. Mervyn Frost, *Ethics in International Relations*, Cambridge: Cambridge University Press, 1996.
3. Another example I often use is provided by people I knew at an essentially Calvinist university in South Africa in the late 1960s who wanted to maintain their standing both as good Christians within the Christian practice (which required their accepting as a matter of faith that the creation took place in six days) and as scientists in the practice of modern science, which was committed to the Darwinian explanation of evolution. The ethical dilemma faced by people in such cases is/was acute indeed.
4. In the closing decade of apartheid in South Africa, many staunch nationalists undertook just such a reinterpretation of nationalism to show that it was not at all in conflict with global capitalism.
5. "Thus the right of asylum is generally considered to be a right of states to grant asylum and not a right of individuals to be granted asylum." Gunnel Stenberg, *Non-Expulsion and Non-Refoulement*, Uppsala: Iustus Forlag, 1989, p. 16.
6. See John Dugard, *International Law: A South African Perspective*, Cape Town: Juta, 2001, p. 268.
7. I am aware that the word "civilian" has a number of different meanings in everyday English usage, but for the purposes of this chapter I use it in the narrow way I have specified here.
8. G. W. F. Hegel, *The Philosophy of Right*, Oxford: Oxford University Press, 1952.
9. David Held, *Democracy and Global Order*, Cambridge: Polity Press, 1996; Andrew Linklater, *The Transformation of Political Community*, Columbia: University of South Carolina Press, 1998.
10. Of course, states have a right to record all border crossings, for it is essential to the functioning of any state that it has accurate knowledge of who and how many people are within its territory. This kind of knowledge is necessary for all the normal functions states are expected to perform.

7

The early warning of forced migration: State or human security?

Susanne Schmeidl

The protection of territory and people against threats, attacks, and unwanted intrusion is one of the oldest human instincts. Although hospitality to guests (even the granting of refuge to those persecuted) is valued in many cultures, there is often also a natural distrust of those we do not know and whose culture is different from ours. These somewhat conflicting concerns between state and human security have led to the rise of intelligence services trying to anticipate threats against state integrity on the one hand, and of early warning systems trying to anticipate threats to the integrity and livelihood of human beings on the other. Despite the different goals of both ideal types of forecasting mechanisms,[1] their methodology – collecting and analysing information, scenario-building, and recommending options to decision makers for preventive action and intervention – is similar. This has led to a cross-fertilization of approaches, with some "hard" early warning systems tending toward the ideal type of intelligence that emphasizes the protection of states (e.g. against the influx of refugees) more than human security.

Forced displacement is a good example of the dual purpose early warning systems can serve when attempting to forecast humanitarian disasters that might affect more than one country, and thus one security concern, simultaneously (those sending and those receiving refugees). In the purest sense, refugee early warning should be aimed at avoiding human suffering. However, it often appears to be, at least partly, also applied to alleviate or even prevent the pressures and destabilizing

130

potential stemming from large-scale refugee movements, and/or to secure the speedy and "safe" return of the refugees and displaced persons (of which Kosovo and to some degree Afghanistan are the most recent examples).

The defensive application poses a dilemma to humanitarian concerns if early warning models are used to understand where refugees might go in order to block exit/entry. However, if the focus is on early preventive efforts that would avoid the need for migration, we may achieve a balance between human and state security – or at least find an area of fruitful coexistence between state and human security that could alleviate humanitarian disasters.

In light of this, the basic premise of this chapter is to show that early warning is the *sine qua non* of effective conflict prevention and can be mutually beneficial to state and humanitarian actors. It critically discusses the emergence of early warning, scrutinizing its aims and objectives. By reviewing existing methodologies of early warning, the chapter tries to show what can and cannot be achieved by early warning and why. It also focuses on the non-technical or more political obstacles to early warning, which ultimately may be the key reason for the failure of the prevention of humanitarian emergencies, rather than methodological flaws. The discussion of political obstacles has become more pressing owing to the 11 September 2001 attacks on the United States, as politicians begin to reconsider the "softer" approach to intelligence and state protection.

Early warning – A brief historical sketch

Humanitarian early warning (in contrast to intelligence) has its roots in climatological (the forecasting of floods, hurricanes, volcanoes, and earthquakes) and economic (the prediction of stock market crashes) forecasting. Whereas academics attempted to understand the causes of wars in the 1970s through indicator systems,[2] early warning was first introduced into humanitarian affairs in the area of famine prediction. Models were strongly linked to hard sciences and an initial focus was to understand the formation of natural disasters in order to prepare relief assistance.[3] The idea was not to prevent the actual disaster (because this was impossible) but to minimize damage and human suffering.

Following in the footsteps of famine early warning, refugee early warning emerged with a similar focus on victim assistance rather than disaster prevention. One could argue that the interest in refugee early warning came during a time when forced displacement (both international and internal), as well as the number of countries afflicted with this

Figure 7.1 Forced migration: refugees and internal displacement in comparison, 1969–2000.
Data sources: US Committee for Refugees, *World Refugee Report*, Washington DC: USCR, 1964–1974; US Committee for Refugees, *World Refugee Survey Report*, Washington DC: USCR, 1967–1978; US Committee for Refugees, *World Refugee Survey*, Washington DC: USCR, 1980–2000; United Nations High Commissioner for Refugees, *Populations of Concern to UNHCR: A Statistical Overview*, Geneva: UNHCR, 1993–2000.

phenomenon, began to grow in the late 1970s and early 1980s (see figures 7.1 and 7.2).[4]

The first study came from within the UN system, by Prince Sadruddin Aga Khan, Special Rapporteur of the UN Commission on Human Rights, in 1981.[5] Utilizing a case-study approach, the initial goal of refugee early warning was more to understand the patterns of such disasters (direction of flow, size of population) than to prevent the disasters themselves. Although Aga Khan's study focused primarily on human rights and the political context, he pointed to other fundamental problems and push factors in forced migration (for example, inadequate economic opportunities owing to the rate of population growth, global food insecurity and scarcity, growing inflation and unemployment, and ecological deterioration). Finally, he also added some possible pull factors to the explanations of refugee flight for the first time, something that thus far had been more common in the study of voluntary than of forced (refugee) migration. These factors included sophisticated information systems, travel networks, liberalization of immigration policies, and institutionalized aid such as refugee camps.

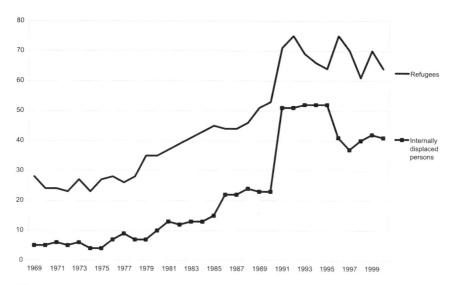

Figure 7.2 Number of countries with forced migration: Internal and external displacement in comparison, 1969–2000.
Data sources: US Committee for Refugees, *World Refugee Report*, Washington DC: USCR, 1964–1974; US Committee for Refugees, *World Refugee Survey Report*, Washington DC: USCR, 1967–1978; US Committee for Refugees, *World Refugee Survey*, Washington DC: USCR, 1980–2000; United Nations High Commissioner for Refugees, *Populations of Concern to UNHCR: A Statistical Overview*, Geneva: UNHCR, 1993–2000.

A more systematic development of refugee early warning, at least on a theoretical level, occurred outside the UN system at the Refugee Policy Group[6] under the leadership of Lance Clark.[7] Extending, and considerably systematizing, the work by Aga Khan, Clark tried to capture the complex causality of refugee flight (push–pull) by identifying underlying causes (root causes), differentiating them from proximate conditions and intervening factors and triggering events. This model (see figure 7.3) set a standard in early warning research and the classification of indicators.

Many scholars paralleled or extended Clark's efforts.[8] The problem, however, was that they merely elaborated Clark's initial model, remained mainly at a theoretical and not empirical level, and never synthesized their work. The Japanese scholar Onishi is a rare exception: he developed an impressive and elaborate early warning model based on Aga Khan's reference study.[9] He tested his model with a combination of case studies and computer analysis. Onishi wanted to create computer outputs or "radar charts," from which it would be possible to tell whether or not the country was in "future danger of generating displaced people."[10] Using many variables in his case studies, he highlighted four areas: (1)

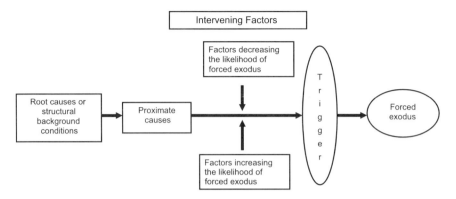

Figure 7.3 Early warning model of forced migration.
Source: Lance Clark, *Early Warning of Refugee Flows*, Washington DC: Refugee Policy Group, 1989.

destruction of the environment (ecological imbalance), (2) failures in development (mass poverty, socio-economic disparities), (3) failures in peace and security (absence of the rule of law), and (4) violation of human rights (absence of respect for human life and cultural rights).[11] Yet the complexity of the model, the multitude of variables, and the fact that he lacked a proper dependent variable made his model less useful to policy makers. In addition, Onishi's work has never been very accessible outside of Japan.

It was not until 1995 that Schmeidl's dissertation lifted the early warning of forced migration to a truly quantitative level, merging knowledge from several bodies of literature (refugees, migration, political instability, human rights violations, and wars). Building upon Clark's original model, she empirically tested root, proximate, and facilitating factors of forced migration and found support for several propositions, such as the association between forced exodus and genocides, internal conflict, and international military interventions into conflicts.[12] Human rights violations seem to push people out only when they are on a physical rather than an institutional level (actual persecution as against an aura of terror). In addition, poverty was found not to be a traditional root cause but more the catalyst in a difficult political environment.

Little has been done since in this area, as refugee early warning slowly began to shift to an understanding of the root causes of forced displacement and conflict prevention. This can be largely attributed to three interconnected factors. First, research revealed that the growth of the world refugee population was linked not simply to the rise of warmongering states but also to an increasing duration of displacement owing to protracted conflicts and a lack permanent solutions. Whereas in

1970 only 4 refugee populations had been in place for over a decade,[13] there were 13 by 1980, 31 by 1990, and almost 50 by 2000. The 1970s and 1980s featured a total of 56 and 57 countries with refugee migration, respectively, and the 1990s had 97 countries with populations in exile. This trend is paralleled by forced internal displacement, with 15 countries in the 1970s, 30 in the 1980s, and 69 in the 1990s.[14]

Second, permanent solutions began to fail, as is reflected in slowing repatriation and resettlement figures. According to the United Nations High Commissioner for Refugees (UNHCR), annual repatriations in the early 1970s constituted a quarter of the world refugee population. By the late 1970s they had dropped to only 3.5 per cent and throughout the 1980s they remained below 2.5 per cent. Although the number of repatriations rose once again to about 30–35 per cent in the 1990s, these can be attributed mainly to refugees from Afghanistan, Ethiopia, and Mozambique.[15] A clear shift from the humanitarian years in the 1970s (when 2 million Indo-Chinese refugees were accepted into the United States, Canada, and Australia, and roughly 75,000 "boat people" or Vietnamese refugees into Europe) became apparent in the 1980s, when resettlement became an exception and states began to tighten their immigration and asylum laws.

Third, the end of the Cold War did not lead to an easing of the world refugee crisis; the numbers forcibly displaced declined only temporarily in 1994 for four years.[16] These trends led Newland to conclude that we are experiencing a "failure or break-down" of the classic refugee and humanitarian regime.[17] They may have also influenced politicians, analysts, and practitioners to realize that the knowledge of "how many refugees would go where when" was a matter of late warning, since the conflict had already escalated. Thus, aiming at the prevention of the crisis rather than finding a cure for it encouraged studies in the early warning of genocides/politicides,[18] ethnic discrimination and ethnic conflict, inter- and intra-state war, environmental conflict, and state failure.[19]

The components of an early warning model of forced migration

Based on Lance Clark's work, traditional early warning models distinguish in one way or another between root or underlying causes of conflicts, proximate causes, which are closer in time to forced exodus (or conflict), and intervening factors that either accelerate or decelerate forced migration. Figure 7.4 provides a summary of the most important indicator categories with a set of examples. The list should be seen as an illustration and by no means exhaustive.[20] The only difference from

Clark's model is the emphasis now put on actors and major stakeholders in early warning models, especially spoilers that might benefit from war.[21] This comes from an understanding that individuals may manipulate necessary but not sufficient causes for conflict and forced displacement for their own good. The importance of actors can be seen in the framing of the proximate causes and intervening factors depicted in figure 7.4.

Root causes

Root causes are underlying events and conditions that have existed for many years, such as religious conflicts, long-standing border disputes, difficulty in state-building, or ecological degradation. These factors are hard to change and by themselves do not lead to forced migration. They are thus necessary but not sufficient causes of forced exodus and in many ways are consistent with theories of underlying grievances that can lead to conflict.[22] Their power lies in the interaction with other more proximate factors, and in the fact that they can be instrumentalized by political entrepreneurs to mobilize support for power struggles or to foster exclusionary politics.

Even though there are many other important root causes, such as existing ethnic grievances, historical events (such as the partition between India and Pakistan in 1947), or a history of past conflicts, empirical research has mainly focused on the role of economic and population factors. Underdevelopment or poverty is probably the most cited root cause of forced migration,[23] and has even found some support in empirical studies.[24] Nevertheless, evidence of a direct causal relation between poverty and forced displacement seems to be inconclusive. Although refugees do come from poor countries, not every poor country experiences forced displacement.

Weiner at one point argued that population pressure or growth can also be linked to forced displacement.[25] Again, the empirical evidence is inconclusive, not finding any direct causal relation between population variables and forced exodus. It may be that the population variables have an impact on the size of refugee populations (small countries, by default, can send fewer refugees than big countries); yet population size is not necessarily the best proxy for identifying people at risk of persecution and, in turn, flight.

Proximate causes

Proximate causes interact (often in a complex manner) with root causes and jointly cause forced migration. Clark provided the example of a long-

FORCED EXODUS

DECREASING THE LIKELIHOOD OF EXODUS

- Efforts by civil society to stop conflict and war (war weariness of non-state actors)
- External conflict resolution or peace-building efforts (and support of local efforts)
- Incentives (economic, political) from the outside to put down arms
- Obstacles to flight (difficult territory, security in border areas)
- Alternatives to flight/coping strategies (joining of opposition)
- Cost of flight (not wanting to leave land behind, not being able to afford to leave)
- Expected reception in neighbouring countries (difficult asylum policies)

INCREASING THE LIKELIHOOD OF EXODUS

- Clear government strategy of ethnic cleansing and forced expulsion
- Scapegoating and isolation from the outside
- Existing migration routes
- Existing migration networks abroad
- Expected reception in neighbouring countries (favourable political environment, existing refugee camp, ability to seek refuge with ethnic kin)
- Past tradition of seasonal or labour migration
- Patterns of decision-making ("leaders" decision to leave or stay)

PROXIMATE CAUSES

Political / Governance
- Level of democracy
- Legitimacy of government
- Institutional mechanisms able to deal with diversity
- Level of human rights violations
- Strength of social infrastructure
- Level of corruption

Security
- Localized or regional tensions or small struggles
- Presence of warlordism or paramilitary forces
- Independence/professionalism of police force/military
- Presence of small arms

Societal / Socio-Demographic
- Strength of civil society as "counter-weight" to bad governance
- Level of unemployment, especially among youth (youth bulge)

Economic
- Strength of economy (e.g. dependency on one export crop)
- Financial dependency on drug or arms trade (war economy)
- Balance between public and military expenditures

International
- Abundance of arms trade into country
- Intervention (political, military) from outsiders
- Border disputes

ROOT (SYSTEMIC) CAUSES

Historic
- Past history of conflicts and wars
- Important historical event that influenced country's perception (e.g. partition of India/Pakistan)

Political / Institutional
- Level of democratic experience
- Amount of experience in non-violent conflict resolution

Economic Equality
- Scarce resources or existing resource competition
- Abundance of natural resources that could be looted or exploited for war
- Level of economic development
- Important regional difference in access to resources

Societal / Socio-Demographic
- Ethnic diversity in country
- Ethnic grievances
- Population distribution in country (which could encourage competition)
- Regional diversity

International
- Historical meddling of neighbouring (or other) states

Geographic
- Geographic location, such as potential trade route (Afghanistan) important to outsiders
- Arbitrarily drawn borders or disputes over territory

Figure 7.4 Examples of indicators for the early warning of forced migration.

standing border conflict turning into warfare: the border dispute is at the root of the problem, but the inability (or unwillingness) to resolve the issue eventually causes warfare (and forced exodus).[26] Proximate causes are also often linked to a government's (or other actors') unwillingness or inability to cope with root causes or unfavourable political, economic, or social conditions. In many ways, proximate causes parallel the arguments of resource mobilization theories of collective action: existing grievances (root causes) can lead to conflict only if there are enough resources available to fuel it (money, leadership, etc.).[27]

Studies of forced migration have often focused on both inter- and intra-state wars as a proximate cause of refugee migration. Inter-state wars are more likely to result in internal displacement, because fighting can make border areas insecure, blocking exit.[28] Intra-state war, on the other hand, especially if combined with military intervention from outsiders, is extremely likely to lead to refugee migration. As noted above, in most other early warning models conflict becomes the dependent variable, making it more important to understand the nature of conflicts than the nature of forced displacement. So far, struggles continue to be over power-sharing and resource distribution, particularly along ethnic divisions. The impact of religious strife is also increasingly becoming a central dimension of internal conflict in some areas, such as Algeria, the Middle East, and Central and South Asia. In addition, places such as Angola, Sierra Leone, or Colombia have been linked to war economies or greed-based warfare (as opposed to grievances) fuelled through the rise of warlords within weak or failed states.[29]

Linked to intra-state conflicts, but also to human rights violations, is the lack of institutional means to accommodate differences and grievances shared by parts of the populations. This is an issue of bad governance. With the rise of warlords in decentralized conflicts, non-state actors have often been as guilty as states, if not more so, of violating the rights of civilian populations.[30] In addition, as long as states can control their borders, even more severe human rights violations may not lead to forced exodus. This shows the importance of intervening factors such as border controls when anticipating forced exodus from politically charged environments.

Facilitating factors

As Aga Khan's study showed, the presence of certain political, economic, and social conditions does not necessarily cause refugee movements. Intervening factors either facilitate or prevent refugee flight, in addition to influencing the timing, size, and direction of forced displacement (maybe also ultimately whether displacement is within or across borders). Therefore, it is necessary to examine the factors that influence people's propensity to leave their home country and seek refuge in neighbouring countries. Clark defines these factors as being responsible for "the timing, numbers, and composition of any future flows," and asks, "why did others stay?" rather than the conventional, "why did people leave?"[31] It is these intervening factors that provide a link between early warning and the formulation of preventive action. One could even argue that, without the monitoring of intervening factors, any early warning, especially one of forced migration, is meaningless because the analysis of root and proximate causes does not sufficiently explain why people are leaving and staying or why conflict ultimately escalates. Clark identified five groups of intervening factors:[32]

1. Alternatives (coping strategies) to international flight (e.g. possibility of resistance or internal displacement).
2. Obstacles to international flight (e.g. knowledge of flight route, geographic obstacles, proper transportation, health and food factors, security problems and controlled borders, the controlling of borders, denial of entry, and the restrictions of immigration laws). Obstacles, however, are not necessarily actual difficulties encountered, but could merely be perceived as such.
3. Expected reception in the asylum country (e.g. its economic situation, asylum policies, the existence of cross-border ethnic groups). For example, it could be argued that camps providing international assistance are a potential "pull factor" for refugees.
4. Patterns in decision-making (e.g. tribal leadership, the "bandwagon effect," the demography of the refugees). This was largely the case among the Afghan refugees because mass movement happened when tribal leaders decided to leave.
5. Seasonal factors (e.g. weather patterns, agricultural cycles). This can be linked to either labour migration or the fact that in conflict situations warring parties tend to fight less during the cold winter months (see Afghanistan), potentially briefly halting mass migration.

An additional intervening factor or aspect of (forced) migration, not considered in Clark's model, comes from Peterson's observations regarding voluntary migration.[33] He found that, once the first migrants have explored a route, the growth of the movement becomes "semi-automatic" and individual motives irrelevant. Therefore, the best predictor of large migration streams is small trickles in the years before. Improved transportation facilities and migration networks (such as family, friends, or social ties in the country of destination) also increase the size and likelihood of the migration stream by lowering the cost of migration. Another factor explaining the self-perpetuation of migration is that migrants often leave agricultural land behind that may be neglected and thus reinforces problems of economic development in the sending country. The migrant has no real advantage in returning home; indeed, his/her family might eventually emigrate as well. Finally, the fact that migrants often earn more money in countries of destination increases the relative deprivation felt by the population left behind and thus increases the likelihood of future out-migration.[34] Massey picked up on this idea that migration will eventually become independent from the factors that initially caused it, arguing that the effect is visible only over a longer period of time and only once a migration stream has begun.[35]

A further intervening factor is the nature of stakeholders in (refugee-producing) conflicts. Although incorporated in Clark's fourth category of "decision-making," it is even more crucial to know exactly "who is who" in conflicts in order to gauge who might use forced expulsion as a clear political strategy. The ethnic cleansing practised in the former Yugoslavia is a key example here. As already discussed under proximate factors, the mindset of stakeholders (toward either conflict or peace) alone does not suffice in an analysis; a consideration of the resources at hand to execute specific goals and strategies is also needed. For example, although Milosevic clearly planned the forced expulsion of Kosovo Albanians, the NATO bombing may have prompted a speedy execution of the plan.

Last but not least, early warning usually also includes the concept of an event that triggers the actual refugee exodus but does not cause it by itself, making it less useful for early warning modelling because it cannot be manipulated and is very hard to predict. Clark argues that triggering events can involve a change in push factors (e.g. a new population group becomes affected, a problem spreads to a new geographic region, or the intensity and level of a problem increase significantly) or intervening factors (e.g. exhaustion of coping behaviour, seasonal factors, changes in the viability of flight, or expected reception).[36] This makes the constant monitoring of intervening factors a key task of early warning systems.

The methodology of refugee early warning

Most early warning systems use similar models that structure indicators along root, proximate, and facilitating factors (sometimes also called accelerators/decelerators). An agreement on the steps of early warning has also developed:

- collection of information (specific indicators);
- analysis of information (attaching meaning to indicators, setting it into context, recognition of crisis development);
- formulation of best/worst-case scenarios;
- formulation of response options;
- communication of the above to decision makers.

Although initially much debate in early warning centred on the collection of information, the information revolution and the Internet shifted attention to the type of analysis or the best methodology. It is here where most disagreements have occurred and to some degree still exist. Early warning models that emerged from the study of the occurrence of wars and worked within the "hard" science paradigm have attempted to use quantitative and empirical models that, as accurately as possible, could predict the occurrence of conflict or forced migration. A major problem of these approaches is their retrospective nature, which clashes with the political necessity for prospective analysis. David Singer's study on inter-state wars (later on he added intra-state conflict as well) was one of the first and best-known quantitative studies to use the label of early warning.[37] Ted Gurr's research on ethnic conflicts is among the best-known empirical studies on internal struggle and minorities at risk.[38] Susanne Schmeidl was the first to study forced migration within this tradition, and has since been followed by Zottarelli and by Davenport, Moore, and Poe.[39] The following approaches have been tested:[40]

- **Threshold models** attempt to identify a specific threshold of human rights violations or other types of violence that will lead to forced migration (or conflict). Although this method has an appeal in being rather simplistic, it often cannot truly capture the complexity of most conflict settings. In addition, in order to set a threshold, a lot of other previous information and qualitative analysis is necessary.[41]

- **Sequential models** make the argument that conflicts follow a specific sequence of events until they escalate and cause people to flee. Thus, research attempts to identify a set of accelerating factors that need to be monitored step by step. Again, the appeal here is the simplistic focus on a selected set of indicators, but in reality it might be more difficult to fine-tune such models by properly weighing the importance of each factor.[42]

- **Pattern-recognition models** are still at the stage of exploration because they rely on complex computer systems that learn all possible constellations of factors that have led to conflict in the past. Once the computation achieves a certain level of knowledge it can identify countries at risk by "fitting" them to a specific conflict pattern. Despite many attempts, no comprehensive model has yet been fully developed. However, the related method of cluster analysis, which attempts to cluster similar conflict constellations, has shown some promise in the analysis of the Middle East crises.[43]

Aside from the method of pattern recognition, both threshold and sequential models rely in the early stages of their analysis (generally for the selection of indicators) on case-study analysis, already showing a tendency toward mixed methods. This has made deductive models not only into the most common method for quantitative early warning, but also into the one that is contrasted mostly against case-study analysis. Typically, using multiple regression models, deductive models test hypotheses by making causal inferences based on correlations among indicators. An added strength of these models is the ability for "conjectural causation, *i.e.*, outcomes depending on combinations of multiple factors,"[44] and a generalizability of findings based on the theory of probabilities.

A major criticism of quantitative models is not only their lack of detail and precision in predicting, but also their lack of flexibility across cases and time. One major problem is obviously the assumption of quantitative models that everything remains constant, which rarely is the case in the real world. Nevertheless, we also should not underestimate the importance of "conditional probabilities" when making predictions.[45]

The focus on *predicting* over *anticipating* outcomes already shows the different language (and emphasis) used by quantitative compared with qualitative models. Thus it remains uncontested that case studies, albeit with little ability to generate generalizable findings, still have the major advantage of contextual and temporal sensitivity. They provide in-depth information about conflict formation, key actors, issues, and events that need to be taken into account when attempting to anticipate conflict. They are furthermore flexible enough to adapt to changing circumstance and indicators. Schmeidl and Jenkins illustrated the importance of contextual sensitivity by suggesting that "processes may have quite different meanings depending on their political context;" for example, "non-violent protest in an authoritarian context might lead to state repression and thus refugee flight, while in a democratic or more open regime it might lead to political reform and thus constitutes an alternative to flight."[46]

Interestingly enough, quantitative modellers were quick to realize their own limitations, including that of "late warning" (lagging behind with predictions), arguing that the main purpose and strength of their research was to rank countries on their "risk potential" and to provide key monitoring indicators. Thus, the argument to combine quantitative models and case-study analysis for the purposes of early warning came far from within the quantitative community.[47] This has led to a development of comprehensive approaches that take both kinds of methodologies into account at different stages in the early warning system.[48]

In light of the above, a comprehensive early warning methodology should include the following steps/aspects:

- At the onset of early warning analysis, using a combination of quantitative and qualitative methods, an analytical framework with key indicators for the ongoing monitoring process needs to be developed. It is important to distinguish the longer-term factors (root causes) from medium-term (proximate) factors and more immediate facilitating or triggering factors. Within these categories, importance needs to be given to a multitude of areas such as political, social/demographic, economic/ecological, and so on.

- Based on the base-line analysis, the monitoring process needs to be constant and ongoing. As Gupta once said, "it is extremely difficult to forecast, especially the future, but if you forecast, forecast often."[49] This is often best accomplished by using a field monitoring system based on standardized protocols developed by event data systems such as Kansas Event Data System (KEDS)[50] or the Protocol for Assessment of Nonviolent Direct Action (PANDA) which later developed into the IDEA (Integrated Data for Event Analysis) Framework.[51]

- While monitoring events grouped around a certain set of standardized indicators, it is also extremely important to profile stakeholders in conflict – both actors for, or spoilers of, peace. It is equally crucial to know their attitude(s) to the conflict/peace process as well as their resources to accomplish their goals.

- Although "on the ground" information from field monitoring is indispensable, one should nevertheless combine this with analyses from field visits and expert panels.

Despite these advances in early warning methodology, there is one "bastion" that still remains unconquered, which is the ability to predict the exact timing of conflict or forced migration. This has been one of the reasons early warning methodology has chosen the language of anticipating rather than predicting an outcome. Schmeidl and Jenkins argued in 1998 that "this is an area where considerable attention needs to be invested."[52] It may be that we will never be able to predict the exact timing of forced exodus. Nevertheless, a group of researchers at Harvard University, in conjunction with a think-tank in Switzerland (the Swiss Peace Foundation), are currently attempting to improve our understanding of temporal proximity and a more accurate forecasting of conflict escalation or de-escalation using event data analysis.

Political obstacles to (refugee) early warning

Aside from the inability to predict the exact outbreak of conflict or forced migration, the previous discussion has shown that early warning methodology has progressed to the point that most practitioners are reasonably satisfied with the ability to anticipate conflicts and forced migration. The ultimate dilemma of the success of early warning seems to lie on the political front. As emphasized above, early warning is best practised as an ongoing process with constant monitoring of events. Thus, it functions far better when considered long term, with the warning coming far in advance. It is easier to anticipate events than to predict the exact outbreak. Long-term anticipation is best combined with long-term operational preventive actions that ideally eliminate or change the structures that lead to and/or accelerate conflicts, or foster those that lower the chances of conflict escalation. Such thinking and warning, however, seem diametrically opposed to the environment in which political actors have to work. The following points illustrate the existing dilemmas:

- Electoral periods are on average about five years. This encourages short-term thinking and planning because politicians prefer to benefit from their own action, rather than providing this opportunity to others (in the worst case, political opponents).
- Long-term political action receives less public exposure because it is easier to use quick results to gauge the success of any politician or bureaucrat.[53]
- The decision to spend scarce resources is often difficult in an environment where one can choose from multiple conflicts and numerous more potential ones – who can justify preventive action when urgent humanitarian assistance is needed? In particular, small countries prefer to keep their resources for those cases where they could make a noticeable difference. Still, states too often miscalculate the costs and benefits of conflict prevention vs. conflict containment or management.
- Fear of failure or disapproval is also a big obstacle to acting on early warning: nothing is more embarrassing than to make a difficult situation worse (the problem of walking a "slippery slope").[54] Even more difficult might be to make a stand against an unfavourable political environment, or even a Prisoner's Dilemma (e.g. Chechnya).[55]
- Bureaucratic procedures, especially in bodies with many member states, can also severely hamper preventive action despite adequate early warning. The United Nations inactivity during the 1994 Rwanda genocide is the most widely used example here. Despite clear warning signals in numerous faxes sent by General Dallaire of the United Nations Assistance Mission in Rwanda in January and February of 1994, not only alerting the UN Department of Peacekeeping Operations of planned mass killings of Tutsis but also suggesting action that might prevent the disaster, no action was taken.[56] Aside from the political considerations of intervening in Rwanda, or not knowing how to react (despite clear recommendations by Dallaire), the UN system simply did not have a proper mechanism for linking early warning to early response.

Notwithstanding all these obstacles within the political or bureaucratic environment of early warning, the primary cause of failure to act on early warning has been cited as the problem of political will. This, however, is an easy criticism as long as we do not understand the underlying reasons for the lack of political will. Apart from an obvious lack of knowledge, lack of resources, or lack of courage to act (or stand alone), there are clearly sober calculations based on state interests. Although the end of the Cold War did produce a shift in the deadlock between East and West – manifested in the UN Security Council – and opened up the possibility for new alliances between states for the protection of human rights and the prevention of conflicts, many lessons remain to be learned, particularly when it comes to humanitarian early warning and conflict prevention. We have to continue to reckon with certain realities in the world, one being that the United Nations has been, is, and will be an entity that represents the interests of states, particularly the strong ones. This may explain why none of the UN early warning systems has so far been successful (see table 7.1 for a chronology of highlights).

As I have shown in the history of refugee early warning, anticipating forced migration is a good demonstration of the somewhat conflicting interests between state and human security. On the one hand, early warning can attempt to understand the timing, direction, and size of refugee flows in order to prepare relief assistance but also in order to build entry or exit controls for refugees. The idea of "safe zones" or the "right to remain," for example, should not necessarily be seen as a new form of refugee protection, but could also be scrutinized as tools preventing refugees from reaching safe haven abroad. Recent trends have clearly shown that Western states in particular tend to focus more on keeping forced migrations within their own country, or at least in the region they come from (first safe country concept) rather than opening their gates to provide safe haven. One could go so far as to argue that the increased applications of UN Chapter VII operations – initiated for the first time since the Korean war with the 1991 intervention in northern Iraq[57] – fulfil the purpose of bringing "safety to people rather than people to safety, by force if necessary":[58]

- In Kosovo, the fear of massive migration flows into unstable neighbouring countries (Macedonia, Albania) and into Western Europe, NATO unity, and the wish to punish Milosevic were the key issues behind the international response. Many humanitarians saw the protection of Kosovo Albanians as secondary to the intervention, because there was no commitment to ground troops, which would have been necessary to protect civilians.
- The Chapter VII operation in northern Iraq was intended less to protect the Kurdish internally displaced persons than to react to the fears of Turkey (a NATO member) that a massive influx of Kurdish refugees could strengthen Kurdish secessionist forces.
- Operation Turquoise in Rwanda was linked more to France's desire to strengthen its political influence in the region than to protect the Tutsi minority.

Table 7.1 Humanitarian early warning in the United Nations – Important developments

	Initially early warning is similar to intelligence operations, collecting information for the protection of peace-keeping operations.
1981	Reference study by Prince Sadruddin Aga Khan for the UN Commission on Human Rights. Aga Khan's study is followed by two others: one by an Independent Commission on International Humanitarian Issues in 1983, and one by the United Nations High Commissioner for Refugees (UNHCR) in 1986. These reports shift the focus from purely political causes of refugee migration to economic underdevelopment.
1987	UN Secretary-General Pérez de Cuéllar creates ORCI (Office for Research and the Collection of Information) with the purpose of exploring the possibility of monitoring situations within countries and the potential utility of an early warning system for forced migration.
1989	Joint Inspection Unit (JIU) in Geneva initiates a study of the UN capacity for the prevention of refugee movements.
1991	Resolution of the General Assembly (46/182) leads to the creation of the Department of Humanitarian Affairs (DHA) in order to strengthen the coordination of UN humanitarian emergency assistance. The idea of conflict prevention becomes a guiding principle in the United Nations.
1991–1992	The UN Administrative Committee on Coordination (ACC) initiates a working group in order to discuss the basic question of early warning within the UN system.
1992	An ad hoc working group with representatives from various UN organizations is initiated and holds monthly meetings. This group tries to strengthen early warning efforts within United Nations organizations – e.g. the Food and Agriculture Organization of the United Nations (FAO), the United Nations Development Programme (UNDP), the United Nations Children's Fund (UNICEF) – as well as encouraging the use and exchange of existing data. Although the meetings improve contact among the different organizations, it remains ad hoc and on a personal level. A main problem is that the working group lacks any kind of decision-making power.
1992	*The Agenda for Peace* lists early warning and conflict prevention as an official task of the United Nations (A/47/227–S/2411).
1992	A joint UNHCR and International Labour Organization (ILO) conference explores the idea of the linkage between economic imbalance and overall poverty in the "South" and forced migration. The Center for Comparative Social Research in Berlin, Germany, follows this up with another conference in 1994.

Table 7.1 (cont.)

1992/1993	Secretary-General Boutros Boutros Ghali dissolves ORCI and initiates UNDHA. DHA, with funds from Japan, develops the Humanitarian Early Warning System (HEWS) based on an indicator approach. HEWS produces short- and long-term analyses and tries to issue warnings in order to identify humanitarian disasters.
1995	The Secretary-General drafts a supplement to the Agenda for Peace for the fiftieth anniversary of the United Nations. The importance of early warning for conflict prevention is highlighted again in paragraph 26 (A/50/60–S/1995/1).
1995	UNDHA and ReliefWeb create IRIN (Integrated Regional Information Network) in order to improve the information feed in the Great Lakes area of Africa. West Africa is added in 1997, and by 2000 IRIN covers all African states and begins to expand to Central and South Asia (http://www.reliefweb.int/IRIN).
1996	UNDHA officially creates ReliefWeb (which is confirmed by the General Assembly in 1997, 51/194). ReliefWeb is the first worldwide clearing-house for timely information about humanitarian emergencies and natural disasters. In 2001 ReliefWeb expands to Asia (http://www.reliefweb.int).
1996	Parallel to UNDHA, UNHCR creates REFWORLD, a CD-ROM representing an authoritative resource comprising all earlier electronic efforts and supplementing these with a great number of new databases and sources of information.
1997	UNDHA is reorganized into the Office for the Coordination of Humanitarian Affairs (UNOCHA) with the following main tasks: (a) policy development and coordination functions in support of the Secretary-General, ensuring that all humanitarian issues, including those that fall between gaps in existing mandates of agencies such as protection and assistance for internally displaced persons, are addressed; (b) advocacy of humanitarian issues with political organs, notably the Security Council; and (c) coordination of humanitarian emergency response, by ensuring that an appropriate response mechanism is established, through Inter-Agency Standing Committee (IASC) consultations, on the ground.
1997	The Executive Committee on Peace and Security (ECPS) is created as part of the reform agenda by the UN Secretary-General Kofi Annan. ECPS is tasked with improving information exchange and cooperation among departments (see A/51/829, Section A), but does not have any decision-making powers as originally envisioned.

Table 7.1 (cont.)

1997 and 1999	The annual report of the Secretary-General specifically deals with crisis prevention (A/52/1 and A/54/1).
1998	ECPS creates an Inter-Agency/Interdepartmental Framework for Coordination. Ten departments, funds, and programmes currently participate in monthly meetings in order to identify crisis areas, plan the evaluation of countries, and discuss preventive methods. Even though this increases contact within the United Nations, it has no capacity for cumulative knowledge or strategic planning.
1998	The president of the UN Security Council re-emphasizes the importance of prevention and credits early warning as a strategy to achieve this (S/PRST/1999/34).
1998–1999	The Executive Office of the Secretary-General initiates the Early Warning and Preventive Measures (EWPM) project with support from the British government. EWPM develops an early warning methodology which can serve as a common analytical language for various UN departments and agencies.
1998–2000	The EWPM programme of the UN Staff College in Turin (http://www.itcilo.it/UNSCP/programmefocus/ earlywarning/) initiates a set of pilot workshops, headquarter-focused workshops, and field-based/focused workshops on early warning and conflict prevention. The United Nations Institute for Training and Research (UNITAR, http://www.unitar.org/) parallels this effort on conflict resolution.
1998–2000	The Security Council re-emphasizes its commitment to the prevention of armed conflicts and recognizes the role of early warning in this (S/PRST/1998/28, S/PRST/1998/29, and S/PRST/1998/35; S/PRST/1999/34; S/PRST/2000/35, S/PRST/2000/34, S/PRST/2000/28, S/PRST/2000/29, and S/PRST/2000/10; and resolutions 1196, 1197, 1208, 1209).
2000	UN Secretary-General Kofi Annan highlights the importance of conflict prevention in several documents, including the *Millennium Report* (A/54/2000). He calls for a culture of prevention, which includes strengthening of early warning and conflict prevention within the United Nations (see also A/55/1).
2000	UNOCHA, under new leadership, dissolves HEWS in order to refocus on key indicators, training of UN field personnel, and improving contact with the Office of the Secretary-General. The establishment of institutional information channels is geared to bridging the warning–response gap.

Table 7.1 (cont.)

2000	The Brahimi Report evaluating the UN peace-keeping operations (A/55/305–S/2000/809) emphasizes the importance of early warning and conflict prevention. One of the main recommendations is the creation of a professional system in the Information and Strategic Analysis Secretariat (EISAS) in order to collect information, improve analysis, and develop long-term strategies. It is proposed that EISAS consolidate the various bodies that are currently responsible for policy and information analysis in the area of peace and security: • Policy Analysis Unit and Situation Center of the Department of Peacekeeping Operations (DPKO) • Policy Planning Unit of the Department of Political Affairs (DPA) • Policy Development Unit of the Office for the Coordination of Humanitarian Affairs (OCHA) • Media Monitoring and Analysis Section of the Department of Public Information (DPI)
2001	Renewed efforts by the Inter-Agency Framework Team to come up with an indicator approach to early warning to be utilized by field personnel.
11 September 2001	Impact on UN system is to prompt reconsideration of the utilization of early warning mechanisms.

On the other hand, early warning can be employed to anticipate factors leading to forced displacement in an attempt to prevent them from occurring. For example, by removing push factors such as poor governance, human rights violations, and armed conflict, forced migration could be prevented. Whereas refugee scholars and practitioners have shifted in this direction for the sake of human security, politicians most likely did it for the sake of protecting their territories and borders.

It seems it is here that early warners need to pay greater attention. Rather than lamenting state actors' lack of human compassion, it might be more beneficial to begin a merging of interests between intelligence-oriented prediction and humanitarian early warning. The *pièce de résistance* may be to frame humanitarian concerns in the language of state security. Sadly, the 11 September 2001 attack on the United States may have dealt the necessary cards here.

Although September 11 was seen as a failure within intelligence systems, it was not necessarily a failure in early warning. Intelligence may have failed to follow up on clues about the movements of terrorists across borders, but early warning would never have bothered to look into this area in the first place because it relies on publicly available information without touching classified information and state secrets. Crucially, however, early warning would have focused not on trying accurately to predict an event such as September 11, but more on anticipating the possibility of such events far in advance in order to find long-term preventive mechanisms to decrease the likelihood of their occurring in the first place.

Even though it is not yet fully clear whether terrorism grows out of unaddressed grievances and conflicts, especially conflicts that seem forgotten by the world (e.g. Chechnya, or even Palestine), terrorist organizations do seem to flourish in situations of turmoil and chaos. Thus, rather than tracking the movement of the al-Qaida terrorist network run by Osama bin Laden, early warners focusing on Afghanistan had long been documenting the dangerous impact of sanctions and political isolation on the Taliban regime.[59] By isolating, and to some degree ignoring, the Taliban in Afghanistan, we may have contributed to an increased radicalization of the movement, allowing it to be hijacked not only by Pakistan but also by Osama bin Laden's al-Qaida terrorist network. Analysis clearly shows the changes in the Taliban movement to the point where they were neither willing nor able to curb terrorist activity within their own borders.

In light of the above, the inability accurately to predict the exact occurrence of a violent event, or being honest about the impossibility of doing so, may in the past have led to early warning being perceived as "soft" and "weak" in comparison with intelligence analysis. However, the failure of intelligence accurately to predict and prevent September 11 may have given early warning an added boost. Consideration is being given to whether the more long-term focus of this methodology and the stress on operational prevention of unknown events could ultimately be a more feasible approach, or whether at least early warning should also be given a chance alongside intelligence analysis. At a minimum it seems that more attention is now paid to early warning analysis, and that there is more political interest or will to tackle the root causes of conflict because it clearly does not stop at Western borders any longer. The intense international involvement in Afghanistan is proof of this. The only remaining question is whether international interest has enough stamina for long-term engagement in order really to prevent future conflict in the war-torn region.

Conclusion

The early warning of refugee migration was initially developed more as an anticipatory system that would assist the humanitarian aid community to provide better refugee relief, but the end of the Cold War has clearly produced a shift in the direction of preventing the causes that lead to mass exodus. Because refugee migration is linked to human rights violations and armed conflict (among other factors), early warning models have developed in a more generic fashion, seeing refugee migration as one of the humanitarian disasters that need to be prevented. Although this has brought the issues into the mainstream and merged concerns, it may have halted some of the more refugee-specific analyses that were done in the past.

The potential to use early warning both to prevent humanitarian disaster but also to block the entry of people fleeing terror has led to a dilemma in the early warning of forced migration. Whereas non-governmental organizations, humanitarian agencies, and academic institutions would very much like to contribute to an enhanced understanding of what causes people to leave their homes, there is no guarantee that such knowledge is utilized by states for humanitarian purposes. A solution to this dilemma may very well be a joint effort to push forward early warning models that track the factors that can lead to forced displacement, with the aim of focusing on early preventive efforts that would then avoid the need for migration in the first place, balancing human and state security alike. The 11 September 2001 attack on the United States may have put the necessary spin on the whole discussion of human vs. state security, and the role early warning could play in bridging the two concerns.

A last resort, however, might be a more targeted use of the mass media and the Internet in order both to pressurize policy makers into "early listening" and to educate the general public about the situation in other countries and the options for conflict prevention. Even if the intervention in Somalia eventually failed, it is a powerful example of what can be achieved with targeted pressure through the media. As long as policy makers are the only ones who know about impending conflicts, they can try to pretend they did not know (as in the case of Rwanda), because there is nothing more embarrassing than others knowing that one knew and did not react. Achieving adequate pressure, obviously linked to adequate response options, may be the ultimate challenge for early warning and the protection of human security. It may still be possible to realize humanitarian early warning goals if technical and institutional obstacles are minimized, thus providing policy makers with few excuses not to act.

Notes

1. "Early warning serves the common good and thus differs from traditional intelligence" (Howard Adelman and Astri Suhrke, *The International Response to Conflict and Geno-*

cide: Lessons from the Rwanda Experience. Part 2: Early Warning and Conflict Management: Genocide in Rwanda, Joint Evaluation of Emergency Assistance to Rwanda, Copenhagen, DANIDA, 1996); "Humanitarian early warning is based on protecting interests of others who are at risk" (Susanne Schmeidl and J. Craig Jenkins, "The Early Warning of Humanitarian Disasters: Problems in Building an Early Warning System," *International Migration Review*, vol. 32, 1998, pp. 471–486, at p. 482).

2. J. David Singer and Michael D. Wallace, eds., *To Augur Well. Early Warning Indicators in World Politics*, London: Sage, 1979; J. David Singer and Richard J. Stoll, eds., *Quantitative Indicators in World Politics: Timely Assurance and Early Warning*, New York: Praeger, 1984.

3. The United Nations Disaster Relief Organization began in 1972 and the United Nations Environment Programme created the Global Environmental Monitoring System (GEMS) in 1975; see B. G. Ramcharan, *The International Law and Practice of Early Warning and Preventive Diplomacy*, Dordrecht: Martinus Nijhoff, 1991. In the same year, the Food and Agriculture Organization of the United Nations (FAO) established the Global Information and Early Warning System on Food and Agriculture (GIEWS) and in the late 1980s the US Agency for International Development designed a Famine Early Warning System (FEWS) in order to avoid a repeat of the drought and famine disaster in the Sahel and Ethiopia; see Abdur Rashid, "The Global Information and Early Warning System on Food and Agriculture," and William P. Whelan, "USAID's Famine Early Warning System: From Concept to Practice," both in John L. Davies and Ted Robert Gurr, eds., *Preventive Measures: Building Risk Assessment and Crises Early Warning Systems*, Lanham, MD: Rowman & Littlefield, 1998.

4. Internal displacement shows greater variations owing to the fluidity of the situation but also owing to problems in estimating this population.

5. Prince Sadruddin Aga Khan, *Study on Human Rights and Massive Exodus: Question of the Violation of Human Rights and Fundamental Freedoms in Any Part of the World, with Particular Reference to Colonial and Other Dependent Countries and Territories*, Special Report to the Commission on Human Rights, 38th session, United Nations Economic and Social Council, GE.82-10252, 1981.

6. *Early Warning of Refugee Mass Influx Emergencies*, Washington DC: Refugee Policy Group, 1983; *Early Warning of Mass Refugee Flow*, Washington DC: Refugee Policy Group, 1987.

7. Lance Clark, *Early Warning of Refugee Flows*, Washington DC: Refugee Policy Group, 1989.

8. Gervase Coles, "Pre-Flow Aspects of the Refugee Phenomenon," internal background paper, International Institute for Humanitarian Affairs, San Remo, Italy, 1982; Akira Onishi, "Global Early Warning System for Displaced Persons: Interlinkages of Environment, Development, Peace and Human Rights," *Technological Forecasting and Social Change*, vol. 31, no. 3, 1987, pp. 269–299.

9. Onishi, "Global Early Warning System for Displaced Persons."

10. Ibid., p. 275.

11. Ibid., p. 288.

12. Susanne Schmeidl, "From Root Cause Assessment to Preventive Diplomacy: The Possibilities and Limitations of the Early Warning of Forced Migration," Ph.D. dissertation, Department of Sociology, The Ohio State University, 1995; J. Craig Jenkins and Susanne Schmeidl, "Flight from Violence: The Origins and Implications of the World Refugee Crisis," *Sociological Focus*, vol. 28, no. 1, 1995, pp. 63–82.

13. Harto Hakovirta, *Third World Conflicts and Refugeeism: Dimensions, Dynamics and Trends of the World Refugee Problem*, Helsinki: Finnish Society of Sciences, 1986.

14. Susanne Schmeidl, "Plus ça change, plus c'est la même chose: Trends and Changes of

Refugee Migration in the 21st Century," presented at the Special Session "Refugee Movements in the 21st Century" at the Annual Meeting of the American Sociological Association, Anaheim, California, 18–21 August 2001.

15. Nevertheless, as trends from Afghanistan (but also Ethiopia and Eritrea) in the past have indicated, repatriation into unresolved conflicts often is not permanent and can lead to renewed displacement.

16. Scrutinizing refugee figures, the decline needs to be seen in the light of the relatively short-term displacement from former Eastern bloc and Soviet successor states and a few (partial) settlements of protracted armed disputes (mainly Afghanistan, Ethiopia, and Mozambique), both leading to (temporary) large-scale repatriations (often in instable environments).

17. Kathleen Newland, "The Decade in Review," in *World Refugee Survey*, Washington DC: US Committee for Refugees, 1999.

18. "Politicide" is a term used where political orientation is the predominant reason for singling out populations for mass extermination. See Barbara Harff, "A Theoretical Model of Genocides and Politicides," *Journal of Ethno-Development*, vol. 4, no. 1, 1994, pp. 25–30.

19. Helen Fein, *Genocide: A Sociological Perspective*, London: Sage, 1993; Helen Fein, "Tools of Alarms: Uses of Models and Explanations and Anticipation," *Journal of Ethno-Development*, vol. 4, no. 1, 1994, pp. 31–36.

20. For a more exhaustive list, see Alex P. Schmid, *PIOOM's Master List of Potential and "Good Prospect" Domestic Conflict (De)Escalation Indicators*, Leiden: PIOOM, 1996.

21. Stephen John Stedman, "Spoiler Problems in Peace Processes," *International Security*, vol. 22, 1997, pp. 5–53.

22. Ted Robert Gurr, *Why Men Rebel*, Princeton, NJ: Princeton University Press, 1970.

23. Myron Weiner and Rainer Münz, "Migrants, Refugees and Foreign Policy: Prevention and Intervention Strategies," *Third World Quarterly*, vol. 18, 1997, pp. 25–51.

24. Edmonston demonstrated a possible relationship between economic hardship and refugee migration in two panel regressions for the years 1986 and 1990. See "Why Refugees Flee: An Analysis of Refugee Emigration Data," paper presented at the Annual Meeting of the Social Science History Association, Chicago, 5–8 November 1992.

25. Myron Weiner, "Bad Neighbors, Bad Neighborhoods: An Inquiry in the Causes of Refugee Flows," *International Security*, vol. 21, no. 1, 1996, pp. 5–42.

26. Clark, *Early Warning of Refugee Flows*.

27. J. Craig Jenkins, "Resource Mobilization Theory and the Study of Social Movements," *Annual Review of Sociology*, vol. 9, 1983, pp. 527–553.

28. Susanne Schmeidl, "Exploring the Causes of Forced Migration: A Pooled Time Series Analysis, 1971–1990," *Social Science Quarterly*, vol. 78, no. 2, 1997, pp. 284–308.

29. David Keen, *The Economic Functions of Violence in Civil Wars*, Adelphi Paper 320, Oxford: International Institute for Strategic Studies/Oxford University Press, 1998.

30. Thus, Serbian warlords were responsible for much of the ethnic cleansing in Bosnia and Herzegovina, and in southern Sudan warlords are also increasingly involved in human rights violations and violence.

31. Clark, *Early Warning of Refugee Flows*, p. 16.

32. Ibid.

33. W. Peterson, "A General Typology of Migration," *American Sociological Review*, vol. 23, no. 3, 1958, pp. 256–266.

34. Douglas S. Massey, "Economic Development and International Migration in Comparative Perspective," *Population and Development Review*, vol. 14, no. 3, 1988, pp. 383–413.

35. Ibid.
36. Clark, *Early Warning of Refugee Flows*.
37. Singer and Wallace, *To Augur Well*.
38. Ted Robert Gurr, *Minorities at Risk: A Global View of Ethnopolitical Conflict*, Washington DC: United States Institute of Peace Press, 1993.
39. Schmeidl, "From Root Cause Assessment to Preventive Diplomacy" and "Exploring the Causes of Forced Migration"; Lisa K. Zottarelli, "Refugee Production: An Exploration of Cold War and Post–Cold War Eras," unpublished manuscript, Department of Sociology, University of North Texas, 1999; Christian A. Davenport, Will H. Moore, and Steven C. Poe, "Sometimes You Just Have to Leave: Threat and Refugee Movements, 1964–1989," paper presented at the Annual Meeting of the American Political Science Association, Atlanta, GA, 1–5 September 1999.
40. For a deeper discussion and examples of these models, see Ted Robert Gurr and Barbara Harff, "Conceptual, Research, and Political Issues in Early Warning: An Overview," in *Journal of Ethno-Development: Special Issue on Early Warning of Communal Conflict and Humanitarian Crises*, vol. 4, 1994, pp. 3–14.
41. Albert J. Jongman, "Mapping Dimensions of Contemporary Conflicts and Human Rights Violations," back of the PIOOM 2002 World Conflict and Human Rights Map, Leiden: University of Leiden, PIOOM, 2002.
42. Barbara Harff, "Early Warning of Humanitarian Crises: Sequential Models and the Role of Accelerators," in Davies and Gurr, eds., *Preventive Measures*.
43. Philip Schrodt and Deborah Gerner, "Validity Assessment of Machine-Coded Event Data Set for the Middle East, 1982–1992," *American Journal of Political Science*, vol. 18, 1994, pp. 825–864.
44. Schmeidl and Jenkins, "The Early Warning of Humanitarian Disasters," p. 477. See also Jack Goldstone, "Explaining Revolution," in Jack Goldstone, Ted Robert Gurr, and F. Mothiri, *Revolutions of the Late Twentieth Century*, Boulder, CO: Westview Press, 1991, pp. 1–17.
45. Schmeidl and Jenkins, "The Early Warning of Humanitarian Disasters."
46. Ibid., p. 477.
47. Ibid. and Ted Robert Gurr and William H. Moore, "Ethnopolitical Rebellion: A Cross-Sectional Analysis of the 1980s with Risk Assessments for the 1990s," *American Journal of Political Science*, vol. 41, no. 4, 1997, pp. 1079–1103.
48. For an example of such an integrated approach, see the early warning unit at the Swiss Peace Foundation, called FAST (German abbreviation for Early Analysis of Tensions and Fact-finding); Heinz Krummenacher and Susanne Schmeidl, *Identifying Armed Conflict. FAST: An Example of a Comprehensive Early-Warning Methodology*, Working Paper, Berne: Swiss Peace Foundation, 2001.
49. Dipak K. Gupta, "An Early Warning about Forecasts: Oracle to Academics," in Susanne Schmeidl and Howard Adelman, eds., *Synergy in Early Warning Conference Proceedings*, York Centre for International and Security Studies, York University, Toronto, 1997, pp. 375–397, at p. 375.
50. Philip Schrodt, *Kansas Event Data System: Codebook*, Lawrence: University of Kansas, 1996; Philip Schrodt, Shannon Davis, and Judith Weddle, "KEDS – A Program for the Machine Coding of Events Data," *Social Science Computer Review*, vol. 12, 1994, pp. 561–574.
51. Doug Bond, J. Craig Jenkins, Charles Taylor, and Kurt Schock, "Mapping Mass Political Conflict and Civil Society," *Journal of Conflict Resolution*, vol. 4, 1997, pp. 553–579; Doug Bond, Joe Bond, Jayson Silva, and Churl Oh, *The VRA Reader*, Weston, MA: VRA Press, 1999.
52. Schmeidl and Jenkins, "The Early Warning of Humanitarian Disasters," p. 477.

53. Jean H. Guilmette, "The Paradox of Prevention: Successful Prevention Erases the Proof of Its Success: A Case for a New Ethic of Evaluation," in Susanne Schmeidl and Howard Adelman, eds., *Early Warning and Early Response*, Columbia International Affairs Online, Columbia University Press, www.ciaonet.org, 1998.

54. Alexander L. George and Jane E. Holl, "The Warning-Response Problem and Missed Opportunities in Preventive Diplomacy," in Jentleson, Bruce W. ed., *Opportunities Missed, Opportunities Seized: Preventive Diplomacy in the Post-Cold War World*, Lanham, MD: Rowman & Littlefield (for the Carnegie Commission on Preventing Deadly Conflict), 2000, pp. 21–39.

55. Gail W. Lapidus, "The War in Chechnya: Opportunities Missed, Lessons to be Learned," in Jentleson, *Opportunities Missed, Opportunities Seized*, pp. 39–68.

56. Adelman and Suhrke, *The International Response to Conflict and Genocide*; Astri Suhrke and Bruce Jones, "Preventive Diplomacy in Rwanda: Failure to Act or Failure of Actions?" in Jentleson, *Opportunities Missed, Opportunities Seized*, pp. 238–265.

57. Thomas G. Weiss, *Military–Civilian Interactions: Intervening in Humanitarian Crises*, Lanham, MD: Rowman & Littlefield, 1999.

58. Newland, "The Decade in Review," p. 17.

59. Barnett R. Rubin, Ashraf Ghani, William Maley, Ahmed Rashid, and Oliver Roy, *Afghanistan: Reconstruction and Peace-building in a Regional Framework*, KOFF Peacebuilding Report 1/2001, Berne: Swiss Peace Foundation, 2001; Ahmed Rashid, *Taliban: Islam, Oil and the New Great Game in Central Asia*, London: I. B. Tauris, 2000; Susanne Schmeidl, "(Human) Security Dilemmas: Long-term Implications of the Afghan Refugee Crisis," *Third World Quarterly*, vol. 23, no. 1, 2002.

Part II

Displacement, return, and resettlement

8

Towards a protection regime for internally displaced persons

Erin D. Mooney

The global crisis of internal displacement is one of the most pressing problems of our time. Worldwide, some 25 million persons are displaced within the borders of their own countries as a result of armed conflict, internal strife, and serious violations of human rights. Essentially, they are "internal refugees" – people who would be considered refugees were they to cross an international border. The reasons why internally displaced persons remain within their country are many, and vary from situation to situation and individual to individual. In conflict situations, for instance, uprooted persons may be unable to reach border areas safely. Geographical obstacles such as mountains and rivers or factors such as age, disability, and health may impede their transit. They may be denied freedom of movement by their own government, or face restrictions by outside countries on their right to seek asylum. This was the case in Afghanistan in the aftermath of the terrorist attacks against the United States on 11 September 2001: while the Taliban severely restricted the ability of Afghans to move freely within the country, surrounding countries closed their borders. As a result, the mass refugee influxes that were anticipated following the events of September 11 simply did not materialize; instead the number of internally displaced Afghans soared from 1.5 million to over 2 million.

Uprooted from their homes, separated from family and community support networks, and shorn of their resource base, internally displaced persons suddenly find themselves stripped of their most basic means

159

of security and survival. Compounding their plight, displacement exposes its victims to additional vulnerabilities and risks. Frequently, internally displaced persons remain caught in areas of armed conflict and under threat of armed attack, physical assault, sexual violence, and forced conscription. Even if they manage to flee areas of hostilities, they often are unable to escape the perception that they are associated with the "enemy" and are targeted on that basis. Many lack adequate food, water, shelter, and medical care. The conditions of danger and deprivation that characterize situations of internal displacement can take a tremendous toll. The highest mortality and malnutrition rates recorded in humanitarian emergencies this past decade have involved internally displaced persons.[1]

Dictates of state sovereignty determine that responsibility for providing protection and assistance to internally displaced persons rests with their government. However, it is often the case that governments are unable to meet these obligations or are unwilling to do so, sometimes even deliberately displacing populations or denying them their rights. Moreover, unlike refugees, internally displaced persons do not benefit from a specific international regime devoted to ensuring their protection and assistance when their own government cannot or will not. Instead, international action on behalf of the internally displaced is ad hoc and therefore not assured. Often, it is obstructed by governmental authorities or insurgent groups. Most critically, where responses do occur, they typically focus predominantly, often exclusively, on assistance, leaving many internally displaced persons without the protection they so vitally need.

Though the phenomenon of internal displacement is not new, in recent years the tragic plight of its growing number of victims[2] has begun to receive the international attention it demands. Indeed, "how to help the millions of the world's most vulnerable people displaced within their own countries" has been singled out as "the hot issue for a new millennium."[3] Addressing this question not only is a humanitarian imperative but increasingly is understood as also a matter of regional and international security. In January 2000, the UN Security Council expressed grave concern that "alarmingly high numbers of ... internally displaced persons do not receive sufficient protection and assistance" and gave particular emphasis to the fact that "there is no comprehensive protection regime for the internally displaced."[4]

An international regime for protecting internally displaced persons worldwide is urgently required. Concretely, this would need to consist of international standards, institutional apparatus, and operational strategies integrated into a coherent and cohesive system of response. This chapter examines the extent to which normative, institutional, and strategic frameworks are in place for protecting internally displaced persons and identifies steps still needed to be taken to further their development and, collectively, that of a comprehensive and effective protection regime.

The normative framework

Protection is fundamentally a legal concept, defined by the rights and entitlements of individuals as provided for by law. For internally displaced persons, unlike for refugees, there does not exist an international convention specific to their plight. However, this is not to say, as sometimes is suggested, that internally displaced persons "are not the concern of international law."[5] In fact, international law has much to offer for the protection of the internally displaced.

To begin with, as human beings, internally displaced persons are automatically entitled to the protection provided for under human rights law, which recognizes and protects the attributes of human dignity inherent to all individuals. States, in turn, are obliged to ensure respect for those universally recognized human rights essential to ensure the survival, well-being, and dignity of all persons subject to their territorial jurisdiction. The Universal Declaration of Human Rights (1948) provides an authoritative statement of the basic tenets of human rights, most of which subsequently have been elaborated and the obligations they entail spelled out in a panoply of international and regional human rights instruments. With human rights concerns cutting across all phases of internal displacement – from its cause, to the conditions of displacement, to the search for solutions – the comprehensive coverage of human rights law is of tremendous importance to the internally displaced.

When internal displacement occurs in situations of armed conflict, whether inter-state or domestic in character, international humanitarian law also comes into effect. Though many provisions of international humanitarian law reflect and reinforce protection provided for under human rights law, because a number of human rights guarantees may be significantly limited or even derogated in situations of armed conflict the protection provided by humanitarian law in these circumstances is particularly valuable. Moreover, unlike human rights law, international humanitarian law contains norms expressly prohibiting displacement.[6] In addition, whereas international human rights law generally is binding only on states and their agents, international humanitarian law specifically applies not only to states but also to insurgent forces.

Refugee law, which spells out the rules for the legal status and treatment of individuals fearing persecution who are *outside of their country of nationality* and unable to avail themselves of its protection, is not directly applicable to the situation of internally displaced persons. Reference to refugee law by analogy nonetheless can be extremely instructive in pointing to the particular types of protection required by persons in refugee-like situations, and which are not necessarily specifically addressed by human rights or international humanitarian law. A particularly important example is the principle of *non-refoulement*, providing protection for refugees against forced return to a situation where they would be at risk of persecution or physical harm. Moreover, internally displaced persons of course are entitled, as a matter of human rights, to seek asylum from persecution in another country and thereby to benefit from the protection of international refugee law.[7]

Although it is undisputed that the coverage of international human rights law and international humanitarian law extends to internally displaced persons, the question arises as to whether these standards adequately address their particular needs. Exploring this issue was among the principal tasks assigned by the United Nations Commission on Human Rights to the Representative of the Secretary-General on Internally Displaced Persons, an independent expert first appointed in 1992 (see below, page 167). Several years of study working with a team of international legal experts in these three branches of law culminated in an elaborate two-part *Compilation and Analysis of Legal Norms* pertaining to internally displaced persons.[8] This study determined that although existing law provides substantial coverage for the internally displaced, there nonetheless remain significant areas in which it fails to provide sufficient legal protection as a result of a number of gaps and grey areas in the law.

The areas of insufficient legal protection for the internally displaced fall into two main categories. The first category concerns gaps that arise out of a lack of explicit norms addressing identifiable needs. Such normative gaps arise in the absence, for instance, of an express right not to be arbitrarily displaced and of a right to restitution of or compensation for property lost as a consequence of displacement during situations of armed conflict. The second category of insufficient coverage concerns those cases where a general norm exists but a corollary provision specifically addressing concerns of particular importance to internally displaced persons has not been articulated that would ensure application of the general norm so as to address these needs. For example, although there is a general human right guaranteeing freedom of movement, for internally displaced persons there is no express guarantee against forcible return to dangerous areas within their own countries comparable to the principle in refugee law of *non-refoulement*. In addition, applicability gaps exist where a legal norm does not apply in its entirety in all circumstances. Serious gaps such as these could arise in situations falling below the threshold of applying humanitarian law, which at the same time are circumstances in which the restriction or even derogation of a number of human rights may be allowed. Finally, what were termed "ratification gaps" in the legal protection of the internally displaced arise where states have not ratified key human rights treaties and/or humanitarian law instruments.

The study concluded that, "where the analysis shows that the needs of internally displaced persons are insufficiently protected by existing international law, it is important to restate general principles of protection in more specific detail and to address clear protection gaps in a future international instrument."[9] The findings and recommendations of the study proved sufficiently compelling to lead the UN Commission on Human Rights as well as the General Assembly to request the Representative to develop "an appropriate normative framework" for the internally displaced.[10] Because the lack of a normative framework was considered by so many UN agencies and non-governmental organizations (NGOs) in the field as requiring urgent attention and remedy, the Representative recommended the drafting of "guiding principles" rather than a convention, which, as other experiences suggested, likely would have taken years – upwards of 10 or 20 – to conclude. With the endorsement of the Commission on Human Rights and the General Assembly, the Representative, together with a team of international lawyers and with input from a broad base of other relevant experts, proceeded to draft what became the *Guiding Principles on Internal Displacement.*[11]

The Guiding Principles bring together in one concise document the many norms of special importance to the internally displaced that previously were diffused in an array of different instruments and, consequently, were not easily accessible or sufficiently understood. The 30 principles spell out what protection should mean for internally displaced persons in all phases of internal displacement: providing protection from arbitrary displacement and protection and assistance during displacement and during return or resettlement and reintegration. Although not a binding document like a treaty, the Guiding Principles reflect and are consistent with international human rights law and international humanitarian law, which is binding. In many instances, the Principles cite verbatim the text of the provisions of human rights and humanitarian law on which they are based.[12] This is especially clear in the cases where the Principles restate a general norm before elaborating what it means to give effect to this right for internally displaced persons. For example, Principle 14 reaffirms the right of every human being to liberty of movement and freedom to choose his or her residence and then specifies that for internally displaced persons this includes a right to move freely in and out of camps and settlements. Similarly, Principle 20 begins by stating the right of every human being to recognition before the law and then proceeds to specify that for internally displaced persons this requires that the authorities facilitate the replacement of documents lost in the course of displacement, without imposing unreasonable conditions such as requiring return to one's area of habitual residence. While reinforcing existing human rights and humanitarian law, the Principles are intended to provide an authoritative statement of how the law should be applied to address the particular needs of internally displaced persons.

For the purpose of the Principles, internally displaced persons are

persons or groups of persons who have been forced or obliged to flee or to leave their homes or places of habitual residence, in particular as a result of or in order to avoid the effects of armed conflict, situations of generalized violence, violations of human rights or natural or human-made disasters, and who have not crossed an internationally recognized state border.[13]

This definition does not confer any special legal status comparable to the determination under international law of an individual as a "refugee." This is not necessary, after all, because unlike refugees, who are outside of their own country and cannot avail themselves of its protection, internally displaced persons remain entitled, as Principle 1 affirms, to "enjoy, in full equality, the same rights and freedoms under international and domestic law as do other persons in their country." They "shall not be discriminated against in the enjoyment of any rights and freedoms on the ground that they are displaced." At the same time, the principle of equality does not preclude the undertaking of special measures to ensure realization of the rights of groups of persons with particular vulnerabilities, such as the internally displaced.[14]

Indeed, the Principles seek to address the particular plight not only of internally displaced persons in general but also of especially vulnerable groups among them. Principle 4 recognizes that "[c]ertain groups of internally displaced persons, such as children, especially unaccompanied minors, expectant mothers, mothers with young children, female heads of household, persons with disabilities and elderly persons, shall be entitled to protection and assistance required by their condition and to treatment which takes into account their special needs." A number of provisions address the special protection, assistance, and development needs of women and children, who in any given situation make up the majority of the internally displaced. For instance, the Principles provide for protection from gender-specific violence, forced prostitution, sale into marriage, sexual exploitation, and forced labour, as well as military recruitment of children (Principles 11 and 13). They also require special efforts to be made to ensure the full and equal participation of women in the planning and management of any planned relocation (Principle 7) and in the planning and distribution of humanitarian supplies (Principle 18), and of women and girls in educational and training programmes (Principle 23).

The Principles underscore that responsibility for ensuring protection and assistance for the internally displaced rests first and foremost with the national authorities. As a general principle, Principle 3 states that national authorities have the primary duty and responsibility to provide protection and assistance to internally displaced persons within their jurisdiction. This responsibility of states is reiterated several times in relation to particular needs of the displaced, for instance regarding the provision of assistance (Principle 25), the establishment of the means to enable internally displaced persons to return voluntarily, in safety and dignity, to their homes or places of habitual residence (Principle 28), and assistance for internally displaced persons in the recovery of or compensation for property and possessions lost as a result of displacement (Principle 29). The use of the term "competent authorities" reflects the broad coverage of the Principles, which intend to provide guidance not only to states but also to insurgent forces, along with "all other authorities, groups and persons in their relations with internally displaced persons."

However, in recognition of the reality that states may lack the ability or even willingness to fulfil their responsibilities towards internally displaced populations, the Principles also are intended to assist international agencies and NGOs working with the internally displaced. Principles 24 to 26 reinforce the right of international organizations to provide humanitarian assistance and to have safe access to populations in need. At the same time, mindful of the problem of inadequate attention paid to protection needs, Principle 27 points out that international humanitarian organizations and other actors providing assistance should give due regard to the protection needs and human rights of internally displaced persons and take appropriate measures in this regard. The Principles thus seek to address not only gaps in the law but also serious shortcomings in programmatic approaches and actual responses on the ground.

Since their formulation in 1998, the Guiding Principles have gained significant international standing and recognition as a valuable tool for furthering protection for internally displaced persons. The UN Commission on Human Rights and the General Assembly have encouraged the wide dissemination and application of the Principles, including their use by the Representative in his dialogue with governments and by international agencies working with the displaced. All of the main international humanitarian, human rights, and development organizations and umbrella groups of NGOs comprising the UN Inter-Agency Standing Committee (IASC) have endorsed the Principles, disseminated them to staff, and decided to integrate them into their activities with the internally displaced. The UN Secretary-General has recommended that in situations of mass displacement the Security Council encourage governments to observe the Guiding Principles, and indeed the Council has begun to do so.[15] Meanwhile, regional intergovernmental organizations, such as the Organization of African Unity (OAU), the Organization for Security and Co-operation in Europe (OSCE), and the Inter-American Commission on Human Rights of the Organization of American States (OAS), have begun to hold seminars on the Principles and apply them to their work.[16] NGOs have been especially active and effective in promoting the Principles, for instance in providing training on them and using them as a tool for advocating the rights of the displaced with governments and non-state actors, monitoring conditions of displacement, and pointing to required changes in national legislation and policy. In all regions, governments of countries with serious situations of internal displacement are making use of the Principles in a number of ways, such as disseminating them as part of public awareness campaigns, requesting seminars and training on them, and incorporating them into national policy and legislation, including constitutional court decisions to protect their internally displaced populations.[17] As perhaps the clearest sign of the Principles' relevance, internally displaced persons around the world are actively using them to advocate on behalf of their communities. To facilitate this, the Principles have been translated into over 25 languages, ranging from Arabic to Georgian to Tamil, with more translations under way. Specifically in the context of Afghanistan, and prior to the intensification of internal displacement in the aftermath of events following 11 September 2001, booklets of the Guiding Principles in Farsi and Pashtu were published and were being disseminated throughout the country.

That the Guiding Principles have so quickly achieved such wide usage – and by a broad range of actors – speaks volumes about what was an urgent need for international standards addressing the plight of internally displaced persons as well as about how the Principles are serving to fill this gap.

The institutional framework

Although protection is based in law, it also requires institutional mechanisms and actors to give it practical effect. For internally displaced persons, unlike refugees, there is no single international organization with a specific mandate and responsibility for ensuring their protection and assistance worldwide. An array of UN humanitarian, human rights, and development agencies and international NGOs are certainly involved in providing assistance, protection, and development aid in situations of internal displacement. None of these organizations, however, has a global mandate to protect and assist internally displaced persons. Moreover, their involvement with the internally displaced occurs on a case-by-case basis, determined by issues of mandate, access, and the availability of resources. Even when these criteria are met, the decision to become involved is discretionary. As a result, international action on behalf of the displaced is highly unpredictable, in terms of not only whether it occurs but also what international actors are involved and what specific role they play.

As earlier noted, in 1992 the UN Secretary-General, at the request of the Commission on Human Rights, appointed a Representative on Internally Displaced Persons.[18] However, as a part-time and voluntary position supported by only one UN professional and no permanent presence in the field, this mandate clearly is not equipped to assume operational responsibility for providing protection and assistance to the world's internally displaced. Instead, the Representative's role is more one of a catalyst seeking to improve national and international responses. In addition to developing a normative framework for the internally displaced, studying and recommending ways of remedying the institutional gap for internally displaced persons has been one of the key areas of the Representative's concern.

Early into his mandate, the Representative of the Secretary-General identified three options for institutional arrangements for the internally displaced.[19] The first of these was the creation of a new agency singularly dedicated to the internally displaced. However as the political and financial feasibility of this option put its realization into doubt, a second option was to assign responsibility for internally displaced persons to an existing agency. It was suggested that the United Nations High Commissioner for Refugees (UNHCR) would be a strong candidate for this role given its expertise in providing protection in situations of displacement and its experience of involvement with the internally displaced since at least the early 1970s. In the 1990s, the UNHCR did indeed prove prepared to increase its involvement on behalf of internally displaced persons significantly, subject to certain criteria.[20] At the same time, however, the UN High Commissioner for Refugees, Sadako Ogata, indicated that her agency did not have the capacity to assume worldwide responsibility for internally displaced persons, who, she pointed out, outnumbered by several millions the global refugee population for whom the agency has a statutory responsibility. A third option consisted of a collaborative approach among the different relevant agencies, coordinated by a central mechanism. To date, this last option has been the preferred approach of the international community.

In many ways, the collaborative approach does appear most appropriate because it allows for a comprehensive and holistic response, involving the various relevant agencies and spanning all phases of displacement, from prevention, to emergency response, to return or resettlement and reintegration. Yet it is also true that coordination of efforts for internally displaced persons repeatedly has proven to be problematic, with the most serious gap arising in the area of protection. Providing protection and assistance to internally displaced persons, the UN Secretary-General underscored in 1997, is a humanitarian issue that has been left to "fall in the gaps of existing mandates of agencies."[21] Towards correcting this problem, the Secretary-General's Programme for UN Reform assigned the Emergency Relief Coordinator (ERC), who heads the Office for the Coordination of Humanitarian Affairs (OCHA), the responsibility of "ensuring" protection and assistance for internally displaced persons.

Under the ERC's leadership, a number of important steps, previously recommended by the Representative of the Secretary-General, for strengthening collaborative arrangements subsequently were implemented. These included the creation of a central database containing information on situations of internal displacement worldwide,[22] the designation of focal points in the various relevant UN agencies and international NGOs, and more regular inter-agency discussion, in particular through the IASC, of specific situations of internal displacement. However, these and other measures undertaken at headquarters in support of the collaborative approach have been slow to translate into effective action in the field.

In January 2000, the need to devise more effective institutional arrangements for the internally displaced was brought to the fore, more precisely to the UN Security Council, with a proposal for major structural reform. The US Representative to the Security Council, Ambassador Richard Holbrooke, forcefully argued that the existing system of diffusing responsibility for the internally displaced among various agencies had created a situation in which accountability was lost and essential leadership lacking.[23] The international response to one of the world's most serious situations of internal displacement, in Angola, which the US Ambassador had appraised first-hand, was cited as illustrative of the problems of coordination and of a general international approach that was failing the internally displaced. In a comment reminiscent of the Secretary-General's Programme for Reform of two and half years earlier, Ambassador Holbrooke lamented that internally displaced persons "fall in between the bureaucratic cracks." To remedy this institutional gap, he advocated, as the Representative had done earlier, the idea of fixing responsibility for the internally displaced in a single agency, specifically the UNHCR. Though the UNHCR did not directly speak to the proposal that it become the global lead agency for internally displaced persons, the agency did indicate that it was "committed to greater engagement with the internally displaced" and "would be ready to take the lead" for the internally displaced in certain circumstances.[24]

In the end, the consensus that emerged among IASC agencies was to continue the conventional approach of a collaborative effort, with the important caveat that concerted efforts needed to be undertaken to mend the now widely exposed shortcomings that continued to arise in practice. As a first step, it was felt that the field-level arrangements for coordination of the UN response to situations of internal displacement needed to be more clearly set out. The existing arrangement whereby the responsibility for coordinating UN action for protecting and assisting internally displaced persons rests with the UN Humanitarian or Resident Coordinator of the country concerned (or, if a lead agency has been designated for that country, the Country Director of that agency) was reaffirmed.[25] However, in recognition that this role, especially as it concerns protection, has not been well understood and still less carried out in the past, it was acknowledged that the specific elements of this responsibility needed to be spelled out.[26] Overall, this responsibility would entail recommending an allocation within the UN country team of responsibilities for protecting and assisting internally displaced persons and ensuring that gaps in the response to their needs are systematically addressed. The effective exercise of this responsibility is now to be reflected in a comprehensive plan of action for each country situation of internal displacement. In addition, the Humanitarian/Resident Coordinator is to engage in dialogue with the national and local authorities to impress upon them their primary responsibility for protecting and assisting the internally displaced in conformity with international human rights and humanitarian law, using the Guiding Principles as a frame of reference. The Coordinator also is to suggest to the national and local authorities ways in which the United Nations can help to strengthen their capacity to provide protection and promote durable solutions. Lobbying the authorities for unimpeded humanitarian access on the part of international agencies to internally displaced populations at risk and in need is expected. Moreover, the Humanitarian/Resident Coordinator may enlist the assistance of the Emergency Relief Coordinator in bringing concerns regarding the protection and assistance of the internally displaced to the Security Council. It is noteworthy that, in a separate development, the Security Council has specifically asked to receive information on situations where internally displaced persons are vulnerable to the threat of harassment.[27]

Given the tendency in the past of the Coordinators, especially the Resident Coordinators, to be extremely reluctant to raise protection issues,[28] it was recognized that they would require support in this regard. To this end, the Humanitarian/Resident Coordinator is expressly encouraged to draw on organizations with special protection expertise, in particular: the Office of the High Commissioner for Human Rights, the International Red Cross and Red Crescent Movement, the United Nations Children's Fund (which has a clear protection mandate under the Convention of the Rights of the Child), and the UNHCR. Ultimately, however, the Humanitarian/Resident Coordinator is responsible for ensuring that the UN country team satisfactorily addresses protection issues. In this connection, it is essential that the Coordinators receive training on human rights and international humanitarian law and have a solid knowledge of the Guiding Principles. Moreover, to promote a greater sense of accountability, their responsibilities for ensuring protection of the internally displaced should, in addition to having been stated in a general directive, be reflected in the terms of reference as well as performance evaluations for each individual Coordinator. At the same time, it is equally important that the Humanitarian/Resident Coordinators be assured that, in exercising leadership and taking stands on protection matters, they will receive the support and backing of the humanitarian and political leadership at UN headquarters.

Clarifying coordination arrangements and responsibility undoubtedly has been a useful exercise in terms of underscoring to Humanitarian/Resident Coordinators the importance of their long-standing responsibility towards the internally displaced and providing them with guidance and a commitment of support for carrying it out effectively. And yet, especially as this exercise essentially restated the coordination arrangements and responsibilities that have been in place for several years now, the challenge remains one of ensuring that these coordination arrangements and responsibilities are actually fulfilled. To this end, in a second important step taken by the IASC, a Senior Inter-Agency Network on Internal Displacement, headed by a Special Coordinator on Internal Displacement attached to OCHA, was established in September 2000. The purpose of this task force is to assess the effectiveness of field-level coordination arrangements for internally displaced persons (IDPs) in a number of specific situations and, on this basis, to make recommendations for improving the overall international response. The Guiding Principles are to serve as a frame of reference for this analysis.

In an interim report of its findings, the Network reported that the review missions "have confirmed that there are serious gaps in the UN and agency humanitarian response to the needs of IDPs – especially their protection."[29] These gaps were attributed to a lack of clear agency responsibilities for some sectors, such as protection and shelter, and inadequate efforts by some agencies in their designated areas of responsibility. Despite the increased attention given to the issue at the level of headquarters, in several cases the problem of internal displacement was found to be a low priority in the field. Nor was it a priority of donors, with the result that resource constraints for protection and other activities for the internally displaced are often considerable. The most critical gap, however, continued to be insufficient attention to protection and human rights concerns. In Burundi, for instance, the Network found that, in a situation in which "serious violations" of human rights were being committed against internally displaced persons with near total impunity, "the majority of humanitarian agencies focus their efforts on the provision of assistance, while inadequate attention is given to the protection needs of the displaced."[30]

To address these serious shortcomings in the international humanitarian response, the Network recommended the establishment of an Office or Unit for IDP Coordination in OCHA, headed by a senior official and supported mostly by staff seconded by key UN agencies and NGOs. Its functions would include: monitoring situations of internal displacement worldwide; undertaking systematic reviews of selected countries and making recommendations to address identified operational gaps; providing training, guidance, and expertise to the Humanitarian/Resident Coordinators, UN country teams, and other humanitarian agencies on issues of internal displacement; supporting resource mobilization for responding to particular situations; global awareness-raising and advocacy efforts; and developing inter-agency policy on internal displacement. In situations where the Unit determines there to be a clear operational gap in the international response to internal displacement and/or a clearly identified need for strengthened coordination, two options are available. Either an adviser on internal displacement will be appointed to support the Humanitarian/Resident Coordinator in carrying out her/his responsibility of ensuring the coordination of international action to protect and assist internally displaced populations, or one of the operational agencies will be assigned primary responsibility for fulfilling this task. In effect, it should perform the function of a central mechanism for coordinating the international humanitarian response to internal displacement – a component that, as noted above, always has been considered by the Representative of the Secretary-General to be essential to an effective collaborative approach. The IDP Unit became fully operational in January 2002. It remains to be seen whether the unit will manage to bridge the coordination gap that has so often hampered effective responses to the protection and assistance of internally displaced persons. As regards the situation of Afghanistan, despite it being at the centre of international attention in late 2001 and into 2002, in February 2002 the critical issue of international institutional arrangements and responsibility for the more than 1 million internally displaced Afghans remained unclear and unsettled.

In addition to ensuring effective coordination, it is also critical that collective institutional approaches to internal displacement be universal and unbiased. Notwithstanding the increased attention to the issue of internal displacement in recent years, many serious situations, including in countries where UN agencies and other international humanitarian organizations are present and conceivably could respond, have remained off the agenda of inter-agency discussions to date. The mandate of the new Unit reinforces this selectivity bias. According to its terms of reference, the office will undertake to review the international response and make recommendations for its improvement regarding "selected countries." Criteria for the selection of the countries with which it is to be concerned have not yet been specified. With limited staff (eight professionals), the Unit inevitably will need to set priorities. Arguably, situations of internal displacement that traditionally have been neglected by the humanitarian community are all the more in need of focused international attention and support. By including such situations in its review process, the new IDP Unit could make an important contribution to a more consistent worldwide response.

Institutional arrangements for responding to the global crisis of internal displacement need to be comprehensive in another sense. More specifically, efforts to improve institutional arrangements should not be limited to the humanitarian, human rights, and development communities alone. The conflict situations to which peace-keeping and peace-enforcement operations are deployed invariably involve situations of actual or potential internal displacement; their personnel should, as a matter of course, be assigned protection responsibilities for the internally displaced and receive training on the Guiding Principles. The role of international financial institutions also must be taken into account. Moreover, collaborative relationships regarding internal displacement need to be fostered with regional and sub-regional organizations, which are becoming increasingly engaged in the issue and have a valuable role to play. Civil society, which is at the forefront of efforts to protect and assist internally displaced persons, must be more actively engaged, especially at the local level. The sheer enormity of the global crisis of internal displacement means that efforts to address it effectively will depend on the collective efforts of the various relevant actors within and across the international, regional, national, and local institutional frameworks for response.

Protection strategies

As the Network's missions and many other analyses of situations of internal displacement worldwide have found, addressing the protection needs of internally displaced persons traditionally has not been a priority of the international response. Relief and development agencies have not considered the protection of human rights to be among their responsibilities.[31] Moreover, they have been reluctant to take up protection issues, out of concern that doing so risks jeopardizing their relationship with the authorities and, as a consequence, perhaps also their safe access to populations in need. And yet, as an official of the International Committee of the Red Cross (ICRC) once asserted, and as has repeatedly been found, protection is "a prerequisite for the efficacy of assistance."[32] Simply providing aid to persons whose physical security is under threat not only neglects their protection needs but can actually exacerbate and perpetuate their plight, for instance by providing a false sense of security, shoring up repressive regimes, fostering long-term dependency, and even resulting in so-called "well-fed dead." Persons at risk of internal displacement – and worse – have argued this point powerfully. A Muslim under threat of "ethnic cleansing" in Bosnia once urged: "We do not need food, we are not starving to death. We are being persecuted and we prefer to be hungry for a week than not to sleep every night, in fear of being beaten, raped, or killed."[33] One analyst has likened the required response to internal displacement to a tripod, with relief, development, and protection each forming a leg; whereas the relief and development legs are more less at full length, the protection leg is severely stunted and as a result the whole apparatus is unstable.[34]

Recently, however, significant headway has been made towards lengthening the protection "leg." An important catalyst for this process has been the Secretary-General's Programme for UN Reform, in which a central theme is that responsibility for addressing human rights concerns is no longer to be limited to the human rights machinery of the United Nations (which in any case remains poorly funded and with only limited field capacity) but shared by the entire UN system. This insistence on the integration or "mainstreaming" of human rights has given concrete meaning to Article 1 of the UN Charter specifying that "promoting and encouraging respect for human rights and for fundamental freedoms for all" counts among the main purposes of the world body. When considered together with the Programme for Reform's conclusion that the protection of the internally displaced was an issue falling in the gaps between the mandates of existing agencies, the directive to integrate responsibility for human rights throughout the UN system also points the way towards filling this protection gap.

Although the language of "mainstreaming human rights" has been taken on board by relief and development agencies, the translation of these words into meaningful action in situations of internal displacement has been impeded by a lack of clarity as to the meaning of protection for internally displaced persons. To tackle this problem, in 1998 the Representative of the Secretary-General, the Emergency Relief Coordinator, and the High Commissioner for Human Rights jointly prepared a discussion paper setting out their understanding of the meaning of protection for the internally displaced and of their respective roles in providing it. The scope of this exercise then was expanded to encompass the IASC as a whole, which in 1999 adopted a common policy paper on the protection of internally displaced persons.[35] Considering the traditional reluctance in inter-agency forums even to discuss issues of protection, this policy paper breaks important ground in the international response to internal displacement.

The IASC policy paper represents the first concerted attempt by international human rights, humanitarian, and development organizations to come to grips conceptually with their collective responsibility to ensure protection for internally displaced persons. The paper presents itself as "part of a growing effort on the part of international organizations to address more proactively the needs of internally displaced persons ... and to act when the rights of internally displaced persons are being violated."[36] The Guiding Principles, which the IASC earlier had endorsed and encouraged agencies to apply, provided critical guidance in this exercise. Recall that the Principles elaborate what protection should mean for the internally displaced. Furthermore, the Principles' embodiment of a comprehensive concept of protection, encompassing not only political and civil rights but also economic, social, and cultural rights, helped to place issues related to the delivery of relief and development assistance in a human rights framework. They articulate, for instance, the right of internally displaced persons to food, to medical care, and to income-generating opportunities. Moreover, as noted earlier, the Principles reinforce the responsibility of humanitarian agencies "to give due regard to the protection needs and human rights of internally displaced persons and take appropriate measures in this regard" (Principle 27). Indeed, while recognizing the specific protection mandate and expertise of particular agencies such as the Office of the High Commissioner for Human Rights and the International Committee of the Red Cross, the IASC policy insists that "[a]ll agencies providing humanitarian assistance to internally displaced persons have a responsibility to consider how the design and implementation of their assistance activities might best contribute to promoting protection of the internally displaced." An annex to the policy paper outlines how each individual IASC member agency and NGO defines its protection role with the internally displaced.

Drawing on a framework for protection developed by the ICRC, the IASC policy paper sets out three sequential but overlapping strategic areas of protection for internally displaced persons: environment-building, responsive action, and remedial action.[37] The first strategy of environment-building seeks to create and consolidate a global environment conducive to full respect for the rights of internally displaced persons. Activities of this nature include: dissemination and promotion of the Guiding Principles; training on the Principles; support to strengthen national and local protection capacity; early warning and preventive action to protect populations against arbitrary displacement; and "active and assertive" advocacy of the rights of the internally displaced vis-à-vis the national and local authorities, non-state actors, and the international community. Responsive protection action, meanwhile, seeks to prevent and/or alleviate the immediate effects of an emerging or established pattern of abuse. In addition to continuing a number of the activities of environment-building, such as advocacy, responsive action by IASC agencies for protecting internally displaced persons would include: establishing an international presence among populations whose physical safety is under threat; transmitting information on human rights violations to the UN human rights machinery; integrating protection in the design of assistance programmes; supporting community-based protection; and addressing the particular protection needs of women and children. Finally, remedial action aims at restoring dignified living conditions through rehabilitation, restitution, and reparation. In situations of internal displacement, this would include: advocacy of the right of the displaced to safe and voluntary return or resettlement as well as of their right to restitution of or compensation for property lost in the course of displacement; providing reintegration and development assistance; and supporting peace-building and conflict resolution efforts.

Efforts are now required to support the translation of this protection policy into practice. A particularly important mechanism in this regard should be the comprehensive plan that is to be developed by the Humanitarian/Resident Coordinator in order to address the protection and assistance needs of internally displaced persons in each situation of internal displacement. Similarly, the IASC protection policy should serve as a frame of reference in the work of the inter-agency IDP Unit in recommending strategies for addressing protection gaps arising on the ground. Concrete examples of protection strategies, which should be drawn upon, are provided in the *Manual on Field Practice in Internal Displacement* and the *Handbook on Applying the Guiding Principles on Internal Displacement*, which were developed in response to requests from operational agencies and NGOs for guidance on measures they could take to promote and protect the rights of internally displaced persons.[38] For the moment, however, there is much evidence to suggest that a critical gap remains between the agencies' description in the IASC policy paper of their respective protection role with the internally displaced and the actual fulfilment of this role in specific situations. Herein lies the particular value of the protection paper: in addition to providing guidance to the IASC members on what protection means for internally displaced persons, it provides a strong basis for holding them accountable for fulfilling the protection role that they have indicated they are prepared to perform, both individually and collectively. If consistently applied, the protection policy would go a long way towards ensuring a more predictable and effective international response to the most neglected and critical need of the internally displaced.

The IASC policy paper on protection makes an important contribution to developing a strategic framework for protection as well as to promoting a more predictable and coordinated international response to the protection needs of internally displaced persons. Still further thought is required, however, to develop additional protection strategies for responding to the various circumstances and protection needs that arise in situations of internal displacement. For example, strategies must be developed for addressing situations of internal displacement occurring in countries where state consent, which is a key criterion of humanitarian response by the UN agencies and most international humanitarian organizations and NGOs, is not forthcoming. Many of the world's most serious situations of internal displacement occur in countries where the government refuses international offers of assistance in addressing the plight of internally displaced persons, sometimes even denying the very existence of these populations. The international system must find ways of engaging these countries and persuading them to address the protection and assistance needs of their internally displaced populations in partnership with international agencies. Strategies also need to be developed with respect to non-state actors, including not only insurgent forces but also corporate entities, which, it is increasingly apparent, are often implicated in the displacing actions of government and insurgent forces. Most critically, greater attention must be paid to developing and implementing preventive strategies for protecting populations against arbitrary displacement and stemming the growing numbers of persons afflicted by this tragic phenomenon.

Conclusion

The international community is unquestionably better equipped today to address the protection needs of the internally displaced than it was 10 years ago when the issue was first placed on the international agenda. A normative framework has been developed with the formulation of the Guiding Principles on Internal Displacement, which spell out the rights of the internally displaced and the obligations of states, insurgent forces, and international actors towards them. Institutional arrangements, though by no means fully defined or dependable in ensuring international protection and assistance for internally displaced persons worldwide, nonetheless have been tested and are being strengthened. Protection is finally now recognized as a priority concern for the internally displaced and strategies are beginning to be drawn up in order to provide it. An international protection regime for internally displaced persons has begun to take shape. This chapter has traced these developments in the normative, institutional, and strategic frameworks for protecting internally displaced persons and particularly as regards the latter two elements, which are still at a formative stage, identified a number of steps for furthering this process.

Even so, to constitute a comprehensive regime, the three separate components of standards, institutional mechanisms, and strategies of protection, once firmly in place, must collectively amount to a cohesive and consistent system of effective response. The Guiding Principles on Internal Displacement, which not only are the culmination of efforts to develop a normative framework but also have acted as a catalyst in the development of more effective institutional arrangements and the design of protection strategies, are already proving to be an important unifying thread. Beyond simply consolidating and clarifying the norms of special importance to internally displaced persons and thereby laying down the legal foundation of protection, the Principles are serving as a tool for building an entire protection regime for internally displaced persons. They are helping to raise international awareness and concern regarding the problem of internal displacement. The Principles are enabling more systematic and informed monitoring of situations of internal displacement worldwide, serving as a benchmark against which to measure the actions of governments, local actors, and international agencies, and thereby promoting greater accountability. They also are facilitating advocacy efforts seeking to address identified shortcomings of response and, at the same time, are fostering the development of strategies and field practices for remedying these. By providing local, regional, national, and international actors with a common framework through which to analyse and address situations of internal displacement, the Principles are providing a basis for forging critical partnerships within and among these different levels of response. Moreover, as universal norms of protection, the Principles could contribute greatly to ensuring a non-discriminatory response. The global crisis of internal displacement requires no less than a truly global solution.

Notes

1. Peter Salama, Paul Spiegel, and Richard Brennan of the Epidemic Intelligence Service and International Emergency and Health Branch, National Center for Environmental Health, Centers for Disease Control and Prevention, and the Health Unit of the International Rescue Committee, "No Less Vulnerable: The Internally Displaced in Humanitarian Emergencies," *The Lancet*, vol. 357, no. 9266, 5 May 2001.
2. From a first count in 1982, which found 1.2 million internally displaced persons in 11 countries, by 1986 the total had risen to an estimated 11.5–14.0 million in 20 countries, and by 1997 to more than 20 million in over 35 countries. By 2001, there were upwards of 25 million persons in more than 40 countries who were internally displaced as a result of armed conflict and persecution. These figures do not include the many millions more persons uprooted within their own countries as a result of other causes, such as natural or human-made disasters and large-scale development projects. Figures from Roberta Cohen and Francis M. Deng, *Masses in Flight: The Global Crisis of Internal Displacement*, Washington DC: Brookings Institution, 1998, p. 5, citing US Committee for Refugees (USCR), "State of the World's IDPs," paper prepared for Brookings, 1996; "Principal Sources of Internally Displaced Persons as of December 31, 2000," Table 5 in USCR, *World Refugee Survey 2001*, Washington DC: Immigration and Refugee Services of America, 2001, p. 8.
3. UNHCR, *Refugees*, issue 117, Winter 1999, front and back cover.
4. United Nations Security Council, "Presidential Statement, 13 January 2000," UN Doc. S/PRST/2000/1, 13 January 2000.
5. "When Is a Refugee Not a Refugee," *The Economist*, 3 March 2001, p. 22.
6. See *Compilation and Analysis of Legal Norms, Part II: Legal Aspects Relating to the Protection against Arbitrary Displacement. Report of the Representative of the Secretary-General on Internally Displaced Persons*, UN Doc. E/CN.4/1998/53/Add.2, 11 February 1998, paras. 56–64.
7. Universal Declaration of Human Rights, Article 14 (1).
8. *Compilation and Analysis of Legal Norms. Report of the Representative of the Secretary-General on Internally Displaced Persons*, UN Doc. E/CN.4/1996/52/Add.2, 5 December 1995; and *Compilation and Analysis of Legal Norms, Part II: Legal Aspects Relating to the Protection against Arbitrary Displacement*, 1998.
9. *Compilation and Analysis*, Part I, para. 413.
10. UN Commission on Human Rights Resolution 1996/52, 19 April 1996; UN General Assembly Resolution 52/130, 12 December 1997.
11. *Guiding Principles on Internal Displacement. Report of the Representative of the Secretary-General on Internally Displaced Persons to the UN Commission on Human Rights*, UN Doc. E/CN.4/1998/54/Add.2, 11 February 1998.
12. The legal basis of each of the Principles is detailed in the *Compilation and Analysis* and summarized in the *Annotations* to them. See *Compilation and Analysis*; and Walter Kälin, *Guiding Principles on Internal Displacement: Annotations*, Studies in Transnational Legal Policy, no. 32, Washington DC: American Society of International Law and the Brookings Institution Project on Internal Displacement, 2000 (which also reproduces the *Compilation and Analysis* in Annex II).
13. *Guiding Principles on Internal Displacement*, "Introduction: Scope and Purpose," para. 2.
14. Kälin, *Annotations*, pp. 3 and 12.
15. *Report of the Secretary-General on the Protection of Civilians in Armed Conflict*, UN Doc. S/1999/957, 8 September 1999, Recommendation 7; UN Security Council Resolution 1286 (2000) regarding "*regroupement*," or forcible relocation, in Burundi.

16. See *Report of the Representative of the Secretary-General on Internally Displaced Persons to the UN Commission on Human Rights at its Fifty-Seventh Session*, UN Doc. E/CN.4/2001/5, 17 January 2001, paras. 37–49.
17. Ibid., paras. 29–36.
18. For resolutions, reports, and other information regarding the mandate of the Representative of the Secretary-General on Internally Displaced Persons, see www.unhchr.ch/html/menu2/7/b/midp.htm.
19. See *Report of the Representative of the Secretary-General on Internally Displaced Persons to the Commission on Human Rights at its Forty-Ninth Session*, UN Doc. E/CN. 4/1993/35, 21 January 1993.
20. In 1993, the General Assembly recognized that the UNHCR's activities could be extended to internally displaced persons when refugee and internally displaced populations are so intertwined that it would be practically impossible or inappropriate, that is inhumane, to assist one group and not the other. See General Assembly, "Office of the United Nations High Commissioner for Refugees," Resolution 48/116, 20 December 1993. In a staff directive, the UNHCR specified that, in addition to this "refugee link," its involvement with the internally displaced would require; a request or authorization from the Secretary-General or a competent principal organ of the United Nations; the consent of the state concerned, safe access to the populations concerned; and adequate resources and capacity. See UNHCR, IOM-FOM 33/93, Geneva, 28 April 1993, reproduced in UNHCR, Division of International Protection, *UNHCR's Operational Experience with Internally Displaced Persons*, Geneva: UNHCR, September 1994.
21. United Nations Secretary-General, *Programme for UN Reform*, UN Doc. A/51/950, July 1997, para. 186.
22. Namely, the Global IDP Database operated by the Norwegian Refugee Council on behalf of the IASC; see www.idpproject.org.
23. Statement by United States Ambassador Richard C. Holbrooke, Permanent Representative of the United States to the United Nations, to the UN Security Council debate on Promoting Peace and Security: Humanitarian Assistance to Refugees in Africa, 13 January 2000, *USUN Press Release #6(00)*, 13 January 2000.
24. See UNHCR, "Internally Displaced Persons: The Role of the United Nations High Commissioner for Refugees," Geneva, 6 March 2000; available at www.unhcr.org.
25. UN Resident Coordinators were first charged with the responsibility of coordinating assistance for internally displaced persons by General Assembly Resolution 44/136 of 15 December 1989. Humanitarian Coordinators, meanwhile, have had an express responsibility for monitoring, facilitating, and coordinating UN assistance to internally displaced persons since 1994; see Inter-Agency Standing Committee, "Terms of Reference of the Humanitarian Coordinator, 9 December 1994." The Secretary-General's 1997 *Programme for UN Reform* specified that the responsibility of the Humanitarian/ Resident Coordinators for the internally displaced included protection as well as assistance. It also allowed for the possibility of designating, in individual country situations, a lead agency to assume this responsibility. *Programme for UN Reform*, para. 192.
26. Inter-Agency Standing Committee, "Supplementary Guidance to Humanitarian/ Resident Coordinators on their Responsibilities in Relation to Internally Displaced Persons," April 2000; available at www.idpproject.org/links_UN.htm#15.
27. UN Security Council Resolution 1296, 19 April 2000, on the protection of civilians in armed conflict.
28. "Most resident coordinators," it was observed in 1995, "do not consider protection of human rights concerns to be compatible with their responsibility of serving as Resident Representative of UNDP [United Nations Development Programme]. In this position, they work closely with Governments on development programmes and fear that

involvement with protection issues will exceed their mandate or result in their expulsion." *Report of the Representative of the Secretary-General on Internally Displaced Persons to the Commission on Human Rights at its Fifty-First Session*, UN Doc. E/CN. 4/1995/50, para. 159.

29. "Interim Report from the Special Coordinator of the Network on Internal Displacement," April 2001, p. 2; available at www.idpproject.org/links_UN.htm#16.

30. "Report of the Senior Inter-Agency Network on Internal Displacement, Mission to Burundi, 18–22 December 2000, Findings and Recommendations," 23 December 2000; available at www.idpproject.org/links_UN.htm#16.

31. In 1995, for instance, the Representative observed that "because human rights protection is not a central concern or function for most relief and development agencies ... protection has not received the attention it deserves." *Report of the Representative of the Secretary-General on Internally Displaced Persons to the Commission on Human Rights at its Fifty-First Session*, UN Doc. E/CN.4/1995/50, para. 184.

32. Jean-Luc Blondel, "Assistance to Protected Persons," *International Review of the Red Cross*, September–October 1987, p. 453.

33. UNHCR, *Information Notes on Former Yugoslavia*, no. 1/94, January 1994, p. ii.

34. Jacques Cuenod, Refugee Policy Group, interview in Geneva, 1996, cited in Cohen and Deng, *Masses in Flight*, p. 255.

35. IASC, "Policy Paper on the Protection of Internally Displaced Persons," adopted 6 December 1999; available at www.idpproject.org/links_UN.htm#16.

36. Ibid.

37. International Committee of the Red Cross, *Protection: Doing Something about It and Doing It Well. Report of the Workshop, 18–20 January 1999*, Geneva: ICRC, 1999.

38. *Manual on Field Practice in Internal Displacement: Examples from UN Agencies and Partner Organizations of Field-based Initiatives Supporting Internally Displaced Persons*, Inter-Agency Standing Committee Policy Paper Series no. 1, New York: United Nations Office for the Coordination of Humanitarian Affairs, 1999; Susan Forbes Martin, *Handbook on Applying the Guiding Principles on Internal Displacement*, New York: Brookings Institution Project on Internal Displacement and the United Nations Office for the Coordination of Humanitarian Affairs, 2000.

9

Reconciling control and compassion? Human smuggling and the right to asylum

Khalid Koser

Even before the events of 11 September 2001, most industrialized states were rushing to legislate against human smuggling. Human smuggling represented a "threat" to state borders. It threatened to undermine immigration controls and, in the words of the Western media at least, to produce a "flood" of illegal immigrants. At the same time, state measures against smuggling were implicitly supported by evidence that smugglers can exploit their "clients." In the aftermath of September 11, still further impetus has been added to the concern to combat smuggling, because it has been suggested this is one way that potential terrorists might cross international boundaries.

The momentum among industrialized states to put an end to human smuggling has left asylum advocates in a quandary. There is growing evidence that a significant proportion of asylum seekers rely on smugglers to enter industrialized nations. At the same time, smuggling clearly can and often does expose them to vulnerability. On the one hand, advocates are concerned that successfully stamping out smuggling would deprive many people of the possibility of seeking asylum in the industrialized nations, but on the other hand they can hardly be seen to support a system that exploits asylum seekers. At least partly as a result of this quandary, asylum advocates – including the United Nations High Commissioner for Refugees – have been surprisingly reticent in the human smuggling debate, and legislation by states to stop smuggling has advanced more or less unchallenged, despite its implications for asylum seekers. As a result, some advocates have begun to lament that the debate has already been lost, and that asylum in industrialized nations may be doomed.

In contrast, this chapter adopts a rather more optimistic perspective. It proceeds from a state-centred perspective, and accepts (and supports) the inevitable momentum towards trying to combat human smuggling. At the same time, it tries to demonstrate that human smuggling cannot be stopped unless asylum is centralized in the policy framework. In other words, the rise of human smuggling on political agendas actually presents a fairly unusual opportunity for state security and the individual security of asylum seekers to be combined – for control and compassion to be reconciled. The role of asylum advocates, it is suggested, should be to suggest realistic asylum policies that might operate in tandem with anti-smuggling policies.

Human smuggling and asylum: An impasse

It has become almost axiomatic to state that the study of human smuggling is in its infancy, and lacks conceptual clarity and an empirical base. In fact this is no longer quite true. There is a growing body of empirical literature, with a global focus, that has begun to reveal some of the complexities of human smuggling.[1] There has been one serious attempt at theoretical analysis, which perceives migration as a business and represents smuggling as the illicit aspect of that business.[2] A wide range of policy reports and documents have been published on the subject, culminating in two substantial reports commissioned by the International Organization for Migration (IOM)[3] and the United Nations High Commissioner for Refugees (UNHCR).[4] Finally, policies are currently being developed, especially in Europe, to combat smuggling. Of particular note is the growing distinction within the policy framework between human smuggling and trafficking. Trafficking is associated with the clandestine movement of people in order to place them in an exploited position in the labour market – for example as a prostitute. Human smuggling is simply the clandestine movement of people across international borders.

Asylum has received rather less attention in the human smuggling debate. The first point to make is that no research has seriously considered the links between asylum and trafficking; instead the focus of the limited existing research has been on human smuggling. A small number of case studies, relying only on small samples, suggests that an increasing proportion of asylum seekers in Europe rely on the services of smugglers, at least in part as a result of restrictive asylum policies.[5] In his report for the UNHCR, John Morrison went so far as to suggest that asylum seekers are so reliant on smugglers to enter Western Europe that to stamp out smuggling would in effect bring an end to asylum there.

At the same time, this limited empirical research has suggested that, through their exposure to smugglers, asylum seekers may be exposed to sources of economic, social, and political insecurity.[6] The principal source of economic vulnerability identified by Koser resulted from the high prices charged by smugglers: in his case study, Iranians had paid between US$4,000 and US$6,000 to be smuggled to the Netherlands. This indebted either asylum seekers or their friends and family at home to money lenders, and one implication is that asylum seekers can spend their first years in destination countries in poverty as they send home any income. For some respondents, economic vulnerability was heightened by the significant periods they spent in transit countries *en route* to the Netherlands, where they also became exposed to a source of political vulnerability, namely the risk of being identified and repatriated by the local authorities. Finally, social vulnerability arose where, largely as a result of the migration routes used by smugglers, a significant number of asylum seekers had arrived in a destination country to which they had not planned to migrate. In some cases they were thus isolated from potentially supportive social networks based on friends and family in other West European countries.

Faced with this dilemma, asylum advocates have been unsure how to intervene in recent policy debates. Put simply, to stop human smuggling would relieve asylum seekers from increased insecurity, but might at the same time close the door on one of the last possibilities for seeking asylum – at least in Europe. In contrast, policy makers are pressing ahead to combat both human smuggling and trafficking. Policy is being made at both the unilateral and multilateral level. It is focusing in particular on penalizing smugglers, intercepting smuggled migrants in transit countries, and returning the victims of smuggling from destination countries.

The intervention of asylum advocates in the policy debate has been largely ineffectual. Some have questioned the assumptions on which policy is currently being made. For example, one of the impetuses for policy action has been the idea that human smuggling is inextricably linked with the smuggling of drugs and arms, yet there is very insubstantial evidence. States have spoken in vague terms about a threat to state security, yet existing data do not even allow an accurate estimate of the scale of human smuggling. Nevertheless, policy makers are forging ahead. Other advocates have asked that policy makers think through in greater detail the implications for asylum of stopping smuggling – yet, as Morrison puts it, states seem willing to sacrifice asylum to put an to end smuggling. Still other advocates have argued for a relaxation of asylum policies, so that asylum seekers no longer need to rely on smugglers to reach Western Europe. Given the political climate in particular, it is hard to envisage any government in the industrialized countries seriously countenancing a relaxation of asylum regulations.

In the spirit of being forward-looking, this chapter proposes an alternative strategy for intervening in the human smuggling policy debate. Its starting point is to be realistic. Whatever the reservations of asylum and other advocates, states are trying, and will continue to try, to stop smuggling. This impetus has only increased in the aftermath of the events of 11 September 2001. For any policy intervention to be taken seriously, it needs to support this overarching aim. What this paper tries to demonstrate, therefore, is that anti-smuggling policies cannot succeed unless asylum is centralized in policy frameworks. In other words, the goal of state security cannot properly be satisfied without incorporating the asylum agenda. Far from accelerating the end of asylum in Europe, the concern to stop smuggling provides an opportunity to revisit asylum.

There are three main arguments. First, asylum seekers may well comprise the single largest group of migrants currently being smuggled, particularly in Europe. Any attempt to combat smuggling without focusing attention on the particular circumstances of the group most affected by the process is unlikely to succeed. Second, the rise of smuggling is at least in part an unintended consequence of restrictive asylum policies. The implication is not necessarily that asylum policies should be relaxed, but that it is impossible to de-couple anti-smuggling policies from asylum policies; they are inextricably linked. Third, current anti-smuggling initiatives address the symptom and not the cause of the problem. It is unlikely that penalizing smugglers and intercepting or even returning migrants will stop smuggling. Instead, human smuggling needs to be understood as a business, which is quickly developing its own momentum. A better way to undermine this business is to remove demand for its services – and this demand is largely from asylum seekers.

The growing reliance of asylum seekers on smugglers

Any attempt to estimate the number of migrants who are smuggled – let alone more specifically the number of asylum seekers who are smuggled – is hounded by problems of an empirical and conceptual nature. Where data do exist they are mainly in the European context. For this reason alone, this section and the remainder of this chapter focus on this region. That is not to underestimate the global significance of smuggling or the growing incidence of the smuggling of asylum seekers throughout the industrialized world.[7]

A starting point is data on illegal migration. Even in Europe, and even for legal migration, data are often inaccurate, out of date, and incomparable. Obviously these problems are amplified for data on illegal or irregular migration.[8] For example, different states in the European Union use different methods for deriving their data. One of the most common sources is data on apprehensions at the border. Thus, 40,201 migrants were apprehended in 1998 after illegally entering Germany,[9] 9,700 during the period January–May 1999 in Austria,[10] and 16,500 in 1998 in the United Kingdom.[11]

However, there are real difficulties in translating these data into an estimate of the number of migrants who have been smuggled. Perhaps the most important is that many, perhaps the majority, of those who have been smuggled may not be apprehended at the border. Where smuggling is successful – and indications are that it often is – migrants often elude border controls. Thus data on apprehensions at the border would need to be combined with data on in-country apprehensions to provide a base figure from which to try to derive a proportion for those who have been smuggled.

The most widely quoted figure for the scale of human smuggling in Europe was produced in 1994 by Jonas Widgren, who tried to overcome some of these data problems.[12] It is worth briefly rehearsing how he arrived at his numbers.[13] He estimated in 1993 that there were 240,000–360,000 illegal migrant entries in Western Europe. The figure was calculated on the basis of extrapolations of how many illegal migrants were apprehended in a destination and the known number of migrants apprehended in transit countries on their way to that destination. Analysis of border control data showed about 60,000 apprehensions. Widgren then estimated, based on discussions with border control authorities, that at least four to six times that number entered their destination undetected. Of this total, Widgren further estimated that between 15 and 30 per cent had used the services of smugglers during part of their journey, amounting to a total of between 36,000 and 108,000 smuggled migrants in 1993.

If Widgren's multipliers are applied to the more recent data on border apprehensions provided above, then the estimate needs to be updated significantly. Approximately the same ranges – 250,000–350,000 illegal migrants, of whom about 35,000–100,00 have been smuggled – are reached using data only for Germany, Austria, and the United Kingdom. Although plainly the basis for these calculations is open to question, this preliminary longitudinal analysis would seem to reinforce a growing consensus that the scale of human smuggling has grown substantially since Widgren made his estimate in 1994.

At the same time, Widgren made a separate calculation for the proportion of asylum seekers who had been smuggled. In 1993 there were about 690,000 asylum seekers in Western Europe, of whom Widgren estimated about half were not in need of protection. Of those without a well-founded claim for asylum, Widgren estimated that 20–40 per cent had been smuggled, amounting to between 70,000 and 140,000 smuggled asylum seekers in Western Europe in 1993. Again, the number of asylum seekers in Europe has increased dramatically since 1993 – given rising applications combined with continuing backlogs – and an update of Widgren's calculations would show a significant increase in the number of smuggled asylum seekers.

Other observations can be made on Widgren's data. First, it is interesting that he made an estimate of the smuggled proportion only of those asylum seekers whose applications he estimated to be unfounded. The limited available research suggests that there are no grounds to assume a distinction in terms of their interaction with smugglers between those who do and do not have a well-founded claim for asylum. In an admittedly small-scale study, for example, Morrison found a high incidence of smuggling among a group of respondents who had been granted refugee status in the United Kingdom.[14]

Additionally, and centrally for the thrust of the argument of this chapter, it is significant that Widgren estimated that there were more asylum seekers in Europe than illegal migrants, and that a greater proportion of asylum seekers (without a well-founded claim) than of illegal migrants had been smuggled (20–40 per cent compared with 15–30 per cent). According to his lowest estimation, a total of 106,000 smuggled migrants included 70,000 asylum seekers (or 66 per cent). His highest estimation was of a total of 248,000 smuggled migrants, including 140,000 asylum seekers (or 56 per cent). In other words, asylum seekers account for the majority of those who are smuggled.

Moreover, there are several reasons to believe that a significantly larger proportion of asylum seekers than estimated by Widgren have used smugglers since he made his estimate. One is empirical: the German Federal Refugee Office estimated in December 1997 that about 50 per cent of asylum seekers in Germany were smuggled into the country; the Dutch Immigration Service upgraded its estimate of 30 per cent in 1996 to 60–70 per cent in 1998.[15]

The second reason is more conceptual and less quantifiable. The proposition is that the distinction between illegal migrants and asylum seekers may no longer be as clear as was proposed by Widgren. Even though the 1951 Convention Relating to the Status of Refugees specifically guards against it, there are indications that asylum seekers' use of smugglers may sometimes negatively affect their claims in some countries. For example, recent grounds for rejecting asylum applications in the United Kingdom have been reported to include the failure to present supporting documentation and the presentation of fraudulent documentation. Yet empirical research has identified both of these as specific outcomes of smuggling.[16] The implication is that a proportion of people who have fled their country of origin as "refugees" are not lodging asylum claims in their country of destination because of their means of arrival. In other words, at least a part of the illegal migrant population is composed of people who should be applying for asylum.

The principal conclusion to carry forward from this section is that the limited available data indicate that the majority of people who use the services of smugglers in Western Europe are asylum seekers. The implication is that any attempt to combat smuggling, at least in Western Europe, cannot ignore asylum. A lack of data precludes an extension of this argument to industrialized nations in any other parts of the world.

Smuggling as an unintended consequence of asylum policy

Further support is added to the conclusion from the preceding section when the focus is narrowed from the level of large-scale data to that of the individual experiences of asylum seekers. This section draws on earlier in-depth research among a sample of 32 smuggled Iranian asylum seekers in the Netherlands.[17] Just as there are reservations about the large-scale data, so there are reservations about small-scale research that relies on an unrepresentative sample. Still, many of the findings from this research have since been supported by research in other contexts (especially Morrison[18]). They demonstrate in an empirical sense why asylum seekers need to rely on the services of smugglers in Europe. In addition to supporting the findings in the previous section, this section adds another argument for centralizing asylum in the human smuggling policy framework. The point is to show that, to a large extent, the growth of smuggling has been a direct result of restrictive asylum policies.[19]

It is important to stress at once that the suggestion here is not that the smuggling of asylum seekers has evolved only as a result of restrictive asylum policies in Europe (and elsewhere in the industrialized world). In some senses there is nothing new about smuggling – Jewish refugees were smuggled out of Germany and occupied Europe before and during the Second World War. In this case, the purpose of smuggling was to assist people to escape from a regime; this was also one of the purposes served by smugglers in the Iranian case study.[20] Smugglers concealed people temporarily in Iran, moved them clandestinely across borders into neighbouring Turkey and Pakistan, and organized tickets, visas, and other documents to help people escape.

What is different is the contemporary political context in receiving countries. Jewish refugees, and after them refugees smuggled from the communist bloc, were openly resettled in Western Europe or North America. They comprised one element in what has been described as an interest-convergence between refugees and receiving states, where it was politically and economically beneficial to settle refugees. Rightly or wrongly, this is clearly no longer perceived to be the case. West European countries have spent the past decade or so reducing or completely closing formal resettlement quotas for refugees and introducing a wide range of policies targeted at reducing the number of asylum seekers and changing their distribution.[21] These policies include the imposition of visa requirements, carrier sanctions, the closure of resettlement channels, Readmission Agreements, and exclusion from state welfare and support after arrival. For earlier refugees, the main purpose of smuggling was to assist them to leave their country of origin and escape persecution. For contemporary asylum seekers, assisting them to enter destination countries and overcome restrictive asylum policies is just as important.

Empirical evidence for this assertion can briefly be provided through a focus on the interaction between asylum seekers and smugglers in the Iranian case study. Besides assisting asylum seekers to escape Iran, smugglers served two other main purposes. The first was to plan migration routes across Europe. Only 18 of the 32 respondents were willing to answer detailed questions about their migration routes, although all but one nevertheless reported that smugglers had been involved in planning the route. Only three had flown directly from Iran to the Netherlands; the remainder had arrived via transit countries, namely Turkey, Pakistan, Romania, or Hungary, and in some cases a combination of these. A relatively restricted number of routes were therefore used, which may be an indication that a limited number of routes have become well established and maintained by smugglers. For 24 of the 32 respondents, smugglers also played a part in the choice of destination. In most cases smugglers apparently provided information about the Netherlands, which added to impressions already formed by asylum seekers. In the case of 11 respondents, however, the choice of a final destination was in effect taken out of their hands, being determined by the routes operated by smugglers at that time.

The second additional function of smugglers was to facilitate migration and entry into transit and destination countries. Facilitating migration included organizing travel tickets and documents. The three principal entry strategies employed by smugglers were clandestine entry, entry with false documentation, or entry without documentation. In general these different strategies coincided with different migration routes. Clandestine entry was the main strategy for entering neighbouring Turkey or Pakistan from Iran. In contrast, a majority of respondents reported using false documentation to enter Romania or Hungary. The dominant strategy for entering the Netherlands was to present oneself to the immigration police without a passport.

This last strategy illustrates that smugglers not only assisted asylum seekers to enter the Netherlands, but also often provided information on how to remain in the Netherlands after arrival. For example, the absence of a passport hinders personal identification, the identification of a country of origin, and the identification of transit countries. The strategy thus offsets the possibility for immediate deportation. Most smugglers were reported to have had very accurate information on the asylum procedure in the Netherlands. Some respondents had even been advised how to respond during interviews with immigration officials, for example by not naming as transit countries those countries with which the Netherlands had signed a Readmission Agreement.

As asylum policies have become more restrictive, it has become increasingly difficult for asylum seekers legally to arrive in Western Europe independently. Indeed so-called "spontaneous" asylum seekers have been one of the primary targets of asylum policy since the early 1990s:[22] visa requirements and carrier sanctions delimit legal access to most EU countries from many countries of origin; the Dublin Convention, which came into force on 1 September 1997, provides a mechanism for determining which country in Europe is responsible for examining an application for refugee status and combines with Readmission Agreements to restrict movement within Europe; and tighter border controls restrict entry into destination states. One outcome has been that, in order to reach and enter a West European state, asylum seekers have few options other than to migrate illegally. And illegal migration channels appear to be dominated by smugglers. In this context, the primary conclusion to be taken from this section is that the growth of smuggling has been one of the unintended consequences of restrictive asylum policies. Policies to combat smuggling are unlikely to succeed without addressing the causes of smuggling, one of which is current asylum policies.

Smuggling as a business

It is precisely the failure of current initiatives to combat smuggling to address the root causes of smuggling that makes many commentators suspect that these initiatives are unlikely to succeed. To reiterate, there are three principal targets for current policies. The first is the stricter penalization of smugglers, including operatives such as truck drivers who knowingly transport migrants. It has been argued for quite some time that, in the absence of a serious penalty, smugglers face few disincentives – smuggling for them is often relatively risk-free. The second is to try to intercept smuggled migrants in transit countries, and a particular emphasis has recently been placed on stiffening border controls in Central and Eastern Europe, and especially in the Balkans.[23] The third policy target is to return smuggled migrants and the victims of trafficking.

Each of these three approaches proceeds from assumptions that have not yet been properly tested through empirical research. Another way of stating this is that there is not yet enough empirical research with which to refute the basis of these policies. Limited research, however, does at least raise questions about the longer-term efficacy of each policy.

One assumption that even limited research can undermine is the monolithic view of smuggling as a large, organized, and multinational network. It is clear that smugglers have diverse motivations and resources, and that organization levels vary widely. They range from what appear to be transnational criminal networks, for example in the case of smuggling from Fujian Province in China, to what have been described in the United States as "mom and pop" outfits, where smuggling originating in Latin America can be a low-level family or local community affair. What is ironic here is that policy tends towards the assumption that all smuggling is of the former character, yet the policy of penalizing smugglers and their operatives is far more likely to be effective against the latter type of organization.

One anecdote from the Iranian research illustrates the point. The view of most respondents in this case was that smuggling between Iran and the Netherlands was well organized at a transnational scale. They were effectively handed on through a chain of smugglers located in the origin, transit, and destination countries. Interestingly, most reported that smugglers were nationals of the countries in which they operated. One respondent reported that she had spent 90 days in Hungary before eventually moving on to the Netherlands. It transpired that, soon after she had arrived there, the person who was supposed to be organizing her onward travel had been arrested. She received a call from an individual in Turkey, who advised her to wait until another person contacted her in Hungary. Within 30 days contact was made, and the "new smuggler" went about making the necessary arrangements for travel to the Netherlands. The point is that arresting a single smuggler in this sort of organization is unlikely to have any impact other than to delay migration by a few weeks while a replacement is activated.

Similarly, although closing down smuggling routes by controlling borders in transit countries may have a short-term effect, the policy is unlikely to have a lasting effect. As mentioned in the previous section, the Iranian asylum seekers interviewed by Koser who had been smuggled to the Netherlands had arrived through a limited number of routes. What is interesting is that one respondent reported that a friend of hers had been smuggled from Iran to the Netherlands three years earlier, and that her route had been completely different, via Spain. The implication would seem to be that smugglers are responsive to opening and closing opportunities for negotiating entry into Western Europe. Again, it is worth making the point that this probably applies only to well-organized and relatively large-scale smuggling outfits, and nobody knows how important these are in the totality of smuggling in Europe.

The third strand of the current policy approach is to return smuggled migrants and the victims of trafficking. Previously, the return of other irregular migrants has proceeded in most West European states on an ad hoc basis, and significant numbers have rarely been returned. Partly in response to these experiences, a number of states are taking more innovative approaches, by providing assistance for returnees and focusing on their sustainable reintegration in the country of origin.[24] The underlying assumption for these policies is that return is an important anti-smuggling weapon: returning migrants who have often paid large sums to be smuggled, and showing that their investment has in effect been wasted, should be a disincentive for them and others to pay smugglers.

There are several question marks over this assumption, even if return could be achieved on a significant scale. There are several reasons, for example, to suppose that returnees may re-migrate and even employ smugglers once more. One is that in certain countries – Iran is one example – returnees can face the risk of persecution simply by virtue of having claimed asylum abroad. In other words, even if their claims were not well founded when they first migrated, returning them in effect puts them under threat and in a situation in which their claims would be better founded. The implication is that these returnees might genuinely need to escape Iran, and might have no option other than to turn once again to smugglers. Another reason returnees may be threatened, and may need to escape once again, is that when return is prompt they are likely to go back to their country of origin heavily in debt, having borrowed money in order to pay for a smuggler in the first place. Finally, evidence at least from the Iranian case study was that asylum seekers increasingly adopt a fairly sanguine attitude. When I asked respondents what would happen were they to be returned, many said that they would raise more money and "try again." They said that they probably would not try the Netherlands again, but instead would head for another West European country.

There are similarly reasons to question whether the example set by returning one migrant really would be a disincentive for others in the local community to migrate. Again the unfortunate assumption is that all asylum seekers are voluntary migrants. Put simply, whatever the experiences of others, if an individual believes that his or her life is at threat, then he or she is probably willing to take a risk to escape. It may be that an effort is made to avoid the smuggler used by the unsuccessful migrant, but the impression from many origin countries is that there is often a substantial market in smuggling from which to choose. Alternative analyses suggest that smugglers actively recruit migrants. Even where asylum seekers are not leaving for broadly political reasons, the reality is that it can take years before rejected asylum seekers are returned from destination countries in Western Europe. These are years during which a debt to a smuggler can be paid off and additional money earned.

The implication of the preceding analysis is that current policy initiatives, even when combined as an integrated set of strategies, seem unlikely to have a lasting impact on smuggling. The reasons that have been alluded to add up to a picture of smuggling as an emerging "business," which can be organized at a transnational level, can overcome policy interventions and can compete for migrants in origin countries. This notion tallies closely with that of Salt and Stein,[25] who view smuggling (they used the term "trafficking") as the illegitimate aspect of a set of institutions that can manage migration and that move people primarily for the motive of profit. Kyle adopts a broadly similar approach,[26] arguing that smuggling has emerged as a consequence of the commodification of migration.

The conception of smuggling as a business is certainly open to criticism, although empirical efforts to test the model of Salt and Stein have largely endorsed it.[27] Nevertheless, it holds some interesting implications for policy interventions. Arguably the most effective way to stop the momentum associated with a successful business is to attack its demand base. Smuggling, in other words, flourishes because there is a demand for it. Penalizing smugglers, imposing border controls, and returning smuggled migrants are unlikely substantially to affect demand. Where is the demand for smugglers? In large part it is with asylum seekers.

Conclusions

This chapter has deliberately proceeded from a state-centred perspective with a focus on combating human smuggling. The alternative perspective – centred on the individual and focusing on the right to asylum – would have yielded different conclusions, for example concerning the growing vulnerability of asylum seekers exposed to smugglers and the threat to asylum of combating smugglers. Yet, by focusing on a state perspective, the chapter has demonstrated the importance of bridging the gap between these two perspectives. It has been argued that to combat smuggling successfully necessitates centralizing asylum in the policy framework. Asylum seekers probably account for over half of all those smuggled into Western Europe. Smuggling has evolved in part as an unintended consequence of restrictive asylum policies. And, from a business perspective, asylum seekers comprise the core demand for the services of smugglers. The smuggling and asylum agendas cannot be decoupled. The smuggling agenda cannot "sacrifice" asylum, because it cannot proceed without centralizing asylum. Perhaps ironically, the inextricability of the links between smuggling and asylum open up a genuine opportunity for reconciling state security with the individual security of asylum seekers and refugees.

For asylum advocates, attempting to convince policy makers that they cannot successfully combat human smuggling without focusing on asylum is, however, just the first step. The most important next step is to try to suggest realistic policy proposals. Not to combat human smuggling is not a realistic proposal; neither is decriminalizing smuggling; and neither is relaxing asylum policies. There are at least three other options, however, that are seriously worth considering, each of which could be exercised in parallel with ongoing anti-smuggling policies.

One is in-country processing – or alternatively perhaps in-country protection. The only reason asylum seekers need to employ smugglers is because they need to move. If movement can be eliminated from asylum, then so can smuggling. Proceeding from the same logic, a second option is processing in a local country, to which legal access can be guaranteed. A third is to reintroduce quotas in West European countries. As has been established, another reason asylum seekers employ smugglers is because they have no legal alternatives. Quotas would mean that at least a proportion of asylum seekers could enter asylum countries legally.

None of these options is new, which means that states have at some time been willing to consider them. At the same time, experience has shown that each option can be very problematic. Furthermore, they would need to be implemented at a scale so significant as probably to be politically unpalatable. Australia's relatively generous resettlement quota, for example, has made no impact on the number of people arriving "spontaneously" to apply for asylum. The conclusion from this chapter is that, if there is a political will to stop smuggling, there also needs to be the will to provide alternatives for asylum seekers.

Faced with this conclusion, policy makers may decide that it is better simply to turn a blind eye to human smuggling. Popular support can be won through isolated successes and buoyant labour markets can continue to exploit illegal immigrants. Pity the poor asylum seekers.

Notes

1. David Kyle and Rey Koslowski, eds., *Human Smuggling: A Global Perspective*, Baltimore, MD: Johns Hopkins University Press, 2001.

2. John Salt and Jeremy Stein, "Migration as a Business: The Case of Trafficking," *International Migration*, vol. 35, no. 4, 1997, pp. 467–494.
3. John Salt and Jennifer Hogarth, *Migrant Trafficking in Europe*, Final Report for the Internation Organization for Migration, 2000.
4. John Morrison, *The Trafficking and Smuggling of Refugees*, Final Report for the UNHCR, 2000.
5. Khalid Koser, "Social Networks and the Asylum Cycle," *International Migration Review*, vol. 31, no. 3, 1997, pp. 591–611; Khalid Koser, "Negotiating Entry into 'Fortress Europe'," in Philip Muus, ed., *Exclusion and Inclusion of Refugees in Contemporary Europe*, Utrecht: ERCOMER, 1997; John Morrison, *The Cost of Survival*, London: Refugee Council, 1998.
6. Khalid Koser, "Out of the Frying Pan and into the Fire," in Khalid Koser and Helma Lutz, eds., *The New Migration in Europe*, London: Macmillan, 1998, pp. 185–198.
7. Kyle and Koslowski, *Human Smuggling: A Global Perspective*.
8. James Clarke, "The Problems of Evaluating Numbers of Illegal Migrants in the EU," in Philippe de Bruycker, ed., *Regularisations of Illegal Immigrants in the EU*, Brussels: Free University of Brussels, 2000, pp. 13–22.
9. Barbara Fröhlich, SOPEMI (Système d'Observatoire Permanent des Migrations Internationales) report for Germany, 1999.
10. Gudrun Biffl, SOPEMI report for Austria, 1999.
11. John Salt, SOPEMI report for the UK, 1999.
12. Jonas Widgren, "Multilateral Cooperation to Combat Trafficking in Migrants and the Role of International Organizations," discussion paper presented to the IOM Seminar on International Responses to Trafficking in Migrants and the Safeguarding of Migrant Rights, Geneva, 1994.
13. Salt and Hogarth, *Migrant Trafficking in Europe*.
14. Morrison, *The Cost of Survival*.
15. Morrison, *The Trafficking and Smuggling of Refugees*.
16. Koser, "Social Networks and the Asylum Cycle."
17. Ibid.
18. Morrison, *The Cost of Survival*.
19. Khalid Koser, "Asylum Policies, Trafficking and Vulnerability," *International Migration*, vol. 38, no. 3, 2000, pp. 91–112.
20. Koser, "Social Networks and the Asylum Cycle."
21. Koser, "Out of the Frying Pan and into the Fire."
22. Khalid Koser, "Recent Asylum Migration in Europe: Patterns and Processes of Change," *New Community*, vol. 22, no. 1, 1996, pp. 151–158.
23. International Organization for Migration, *Migrant Trafficking and Human Smuggling in Europe*, Geneva: IOM, 2000.
24. Khalid Koser, *The Return of Rejected Asylum Seekers and Irregular Migrants*, Geneva: IOM, 2001.
25. Salt and Stein, "Migration as a Business: The Case of Trafficking."
26. David Kyle, *Transnational Peasants: Migrations, Networks and Ethnicity in Andean Ecuador*, Baltimore, MD: Johns Hopkins University Press, 2000.
27. International Organization for Migration, *Migrant Trafficking and Human Smuggling in Europe*.

10

Post-conflict peace-building and the return of refugees: Concepts, practices, and institutions

B. S. Chimni

Over the past two decades repatriation has come to be designated by the international community of states and the Office of the United Nations High Commissioner for Refugees (UNHCR) as *the* solution to the global refugee problem. Local integration and resettlement in third countries have been de-emphasized and remain only in name; these are applicable to less than 1 per cent of the world's refugees. The reasons for this are widely known. In the case of the North, it is because, put bluntly, the refugee no longer conforms to the acceptable demographic or political profile of being male, white, Christian, and anti-communist. In the case of the South, the emphasis on repatriation is, among other things, a function of its impoverishment and the absence of international burden-sharing. Consequently, the UNHCR has been under great pressure to facilitate and promote the return of refugees even when conditions in the countries of origin are far from ideal. Indeed, the organization admits that, in recent years, "repatriation has frequently involved various forms of pressure or duress."[1]

The current focus on repatriation has ensured that research on the subject is driven by the objective not of promoting the goal of protection but of ensuring early return. Legal experts have given relevant texts suitable interpretations[2] and social scientists have grounded the need to return refugees in the discourse of human rights.[3] On the other hand, little information is available about what has happened to those refugees who have returned home, as few authors have attempted to investigate the experiences of the returnees themselves.[4] Although repatriation may bring to an end the "refugee cycle," "it also coincides with the beginning of a new cycle."[5] Despite this, even the UNHCR initially failed to undertake a review of the consequences of withdrawal from a returnee-populated area or the scaling down of its presence.[6] As a result, the organization was unable to assess the longer-term consequences of its interventions, albeit in the past few years it has undertaken a more systematic survey of returnees and their concerns, and issued guidelines on returnee monitoring.[7]

But there is a more fundamental problem that afflicts returnees, especially in post-conflict situations. The absence of any systematic theoretical and legal framework regarding "post-conflict" situations precludes the possibility of the "peace-building" strategy being derived from a critical and integral understanding of the problems that characterize "post-conflict" societies or of refugees who return to them. The result is an array of measures that have rarely been arrived at in consultation with refugees and returnees, are often coercive or work at cross purposes with each other, and have been assembled in the matrix of a neo-liberal economic vision which, among other things, does not focus on the international causes of internal conflicts and excludes the possibility of building a participatory "post-conflict" state. To put it differently, the basic problem with the policies relating to the return of refugees to "post-conflict" societies and their reintegration is the poverty of the epistemology deployed to identify suitable measures that will go to promote "sustainable return." This is the underlying and unifying theme of the chapter, which also suggests ways of moving forward.

The chapter is structured as follows. First, I critically examine the concepts of a "post-conflict society," "peace-building," and "sustainable return," and I review the contemporary debate on the subject of the international law of repatriation. I then look at the dynamics of return and explore possible policy solutions to promote sustainable return. Certain specific problems of returnees are dealt with, such as land and property rights, the existence of land mines, the issue of the disarmament, demobilization, and reintegration of former combatants, and the problem of statelessness. This is followed by an examination of the role of UN agencies such as the UNHCR and the Security Council and the problems of coordination arising from numerous UN agencies being involved in peace-building. The final section suggests conclusions and recommendations.

Post-conflict building and repatriation – A critical view

What is a "post-conflict" society?

Since the early 1980s – around the time of the increased flow of refugees from the South to the North in a non–Cold War context – the solution of voluntary repatriation has come to be designated by the UNHCR as the "ideal solution."[8] By the 1990s, however, states had become increasingly impatient with the standard of "voluntariness," for it constrained return in less than ideal conditions, in particular to societies experiencing internal conflicts. This invited a research focus on repatriation under conflict and yielded the somewhat convenient conclusion that most refugees return spontaneously to their country of origin and that they do so even when the conflict has not ended; the real question was whether the policies of host states left the refugees with any alternative.[9] Be that as it may, the movement of "spontaneous" refugees still left large numbers of refugees in host states. Therefore, at some point, the distinction between spontaneous and involuntary returns had to blur.

The need to legitimize return called for the invention of new and flexible conceptual categories. One such concept is that of a "post-conflict" society. Its elastic nature is best illustrated with reference to a World Bank review in 1998 of its activities in "post-conflict" countries that included Angola, Bosnia, Burundi, Cambodia, Rwanda, and Uganda, all of which, as Crisp points out, "continue[d] to experience high levels of social conflict, violence, human rights abuse and large-scale population displacement."[10] Indeed, the World Bank itself was forced to admit that "drawing a line between 'conflict' and 'post-conflict' is difficult."[11] The UNHCR also accepts this fact but does not abandon the term "post-conflict":

As some of these conflicts subside, states re-emerging from the ashes of destruction may still undergo periods of intense if sporadic fighting. It may therefore be inaccurate, even misleading to talk about "post-conflict situations" as such as situations do not pass directly from conflict to post-conflict conditions. *We shall however retain the term "post-conflict" to indicate those war-torn societies that are undergoing some form of transition towards a more peaceful and stable situation.*[12]

According to Macrae, what is "problematic is the fact that no criteria are given in UNHCR policy statements which indicate when a particular state might be accurately identified as embarking on 'some form of transition', nor when it is seen to end."[13] What then are the meaning and purpose of blurring the distinction between war and peace? These appear to be fourfold: first, and most obvious, it legitimizes the involuntary repatriation of refugees; second, the representation of conflict situations as normal allows donor states to disengage from them; third, the assumption of normalcy allows structural adjustment programmes to be launched by the international financial institutions (IFIs); fourth, it helps circumscribe the meaning of "peace-building" by equating it with a rudimentarily accountable state. This last conclusion calls for further elaboration.

The meaning of "peace-building"

"Peace-building," according to the UNHCR, refers "to the process whereby national protection and the rule of law are re-established. More specifically, it entails an absence of social and political violence, the establishment of effective judicial procedures, the introduction of pluralistic forms of government, and the equitable distribution of resources."[14] Likewise, the UN Secretary-General (UNSG) has noted that "peace-building may involve the creation or strengthening of national institutions, monitoring elections, promoting human rights, providing for reintegration and rehabilitation programmes, and creating conditions for resumed development."[15] But, in the absence of serious effort on the part of the international community to assist "post-conflict" societies (as has been the experience from Afghanistan to Rwanda), the possibilities of reconstruction and peace-building are dim. The UNSG has himself noted in this regard the lack of support for a number of key reconstruction and development projects in post-conflict societies. Although a dozen bilateral agencies are said to have created "peace-building funds," "only a small proportion – less than 15 per cent – of all emergency assistance is being devoted to anything like reconstruction or peace-building."[16] To put it differently, the developed North appears to have successfully disengaged from post-conflict situations even as it incessantly talks of "peace-building." Highly visible situations such as Afghanistan in early 2002 may appear to challenge such a conclusion, but this represents the minority of cases; moreover, the level of actual investment and support is often not what is promised. The absence of aid has compelled post-conflict societies to turn to IFIs for succour. Unfortunately, however, the IFIs prescribe conditions that, in the final analysis, tend to reproduce the general environment for conflict. So often the meaning of "an accountable post-conflict state" turns out to be a state that can come to terms with the legitimacy crises and social protest generated by the implementation of a neo-liberal adjustment programme and greater integration into the world economy. In the circumstances, formal compliance with the norms of liberal democracy changes very little. The parties that participate in "post-conflict" elections either lack any alternative programme to neo-liberalism or do not have the resources to push it through. In most cases "there is a pathological fixation on aping World Bank and IMF prescriptions."[17] The contesting political parties are, in other words, not interested in the dismantling and reconstruction of "the unstable, non-hegemonic, violent, exploitative and inefficient neo-colonial state."[18] The state may well continue to be repressive and its resources continue to be privatized. There is therefore little possibility of implementing a social agenda that pays heed to people's needs and frames policies with their participation. Instead, the state continues to manipulate divisions within society, making the renewal of conflict a distinct possibility.

"Post-conflict" Afghanistan, with an interim government in office in early 2002, exemplified the absence of alternative policies even more. The reconstruction effort there was led by the United Nations Development Programme (UNDP), the World Bank, and the Asian Development Bank in the absence of any capacity of the Afghan state to shape policies. According to Woodward, "a fatal flaw in all 'post-conflict' economic policy is the prior need of a functioning government and functioning proper financial and legal institutions – to absorb the aid delivered, adopt the necessary policies, and implement those decisions. Such governments do not exist under conditions of war and severe war damage – human capital is the scarcest commodity after wartime, but the Afghan case may well be the worst."[19] This has compelled others to insist on the need to make use of local capacities and agencies.[20] Yet mere local participation, in the absence of a state-led policy of self-reliance, will not guarantee development. Bosnia–Herzegovina "provides a clear object lesson": despite a relatively high level of donor financing, "a fully successful five-year World Bank-led program of recovery and reconstruction has not yet, six years after the peace agreement, generated economic development."[21]

Unfortunately, even those concerned with the protection of returnees are now hoping to collaborate closely with the IFIs. The UNHCR has initiated "a common dialogue" with the World Bank in order to develop a coherent approach to reintegration and on the funding instruments required to finance this strategy.[22] This is difficult to understand, because the World Bank can provide leadership only on macroeconomic and external debt issues. Furthermore, the UNHCR "lacks the legal or ethical framework offered by international refugee law or equivalent humanitarian principles to guide its interventions in this area of its work."[23] This framework is necessary because, as the UNHCR itself concedes, "structural adjustment programmes may in the … short run … exacerbate the causes of conflict":[24]

[E]conomies wrecked by years of war, famine and/or military dictatorships, which lack infrastructure and management skills, cannot overnight adjust to the changing dynamics of the global economy. The primary objective of external and local efforts in post-conflict countries should, therefore, be the establishment of peace with justice. It is unrealistic to ask countries like Rwanda, Somalia or Sierra Leone to embrace an "orthodox" adjustment programme to rebuild their devastated economies when healing the deep scars of war and genocide alone is such a daunting task.[25]

Even the UN Secretary-General apparently recognizes the potential role of IFIs in creating or exacerbating conditions of conflict in Africa. He has therefore pleaded with the IFIs to ease the conditionalities that normally accompany loans and to initiate "a 'peace-friendly' structural adjustment programme."[26] Indeed, the World Bank has assessed its own experience in post-conflict situations and concluded that conventional wisdom can turn into folly during post-conflict periods. Criticisms arose from inside and outside the Bank that "too much emphasis was put on a rapid pace of reforms in Haiti, Rwanda, and Uganda, as opposed to concentrating on maintaining low inflation and a convertible currency, and approaching other reforms more incrementally."[27] The World Bank thus concluded, for example, that an emphasis on immediate and widespread privatization in post-conflict situations "may well not enhance the prospects for sustained, equitable development, and may even make them worse."[28] How, then, are conditions of "sustainable return" to be created without heavy doses of non-conditional development aid?

Ensuring "sustainable return"

"Sustainable return" is, in any case, more than simple development. It has been described as a situation which, ideally, assures returnees' physical and material security and consolidates a constructive relationship between returnees, civil society, and the state.[29] It calls for four kinds of insecurities to be addressed, namely, physical insecurity, social and psychological insecurity, legal insecurity, and material insecurity.[30] The absence of conditions that ensure security on all these fronts could compel the refugee to seek asylum again. The elimination of these insecurities anticipates "peace building" and "reconciliation" leading to "reintegration." "Reconciliation" "refers to the consolidation of constructive social relations between different groups of the population, including parties to the conflict."[31] The relationship between reconciliation and reintegration is critical because reconciliation has to precede reintegration.[32] "Reintegration" is described as "a process which enables formerly displaced people and other members of their community to enjoy a progressively greater degree of physical, social, legal and material security."[33]

This holistic understanding points, first, to the need to view repatriation and reintegration as an integral process in order to ensure sustainable return. This is borne out by experience in the field. The Mozambican repatriation and reintegration programme (1992–1996) was the largest undertaken by the UNHCR, involving 1.7 million returnees. In its review of the programme, the UNHCR noted (i) that "the organization had a tendency to treat repatriation and reintegration as two distinct and consecutive tasks, with the latter being considered in a systematic manner only when the former was well on the way to completion";[34] and (ii) that "the planning of the Mozambican operation might have been more effective if the repatriation and reintegration program had been conceived in an integrated manner, involving not only the country of origin, but also the countries of asylum."[35] In its *General Conclusion on International Protection* of 1994, the UNHCR's Executive Committee also stressed the fact that "for repatriation to be a sustainable and thus truly durable solution to refugee problems it is essential that the need for rehabilitation, reconstruction, and national reconciliation be addressed in a comprehensive and effective manner." If this understanding is correct, it only goes to underline the limits of the role of the UNHCR in creating conditions of sustainable return; the UNHCR possesses neither the human nor the material resources to undertake this task. Second, "sustainable return" requires that problems relating to property and housing rights, land mines, the demobilization and disarming of combatants, and statelessness be resolved. In both these respects, a coordinated response by UN agencies is needed. I shall return to these matters later.

International law of repatriation and post-conflict return

Meanwhile, the category "post-conflict society" continues to undermine the international law of repatriation with the idea of voluntariness at its core. Scholars of international law – especially those of industrialized countries – have invoked the changed historical and political context (the end of the Cold War) to revert to an arid positivism to contest that repatriation has to be voluntary under the 1951 Convention. Earlier, the category "safe return" was invented in the context of "temporary protection" regimes to give legitimacy to involuntary return. A critical review of these developments is therefore in order.

The standard of voluntary repatriation

The General Assembly of the United Nations resolved in Resolution 8(I) of 1946 as follows:

[N]o refugees or displaced persons who have finally and definitely, *in complete freedom*, and after receiving full knowledge of the facts, including adequate information from the governments of their countries of origin, expressed valid objections to returning to their countries of origin ... shall be compelled to return to their country of origin. (Emphasis added)

Later, the Statute establishing the Office of the High Commissioner for Refugees (1950) called upon governments to cooperate with it *inter alia* through "assisting the High Commissioner in his efforts to promote *voluntary* repatriation." The need to respect the voluntary character of repatriation has since been reaffirmed in Conclusions adopted by the Executive Committee of the High Commissioner's Programme. Although these conclusions represent "soft law," they have a binding character so far as UNHCR is concerned. The two well-known texts are Conclusion No. 18 (XXXI) and Conclusion No. 40 (XXXVI), both of which emphasized the *voluntary* character of refugee repatriation. Thus, Conclusion No. 18 "stressed that the essentially voluntary character of repatriation should always be respected." Likewise, Conclusion No. 40 states:

The repatriation of refugees should only take place at their *freely expressed wish*; the voluntary and individual character of repatriation of refugees and the need for it to be carried out *under conditions of absolute safety*, preferably to the place of residence of the refugee in his country of origin, should always be respected. (Emphasis added)

At the regional level, Article V of the Organization of African Unity's 1969 Convention Governing the Specific Aspects of Refugee Problems in Africa is categorical: "The essentially voluntary character of repatriation shall be respected in all cases and no refugee shall be repatriated against his will."

In the same vein, the influential 1984 Cartagena Declaration on Refugees affirmed "the voluntary and individual character of repatriation of refugees and the need for it to be carried out in conditions of absolute safety." In short, there was for long little doubt that international law prescribed the standard of voluntary repatriation to states and international institutions.

The 1951 Convention, "safe return," and the standard of voluntary repatriation

In recent years it has been argued with reference to the 1951 Convention on the Status of Refugees that it does not call for the application of the standard of voluntary repatriation because the requirement of voluntariness is not mentioned therein; it finds a place only in the Statute of the Office of the High Commissioner for Refugees. Therefore, according to Hathaway, "it is wishful legal thinking to suggest that a voluntariness requirement can be superimposed on the text of the Refugee Convention."[36] In his opinion, "once a receiving State determines that protection in the country of origin is viable, it is entitled to withdraw refugee status."[37] The need to respect the standard of voluntariness was more easily dispensed with in the context of temporary protection regimes established in Europe to deal with a mass influx of refugees from former Yugoslavia; the concept of "safe return" was invented and replaced the standard of voluntary repatriation.

What both the Hathaway thesis and the concept of "safe return" do is to substitute the judgement of the refugee with the decision of the host state. First, this view entirely overlooks the fact that, although there is no reference to voluntary repatriation in the text of the 1951 Convention, the involuntary return of refugees would in practice amount to *refoulement*.

Second, by denying that the refugees' subjective assessment of the situation is an important element to be taken into account in the decision to return, it proceeds to redefine the meaning of the term "refugee." As Goodwin-Gill has perceptively observed, such a view "effectively substitute[s] 'objective' (change of) circumstances for the refugee's subjective assessment, thereby crossing the refugee/non-refugee line."[38] In other words, the objectivism that characterizes the concept of "safe return" disenfranchises refugees by eliminating their voice in the process leading to the decision to deny or terminate protection. Indeed, it tends to substitute the subjective perception of state authorities for the experience of the refugee. It also allows the state to decide whether it is necessary for refugees to return to the place from where they fled. A negative determination merely carries the disenfranchisement of the refugee a step further. It means not only forcible return but also a whole host of difficult problems relating to property claims, employment, and education, which deny returnees a life of dignity.

Third, it is forgotten that voluntary repatriation by definition does *not* take place in ideal circumstances and for that reason operates prior to the use of cessation clauses. The latter *inter alia* come into play when "the circumstances in connection with which he has been recognized as a refugee have ceased to exist" (Article 1C(5) of the 1951 Convention). Since repatriation takes place prior to the moment when the cessation clause can be invoked, there is an understandable emphasis on voluntariness, which is precisely why involuntary return amounts to *refoulement.*

Fourth, it disregards the fact that for decades industrialized states gave an "exilic" interpretation to the 1951 Convention. As Hathaway himself concedes, "the formal distinction between refugee status and permanent asylum remained intact, but the right to revoke status due to change of circumstances fell into disuse."[39] The past practice of states has to be taken into account in giving the Convention meaning today. This practice not only has probative value but arguably modified the content of the treaty.[40]

Fifth, it is the element of voluntariness that ensures the sustainability of return, especially in a post-conflict situation. Involuntary return tends to inject an element of instability into the situation, in particular when it involves large numbers of refugees. It also accentuates the problem through a containment effect because it discourages people to leave and seek asylum. Furthermore, the increasing presence of the UNHCR in the country of origin makes it easy to classify asylum seekers as economic migrants rather than refugees.

The developing world and involuntary repatriation

The ongoing effort to modify the standard of voluntary repatriation is increasingly supported in practice by developing countries that seek to return refugees in less than ideal conditions. Impoverished host states seek to return refugees for a whole range of reasons. These include concerns that the presence of displaced people can be a source of instability or insurgency, economic concerns, concerns about environmental degradation, problems of unemployment of host populations, and the possibility of political conflict. Refugees, on the other hand, want to return because "the alternative is to languish in camps and to live indefinitely off handouts, or to suffer from harassment, round-ups, arbitrary detention, extortion and even deportation."[41] Of course, going back "home" also means regaining citizenship rights and often meeting an emotional need. But, as would be evident, the refugee will be able to regain citizenship rights and feel at home only if the preconditions for sustainable return prevail, and these are most often marked by their absence. To put it differently, the principal reason for refugees returning against their wishes is the economic crisis that afflicts much of the third world and the absence of international burden-sharing, which leads poor host states to take measures (inexcusable nevertheless) that compel refugees to return. The Northern states, on the other hand, support this process because it is more economical than sustaining camps and also legitimizes involuntary return from their own territories.

Mass influx and involuntary repatriation

It is sometimes argued that, from the point of view of international law, where *prima facie* determination of refugee status is arrived at in the context of a mass influx, it might be odd to insist that repatriation must be viewed from an individual angle.[42] But the fact of mass influx has no direct bearing on the standard that controls return. The standard of return should be linked to the principle of *non-refoulement*, which applies not merely to those granted refugee status or an intermediate humanitarian status but also to asylum seekers. Furthermore, as was seen, the OAU Convention prescribes the standard of voluntary repatriation. Finally, in the context of mass influx and return there is available, as Zieck has pointed out, "a body of *leges speciales*" constituted by the numerous bilateral and tripartite agreements entered into by the UNHCR, the country of asylum, and the country of origin to regulate the modalities of return.[43] According to Zieck,

[the agreements] presuppose that the refugees whose return is thus regulated (regardless of whether or not their entitlements derive simultaneously from other applicable agreements, universal or regional customary international law, or even *comitas gentium*) are unrepatriable ... and that both UNHCR and the country of refuge are *bound* to observe the prohibition of *refoulement* (regardless of whether or not that obligation may be derived from other sources of law).[44]

The UNHCR and spontaneous repatriation

Although the standard of voluntary repatriation binds the UNHCR, should it stand by when refugees take the decision to go back to conditions that are less than ideal? In its *Handbook on Voluntary Repatriation: International Protection*, the UNHCR specifies the circumstances in which it would "facilitate" voluntary repatriation of refugees during conflict:

Respecting the refugees' right to return to their country at any time, UNHCR may facilitate voluntary repatriation when refugees indicate a strong desire to return voluntarily and/or have begun to do so on their own initiative, even where UNHCR does not consider that, objectively, it is safe for most refugees to return. *This term should be used only when UNHCR is satisfied that refugees' wish to return is indeed voluntary and not driven by coercion.*[45]

However, in a non-ideal world is the UNHCR bound to make this distinction? Although the right of a national to return is an integral part of human rights law, the role of the UNHCR is subject to its mandate and it should ensure that the right is not compromised. In this context, it also needs to be mentioned that, so far as the UNHCR's role in monitoring returns is concerned, it is of help only when conditions inside the country of return at least resemble a state of normalcy. It is beside the point when, as for example in Afghanistan, the idea of a "post-conflict" society is fundamentally flawed. It is then an idea superimposed by the international community on conditions that defy such categorization. The result is the return of the returnees to seek refuge. At this point, the idea that the UNHCR intervenes with state authorities to protect returnees, or negotiates in order to bring about a better climate of return, loses all meaning. The UNHCR, however, increasingly ignores the phenomenon of involuntary return because it allows the organization, among other things, to reduce its involvement in post-conflict societies. As we shall see later, the principal reason for the organization becoming involved in "peace-building" and "development" activities was to promote return. But, if return can take place without the UNHCR's involvement in these activities, it would welcome it and refocus itself on "international protection," whatever this may mean in contemporary times. In other words, in the future we will see a lean and mean UNHCR that is less committed on all fronts – assistance, peace-building, and protection.

The dynamics of return: Exploring innovative solutions

In an era in which the principle of voluntary repatriation is under increasing stress, where does the solution lie? If interpretative flexibility has to have legitimacy the standard of voluntary repatriation must be interpreted in dialogue with refugees and returnees: refugees are not a homogeneous group and respond differently to post-conflict conditions. Lubkemann distinguishes two kinds of models with respect to refugee repatriation: the "kinetic" and the "dynamic" models. In a kinetic model, "forces external to and beyond the influence of migrants themselves are seen as determining migration behavior entirely apart from the migrants' own internal motivations."[46] This model frames the problem of return "by assumptions based on the political structure of the international system."[47] It "treats refugees as largely homogeneous groups, with little attention to the differences between or within displaced populations."[48] It ignores internal differentiation with regard to gender, class, or generation. By treating all refugees alike, it is not able to appreciate that different refugee groups return in varying conditions and possess different needs. The dynamic model, on the other hand, views internal motivation as influencing migration behaviour and outcome. It does not consider external change as determinative of refugee behaviour. However, "though desperately needed, even the most rudimentary information on demographic differentiation is generally lacking."[49] This information is necessary, among other things, in order to implement the norm of participation. Mechanisms need to be devised to ensure that those participating in the consultations and negotiation are representative of the internal differentiation that marks them. There is particular need to be sensitive to the gender factor. Only participation can lead to taking into account the peculiar social realities that confront different groups of returnees. To treat returnees marked by the urban/rural and class and gender divides similarly is to reproduce the inequities in the pre-conflict situation and to disadvantage some groups as against others. Above all, it offers no insight into which refugees can return in relative safety and dignity.

At present, refugee representation is not seriously considered in the Tripartite Commission, which is made up of the UNHCR, the country of origin, and the receiving/host country. The UNHCR *Handbook* merely states that "the refugee community should be kept informed of the progress of repatriation negotiations. Formal representation of the refugee community can be considered."[50] However, at an earlier point, the UNHCR had talked about establishing a quadripartite commission.[51] Although states may be averse to granting refugees formal status by making them a party to an international agreement, refugee representation in a Tripartite Commission should at least be considered. There is only one previous instance of such participation: the representatives of Guatemalan refugees participated in the eleventh meeting in 1990 of the Tripartite Commission deliberating on their repatriation from Mexico. There is no reason why this cannot be the norm. Representation must also be considered for returnees who can reflect on their own experience in terms of conditions at home and the usefulness of the kind of assistance given to them.

The significance of the dynamic model goes beyond simply factoring in refugee and returnee behaviour. It emphasizes that the options of return and non-return do not have to be structured as mutually exclusive categories. Indeed, "return" could be used in a double sense to suggest a form of *incipient* dual membership of the host state and the state of origin. The idea would be to accommodate multiple identities and entitlements. If the solution to the refugee problem has always been in particular historical and political contexts, then in the era of globalization it is worth recognizing that for many refugees there is no single meaning assigned to "home." It may be necessary to think of ways to avoid a complete rupture with the host country. The fact that there is no clean break would encourage refugees to return, because they would have the alternative of returning to the host country, albeit not as refugees and for a limited period of time.

Some problems related to return: Land, property, and nationality issues in peace-building

I will now turn to a narrower set of issues pertaining to the creation of more immediate conditions that could ensure sustainable return: the restitution of housing and property rights, the removal of land mines, the disarmament, demobilization, and reintegration of former combatants, and the problem of statelessness.

Housing and property rights

It has been aptly observed that "housing and property restitution has emerged as one of the most important components of post-conflict reconciliation and rehabilitation."[52] Indeed, property problems are at the heart of the return process.[53] There is a general obligation placed upon states of origin to safeguard the property rights of the returnees. On 26 August 1998, the UN Sub-Commission on Prevention of Discrimination and Protection of Minorities adopted Resolution 1998/26, entitled *Housing and Property Restitution in the Context of the Return of Refugees and Internally Displaced Persons*. The resolution recognized that "the right of refugees and internally displaced persons to return freely to their homes and places of habitual residence in safety and security forms an indispensable element of national reconciliation and reconstruction and that the recognition of such rights should be included within peace agreements ending armed conflicts."[54] It urged states to develop effective and expeditious legal, administrative, and other procedures, including fair and effective mechanisms designed to resolve outstanding housing and property problems. It also called upon the UNHCR and the UNHCHR (United Nations High Commissioner for Human Rights) to develop policy guidelines to promote and facilitate the rights of all refugees. This resolution has been affirmed in subsequent years.

Yet, in many situations thousands of returnees cannot return to their original homes or recover their property or receive compensation in lieu of it. This is because the issue of enforcement has not always been sufficiently addressed. Peace agreements that have made a provision for the return of property and land rights have not included effective enforcement mechanisms. Thus, even though the Dayton Accords established the Commission on Real Property Claims of Refugees and Displaced Persons (CRPC),[55] it is reported that, of the 50,000 claim certificates issued by the CRPC, only a "small minority of them, three percent according to the International Crisis Group, resulted in the claimant actually recovering his property."[56] Therefore, minority returnees have found it difficult to return to their original homes, despite changes in national property laws.[57] On the other hand, compensation has not been paid because it was not "compatible with the overall strategy of trying to reverse effects of ethnic cleansing by encouraging return to minority areas."[58] In brief, despite the effort to develop appropriate norms on the international plane, it is difficult to see housing and property disputes being resolved in a fair and free manner in post-conflict societies. Property issues are central political issues as well.[59] The lesson it points to is the need to devise effective preventive strategies because "post-conflict societies" are hostile spaces for the restoration of property rights.

Removal of land mines, disarmament, demobilization, and reintegration

Land mines represent a key obstacle to the return of refugees and displaced persons and to reconstruction activities. This has been the experience of returns to all post-conflict societies, including Cambodia, Afghanistan, Mozambique, and Angola. The UN General Assembly (UNGA) has, for example, noted the "devastating consequences and destabilizing effects of the use of anti-personnel landmines on Cambodian society" and called for greater contributions from donor countries.[60] It has also expressed concern "about the problem of millions of anti-personnel landmines and unexploded ordnance as well as the continued laying of new landmines in Afghanistan, which continue to prevent many Afghan refugees and internally displaced persons from returning to their villages and working in their fields."[61] The answer lies in, first, devoting greater funds to de-mining operations. It is estimated that US$500 million is required to clear Afghanistan of land mines; but it is doubtful whether that kind of funding will be forthcoming. Second, de-mining should be stressed in the terms of reference of peace-keeping operations.

The UN Secretary-General has noted that the effective disarmament, demobilization, and reintegration (DDR) of former combatants is often crucial to the success of a peace process but, without some degree of predictability of funding for such operations, the entire enterprise can end in failure.[62] The UN Security Council (UNSC) has recognized that adequate and timely funding for disarmament, demobilization, and reintegration is critical to the successful implementation of a peace process.[63] Taking all these recommendations into account, the UNSG has proposed to "include comprehensive disarmament, demobilization and reintegration programmes ... for future peace operations ... so that the Security Council can consider including aspects of the disarmament, demobilization and reintegration programmes in the operations' mandates and the General Assembly can review proposals for funding demobilization and reintegration programmes, in the start-up phase, through the mission budgets."[64] These are moves in the right direction. However, it needs to be recognized that the effectiveness of DDR measures depends on success in generating income-generating activities. In its absence, DDR could actually lead to the deterioration of the law and order situation. This is a major challenge in post-Taliban Afghanistan.

Resolving the problem of statelessness

There is little possibility of sustainable return when the state of origin refuses to recognize returnees as its own nationals. A stateless person has been defined in international law as one "who is not considered as a national by any state under the operation of its law" (Article 1 of the 1954 Convention Relating to the Status of Stateless Persons). But this definition is confined to what are termed *de jure* stateless persons. There are in addition de facto stateless persons, who are unable to establish their nationality or whose citizenship is disputed by one or more countries; that is, all those who lack "effective nationality." In this context, the accession to the 1954 and 1961 conventions on statelessness, as well as the expansion of their ambit through amendment, needs to be explored. The UN Sub-Commission on Prevention of Discrimination and Protection of Minorities has in this regard emphasized "the crucial importance of the right to return voluntarily to one's country or place of origin as a principal means of long-term resolution of the plight of refugees and internally displaced persons."[65] The campaign against statelessness by the UNHCR and other agencies appears to have had some effect. In the recent past, Chad, Latvia, Lithuania, Mexico, St. Vincent and Grenadines, Slovakia, and Swaziland have acceded to the 1954 Convention Relating to the Status of Stateless Persons, bringing the total number of states party to this instrument to 52. Chad, Slovakia, Swaziland, and Tunisia have also acceded to the 1961 Convention on the Reduction of Statelessness, which now has 23 states party to this instrument.[66] The UNHCR has, however, pointed to the absence of adequate resources devoted to the problem of statelessness.[67] This situation needs to be rectified.

The United Nations, repatriation, and return: Multiple roles

What role should the United Nations system play in ensuring sustainable return to post-conflict societies? At present, according to UNSG:

Virtually every part of the United Nations system, including the Bretton Woods institutions, is currently engaged in one form of peace-building or another, including in the fields of: disarmament, demobilization and reintegration of former combatants, including children; strengthening of rule of law institutions; human rights; electoral and governance assistance, including to national human rights institutions and national machineries for the advancement of women; the development of civil society and the support of free media; and the promotion of conflict resolution and reconciliation techniques.[68]

However, I shall consider here only the role of the UNHCR and the UNSC and underline the need for greater coordination. Subsequently, I shall stress the need to evolve a law of responsibility of international institutions.

The UNHCR and sustainable return: The limits of involvement

It was in 1985 that the Executive Committee of the UNHCR noted the legitimate concern of the High Commissioner about the consequences of refugee return. At this time, "legitimate concern" was interpreted primarily in relation to protection, in particular to the adherence by states of origin to given guarantees and amnesties to returnees.[69] Until the beginning of the 1990s, "returnee aid and development was a derived concept. It did not have a meaning independent of refugee aid and development."[70] The reasons for UNHCR non-involvement in returnee reintegration till the early 1990s were sixfold. First, because the exile bias prevailed in the first decades of its existence, there was little opportunity for the UNHCR to be involved in such activities. It was only after voluntary repatriation became the central preoccupation of the UNHCR in the post–Cold War period and the UNDP declared the 1990s as the decade of returnees that "the concept of returnee aid and development began to gain currency among those administering development aid and those responding to humanitarian needs."[71] Second, in the 1960s and 1970s, when refugees did return in large numbers in Africa, it was often a result of the decolonization process, and the newly independent states began to accept the responsibilities of meeting the concerns of returnees. Third, even when the state demurred in these times, the UNHCR thought it squarely the task of the state of origin to ensure the "reintegration" of returnees. Fourth, in the 1990s refugees were returning to the poorest of countries that were in no position to respond to the needs of returnees; according to the World Bank, in this period, 16 of the 20 poorest states were post-conflict countries.[72] Fifth, in this period the UNHCR became increasingly involved with internally displaced persons. Finally, the involvement in returnee integration was necessary to the strategy of promoting the return of refugees. In the words of Crisp, "the genius of the returnee aid and development strategy was that ... it was unambiguously intended to promote and consolidate the solution of voluntary repatriation."[73] Thus, for example, in 1996 the UNHCR spent US$214 million on reintegration, nearly double the levels in 1994.[74]

Yet, the UNHCR is not a development agency nor is it equipped in material and intellectual terms to address the problem of development of post-conflict societies. Understandably, then, the scope of returnee aid is confined to achieving the objective of establishing minimum material and social conditions in which the return of refugees can be promoted. The strategy was exemplified by Quick Impact Projects (QIPs) executed by the UNHCR to help the reintegration process. QIPs are essentially "emergency development" projects that do not take into account the long-term problems of recurrent costs and sustainability. This weakness of QIPs merely reflects the "outer limit" of the UNHCR's mandate – it is involved in an activity that takes it far away from its protection role. Furthermore, there is often the assumption that the UNHCR's multilateral partners would be willing and able to build on activities initiated by the UNHCR. In reality, the priorities, objectives and approaches of other agencies often diverge from UNHCR's specific concerns.[75] Moreover, as a former High Commissioner for Refugees has pointed out, the UNHCR has been "very frustrated by lack of funding in the post-emergency phase in places like Rwanda, Liberia and Bosnia."[76]

This has led to attempts at collaboration with the World Bank on the reconstruction of "post-conflict societies." But the attempts to collaborate with the World Bank, as has already been pointed out, overlook the fact that at least one factor fuelling the ethnic conflict was that "international financial institutions imposed programs that exacerbated inflation, unemployment, land scarcity, and unemployment."[77] The international community therefore needs to ensure that enough funds are available that are not subject to traditional conditionalities imposed by IFIs. More significantly, it has urgently to address the inequities in the international economic system that *inter alia* translate into low primary commodity prices and huge debts for poor third world countries.

The UNSC and post-conflict peace-building

Through a presidential statement on the subject of post-conflict peace-building in 1998, the UNSC outlined its approach to peace-building.[78]

First, the UNSC recognized "the importance of the post-conflict peace-building efforts of the United Nations ... with due involvement of all United Nations bodies." In particular, it welcomed the role played by the UNSG in this field. Second, it encouraged the UNSG "to explore the possibility of establishing post-conflict peace-building structures as part of efforts by the United Nations system to achieve a lasting peaceful solution to conflicts, including in order to ensure a smooth transition from peacekeeping to peace-building and lasting peace." Third, it noted "the value of including, as appropriate, peace-building elements in the mandates of peacekeeping operations." It agreed with the UNSG that "relevant post-conflict peace-building elements should be explicitly and clearly identified and could be integrated into the mandates of peacekeeping operations."[79] Fourth, the UNSC recognized "the need for close cooperation and dialogue between the bodies of the United Nations system, in particular those directly concerned in the field of post-conflict peace-building, in accordance with their respective responsibilities and expresses its willingness to consider ways to improve such cooperation."

In February 2001, subsequent to a debate on the subject, another presidential statement was issued on the need for a comprehensive and integrated approach to peace-building. The Security Council presidential statement noted that "the quest for peace requires a comprehensive, concerted and determined approach that addresses the root causes of conflicts, including their economic and social dimensions."[80] It also pointed out that peace-building called for "short and long-term actions tailored to address the particular needs of societies sliding into conflict or emerging from it" and "should focus on fostering sustainable institutions and processes in areas such as sustainable development, the eradication of poverty and inequalities, transparent and accountable governance, the promotion of democracy, respect for human rights and the rule of law and the promotion of a culture of peace and non-violence." The Security Council expressed "its willingness to consider ways to improve its cooperation with other United Nations bodies and organs directly concerned by peace-building, in particular the General Assembly and the Economic and Social Council which have a primary role in this field." Of course, all the activities were to be initiated with "the consent and cooperation of the authorities of the State concerned" (where it exists).

As statements go, these are fine. But it will all eventually depend on how these are interpreted by the international community. Although the UNSC does talk of root causes of conflicts, it is mainly directed at the internal causes of conflicts. But, as I have suggested, without recognizing the *international* causes of internal conflicts, peace-building is impossible in the long run. Here the UNSC statement emphasizes the "comparative advantage" of the actors involved in peace-building, meaning thereby that IFIs will continue to play a key role in devising economic policies. This is deeply problematic unless these institutions change their approach and conditionalities.

Need for coordination among UN agencies

According to the UNDP, "a consensus is falling into place on the urgency of improved coordination during post-conflict situations, partly as a result of pressure created by several well-publicized incidents" such as the shelter programme in Rwanda.[81] Thus, in the case of the UNDP, coordination is called for because, first, it "tends to focus on long-term development issues.... It is not institutionally well equipped to undertake the speedy and local-level rehabilitation activities which are required when large numbers of people suddenly return to areas which have been devastated by war."[82] Second, it targets not individuals but state structures. Third, its mandate has not included any protection role, albeit in recent agreements with the Office of the UN High Commissioner for Human Rights the UNDP has sought to integrate human rights and sustainable development into its work.[83] However, it does not have the institutional capacity to tackle contentious protection issues. In view of these constraints, the UNDP needs, as it itself recognizes, to work more closely with UNHCR representatives on reintegration efforts.[84] In brief, it "should formulate and distribute an overall policy statement on its role in post-conflict situations."[85]

Law of organizational responsibility

In order to ensure effective peace-building and sustainable return, the international institutions responsible for well-defined activities must be made more accountable for their actions. In instances when the acts and omissions of an international institution lead to the violation of human rights it should be held responsible in international law. For example, the UNHCR should incur responsibility in international law for violating its mandate. Unfortunately, this is not the case today. Thus, it is not responsible in international law if it incorrectly declares that a source state is safe for return, and permits or facilitates the repatriation of the refugee population, who suffer persecution on return. The law on the subject of the responsibility of international institutions is still undeveloped. This situation needs to be urgently rectified because it does not stand to reason that states are held responsible for the violations of human rights but their creatures are not.

Conclusions and recommendations

Recommendations are often grossly inadequate to the situation. Sometimes they risk reproducing the societal dynamics that engendered the original violence. Indeed, the United Nations system hopes virtually to (re)produce a sustainable society and state without addressing the *international* causes of structural violence. Be that as it may, the overlapping conclusions and suggestions that emerge from the above analysis are as follows:

General

* There is a need to revisit and rethink the concept of "post-conflict" societies and the implications of deploying it.
* The meaning of the concepts of "peace-building" and "sustainable return" needs to be clarified.
* The United Nations must effectively move "from a culture of reaction to a culture of prevention."
* The international causes of internal conflict need to be identified and addressed.

On standards of repatriation

* The principle of voluntary repatriation must be respected.
* There is the need to research plural legal solutions to deal with refugees who are returned in less than ideal conditions or are unable to integrate into the country of origin.
* Provision should be made for formal refugee and returnee participation in trilateral commissions.

On returnees

* There is a need to conduct extensive research on the experience of returnees.
* The possibility of dual membership of returnees in the host country and the country of origin needs to be explored.
* Cognizance must be taken of the internal differentiation among refugees in order to determine their different assistance and protection needs.
* The needs of women call for particular attention in terms of making productive resources available to them and ensuring greater political participation.

- UN development agencies should have a clear mandate and focus on returnees in order to ensure sustainable return.
- Provision should be made in peace accords and national laws for the effective enforcement of land and property rights.
- Greater resources need to be devoted to de-mining operations to facilitate safe and sustainable return. De-mining can be included in the agenda of peace-keeping operations.
- There must be greater focus on the reintegration of disarmed demobilized soldiers. DDR programmes must be integrated into peace-keeping operations and more funds devoted to them. Their success depends on income-generating activities.
- The problem of statelessness must be addressed, *inter alia*, through ratification of appropriate international instruments.

On peace-building

- Repatriation and reintegration should not be seen as two separate tasks but be addressed in an integrated manner. Planning for repatriation must begin long in advance.
- The principle of burden-sharing must be respected. More non-conditional financial assistance should be made available to undertake developmental activities.
- The international financial institutions must ensure *peaceful* structural adjustment programmes.
- Peace-building needs to be integrated into the mandates of peace-keeping operations.
- Regional peace-keeping capacities may be enhanced, albeit not at the expense of international peace-keeping.

On the United Nations

- The United Nations system needs to address the structural or root causes of internal violence.
- The Security Council must outline its own role and that of peace-keeping in peace-building. All action must, however, be taken with the consent of the host state.
- Extensive peace-keeping mandates call for the democratization of the Security Council.
- There is a greater need for dialogue and coordination among UN agencies in the pursuit of peace-building and reintegration activities.
- The UNDP needs to clarify if it has a protection role and what it is to be.
- There is an urgent need to develop the law of state responsibility with respect to international organizations.

On the UNHCR

- The voluntary nature of repatriation must be ensured. To this end, a greater role should be assigned to the Department of International Protection in the repatriation process.
- There should be a clear definition of the role of the UNHCR in the return and reintegration process. Legal and ethical guidelines should be spelt out in this regard.
- Responsible phasing-out of an existing reintegration programme must be ensured.
- There is a need to rethink its collaboration with the IFIs and the transnational corporate sector.

Notes

1. Executive Committee of the High Commissioner's Programme: Forty-Eighth Session – Annual Theme: *Repatriation Challenges*, GA Doc. A/AC.96/887, 1997, p. 1. More recently, Crisp, of the evaluation unit of the UNHCR, has written that, "despite a well-established legal principle that refugee repatriation should take place on a wholly voluntary basis and in conditions of safety and dignity, a substantial proportion of Africa's most recent returnees have gone back to their homes in conditions which do not meet these standards" (J. Crisp, "Africa's Refugees: Patterns, Problems and Policy Challenges," New Issues in Refugee Research, UNHCR Working Paper no. 28, August 2000, p. 16).
2. For example, James C. Hathaway, "The Meaning of Repatriation," *International Journal of Refugee Law*, vol. 9, no. 4, 1997, pp. 551–558.
3. G. J. L. Coles, "Approaching the Refugee Problem Today," in G. Loescher and L. Monahan, eds., *Refugees and International Relations*, Oxford: Oxford University Press, 1989, pp. 373–410.
4. F. Cornish, K. Peltzer, and M. MacLachlan, "Returning Strangers: The Children of Malawian Refugees Come 'Home'?" *Journal of Refugee Studies*, vol. 12, no. 3, 1999, pp. 237–264, at p. 265; emphasis in original.
5. R. Black and K. Koser, eds., *Refugee Repatriation and Reconstruction*, New York: Berghahn Books, 1999, pp. 11–12.
6. J. Crisp, "Mind the Gap! UNHCR, Humanitarian Assistance and the Development Process," paper prepared for the Center for Migration Studies conference, Commemorating UNHCR at 50: Past, Present and Future of Refugee Assistance, New York, 16–18 May 2000 (on file with the author).
7. UNHCR, *Executive Committee of the High Commissioner's Programme: Note on International Protection*, A/AC.96/930, 2000, para 51.
8. See, generally, B. S. Chimni, "The Geopolitics of Refugee Studies: A View from the South," *Journal of Refugee Studies*, vol. 11, no. 4, 1998, pp. 350–375; B. S. Chimni, "From Resettlement to Involuntary Repatriation: Towards a Critical History of Durable Solutions to Refugee Problems," UNHCR Working Paper no. 2, February 1999.
9. Barry N. Stein and Fred C. Cuny, "Repatriation under Conflict," *World Refugee Survey, 1991*, Washington DC: US Committee for Refugees, 1991, pp. 15–21. Of course, the category of "spontaneous refugees" was not new. It had received mention, for example,

even in the 1985 Conclusion (No. 40) on voluntary repatriation adopted by the Executive Committee of the UNHCR. But now the focus was on "repatriation under conflict."

10. J. Crisp, "The 'Post-Conflict' Concept: Some Critical Observations," PRU Discussion Paper, 21 August 1998, p. 2 (on file with the author).

11. World Bank, *Post-Conflict Fund: Guidelines and Procedure*, Washington DC: World Bank, August 1999.

12. *UNHCR Operational Framework for Repatriation and Reintegration Activities in Post-Conflict Situations*, Geneva: UNHCR, Division of Operational Support, Reintegration Section, 1999, p. xvii, emphasis added.

13. Joanna Macrae, "Aiding Peace ... and War: UNHCR, Returnee Reintegration, and the Relief–Development Debate," New Issues in Refugee Research, Working Paper no. 14, Geneva: UNHCR, 1999, p. 15. According to Macrae, "the persistence of this terminology is very misleading, since the majority of refugees return to situations of on-going conflict."

14. UNHCR, *The State of the World's Refugees: A Humanitarian Agenda*, Oxford: Oxford University Press, 1997, p. 159.

15. Kofi Annan, *The Causes of Conflict and the Promotion of Durable Peace and Sustainable Development in Africa*, New York: United Nations, 1998, p. 14.

16. Inter-Agency Standing Committee, *Global Humanitarian Assistance 2000: An Independent Report Commissioned by the IASC from Development Initiatives*, Geneva: IASC, 2000, p. 51.

17. J. O. Ihonvbere, "The State, Constitutionalism and Democratization," *Seminar*, no. 490, June 2000, pp. 21–32, at p. 24.

18. Ibid., p. 25.

19. Susan Woodward, "On War and Peacebuilding: Unfinished Legacy of the 1990s," at www.ssrc.org/Sept11/Essays/Woodward.htm.

20. Astri Suhrke, Arne Strand, and Kristain Berg Harpviken, *Peace Building Strategies for Afghanistan*, Report Prepared for the Norwegian Ministry of Foreign Affairs, 14 January 2002, pp. iii and 24.

21. Woodward, "On War and Peacebuilding."

22. The Roundtable co-convened by the two organizations at the Brookings Institution in early 1999 was a first step in trying to facilitate a system-wide discussion on these issues, and it has been followed up by subsequent meetings and papers. See UNHCR and World Bank, *Report on the Roundtable on the Gap between Humanitarian Assistance and Long-term Development*, Washington DC: Brookings Institution, 1999.

23. Macrae, "Aiding Peace ... and War."

24. UNHCR, *Oversight Issues: Reintegration*, EC/48/SC/CRP.15, 1998.

25. UNHCR, Executive Committee of the High Commissioner's Programme, Standing Committee, 14th Meeting, *The Security, Civilian and Humanitarian Character of Refugee Camps and Settlements*, EC/49/SC/INF.2, 14 January 1999.

26. Annan, *The Causes of Conflict*.

27. Cited in UNDP, *Sharing New Ground in Post-Conflict Situations: The Role of UNDP in Support of Reintegration Programmes*, New York: UNDP, January 2000, p. 49.

28. Ibid.

29. UNHCR, *Oversight Issues*.

30. UNHCR, *The State of the World's Refugees*, pp. 154–160.

31. Ibid., p. 159.

32. UNHCR, *Oversight Issues*.

33. UNHCR, *The State of the World's Refugees*, p. 159.

34. Ibid., p. 18.

35. Ibid., p. 24.

36. Hathaway, "The Meaning of Repatriation," p. 553.
37. Ibid., p. 551.
38. Guy Goodwin-Gill, *The Refugee in International Law*, 2nd edn, Oxford: Clarendon Press, 1997, p. 276.
39. Hathaway, "The Meaning of Repatriation," p. 552.
40. I. Brownlie, *Principles of Public International Law*, 4th edn, Oxford: Oxford University Press, 1990, pp. 626 and 629.
41. G. Kibreab, "Revisiting the Debate on People, Place Identity and Displacement," *Journal of Refugee Studies*, vol. 12, 1999, pp. 384–411, at p. 390.
42. J. Boutroue, *Missed Opportunities: The Role of the International Community in the Return of the Rwandan Refugees from Eastern Zaire*, Working Paper no. 1, Cambridge, MA: Massachusetts Institute of Technology, 1998, p. 20, fn. 63.
43. M. Zieck, *UNHCR and Voluntary Repatriation of Refugees: A Legal Analysis*, The Hague: Martinus Nijhoff, 1999, p. 107.
44. Ibid., p. 108.
45. UNHCR, *Handbook on Voluntary Repatriation: International Protection*, Geneva: International Protection Unit, 1996, p. 17, emphasis added.
46. S. C. Lubkemann, "Sociocultural Factors Shaping the Mozambican Repatriation Process," in S. C. Lubkemann, L. Minear, and T. G. Weiss, eds., *Humanitarian Action: Social Science Connections*, Occasional Paper no. 57, Thomas J. Watson Institute of International Studies, 2000, p. 99.
47. Ibid., p. 103.
48. Ibid., pp. 101–102.
49. S. C. Lubkemann, L. Minear, and T. G. Weiss, "Understanding Forced Migration: Rethinking Collaborative Arrangements," in Lubkemann, Minear, and Weiss, *Humanitarian Action*, pp. 1–32, p. 3.
50. UNHCR, *Handbook on Voluntary Repatriation*, p. 34.
51. UNHCR, "Protection Guidelines on Voluntary Repatriation" (draft), September 1993, pp. 4 and 47.
52. S. Leckie, "Introduction: Land and Property Issues," *Forced Migration Review*, April 2000, pp. 4–5, at p. 4.
53. Catherine Phuong, "'Freely to Return': Reversing Ethnic Cleansing in Bosnia–Herzegovina," *Journal of Refugee Studies*, vol. 13, no. 2, 2000, pp. 165–183, at p. 169.
54. Economic and Social Council, *Housing and Property Restitution in the Context of the Return of Refugees and Internally Displaced Persons*, Sub-Commission Resolution 1998/26, E/CN.4/Sub.2/Res/1998/26, 26 August 1998.
55. Its mandate, as laid down in Article XI of Annex 7 of the Dayton Accord, is as follows:

    The Commission shall receive and decide any claims for real property in Bosnia and Herzegovina, where the property has not voluntarily been sold or otherwise transferred since 1st April 1992, and where the claimant does not now enjoy possession of that property. Claims may be for return of the property or for just compensation in lieu of return.

56. Phuong, "'Freely to Return'," p. 169. See also Lene Madsen, "Homes of Origin: Return and Property Rights in Post-Dayton Bosnia and Herzegovina," *Refuge*, vol. 19, no. 3, December 2000, pp. 8–17.
57. Madsen, "Homes of Origin," p. 10 ff.
58. Phuong, "'Freely to Return'," p. 170.
59. Catherine Phuong, "At the Heart of the Return Process: Solving Property Issues in Bosnia Herzegovina," *Forced Migration Review*, April 2000, pp. 5–8, at pp. 6–7.

60. UNGA Res. A/RES/53/145, 8 March 1999, adopted on the Report of the Third Committee, A/53/625/Add.2, 53/145.
61. UNGA, *Comprehensive Review of the Whole Question of Peacekeeping Operations in All Its Aspects: Enhancement of African Peacekeeping Capacity – Report of the Secretary-General*, A/54/63 S/1999/171, 12 February 1999.
62. UNSG, *Report of the Secretary-General on the Work of the Organization*, GAOR: fifty-fifth session Supp. no. 1, A/55/1, 2000, para. 72.
63. United Nations, *Report of the Secretary-General on the Implementation of the Report of the Panel on United Nations Peace Operations*, S/2000/108, 20 October 2000, para. 26.
64. Ibid.
65. UN Sub-Commission on Prevention of Discrimination and Protection of Minorities, *The Right to Return*, ECOSOC E/CN.4/Sub.2/Res/1997/31, 28 August 1997.
66. UNHCR, *Note on International Protection*, para. 65.
67. Ibid.
68. Ibid., para. 21.
69. Conclusion No. 40 (XXXVI)-1985, *Voluntary Repatriation*, adopted by the Executive Committee of the UNHCR.
70. R. F. Gorman and G. Kibreab, "Repatriation Aid and Development Assistance," in James C. Hathaway, ed., *Reconceiving International Refugee Law*, The Hague: Martinus Nijhoff, 1997, pp. 35–82, at p. 64.
71. Ibid.
72. World Bank, *Post-Conflict Fund*.
73. Crisp, "Mind the Gap!"
74. Macrae, "Aiding Peace … and War."
75. Tajikistan provides a clear example of an unworkable gap between the expectations of the UNDP and the UNHCR in the field of reintegration. The UNDP did not continue many of the projects that the UNHCR had initiated with grass-roots community actors (UNHCR, *Oversight Issues*).
76. Speaking to the UN Security Council in November 2000 (her last speech as High Commissioner to the body), Sadako Ogata observed:

Our problem, as I have said many times, is that we do not have the resources, nor indeed the expertise, to run development programmes – and yet, development agencies are slow to come once emergencies have ended. There is a gap between emergency, short-term humanitarian activities and the implementation of medium to long-term development and reconstruction programmes. During this gap, societies can unravel again very easily, and conflicts re-start.

77. OAU, *Report of the International Panel of Eminent Personalities: Rwanda – The Preventable Genocide*, Addis Ababa, 29 May 2000.
78. UNSC, *Statement by the President of the Security Council*, S/PRST/1998/38, 29 December 1998.
79. For the Secretary-General's view to this effect, see Annan, *The Causes of Conflict*, p. 15.
80. Security Council, *Presidential Statement*, SC/7014, 4278th Meeting (AM), 20 February 2001. The text is available at www.un.org/News/Press/docs/2001/sc7014.doc.htm. All subsequent quotations in this paragraph are from this source.
81. UNDP, *Sharing New Ground in Post-Conflict Situations*, p. 40.
82. UNHCR, *The State of the World's Refugees*, p. 166.
83. Human Rights Watch, *Burmese Refugees in Bangladesh: Still No Durable Solution*, HRW Report, May 2000, at www.hrw.org/reports/2000/burma/.
84. Ibid.
85. UNDP, *Sharing New Ground in Post-Conflict Situations*, p. 53.

11

The long-term challenges of reconstruction and reintegration: Case studies of Haiti and Bosnia– Herzegovina

Patricia Weiss Fagen

Actions intended to avert refugee flows when violent conflict threatens to escalate and actions intended to enable war-uprooted people to reintegrate when the fighting ends are, in effect, the bookends of international refugee policies. At one end, societies lacking basic conditions for citizen security, rule of law, responsive and effective governance, an active civil society, and basic trust among national groups are vulnerable to civil conflict and consequent refugee outflows. At the other end, these conditions may wholly or partially persist even after peace agreements are made and refugees return. Over the past decade, political instabilities, lingering hostilities, and social and economic dislocations have impeded peace from taking firm root in a number of countries long plagued by conflict. Measures designed to contribute to conflict prevention and programmes to assist war-to-peace transitions are intended to help national leaders address the root causes that give rise to conflicts and motivate refugee flight.

The mandate of the refugee agency, the United Nations High Commissioner for Refugees (UNHCR), does not officially encompass either of the two bookends. However, since resolving refugee/returnee issues merges with the revitalization of the society as a whole, UNHCR, along with several international agencies and institutions, has channelled its efforts and resources to broad-based initiatives in a number of war-torn societies.

That UNHCR has a significant role to play in conflict prevention and reconstruction is a fairly new phenomenon. UNHCR involvement in reintegrating returnees expanded during the 1990s and was recognized to be essential to future peace and progress. At the time, there was growing interest within the organization in conflict prevention as well. Since the late 1990s, however, UNHCR has been curtailing responsibilities beyond core refugee protection and assistance, and, overall, the contributions of international actors to prevention and reconstruction remain inadequate. Despite prominent institutional rhetoric and needs assessments, international commitments to long-term revitalization and reintegration take a back seat to the short-term mobilization of human and material resources for emergency responses to humanitarian crises.

Donors and operational agencies maintain they can and should establish the foundations of good governance, security, civil society organizations, and economic development as quickly as possible, during the emergency phase and even during actual conflict. In practice, unsurprisingly, the "massive intervention and quick fix" approaches typical of humanitarian emergency actions rarely yield durable results. Scholars, practitioners, and evaluators continue to document the disappointing performance of international assistance during emergencies, underscoring the prevalent lack of coordination, duplication of efforts, fragmented programmes, and expenditures that are too large to be absorbed locally that so often characterize these situations.[1]

This chapter will discuss international interventions in two countries, Haiti and Bosnia–Herzegovina (BiH), both of which have refugee issues at their core. In Haiti, the intervention was mounted to restore the former president and establish levels of stability and security sufficient to stem the continuing refugee flows, primarily to the United States. In BiH, the central goal of a massive internationally supported post-conflict rebuilding programme was to make possible the return of refugees to a multi-ethnic society that had been destroyed by ethnic cleansing, war, and nationalist repression. In Haiti, the UNHCR has been minimally involved, whereas in BiH it has been one of the most essential players. The intention here is to illustrate how, in two very different countries, international actors invested major resources during the early phase of their involvement, but did not achieve the results they sought because they failed to plan comprehensively and reduced resources too quickly. Haiti and Bosnia–Herzegovina are far from the least successful examples of international humanitarian interventions. Yet they illustrate the limited understanding of, or preparation for, the challenges of long-term transition periods. Features common to both, and to many other cases, include:

1. Donors and agencies have proposed to lay the foundations for political, social, and economic objectives (which require a decade or more

to achieve under favourable conditions) but to do so on the basis of planning, funding, and mandates that change from year to year.

2. Even where there are indications that international interventions are producing favourable results, the supporting agencies have found themselves unable to capitalize on this success owing to arbitrarily determined phase-out projections.

3. Continued funding for fundamental changes is still programmed according to unrealistic indicators that are supposed to establish year-to-year progress, although in nearly all cases improvements in one area are accompanied by – or cause – regressions in another.

4. Donor fatigue sets in when it is perceived that an emergency has been managed, but well before the desired durable changes can reasonably be expected.

These constraints affect outcomes when projects are undertaken by development as well as relief agencies in so far as both are bound by time-limited project cycles and changing donor priorities. Conflict prevention and mitigation and post-conflict reconstruction are almost always unevenly and/or poorly funded. Nevertheless, as will be shown, a smooth transition process from war to peace is a function not solely of the amount of funding, but also of how and at what pace the funding is targeted to the multiple problems of difficult war-to-peace transitions.

Restoring democracy in Haiti

Intervention

From the outset, following the slave-led war of independence against France in the late eighteenth century, dysfunctional and dictatorial government, extreme inequalities, and internal conflict have plagued Haiti. The overwhelming poverty of the majority of Haiti's people has generated economic migration, while widespread political repression has generated refugees. Haitians fleeing repression or poverty, or often both, have been arriving on US shores in substantial numbers for the past 40 years. The coup of General Cedras against Aristide convinced the US government in 1994 to resolve the Haitian crisis and its consequent refugee outflow with force.[2]

United Nations Security Resolution No. 940 of 31 July 1994 cited a "further deterioration of the humanitarian situation in Haiti" and the desperate situation of Haitian refugees. On these grounds it authorized the creation of a Multinational Force (MNF) under Chapter VII of the Charter. The United States was the leading advocate and executor in this initiative, and its troops constituted the majority in the force. The Resolution authorized the MNF to "use all means" to restore the legitimate authorities to Haiti, to maintain a "secure and stable environment," and to permit implementation of the 1933 agreement. Haiti thereby became the first case in which a Multinational Force under the United Nations was prompted by a refugee flow. The US-led Haitian intervention achieved the mission it assigned for itself and exited on schedule. Within the 18-month period that the Multinational Force remained in Haiti, it removed the military dictatorship, restored Jean Bertrand Aristide to the presidency, re-established civic order, and prepared the ground for the United Nations Mission in Haiti (UNMIH), which took over on 31 March 1995. For the United Nations, both the action itself and the handover demonstrated the relevance of multilateral actions even in a sphere of superpower interests. For the Haitian people, the MNF presence meant removal of the dictatorship, the restoration of Aristide, and, for the first time in many years, hope for a better future. Migration significantly declined.

UNMIH remained in Haiti until February 1996; its core mission was to:
- professionalize the armed forces,
- establish a new police force, and
- prepare for elections (UNMIH with MICIVIH)

Although the UN Secretary-General applauded the work of the MNF/UNMIH in his report of 17 January 1995, he underscored the fragility of what had been achieved in the first year. He called attention to the extremely poor condition of the new and untested security forces, the dire need for more forceful judicial and prison reform, and the likelihood of continuing political tensions. The return of President Aristide, he concluded, combined with promises of important international assistance, "have raised very high expectations of jobs, education and a better life for all."[3] These very high expectations, he implied, could well be disappointed by the limited terms of engagement built into the UN mandate, and thereby undermine what had been achieved.

Following the end of UNMIH's mandate on 31 May 1996, UN operations were no longer under Chapter VII "peace-keeping," and subsequent missions depended on donor voluntary contributions. Each succeeding mission by the United Nations and the Organization of American States (OAS) was smaller in size and resources.

UNSMIH   UN Support Mission in Haiti, 28 June 1996 – 31 July 1997
UNTMIH   UN Transition Mission in Haiti, 30 July – November 1997
MIPONUH UN Police Mission in Haiti, 30 November 1997 – March 2000
MICAH[4]   UN Civilian Support Mission in Haiti, March 2000–

Each mission was a new entity, with its own mission plan and new staff members. The initiatives undertaken by one mission were not necessarily completed by the next, although the general themes of electoral support, police training, and penal reform were common to all. Most UN efforts were devoted to the creation of the new Haitian police force. Other international actors implemented a broader range of economic and institutional projects, including important judicial reform projects. The United States, especially, invested significant resources for judicial reform. For the most part, the bilateral donor initiatives – like those of the UN missions – were designed for circumscribed purposes and quick implementation.

At the outset, the international community raised hopes of support for a political and economic transformation of Haiti. In 1995, donors pledged some US$1.2 billion. This was an unprecedented sum of money for a country of that size and absorptive capacity. Then, at the Paris Club meeting of 1995, they pledged a larger amount, US$2.8 billion. The international financial institutions cleared Haiti's debt so that rapid disbursement would not be impeded.[5] The government agreed to an Emergency Economic Recovery Programme that included privatization, trade liberalization, decentralization, and general economic stabilization, in keeping with the structural adjustment programme recommendations of the World Bank and the International Monetary Fund.

Despite generous pledges, slightly less than half of the promised US$2.8 billion had been disbursed at the end of fiscal year 1996. Much of the funding was delayed on the grounds of Haiti's inadequate compliance with aspects of the economic reform. Privatizing state enterprises was unpopular in Haiti, and the Haitian parliament resisted the passage of the legislation. Some donors criticized Aristide for equivocating on his commitments to overall economic reform,[6] and withheld committed funds. This, in turn, jeopardized major programmes the government and donors were executing in other areas, including the all-important effort firmly to establish the new police force.

The agenda: Achievements and disappointments

Whereas UN missions and other internationally funded projects were usually of short duration, achieving even the limited UN and OAS agendas in Haiti implied institutional and economic transformations that were anything but clear cut or short term.

The armed forces and the security gap

The Haitian Armed Forces (FAd'H) had served as an organ of internal repression for Haiti's authoritarian governments. In April 1995, Aristide disbanded the last of the FAd'H.[7] For the first time in Haiti's history, the armed forces would not be a determining factor in Haitian politics. A few former military troops were incorporated into the National Police.

A USAID/OTI (United States Agency for International Development/ Office of Transition Initiatives) programme, implemented by the International Organization for Migration (IOM),[8] offered vocational training and counselling, and about 5,500 former FAd'H took advantage of the offer. Of those who had accepted the training, only 304 found employment.[9] Without employment or livelihood, the demobilized soldiers, and particularly those who had been trained in specific employment skills that were not marketable, were intensely dissatisfied. Many turned to crime.

An IOM official perceptively questioned the outcomes of the training for demobilized soldiers that his organization had undertaken. The programme was typical of many others in its scope and time-frame. He noted that, although the IOM had successfully fulfilled its training mission, the project was too narrowly conceived to address any of the prevailing conditions affecting the lives of most of the Haitian beneficiaries. He believed that what was needed at that time, rather than a militarily defined operation performed quickly, was a multi-year, multi-layered planning process for the country overall.[10]

The more immediate challenge to peace and progress resulted from the fact that the disappearance of the army created a security vaccuum. As UN military peacekeepers were withdrawn, and with the new police force in the early stages of its formation, security threats in Haiti increased. During 1995, the Front pour l'Avancement et le Progrès Haitien (FRAPH) and paramilitaries – still armed and not faced with prosecution – committed serious and frequent acts of violence. Crime increased sharply in 1995 as the drug trade took greater advantage of the easy access to Haitian territory and the willing collaboration of many Haitians.

Nevertheless, the UN Security Council continued to scale back the UN peace-keeping forces of UNMIH and its successor, UNSMIH. By 1996, the UNSMIH troops were solely concentrated in Port-au-Prince, and could no longer help resolve security problems in the countryside. By 15 September 1996, international troop strength was at 600, plus an additional 672 funded on a voluntary basis, down from over 4,000 troops deployed in 25 locations.

The Haitian national police force

The international policy makers determined that Haitian security would best be served with a reliable and professional police force rather than by a military establishment. Therefore the MNF was charged with creating what would become the Haitian National Police (HNP). The police force was to be the centrepiece of international action.

All the UN missions to Haiti have made it their priority to recruit, train, equip, and generally improve the HNP. So too have the major bilateral donors. The United States alone contributed more than US$70 million to the HNP.[11] Canada, France, and the international agencies have contributed funds as well as personnel. With the appointment of a number of capable and committed officers to leadership positions, early assessments of performance were optimistic.[12] Within about 18 months, there were HNP officers throughout the country. Haiti thereby acquired the first credible police force in its entire history. The United States took the position that a credible police reform programme and an effective and democratic security force justified the withdrawal of the international troops.[13]

By 1998, the HNP reached its peak of some 6,500 officers. Thereafter, performance patterns were worrisome. The police worked for long hours, for little remuneration, with few opportunities to advance, and with inadequate technical or logistical support – significant donor contributions notwithstanding. The low salaries, the possibility of easy drug money, and the lack of effective oversight opened the way to rampant corruption. These and other factors caused the number of police to decline. Political opponents alleged that the HNP had come to serve the aims of the Aristide government, as former police forces had served previous Haitian rulers. International criticism of the HNP mounted between 1998 and 2000.[14] Arguing against further support, a report of 2000 by the US General Accounting Office (GAO) characterized the police as a "largely ineffective law enforcement body."[15] US congressional opponents of Haiti's government voiced considerably more strident criticism.[16] A mid-term Canadian evaluation concluded, more sympathetically, that despite the efforts expended to strengthen the HNP its institutional capacity remained weak and the training had produced minimal results.[17] That evaluation perceptively advised that the Canadian government deepen its involvement, monitor HNP progress more closely over a longer period, and lower expectations of immediate results.

Electoral assistance

Another fundamental goal of the international efforts in Haiti was to replace the pattern of repressive dictatorship with democratic government. UNMIH oversaw two elections for members of parliament and for president in June and December 1995, respectively. Despite serious irregularities, the elections represented major improvements over previous elections in Haiti. When René Préval replaced Jean Bertrand Aristide, the international community hailed the electoral transition from one civilian to another.[18] To their disappointment, electoral procedures and practices in subsequent elections deteriorated rather than improved.

First there was a parliamentary crisis that began in 1997 when the ruling Lavalas coalition fractured and then split. President Préval dissolved the sitting parliament in 1999 and ruled for a year without a legislature. Without the legislature, his own appointments and policies could not be ratified. Haiti paid an extremely high price for this political dispute because international programmes were suspended, investors withdrew, and already approved funding was not disbursed. Donors concluded that the country lacked a functioning government to assume responsibility for the funding it received. Haiti lost US$500 million in loans and aid from the international financial institutions because there was no parliament to ratify the conditions of the funding. Opposition to the ruling government increased among the better-educated urban population.

New local and parliamentary elections were finally held in May 2000. Far from resolving the problems of political paralysis, the manner in which electoral victories were tabulated further undermined confidence in the democratic intentions of Haiti's leadership. Political rivals accused Aristide of engineering a political monopoly that would result in his becoming president for life like his infamous predecessors. The US Congress used the electoral manipulation to ban US public assistance to the Haitian government. Haiti's other major donors have also held back promised assistance, although as before 1994, the economic punishment aimed at Haiti's leadership falls on Haiti's poor.

Judicial system

The judicial sector in Haiti has been inefficient, corrupt, and distrusted by all – outside of the wealthiest segments of the population, whose interests it has served. Observers across the board have referred to it as "dysfunctional." Although judicial reform was not an official activity of the UN missions, the United Nations and all the donors recognized that, without a substantially improved judiciary, there could be no credible criminal prosecutions even if Haiti had an effective police force. Nor would it be possible to adjudicate land and other disputes among citizens. The US government and the United Nations Development Programme (UNDP) in particular supported a wide diversity of judicial reform projects, with little apparent success. Considering the numerous explanations of why the efforts produced few results, the most persuasive seems to be that the proposed changes were grafted onto existing structures and staff. In contrast to the aggressive approach to creating a new security sector, resources went into the pre-existing, hopelessly flawed, institution.

Another obvious need in Haiti was, and still is, prison reform. Outside funding has brought material improvements to Haiti's prisons, but they remain substandard in terms of both conditions and ability to manage the prison population. It is up to the government to take the initiative on an overall penal reform.

Economic progress

As noted, the generous donor investment for reconstruction early on, combined with the positive impacts of security and political reform, were supposed to lead to lasting economic improvement. At the outset, several projects were hastily put in place for repairing damaged infrastructure, including erosion control, potable water, and health and educational structures. These projects were socially useful and provided desperately needed jobs for unskilled and low-skilled workers, but the positive impacts were not sustainable. In order to be ready for immediate execution, the projects were inadequately prepared. Neither local authorities nor already existing local enterprises were taken very much into account, and there was little or no planning for future maintenance.[19] As for the private sector, international investors could not help but notice that the members of the Haitian élite continued to invest their own money outside of the country, indicating their lack of political and economic confidence.

At the outset, the Aristide government acceded in large part to IFI insistence on monetary control and, as a result, was able to clear its arrears with the international banks, as well as to reduce inflation from 30 per cent to 10 per cent between 1994 and 1998. By late 1999, according to the World Bank, both inflation and the fiscal deficit had again increased, and the Haitian *gourde* was depreciating rapidly.[20] This was blamed on the related phenomenon of declining external contributions and neglect of the reform package. Haiti still receives more outside financial support than many similarly poor countries, especially in Africa. Nevertheless, the support is significantly less than was foreseen at the time of the 1994 intervention. Disbursements from international grants and loans from bilateral and multilateral sources have declined by 4.8 per cent each year from 1995.[21] As of 1998, international support accounted for about 10 per cent of the gross national product. Even this small percentage, however, has been extremely important for the Haitian people, representing 85 per cent of government expenditures.[22]

Haiti's economic profile is little different from that of 1994 when the intervention was launched to save the country from authoritarian rule and deepening misery. According to the UNDP, 91 per cent of Haitian households are considered poor and 81 per cent are considered extremely poor.[23] The rural population living in absolute poverty migrates in ever accelerating numbers to the capital city, where conditions of life are scarcely better. Income inequalities also remain extreme: the top 4 per cent of the population possesses 66 per cent of the wealth; 70 per cent of the population has but 20 per cent of national wealth; and the bottom 10 per cent is too poor to count.[24]

Expectations and results

The donor assumption that creating a more secure environment and democratic government in Haiti would be sufficient to attract private investment, which, in turn, would generate jobs, did not come to pass. Investors have been discouraged by the failure of the government to privatize and to follow the reform package to which it had agreed. The donors that have been supporting rebuilding, democratization, and institutional strengthening point to political instability, poor management, politicized development policies, and the uncooperative behaviour of the Haitian government as reasons for the multiple failures. There are ample reasons to blame Haiti's government for much of what has gone wrong. It has neither lived up to its commitments to sustain democratic structures nor provided adequate material and political support to maintain independent and responsive institutions. Although the specific charges are accurate, the international diagnosis contains little self-criticism related to the donors' own programmes or expectations:

Mutually dependent goals

The UN/OAS mission mandates centred on security, electoral performance, and human rights. In practice, significant improvements in the sectors targeted by these missions required complementary improvements in other related sectors. Human rights and an effective civilian police force required comprehensive judicial reform and improvement in the penal system. The productive incorporation of the FAd'H required economic opportunities, of which there were few in Haiti. Donor contributions to all sectors were contingent on confidence in government commitments, beginning with respect for the rule of law and electoral transparency. The international community sought immediate results, but opted against a comprehensive programme that would encompass all these areas.

Broad expectations – narrow commitment

The international intervention and subsequent UN peace-keeping missions were charged with setting Haiti on the road to democracy and establishing the foundations for economic stability. Yet, as we have seen, the missions' activities were narrowly defined and each mission was in place for a brief period. The MNF remained only 18 months. The UN peacekeepers were progressively withdrawn despite clear indications that Haitian security remained fragile, that violence was rising, and that the newly created national police force was insufficiently prepared to meet the challenges placed before it. These problems were entirely predictable and, indeed, had been predicted.

Reprisals

Only six years after the high national and international optimism that greeted the restoration of the Aristide government, donors seemed to have decided that too little had changed for the better to justify continued engagement. Since 2000, US assistance cannot be channelled to the Haitian government, and now goes only through non-governmental organizations (NGOs) and community groups. Other donors are more likely now to channel their assistance through UN projects rather than bilaterally.

The Inter-American Development Bank (IDB), which has long maintained a strong presence in Haiti, especially in social sectors, had projects worth approximately US$200 million signed before the end of 1998 but pending parliamentary approval. Although a new parliament was inaugurated in 2001, its legitimacy is in question at this writing, hence the IDB projects cannot yet be executed. "We have lots of cash," the IDB's Resident Representative commented in 2000, "but no way to provide it."[25]

Haitians' prospects

Although disillusionment regarding economic and political progress and access to justice is very broadly shared, Haitians acknowledge that political expression is more open. Human rights violations, though widespread, are no longer official policy; and locally elected officials, at least in some parts of the country, are more responsive to citizens. Perhaps most significantly, the government is no longer sustained by the armed forces. The HNP is a flawed institution, and will continue to be so while the judicial sector remains unreformed. Yet, the HNP is still an improvement over the terror wrought by the FAd'H and Tonton Macoutes. Despite undemocratic practices on the part of the national government, Haiti today is a politically diverse country, with opposition voices that are heard and sometimes heeded. Opposition candidates have won local office in a number of communities. The media remain varied and often critical. In short, since the international intervention, significant political changes have taken place that affect the general population.

The economic situation is not encouraging. Although internationally financed, mainly privately supported, micro-projects help people to survive in some communities, the projects depend entirely on international support. Haiti's economy provides very little relief from the misery in which the majority still live, and economic indicators remain stagnant. Agriculture, the traditional activity of most Haitians, is proving less and less viable for sustenance, causing record numbers to settle in the vastly overcrowded capital, Port-au-Prince. Unfortunately, Haiti has not recovered from the loss of manufacturing and other economic enterprises that operated during the 1980s. Rural and urban Haitians are ready, as always, to leave for almost any destination that can offer greater economic opportunity. Perhaps in recognition of this likelihood, in September 2002 the Organization of American States, with backing from its US representative, advocated unblocking the millions of dollars in foreign aid that were frozen as a result of the events surrounding the May 2000 elections.[26] The funds could go a long way toward strengthening the government's ability to respond to popular needs.

Haitians fleeing to neighbouring Dominican Republic and other Caribbean destinations encounter increasingly heavily policed borders. The US Coast Guard reports having intercepted increasing numbers of Haitian boats: 480 in 1999; 1,394 in 2000; and 1,956 in 2001.[27] All the evidence indicates increasing efforts to leave, which the UNHCR has attributed to violence, persecution, and instability.[28] As of this writing, there is no massive Haitian entry into the United States, but numbers of interdictions and asylum applications rose in 1999 and in 2000. First-instance approval rates increased from 7.6 per cent to 22.0 per cent between 1999 and 2000.[29] The interdiction rates will certainly continue to rise: since 11 September 2001, the US government has come to perceive Haitian illegal entries in the context of its fear of terrorist incursions. Border security has become a vital issue and the prospect that boats can penetrate US Coast Guard patrols – as they have for so long – is now considered to be an unacceptable risk.

The UN system operating in Haiti is trying to rectify the former pattern of fragmented short-term projects. Haiti is one of the sites for the coordination mechanisms being put in place in selected countries following the Secretary-General's 1997 reform plan. Through the Common Country Assessment (CCA) and the UN Development Assistance Framework (UNDAF), launched in September 2000, the UN agencies in Haiti have laid the groundwork for a multifaceted and coordinated strategy over the long term. The agencies involved have pledged to engage in comprehensive planning for medium- and long-term outcomes, with maximum national execution.[30] Sadly, as the United Nations system is finally preparing its member agencies to participate in this strategy, the funding needed to give the initiative greater impact is unlikely to be forthcoming.

The political future of Haiti may not be encouraging, but it is not doomed to repeat the pattern of the Duvalier past. Yet, if the donors turn their backs both on current problems and on the deeper political and economic roots of these problems, and if Haitian political leaders, including both government and opposition, fail to look beyond their own political interests, life in Haiti will become truly unbearable and likely more explosive.

Minority returns in Bosnia and Herzegovina

Today, nearly five years after Dayton, I am pleased to report that minority returns are finally a reality ... After years in limbo, the refugees and displaced people are tired of waiting (September 2000).[31]

In fact, there are few refugee returns to Bosnia–Herzogovina (BiH), to minority areas or elsewhere (about 13,000 in 2000). However, a number of Bosnians who were ethnically cleansed from minority areas are now seeking to return to their places of origin after years living in majority areas. This movement more than quadrupled between the first quarter of 1999 and the same period of 2000.[32] By September 2002, minority returns numbered 80,711 according to UNHCR and OHR figures.[33] The welcome news, if it becomes a trend, would vindicate international humanitarian support for rebuilding and reconciliation. There are, however, still over 800,000 internally displaced persons in Bosnia.

Without question, the years of international programmes, pressures, and incentives in BiH were fundamental to improving conditions for minority returns. Nevertheless, a review of the international efforts to achieve these ends also demonstrates lack of clarity among donors and agencies about the linkages among their programmes, as well as unrealistic expectations about the feasibility of early refugee returns. Moreover, although it is encouraging that significant numbers of people now are willing and able to move back to areas that were ethnically cleansed, the challenges of integration still lie ahead. Whether adequate international assistance and protection will be available to facilitate that integration is very much in doubt.

Between 1992 and 1995, internal conflict in Bosnia–Herzegovina (BiH)[34] and Croatia, formerly part of Yugoslavia, produced approximately 1.7 million refugees, at least the same number or more internally displaced persons, and 200,000 deaths, from an initial population of about 4.4 million.[35] The population fell by half between 1991 and 1995 and, of those remaining, more than half were displaced from their original areas. Serbian aggression was intended to achieve ethnic uniformity by forcibly displacing the non-Serb population (consisting primarily of Muslims and Croats). By the time the war was brought to a close in December 1995, Bosnian cities, towns, and rural communities were sharply segregated along ethnic lines. Additionally, what had been a moderately prosperous Bosnia was physically in ruins. Close to two-thirds of the housing had been wholly or partially destroyed; factories, schools, mosques, medical facilities, and communications networks were in ruins. The gross domestic product in Bosnia declined some 75 per cent between 1991 and 1995.[36]

The General Framework Agreement on Peace in Bosnia and Herzegovina (GFAP), commonly known as the Dayton Peace Accords, recognized the de facto creation of two separate ethnically defined entities: the Federation of Bosnia and Herzegovina and the Republika Srpska (RS). Bosniacs (Muslims) and Croats shared the former, and the population in the latter was almost exclusively Serb. At the same time, the measures comprising the Dayton Accords were aimed specifically at undoing the ethnic separation caused by the war, and which had been the motor force of the conflict. Annex 7 of the Dayton Accords states the parties' agreement to respect the rights of refugees and internally displaced persons, and to permit them to return to the places in which they had lived prior to the war, without "harassment, intimidation, persecution, or discrimination, particularly on account of their ethnic origin, religious belief or political opinion" (Article 1 (2)).

The Accords established a structure that gives ample space for international interventions in every sphere. At this writing, the Office of the High Representative (OHR) oversees the civilian aspects of international programmes (political, economic, and humanitarian), monitors the compliance of the Bosnian parties,[37] and coordinates strategies and programmes with the other agencies. The UNHCR was given the leading role in refugee repatriations and promoting the right of return for internally displaced persons. The OHR, with the UNHCR, assumed responsibility for accommodating the return of refugees and internally displaced persons, and nearly all donors designed their aid packages to facilitate the return process.

In January 1997, the OHR and the UNHCR created the Reconstruction and Return Task Force (RRTF) to serve as an inter-agency forum to coordinate reconstruction work for returnees.[38] The RRTF established chapters at the local level and divided its international staff between the secretariat and the field. The UNHCR and the OHR, directly or through the RRTF, and often with Stabilization Force (SFOR) participation, have brokered returns by directly assisting persons wishing to go back to their areas of origin and negotiating with the communities that should receive them. The International Organization for Migration and the International Labour Organization also have initiated refugee return programmes. The goals of restoring a multi-ethnic character in BiH and establishing peace and development coincided with national interests: it was expected that creating adequate conditions for return and demonstrating international generosity would bring about the repatriation of tens of thousands of refugees who had gone to Europe and North America.

To address both physical damage and peace-building activities, donors pledged over US$5 billion, which was to be disbursed during the four years following Dayton. Although this aid was not always timely, effective, or efficiently disbursed, it established a pattern of tying support for reconstruction to incentives for peace-building and reintegration. The mandates of almost all the agencies in Bosnia have directly or indirectly affected the course of refugee return. A Peace Implementation Council (PIC) has met regularly to set broad policies. The NATO international Implementation Force, IFOR, later renamed the Stabilisation Force (SFOR), is responsible for military and security issues, with authority to intercede at the local level when needed. The Organization for Security and Co-operation in Europe (OSCE) has monitored disarmament and human rights and organized elections. The United Nations Mission in Bosnia and Herzegovina (UNMIBH) cooperates with the OHR in judicial reform projects and in implementing election results. The UN mission has been responsible for organizing the International Police Task Force (IPTF) charged with training, reforming, and restructuring the Bosnian police.[39] The World Bank and the European Union (EU) became lead agencies in the reconstruction effort. They coordinated the wide array of multilateral and bilateral assistance and the NGOs that implemented the activities. USAID and the European Commission have been the largest donors, but virtually all the major donors have given priority attention to Bosnia and Herzegovina.

Minority returns: Expectations and obstacles

Despite having signed the Dayton Accords, the nationalists steadfastly opposed the efforts of minorities to return and sought to restrict freedom of movement. In addition to the extensive destruction of homes and infrastructure and the scarcity of employment, ethnic minority refugees and internally displaced persons (IDPs) faced local hostility and locally imposed legal obstacles to reclaiming property and rights. Although conditions governing returns differed in each municipality, municipal authorities in neither entity were accommodating to minorities. On the contrary, the leaders frequently used their executive powers to the fullest negative potential, and rarely punished elements in the local population who threatened the lives of former residents from minority families trying to reclaim homes and property.[40] Until nearly the end of the 1990s, minorities seeking to return were typically subjected to practices ranging from a levy of so-called war taxes, the requirement of special visas, discriminatory distribution of public assistance, and onerous registration requirements.[41] In some places, discriminatory practices are still enforced.

Early actions to repair physical damage and revitalize the economy in the Federation communities facilitated the return of elderly persons and families whose reintegration was not complicated either by ethnic factors or by major war damage to homes during 1996. The vast majority of the refugees have chosen, where possible, to remain outside the country.[42] When refugee host countries in Western Europe and in the former Yugoslavia suspended temporary protection for Bosnian refugees between 1996 and 1998, however, over 150,000 Bosnians returned to BiH during this period.[43] They were almost all Bosniacs and Croats who had been ethnically cleansed. These returnees would not and could not recover their homes in minority areas and instead went to communities in the Federation, which became increasingly crowded. They remained there, living as internally displaced persons entirely dependent on international assistance. This trend not only strengthened the ethnic divide in the formerly multi-ethnic society but seriously aggravated the problem of displacement as well. It is this population that began to explore the possibilities of return to the Republika Srpska (RS) and to the areas of the Federation under Croat control during 2000.

The donors laid the groundwork, or so they believed, for refugee and IDP return during 1997 and 1998. Their strategy was to use resources as incentives. Cash advances were made available for returning families from Europe, and Bosnian municipalities and communities willing to collaborate were rewarded. Meanwhile, the OHR, the UNHCR, and other agencies sought to remove physical and economic obstacles to return for those contemplating such action. Major initiatives included:

1. The Reconstruction and Return Task Force (RRTF) selected "cluster areas" for return-related reconstruction projects, costing approximately US$179 million. The areas were chosen on the basis of their capacity to absorb and house returnees, the openness of local government to accommodating returnees, their potential economic development possibilities, and their importance as examples of inter-ethnic reconciliation.[44] It was hoped that up to one-third of the 590,000 believed to have fled would return by the end of 1998.[45] The investment produced disappointingly modest results.

2. The UNHCR increased its investment for the housing reconstruction and rehabilitation programme under way since 1996. The construction activity helped spark local economies, but the programme was costly and the results did not seem to justify the expense. As of the end of 1998, only 30 per cent of the repaired houses were occupied.[46]

3. The "Open Cities" programmes operated separately but along similar principles. The UNHCR and the US Bureau of Population, Refugees,

and Migration aimed to reward those cities and areas that cooperated with minority return policies. The localities participating in the programme could have access to security forces and/or human rights monitors. Donors would invest in basic infrastructure and income-generation projects. The UNHCR predicted that the Open Cities initiative, combined with other improvements that facilitated returns, would yield some 50,000 minority returns by early 1998. Instead, the minority return rates in the selected communities taken as a whole appeared to be no different from those outside the programmes.[47] The UNHCR estimated that only 10,000 returned to minority areas, of whom 4,000 registered with the UNHCR.[48]

Notwithstanding strengthened international determination to promote minority returns, far fewer than expected took advantage of incentives and expanded opportunities to go home. The pattern of majority as opposed to minority returns persisted. In March 1998, the OHR reported that more than 400,000 persons had returned in the first year of Dayton, but acknowledged that 1997 returns were down 40 per cent from 1996.[49]

Return linked to security

Without exception, official and unofficial analyses between 1996 and 1999 underscored inadequate security and human rights protection as the primary reasons for the low rate of minority returns. Funding for rebuilding and reconciliation succeeded only in those few municipalities where incentives and security were linked; i.e. where international protection was strong and visible enough to allay fears.[50] Those who were contemplating return had been the victims of ethnic cleansing and had experienced hostility and brutality, and they were not easily lured into situations in which they and their families would be at risk. The risks were augmented by the poorly functioning judicial system, criminal corruption on the part of many political leaders, and overall institutional weakness throughout BiH.

Prior to 1998, proponents of minority returns looked in vain to the international forces of NATO to take more forceful measures against Dayton's opponents. During the first three years of their occupation, the peacekeepers of the Implementation Forces IFOR/SFOR rarely used their powers to force compliance with Dayton with regard to the illegal obstacles to return or other issues. Nor did NATO forces arrest persons indicted for war crimes or pursue indicted criminals. As late as 1998, the SFOR had arrested only 2 major figures on the list of accused war criminals in the Republika Srpska and some 30 low-level officials.[51] The elections of 1996, predictably, had confirmed the power of the intransigent, anti-democratic, and generally corrupt nationalists who had made the war and used their official positions to preserve ethnic homogeneity and ethnicity-based control. The Republika Srpska was more restrictive than the Federation, but minority returns remained rare and difficult in both areas.

Imposing Dayton

Beginning in December 1998, the SFOR departed from its previous pattern of ignoring war criminals and arrested major figures among the wanted criminals.[52] A number of actions in favour of economic transparency, judicial reform, control of borders, anti-corruption, human rights, and electoral reform were initiated in rapid succession, all aimed at further unifying the territory and diminishing the power of the extreme nationalists.

* In late 1997, the High Representative introduced a common licence plate for vehicles from all areas. The effect of this seemingly modest gesture was dramatic in terms of opening the way to freedom of movement throughout the entire area. The common plates, importantly, allowed potential returnees to return to their places of origin and assess living conditions.

* In order to restructure and regulate the broadcast media, the High Representative, with SFOR support, created an Independent Media Commission, and in 1999 he established the legal framework to govern public radio and television throughout the territory. In 1999, SFOR seized the transmission facilities of the nationalist-controlled media and, with that action, silenced the regular broadcasts of nationalist propaganda.

* Acting directly on the political front, the High Representative used his power to dismiss 22 elected officials, from all ethnic groups, on the grounds that they failed to comply with their obligations under Dayton – usually related to recovery of property – or were involved in criminal operations.

The Dayton Accords received a further boost, and the ultra-nationalists in BiH suffered an unanticipated setback, with the changes of government in both Croatia and the former Yugoslavia during 2000.

In addition to the power of the nationalist leadership, the other major impediment to minority return has been the inability of property owners and renters to reclaim their homes or to evict those illegally inhabiting these homes. The flats and houses abandoned by the Bosnian Muslims in the RS were likely still to be occupied by minority Serbs and Croats who also fled during the war from the areas later encompassed within the Federation and Croatia. On 27 October 1999, the High Representative finally issued decisions that brought together all property legislation in force in both entities, harmonized RS property legislation with that of the Federation in accordance with Annex 7, and established a coherent strategy for property law implementation. Until then, post-war legislation in both entities had permitted property not claimed by the owners within a specified time to be declared abandoned and allocated to new inhabitants. The Property Law Reform package was the result of close collaboration among the OHR, the UNHCR, the OSCE, the UNMIBH, and the Commission for Real Property Claims (CRPC). The new laws, implemented in 2000, called on all 140 municipalities in the country to process claims for restitution of property and to end illegal occupancy through evictions. They also specified the rights returnees could demand of local officials.

Although this property reform legislation is fundamental to opening the way for minority returns, its implementation is still problematic for the majority of urban dwellings occupied for years by squatters. In all, only about 20 per cent of property claims raised had been decided as of March 2001.[53] In the RS especially, municipal capacity remains weak and resistance to evicting illegal occupants is still strong.[54] The rightful owners frequently find themselves spending months or even years trying to establish their legal rights, while living in inadequate temporary dwellings. Most are discouraged.

Therefore, the present upswing in minority returns is directed primarily at rural not urban areas. There are no legal obstacles to returning to the ethnically homogeneous Bosniac villages that were destroyed by the Serbs during the war. Minority families now feel sufficiently secure to return to their villages or, rather, the places where villages once stood – providing their homes can be rebuilt and other needs attended to. Therein lies a problem: the once generous international funding for exactly these purposes was already rapidly disappearing in 2000, just as interest in returning grew.

Paying the price of return and integration

A UNHCR monitoring and evaluation mission sent in early 2000 to observe recent minority returns found relative physical security but an economically fragile population.[55] Returnees sought help with housing construction, employment, in some cases land-mine removal, and other needs. Although building homes prior to return had not brought people back, shelter became the first and most urgent need for families who had made the decision to return. The shortage of housing stock throughout the country has been further exacerbated by the fact that families returning to their places of origin have tried to maintain two homes in case the return proves untenable. As for means of livelihood, only 5.5 per cent of the interviewees or spouses were employed and these almost exclusively in the Federation. Children attended school in the Federation because virtually no appropriate schooling was – or is – available in the RS.[56]

The RS population overall is in difficult circumstances. The donor policies of conditioning assistance on compliance with Dayton principles and acceptance of minority returns resulted in a disproportionate amount of assistance flowing to the more cooperative Federation and far less to the more intransigent RS. Not only did this leave the RS poorer and less able to accommodate returnees, but it also reinforced the isolation – and corruption – of the leadership. By late 1998, the poverty and isolation, combined with SFOR's more vigorous pursuit of war criminals, finally led voters to begin to reject some intransigent nationalist candidates. Slowly, moderate leadership replaced nationalist wartime leadership, at least in the western municipalities. These municipalities were then able to benefit from the various programmes already under way in the Federation. Nevertheless, the economic situation to date remains quite dismal in most of the area. The residents of all ethnic groups lack pensions and health coverage, electricity, education, public transportation, agricultural machinery, etc. There is virtually no private investment in the RS and, for that matter, very little in BiH overall.

The absence of adequate jobs for the returnees and the rest of the population inevitably sharpens tensions and resentments between and among them. Although local police are now more helpful and the general population is more open, security remains problematic. Violence against minority returnees continues in parts of the RS and Croat-controlled areas of Bosnia. As more people return to areas that are difficult to access and likely to be unfriendly to minorities, they will need security that – in the short run at least – only the international forces and police can furnish.

In order to reintegrate and restore the once ethnically diverse society in Bosnia, donors have remained involved over a longer time-span than had been anticipated or is usually sustained in peace-building programmes. It appears to be not long enough. The OHR, the UNHCR, and other operational agencies repeatedly express their concern that funding is diminishing just as their policies are finally beginning to bear fruit. Indeed, the present opportunities notwithstanding, there is a clear trend among donors to reduce their contributions to BiH operations, and to the Balkans generally.

By 2000, donors had already adjusted most of their projects from humanitarian to development-focused assistance, emphasizing legislative and administrative matters over more immediate forms of assistance. The well-justified commitment to institutional change, however, was accompanied by smaller total contributions. The Bosnian donors' conference of May 1999 yielded pledges that covered only 30 per cent of the estimated cost of implementing the reforms planned and requested by the OHR.[57] Over the next two years, the total Consolidated Appeal Process (CAP) submitted progressively lower requests for UN agency projects, but donor responses declined more precipitously than the amounts requested.[58] The CAP request for 2001, reduced by US$200 million from 2001, was US$429 million – with 70 per cent of the total still targeted for the Federal Republic of Yugoslavia – although this time funding requirements for Kosovo were considerably reduced.[59] By all accounts, total funding will fall further in 2002/2003, with a smaller allocation for what are considered relief items, including housing construction and direct assistance to returnees.

The UNHCR's requirements for humanitarian assistance have been rising owing to a modestly increasing case-load of refugee returns and a faster-growing case-load of minority non-refugee returns. The World Bank supports some infrastructure repair for returnee areas, but not individual housing or other important UNHCR programmes that furnish legal advice and information and short-term income generation.

The region-wide Stability Pact for South Eastern Europe has become the major vehicle for securing funding and coordinating donors' contributions in the Balkans, including BiH. The Pact was initiated on 30 July 1999 by the European Union, under the umbrella of the Organization for Security and Co-operation in Europe (OSCE). The European Union and the World Bank jointly coordinate Stability Pact activities. The Pact brings together the foreign ministers of European and North American donor countries and of the Southeast European countries. Its aim is to strengthen regional cooperation, political and economic reform, stability, and national institutions throughout the Southeast European region, with a view to the eventual incorporation of these countries within the European–Atlantic framework. The Stability Pact mobilizes funding for activities encompassing urgent needs (e.g. Quick Start Programme projects in rural villages), institutional strengthening, governance, education, media, and human rights.

Preventing forced displacement and ensuring safe return are among the explicitly stated objectives of the Stability Pact.[60] Aspects of the return scenario emerge in virtually all discussions and, thus far, minority returns have been privileged in terms of attention within the Stability Group framework. For example, in 1999 the European Commission began implementation of an Integrated Return Programme that included housing, infrastructure, social projects, legal aid, and land-mine clearance.

Yet it would seem the Stability Pact, like the OCHA CAP, is meeting the same reticence among donors to invest further resources in BiH. Funding conferences for projects covering the Balkan region have yielded disappointing results. Support for returnee housing is still seriously lacking.

The United States is a case in point. The United States has been a major donor across the entire array of Bosnian reconstruction needs, as well as a steadfast and dependable partner of the UNHCR's programmes. Overall, through USAID and the State Department Bureau of Population, Refugees, and Migration (PRM), it has contributed nearly US$1 billion to support the Dayton Accords. PRM has been the channel for UNHCR and NGO humanitarian activities in support of reconstruction for refugees and the internally displaced. This assistance has continued. By March 2000, however, PRM guidelines for NGOs working in Bosnia and Croatia warned of forthcoming funding reductions, and proposed giving priority in 2000 to projects that could be completed in 12 months so that the NGOs could be phased out.

The UNMBIH terminated its mission at the end of 2002. The Secretary-General has urged international donors to "provide necessary financial resources to enable UNMBIH to complete its work."[61] The remainder of his message enumerated a number of challenges that remained, and probably would remain, after the mission's departure.

Prospects

The improvement in security in much of the Bosnian territory since 2000 has strengthened what may represent an enduring change of attitude among Bosnian citizens toward greater tolerance. It is not yet time to phase out the international vigilance over the Dayton process. Moreover, the very successes in obliging compliance potentially create further tensions. Minority returns, civil society groups demanding their rights, pressures to end discriminatory practices, and the many actions that bring reconciliation closer to reality will inevitably be challenged by still determined opponents. Clearly SFOR still has an essential role to play until reconstruction, reconciliation, and reintegration take root.

The process by which the international presence in Bosnia–Herzegovina will be phased out requires the utmost care, collaboration, and planning. Decisions should be guided by realities on the ground and should allow realistic time-frames for the still essential activities that require international resources and/or presence. Economic progress is now visible in most of Bosnia, but jobs are still scarce; unemployment in 2000 was about 41 per cent in the Federation, and assumed to be much higher in RS.[62] Of fundamental concern to the donors contemplating the medium and long term, however, is the fact that economic growth is still primarily a function of donor transfers. Economic and especially banking reforms remain as continuing challenges. Nevertheless, assuming a gradual evolution toward political stability, security, and improved governance, Bosnia and the other countries of the region – collectively and individually – should attract reasonable levels of international investment in the not too distant future.

There is virtual unanimity among analysts and field workers that Bosnia now needs long-term programmes that strengthen institutions and provide economic bases for reconciliation, rather than short-term projects. It is especially important that international support continues for local capacity-building, as national actors take over their rightful responsibilities. With regard to minority returns, reintegration assistance for basic needs is still critical. The case for continued support for construction and reconstruction of housing and for income generation for at least the next few years could hardly be more compelling. Families returning for the first time since the war to their places of origin need emergency assistance and security support as well as investment in longer-term development. In other words, continued attention to urgent needs should accompany efforts directed at regional development and institutional and structural changes, until such time as the government can mobilize adequate resources to take on the reconstruction itself.

Conclusion

There were strong justifications for the international interventions in Bosnia–Herzegovina and in Haiti. The Balkan conflict had been spreading and it was feared that it would affect other Balkan nations, e.g. Kosovo, bringing added tensions to neighbouring European countries. Moreover, the human rights violations, brutal ethnic cleansing, widespread displacement, and, not least, massive refugee arrivals throughout Europe demanded forceful responses. In the case of Haiti, the combined effects of serious human rights violations during the dictatorship, extreme poverty affecting the majority of citizens, and the counter-productive results of international sanctions had produced a volatile domestic situation and a refugee emergency. The rapidly growing Haitian refugee population in the United States was an important factor motivating international action.

Following the armed interventions, the major powers committed their resources to rebuilding the countries, reconciling and reintegrating mutually hostile and uprooted citizens, and strengthening national institutional capacities in the political, economic, and social spheres. These remain the challenges. This chapter has explored these challenges from a refugee perspective, which means that it has examined the impacts of post-conflict international efforts on the potential for continued flight and/or the conditions for durable return. The two quite different case studies illustrate a number of common strengths and weaknesses. In both cases, refugee and returnee integration and stability were threatened by continuing conditions of fragile security, internal political conflicts, and limited prospects for a viable, long-term economic future.

In both Bosnia–Herzegovina and Haiti, the countries of Europe and North America and Japan have invested significant resources for post-conflict rebuilding. The findings indicate that these resources could have been used to greater effect in addressing these problems. In BiH, establishing citizen security should have been among the first objectives. Despite the fact that humanitarian assistance was plentiful at first, the international community could not induce refugees and displaced minority populations to attempt to reclaim their homes in areas hostile to their ethnic group. Once the peacekeepers and political leaders were prepared to enforce the Dayton Accords more forcefully, a gradual but significant movement to the former minority areas began to take place. By that time, however, the humanitarian assistance was no longer plentiful. Although current evidence indicates that BiH is moving in a more positive direction in political and – more tenuously – in economic terms, international presence and support remain essentials during the next few years.

In Haiti, it was clear that reinforcing political legitimacy and human rights was a *sine qua non* for creating options other than flight for the citizens of the country. And, when internationally induced agreements failed to achieve these objectives, armed international intervention was determined to be the only effective means for doing so. The primary goals of the armed intervention and the subsequent UN missions were to establish a system of security and reliable electoral mechanisms. These ultimately proved too narrow to sustain the transition that Haiti required – and still requires.

With both countries still in the midst of the transition from war to peace, it is not clear that there will be sufficient support to sustain present achievements, much less to spur further progress. International agencies have been cutting back operations and donors reducing support, despite the fact that the specific needs for which international assistance was initially mobilized are still high, and before national institutions and capacities to meet these needs have been established. In the case of BiH, a stronger commitment to "staying the course" would almost certainly produce long-sought goals of greater ethnic diversity. In Haiti, which is a more problematic case, withdrawal of support risks leading to the return of conditions resembling those that brought about the refugee emergency and intervention in the first place.

The conflicts of the past two decades on every continent – South-East Asia, the Horn of Africa, the countries of the Great Lakes region in West Africa, Central America, and the Balkans – are all characterized by terrible destruction and massive human displacement. Authoritarian and repressive governments, weak institutions, and poverty have further complicated recovery in these countries. The major reason for declining international resources and commitments seems to be that donor governments neither anticipate nor plan for long-term involvement. Yet logic as well as history indicates that, following protracted periods of violence, destruction, economic and social disruption, and massive displacement, all war-to-peace transitions are bound to be long and troubled. It is well understood that international funding alone will not be sufficient to produce meaningful political, economic, and social reform. Nevertheless, inadequate commitments of time and funding, combined with an approach based on fragmented and uneven projects, obviously impede significant improvements.

The observations contained in this chapter are not intended to convince donors that staying longer is always better than leaving, or that more involvement is necessarily better than less. There is abundant contrary evidence that international actors sometimes overwhelm and stifle local initiatives. This has occurred in relation to some programmes in the Balkans. The underlying question is how donors and international agencies, working with local actors, determine the impacts of their involvement on a continuing basis; that is, on what bases are decisions taken that support should be modified, reduced, augmented, or eliminated? These issues warrant greater attention from donors and international agencies. In assessing needs, it is essential to take into account how war-uprooted groups are being reabsorbed into political, economic, and social structures. Efforts that have not failed should be brought to a close not through impatience or funding gaps,[63] but rather through informed and deliberative decisions aimed at achieving the best results by means of combined local and international efforts.

Finally, it is important to emphasize that, although peace-building and reintegration are long-term propositions, post-conflict international interventions need not be open-ended in the vast majority of cases. Exit strategies can strengthen rather than weaken national capacities to take on remaining problems. Nonetheless, they must be developed on the basis of comprehensive planning, funding levels must be targeted to priority tasks, and development and institutional assistance must be accompanied by a willingness to pay continued attention to countering the legacies of war, displacement, and violence.

Acknowledgements

The research for this chapter was funded with a grant from the United States Institute for Peace.

Notes

1. Ian Smillie gives a diagnosis of the learning process and its inadequacies in meeting current challenges of war-to-peace transitions in *Relief and Development: The Struggle for Synergy*, Occasional Paper No. 33, Providence, RI: Thomas J. Watson Institute for International Studies, 1998.
2. The policies are described in Andrew Schoenholtz, "Aiding and Abetting Persecutors: The Seizure and Return of Haitian Refugees in Violation of the U.N. Refugee Convention and Protocol," *Georgetown Immigration Law Journal*, vol. 7, no. 1, March 1993, pp. 67–84; Susan Martin et al., "Temporary Protection towards a New Regional and Domestic Framework," *Georgetown Immigration Law Journal*, vol. 12, no. 4, Summer 1998, pp. 552–553; Irwin P. Stotsky, *Silencing the Guns in Haiti: The Promise of Deliberative Democracy*, Chicago: University of Chicago Press, 1997; Robert Maguire et al., *Haiti Held Hostage: International Responses to the Quest for Nationhood, 1986–1996*, Occasional Paper No. 23, Providence, RI: Brown University, Thomas J. Watson Jr. Institute for International Studies and UN University, 1996; David Malone, *Decision-Making in the UN Security Council: The Case of Haiti, 1990–1997*, New York: Oxford University Press, 1998, p. 70.
3. UN Security Council, *Report of the Secretary General on the Question Concerning Haiti*, S/1995/46, 17 January 1995.
4. MICAH consolidated the functions of both the UN Police Mission in Haiti (MIPONUH) and the International Civilian Mission in Haiti (MICIVIH). Although scheduled to begin in March, the mission was not in the field until May 2000.
5. Maguire et al. note 19 multinational institutions and 14 governments (*Haiti Held Hostage*, p. 72). See also Smillie, *Relief and Development*, p. 7.
6. Maguire et al., *Haiti Held Hostage*, p. 74; Johanna Mendelson Forman, "Beyond the Mountains, More Mountains: Demobilizing the Haitian Army," in Tommie Sue Montgomery, ed., *Peace-keeping and Peacemaking in the Western Hemisphere*, Boulder, CO: North South Center/Lynne Rienner, 2000, pp. 67–89.
7. Malone, *Decision-Making in the UN Security Council*, p. 122.
8. The broader US operation was called Operation Restore Democracy. The soldiers who, for a brief time, formed part of the interim police eventually had access to training as well.
9. Smillie, *Relief and Development*, p. 10, notes that many of the former soldiers were trained for skills already over-supplied in Haiti.
10. Interview, 18 October 2000.
11. US General Accounting Office, *Testimony of Jess T. Ford, before the US Congress Committee on International Relations*, House of Representatives, GAO/T-NSIAD-00-257. In the United States, the programme was operated by the Department of Justice's International Criminal Investigative Training and Assistance Program.
12. Hugh Byrne et al., "Haiti and the Limits to Nation Building," *Current History*, March 1999, pp. 127–132; Chetan Kumar, *Building Peace in Haiti*, IPA Occasional Paper Series, Boulder, CO: Lynne Rienner, 1998.

13. Mendelson Forman, "Beyond the Mountains," p. 82.
14. Ibid.; Serge Kovaleski, "Haiti's Police Accused of Lawlessness: US Forces Linked to Killings, Drug Offenses," *Washington Post*, 28 September 1999; Amnesty International, *Amnesty International Reports: Haiti*, at www.amnesty.org. In the reports for 1999, 2000, and 2001, AI criticized the practices of the HNP.
15. US General Accounting Office, *Testimony of Jess T. Ford before the US Congress Committee on International Relations*.
16. Press release from the US House International Relations Committee Hearings, 19 September 2000.
17. Canadian International Development Agency, *Projet d'appui institutionnel à la Police Nationale d'Haiti*, Mid term evaluation, 26 January 2000, p. 57.
18. Kumar, *Building Peace in Haiti*; *Human Rights Watch*, 25 June 1995.
19. Smillie, *Relief and Development*, pp. 8–9. Smillie makes this judgement on the basis of an evaluation conducted in 1998 by L. M. G. Carlier for the World Bank ("Review of the Impact and Effectiveness of Donor-Financed Emergency Poverty Alleviation Projects in Haiti: The Challenge of Poverty Reduction," vol. II, March 1998).
20. World Bank, *Haiti Country Brief*, Washington DC, June 2000.
21. UNDP, *Système Opérationnel pour les Activités de Développement des Nations Unies en Haiti, Rapport Annuel du Coordinateur Résident*, 1999, p. 11, at www.ht.undp.org/pnud-hai/un/rapport/index.html.
22. 1998 figures from UNDP website, at www.ht.undp.org.
23. UNDP, *Cadres de coopération avec les pays et questions connexes. Premier cadre de coopération avec Haiti (1999–2001)*, Report from Resident Coordinator, DP/CCF/HAI/1, 20 July 1999.
24. These figures are recorded in the 2000 annual reports of the Economic and Social Council of the United Nations and the World Bank: *Elaboration and Implementation of the Long-Term Programme of Support for Haiti*, ECOSOC, 5 June 2000; World Bank, *Haiti: Country Brief*, June 2000.
25. Email exchange with Gerard Johnson, the IDB's Resident Representative, 14 December 2000.
26. *New York Times*, 5 September 2002, article by David Gonzalez.
27. "US Coast Guard Migrant Interdictions at Sea, Calendar Years 1982–2000: Haiti Figures," at www.USCG.gov.
28. Cited by the US Committee for Refugees (USCR), at www.refugees.org/world/countryrpt/amer-carib/2001/haiti.html, information for 2000.
29. Ibid. – from 3,000 new applicants in 1999 to 4,700 in 2000.
30. UNDP, *Système Opérationnel*, pp. 17–22.
31. Statement by Mrs. Sadako Ogata to the Humanitarian Issues Working Group of the Peace Implementation Council and the Stability Pact (Geneva), 11 September 2000, at www.unhcr.ch/.
32. USAID, "Country Profile: Bosnia–Herzegovina," August 2000, at www.usaid.gov/country/ee/ba/.
33. Figures at www.unhcr.ba/return/index/.
34. The terms Bosnia–Herzegovina, BiH, and Bosnia are used interchangeably.
35. Walter Irvine, *Review of the UNHCR Housing Programme in Bosnia and Herzegovina*, UNHCR, Evaluation and Policy Analysis, November 1998, p. 10.
36. Nicola Dahrendorf and Hrair Balian, *The Limits and Scope for the Use of Development Assistance and Disincentives for Influencing Conflict Situations: Case Study: Bosnia*, Organisation for Economic Co-operation and Development, Development Assistance Committee (DAC), Task Force on Conflict, Peace and Development Cooperation, Paris, June 1999, pp. 13–14.

37. The OHR, under the auspices of the UN Security Council, is governed by the Peace Implementation Council, consisting of the G-8 countries, the President of the European Union, the European Commission, and the Organization of the Islamic Conference.

38. The Task Force has consisted of bilateral donors, international organizations, and NGOs, with SFOR participation, for programmes aimed at coordinating international support and facilitating return and integration. Funding for the RRTF came from the United States, the European Commission, and the World Bank.

39. See Security Council Resolutions 1031 (1995), 15 December 1995, and 1088 (1996), 12 December 1996; UN Security Council, "Report to the Secretary General," S/1999 1260, 17 December 1999.

40. The actions of local officials to obstruct minority return was a key factor. In 1996, the mayor of one community, Travnik, cooperated with international authorities so that both refugees and displaced persons returned there, bringing benefits to both town and returnees (*Human Rights Watch*, June 1996, p. 14).

41. Smillie, *Relief and Development*, pp. 12–16; US Institute of Peace (USIP), "Balkan Returns: An Overview of Refugee Returns and Minority Repatriation," Special Report, Washington DC, 21 December 1999, pp. 7–8.

42. As of November 2000, the estimated number of refugees who had returned to the country, to both majority and minority areas, was about 190,000 out of the 1.7 million estimated to have left. Of these, most of the approximately 800,000 who went to Serbia and Croatia have probably relocated permanently. Some 70,000 to 90,000 are living in Germany with temporary status, but are likely to be regularized. Thus far, 179,000 have returned from Germany, mainly in 1997 and 1998. Only a few thousand returned in 2000 (figures obtained from the International Organization for Migration, 1996–2000). The USCR estimates that about 250,000 still live abroad and lack durable solutions; at www.refugees.org/world/countryrpt/.

43. Total refugee returns from all countries during 1997 were 60,257 and during 1998 90,503, according to IOM figures. Those from Germany represented by far the largest group.

44. OHR/RRTF, *RRTF: Report, December 1997: Outlook for 1998*, p. 3, at www.ohr.int/rrtf/.

45. Ibid., p. 4.

46. Irvine, *Review of the UNHCR Housing Programme*, pp. 5–6.

47. Dahrendorf and Balian, *The Limits and Scope for the Use of Development Assistance*, pp. 27–28. The DAC study offers some possible explanations, including inadequate selection mechanisms and follow-up, initiation of rewards on the basis of promised cooperation that failed to materialize, and the fact that donors overall did not necessarily invest more in the open cities than in other places.

48. UNHCR, *Bosnia*, 17 June 1997, at www.unhcr.ba/return/index/; unregistered returns are those unassisted by the UNHCR.

49. OHR/RRTF, *RRTF: Report, March 1998*, p. 2, at www.ohr.int/rrtf/.

50. USIP, "Balkan Returns," p. 6. Central Bosnia was among the few areas where the SFOR peacekeepers were actively present and obliged compliance with Dayton returnee projects. This USIP report cites a study by the International Crisis Group showing small numbers of Croats and Bosniacs returning to the towns of Bugojno and Prozor-Rama, respectively, largely owing to effective RRTF presence in those particular places.

51. Sandra Coliver, "The Contribution of the International Criminal Tribunal for the Former Yugoslavia to Reconciliation in Bosnia and Herzegovina: Lessons for the International Criminal Court," in Dinah Shelton, ed., *International Crimes, Peace and Human Rights: The Role of the International Criminal Court*, New York: Transnational Publishers, 2000.

52. The consequences are elaborated in Coliver, "The Contribution of the International Criminal Tribunal for the Former Yugoslavia"; European Stability Initiative, "International Power in Bosnia," Discussion Paper, 30 March 2000, at www.esiweb.org.

53. Interview with Werner Blatter, UNHCR Representative in BiH, *Oslobodjemje*, 2001.

54. Many of those occupying homes illegally are Serbs forced out of the Croat Krajina area.

55. UNHCR, "Returnee Monitoring Study: Minority Returns to the Republika Srpska, Bosnia and Herzegovina," based on interviews 5 January – 3 March 2000 by Michelle Alfaro et al.

56. Ibid.

57. Carlos Westendorp, the High Representative for two years through end July 1999, "Lessons from Bosnia," *Wall Street Journal*, 29 July 1999.

58. The Office for the Coordination of Humanitarian Affairs (OCHA), *Consolidated Inter-Agency Appeal for Southeastern Europe 2001*, Geneva: UN OCHA, 8 November 2000, covers the five countries of the Southeastern region (Albania, Bosnia and Herzegovina, Croatia, the Former Yugoslav Republic of Macedonia, and the Federal Republic of Yugoslavia) and the 16 UN agencies working there. In the 1999 submission for 2000, the initial request was for US$660 million, which was later reduced to US$627 million when the UNHCR reduced its request. The total was one-third less than it had been in 1999. The donor response was disappointing, with less than 50 per cent of the requested amount in place by the end of October 2000.

59. OCHA, *Consolidated Inter-Agency Appeal for Southeastern Europe 2001*.

60. Statement of the Special Coordinator of the Stability Pact for South Eastern Europe, Cologne, 10 June 1999.

61. UN Department of Public Information, 5 December 2000.

62. Norwegian Refugee Council, "Internal Displacement in Bosnia and Herzegovina: Updated Country Profile," 1 December 2000, at www.nrc.no/.

63. The Center on International Cooperation at New York University has been exploring options to facilitate effective humanitarian assistance and overcome fragmented and piecemeal funding patterns; see www.nyu.edu/pages/cic/. See also Shepard Forman and Stewart Patrick, *Good Intentions. Pledges of Aid for Postconflict Recovery*, Boulder, CO: Lynne Rienner, 2000.

12

Sovereignty, gender, and displacement

Julie Mertus

Taking a bath in private is something most people take for granted. For Afghan refugees densely packed into the camps mushrooming around Mazar City, a safe, clean bath is a dream. Sippi Azerbaaijani-Moghdam, a representative of the Women's Commission for Refugee Women and Children, has worked with Afghan women refugees for nearly a decade. The latest trend, she says, is for the international humanitarian organizations setting policy in Afghanistan to have specific projects on women refugees.[1] But nothing really changes. The washrooms, latrines, and wells in the Sakhi camp are still built on a grid pattern that ignores the needs of the women who would use the facilities the most. The facilities are poorly lit and unguarded; women who use them are susceptible to being sexually assaulted. "This is an emergency," the camp planner, a former city planner who now works for an Afghan non-governmental organization (NGO), tells Sippi. "Everyone will get the same ... There is no time for gender." Even after local women are employed as female health care educators in the camp, little changes. "Employing women in such situations fills a gender quota and is a palliative for those who criticize," Sippi observes, "but the women have no power to do anything within the organization or project."

Many of the NGOs at work in Afghanistan have "gender experts" who analyse problems and write fancy monographs but do little to influence the work of their organizations on gender issues. Small business projects channel women into knitting endeavours where there are no markets for women's goods. Sanitation projects neglect women's privacy concerns in constructing bathing facilities. Food distribution procedures overlook women's role in feeding their families; consequently, warring factions siphon off aid and women and children go hungry. Women who have always been the farmers in their communities watch while the men receive the agricultural aid. One after another, the projects most intended to help Afghan women fail.

The main approach of humanitarian and development organizations to gender issues has been to create "special" "women's programmes" for their "special" needs. This wrongly assumes that "men's problems" are the standard against which "women's problems" are measured and that women are concerned with only a limited list of issues specific to their femaleness. Afghan women, for example, are concerned about the mistreatment they have suffered because they are women. But ask any Afghan woman in a refugee camp to list her primary concerns, and she is more likely to talk about the need for peace, health care, food, education, and shelter than about having to wear the burqa. Afghan women do want to have a choice about wearing a burqa, but there are other issues that demand their immediate attention. And these issues are also "women's issues."

Demilitarization, de-mining, infrastructure reconstruction, economic development, reform of police, courts, and judiciary, the redress of past war crimes, and the future integration of international human rights standards into local law and practice – these are all equally women's problems. Women and men should both have a say in solving them. In analysing a problem, women may draw from their particular experiences as women. For example, many women can tap the skills and insight they have gained in their roles as mothers and family caretakers. From this perspective, women may add ideas that would otherwise go overlooked.

However, simply placing more women at the decision-making table does not guarantee that their ideas will be reflected in new programming. New ideas cannot be simply added on to existing programming that structurally resists them. It would be like adding eggs on top of a cake after it has already started to bake. To be more effective, international organizations working in Afghanistan must examine their own institutional gender inclusiveness and consider potential roadblocks to gender-based programming in their own organizational structure. Necessary changes in institutional policy should then be made to ensure that the skills, interests, and experiences of women and men are accounted for in every aspect of programming. In Afghanistan, this approach would entail asking Afghan women and men about their priorities for reconstruction, and involving them as equal partners in efforts to address the problems they identify.

International governmental and non-governmental organizations have come a long way in addressing the concerns of displaced women, but they still have a long way to go. This chapter argues that international organizations would do better if they had a more complete understanding of the nature of the problem, one that concerns not only women organizing as women, but also larger gender issues concerning the socially constructed roles of women *and* men in society. It explains how the experience of displacement is gendered, that is, how it is influenced by real and perceived roles, responsibilities, constraints, opportunities, and needs of men and women in society. The existence of an uprooted and imperilled population should be filtered through a "gender lens," to include root human rights violations and other causes of flight, the type of violence and other rights violations encountered during flight and in temporary encampments, and the consideration of permanent solutions for resettlement or return. At the same time, the mechanisms for both the delivery of humanitarian aid and the protection and resettlement or return of uprooted and imperilled people should disclose a concerted effort to account for the gender dimensions of their work.

The gendered process of displacement occurs within the context of shifting and competing sovereignties described throughout this text. This chapter will consider two interrelated variables: the gender dimensions of displacement and changing approaches to sovereignty. Each dimension has important consequences for displaced populations. The 11 September 2001 terrorist attacks and the responses thereto underscored what many international relations scholars and practitioners had long observed: the impact of the gravest threats to world security reach across state borders, perpetrators are likely to be trans-sovereign in nature (in that they are not bounded by any particular state), and responses are likely to involve the coordinated efforts of trans-sovereign (both multi-state and non-state) actors. The first section of this chapter identifies how and why sovereignty matters to advocates concerned about gender and displacement and, in particular, to the organizational strategies of displaced women. The chapter then explores in greater detail the gendered dimensions of flight and the displacement experience itself, and reviews trends in responses to the gender dimensions of displacement, both within and outside one's state borders. The goal of the chapter is to enhance understanding of policy options for state actors responding unilaterally or collectively to gender in displacement and contribute to an understanding of the political strategies of non-state actors who increasingly assert their concerns about gender and displacement in trans-sovereign spaces.

The importance of sovereignty

Changes in the nature of state sovereignty are of great relevance to displaced women, as they are for all people concerned with gender issues in displacement. Rosalyn Higgins defines sovereignty as "the entitlement of a state to act as it wishes at the international level – the ability to resist intervention from the international community."[2] This traditional concept of sovereignty embodies several assumptions of great concern to displaced communities: that only states are in charge of the creation and implementation of international human rights and humanitarian law, that international law is made exclusively with the consent of states, and that no one is allowed to interfere with the way in which a state treats its own inhabitants.

Displaced women do not seek sovereignty in this traditional sense but, as Higgins points out, "they are interested in international status in order to acquire an external area in which to articulate their claims for internal rights." By talking in terms of sovereignty, displaced women and their advocates can acquire representation and legitimacy in the world. At the same time, by working in ways that challenge traditional notions of sovereignty, displaced women and their advocates can more effectively raise their gender-based concerns and demand participation in decision-making and implementation of solutions to their problems.

The actions of displaced women and their advocates challenge traditional state sovereignty in several fundamental ways. First, in demanding protection in their state of refuge, the actions of displaced women serve to advance and strengthen international legal prescriptions for domestic governance. Human rights and humanitarian laws place obligations on states to treat displaced women with certain minimum standards and, in so doing, temper unilateral state control. Domestic methods for dispute resolution, including domestic courts and administrative procedures, are therefore limited in their decision-making by international law.

Second, in turning to international bodies for protection and support, displaced women foster the development of supranational authority. Transnational authorities – above and beyond the single state – recognize displaced women as subjects and not mere objects of international law and, by restricting domestic control, further undermine the ability of states to act in accordance with their own wishes. International methods for dispute resolution, including mediation, arbitration, and dispute settlement, enforce international standards, thereby limiting state authority.

Third, in networking with other individuals and organizations outside their own state borders, displaced women promote the development of transnational civil society. Although transnational civil society has not, as Jean Bethke Elshtain desires, replaced the state with a "co-exist[ing] of overlapping, porous sovereignties,"[3] non-state actors working within this space are not without power to effect change. Non-state actors shape the content of norms important to displaced women and, through fact-finding, advocacy, and negotiation, help affect their enforcement. Although often acting in concert with individual states and international bodies, transnational civil society also provides a check on individual state and trans-state action and, accordingly, new opportunities for transformative justice.[4]

In all three cases, the locus for the formation of rights or duties, decision-making, and law enforcement has shifted from a space controlled exclusively by the state to one influenced by other entities. In attempting to influence this process so that their concerns are heard and addressed, displaced women and their advocates have tended to draw upon two often conflicting ideas of feminist ethics.

Cultural or relational feminists suggest that women stand to benefit as state borders break down and sovereignty becomes more fragmented and textured over time. These theorists expose the ways in which the maintenance and expansion of the territorially bounded state rely in large part on the silencing and suppression of women.[5] Leading this school of thought, Jean Bethke Elshtain writes that historically "much of the power of the concept of sovereignty" lies in its masculinized nature.[6] Iris Marion Young explains this sentiment:

Founded by men, the modern state and its public realm of citizenship paraded as universal values and norms which were derived from specifically masculine experience: militaristic norms of honor and homoerotic camaraderie; respectful competition and bargaining among independent agents; discourse framed in unemotional tones of dispassionate reason.[7]

States are patriarchal institutions not only because they exclude women from decision-making, but also because they are based on the concentration of power in an élite and the legitimization of a monopoly on the use of force to maintain that control.[8]

International institutions are "functional extensions of states" that are similarly based on male norms. Even if state institutions and practices do not overtly discriminate against women, they in effect exclude or inhibit women's participation by adopting a male world-view as the standard by which behaviour is judged. Under this system, "state sovereignty" grants legitimacy to the subjugation of women. "In an international society peopled by States," Karen Knop asserts, "women are analytically invisible because they belong to the State's sphere of personal autonomy."[9] Christopher Joyner and George Little explain this point:

In the view of feminists, men have legitimated "state autonomy" as a juris-prudential means by which they can remove themselves from its gendered effects. That is, men can point to the "depersonalized state" as an actor that normatively functions independently of human control. In reality, however, males decide and direct (in general) the course of "state" action. As feminists see it, the conceptual divorce of the independent "state" from its male masters cleverly masks gender bias in international law.[10]

The movement away from the inviolable state to a more permeable and fluid entity thus opens new opportunities for dismantling the institutionalized subordination of women in international law, international institutions, and their processes. Moreover, cultural and relational theorists believe, this shift demonstrates that the international environment is moving toward an appreciation of the interconnectedness of actors in world politics and a feminist morality grounded in an ethic of care.[11] Extrapolating from a domestic analogy, these thinkers argue that, as with individuals, an ethic of care should apply to relations between states.[12]

For those concerned about gender issues in displacement, the emphasis on caretaking and responsibility can be an important moral argument as well as an advocacy strategy that resonates widely.[13] Cultural feminist Robin West emphasizes that, until we place greater value on caretaking and provide better supports for caretakers of dependants, women will continue to be unequal.[14] This insight applies to the issue of gender in displacement. In highlighting the traditional caretaking roles of women and the interconnectedness of women and men in society, observations of relational feminists can help humanitarian organizations so that their work supports indigenous movements for transformative social change. The goal then, as Kathleen Jones has stated, is to "replace the voice of the sovereign master not with babble, but with efforts to recognize and admit responsibility for patterns of relationships that sovereign boundaries aim to negate."[15]

A competing voice in feminist ethics, attributed to radical feminists, views the dismantling of state borders as threatening to women. Radical feminists therefore call into question the extent to which shifts in sovereignty stand to benefit women. As Karen Knop has observed, "the violation of a state's territorial integrity is transformed into the imagery and reality of rape in a number of ways."[16] When state borders are violated militarily, gender-based violence becomes a favourite tool of advancing forces. As explained more fully in this chapter, women become more susceptible to the threat of rape and other forms of gender-based abuse and men become targets of violence designed to be emasculating. In order to sustain itself, the process of militarization deliberately manipulates images of masculinity and femininity.[17] In times of war, the psychological transference of identity to the state through the machinery of patriotism and the language used to describe the event involve sexual imagery, dehumanizing women.

The shift in power from the state to trans-sovereign private and corporate sectors of society can become another, more effective way to exclude women's participation in decision-making. Spike Peterson and Anne Sisson Runyon worry that women have little influence over the international governmental organizations that control their lives.[18] The increased devaluation of the public sector at the state level, they assert, greatly reduces the political space for women to gain power and use it to promote equality. The goal, in their view, should be maintaining and reimagining state boundaries, not dismantling them altogether.

Organizing to address the gender issues facing displaced men and women thus entails working with states, not against them, and strengthening state responsibilities and capacities, not weakening them.[19] What women facing sexual violence often want, for example, is for the state to take corrective and restorative action, and not recede into the background. This argument is often raised in the domestic context, where viewing violence in the family as a private matter preserves the inequality and vulnerability of women within the family.[20] To address the perpetuation of institutionalized inequalities, advocates have demanded that standards of justice be applied to the private realm and the family, as well as to the public realm of state and civil society.[21]

An analogy can be made with the traditional refusal of international law to address state-condoned violence against its own citizens. Just as feminists call for the dismantling of the public/private split in the domestic violence context, they argue that the boundary between international and domestic jurisdiction on human rights questions should be made permeable and, in some cases, dismantled altogether.[22] The notion of humanitarian assistance as an exception to the international legal principle of non-intervention may be treated in the same way as state intervention in the family, in that intervention serves to protect weaker members from isolated instances of abuse.

This argument has particular force for advocates concerned about the gender dimension of displacement. Issues of concern to displaced women and their lived experiences have not been addressed, in part owing to the mistaken belief that such issues are private and beyond state control generally, and because family law and violence against women have been dealt with as private matters of internal national regulation and not as matters of concern between states. Even when international law addresses the experience of women in conflict, its impact is partial and incomplete because women have traditionally been excluded from the law formation and enforcement.

In sum, advocates concerned with gender issues in displacement have a great stake in the shifting sovereignty debate. Because the displaced community is diverse in composition and experience, there is not one single project for addressing sovereignty, but many strategies. In any event, the issue of sovereignty cannot be avoided. States are no longer the only or most important perpetrators of violence and other conditions that cause displacement; states are no longer the only or most important actors responding to displacement. New thinking on sovereignty informs the reasons for flight, the experiences of displaced women in resettlement, and trends in responses. Each of these will be discussed in turn below.

Gender dimensions of displacement

Today an estimated 40–50 million people around the world are uprooted, spilling across state borders and demanding solutions that challenge traditional notions of sovereignty. Approximately 75–80 per cent of the displaced are women and children.[23] The experience of flight and displacement has different implications for male and female members of a population, largely according to the roles they are expected to play in society.

The human rights dimensions leading to flight are gendered. Although women may experience the same human rights deprivations as men, human rights violations often take different forms for women and men because of their perceived gender roles. After the civil war began in Somalia in 1991, for example, over a quarter of the population had fled; 300,000 of these refugees sought safety in Kenya, where hundreds of women were raped in camps in the northeastern provinces.[24] During the 1994 genocide, Rwandan women were also subjected to sexual violence on a massive scale. As many as 5,000 women in Rwanda were impregnated by rape, many of them by the killers of their spouses and family members.[25] In the 1980s, thousands of Mozambican refugee women were raped after they sought shelter in Zimbabwe.[26] Women are far more likely to attempt to leave their country to escape battering in the home that goes unaddressed by their governments or to avoid community practices dangerous to their lives and health, such as female genital mutilation, child brides, forced sterilization and abortion, or other abuse of women in same-sex relationships.

Because of gender-related economic and social circumstances, women are less likely to have the information and means that will enable them to demand accountability for human rights abuses. In some cases, legal and social prohibitions may prevent a woman from reporting sexual violence or other crimes. As a result, abuses against women are far less likely to be reported, investigated, and prosecuted.

The consequences of human rights violations are likewise gender specific. Sexual violence directed against women, for example, can lead to pregnancy and, as a consequence of pregnancy, ostracism from the community. The uprooting of elderly people and persons with disabilities can lead to greater responsibilities for the women of the community, as women are most likely to become their caretakers. In contrast, abuses against men are more likely to lead to loss of life, loss of political position, and interference with traditional roles in community.

Economic catalysts also figure heavily for both male and female flight. For a variety of reasons, however, including the fact that men stay at home to fight (and often to die), women now form the majority of migrant workers. In war-torn countries, women often find themselves unable to support themselves and their family and are thus forced to seek employment opportunities across state borders. In newly deregulated economies, many skilled and educated women workers are unable to find jobs that provide a living wage. They face state-condoned discrimination against women in the workplace, and are pressured into low-paying, stereotypical "women's jobs," such as maid, nanny, or piecework textile worker. Some women are lured into sex-work, often without full information that would enable them to consent.

Both women and men may be pushed from their homes when their government, military, paramilitary troops, or other powers severely discriminate against them and their families for their "subversive" political activities. Yet the context of this government abuse differs for men and women. Women human rights activists are more likely to flee so that their government does not arrest and harass their politically active family members, or women in flight may themselves face gender-based violence owing to their personal relationship with political activists.[27] Some Albanian women in Kosovo, for example, have been forced to flee with their families after the Serbian authorities accused them of supporting militant factions and targeted them for reprisal.

Women and men also leave their homes in order to escape health- and life-threatening forms of discrimination and persecution owing to their religion, race, ethnic group, and political opinion. Examples include growing violence and anti-Semitism against Jews in the former Soviet Union, against Roma or "gypsies" in Central and Eastern Europe, against Muslims in Burma, and against Christians in Sudan. Often gender-based abuse has, at its core, the failure of governments to respect different political or religious views. Women and men who run foul of expected gender roles are particular targets. One most evident example of this is the harassment, torture, and at times killing of gay men and lesbians who, by their very existence, refuse to accept the dominant political or religious view. This phenomenon often acts more to the detriment of gay men because they are more visible than lesbians in public places.

Once in flight or temporarily settled in another community or country, men and women confront tremendous challenges in having their immediate needs met and moving on with their lives. Men encounter the most intense pressure to take up arms and support one side in an armed conflict. Owing to their traditional role in society, men face a great risk of forced and involuntary conscription, loss of life on the battlefield, and torture and abuse as prisoners of war. For women, their roles present different challenges. Uprooted women often lose contact with their communities and family members, particularly male members. They may have men folk who have "disappeared" while in combat or in flight. They might know where some of their friends and family members are, but remain unable to contact them for practical or financial reasons. When their men are killed, missing, or imprisoned, women may be forced into new economic roles.

Displacement thus often leads to dramatic changes in family structures and gender roles. If the family is intact and a man is present, women must often deal with changes in male and female roles. Surviving men face threats to their established role as a provider for their family and a decision maker in their communities.[28] Often the man, who used to work outside the home, is left without work or meaning for life, while the woman continues to be productive: cooking, cleaning, taking care of children, shopping, and at times providing for all basic needs of the family. Many times the burden for women increases, as their elderly relatives become more dependent on them. If the men do not readjust their roles, there is a danger of new duties simply being added on to women's roles and women becoming perpetually more and more overworked. At the same time, the new demands placed on women may lead to greater confidence and the development of political consciousness and agency.[29]

Life in a refugee camp or camp for internally displaced persons is influenced by the cultural values of the surrounding community. The change in gender roles experienced by displaced people is particularly dramatic when they seek refuge in an area with a social context alien to their own. Scott Turner has reported that refugees often blame UN agencies for what they experience as "social and moral decay" in refugee camps.[30] To compound the pressures of role shifts, often the host area or country is hostile to the refugee or displaced population. With their normal social structures and support systems broken down, both men and women are vulnerable to discrimination, physical violence, and other forms of abuse.

The manifestation of violence and discrimination against displaced populations is also gendered. Whereas men may face physical attack and discrimination in the so-called "public" sphere, women are more vulnerable to sexual exploitation, domestic violence, and rape.[31] Although in some cases women's status improves during displacement (at least on a temporary basis), in many other cases the long-term effect of displacement is the reinforcement of patriarchal institutions. Men may maintain their social status in the camps, but women may lose their social status so completely that they are re-subordinated owing to their particular physical vulnerability. Judy Benjamin explains:

Taking advantage of the weakest has long been a key strategy of conflict; fighters are trained to zero in on their enemy's weak points. In situations of displacement, women and girls become easy targets of aggression, a vulnerable flank upon which aggressors focus their attacks to humiliate and defeat their opponent.[32]

When displaced men are subjected to sexual violence, the goal of the perpetrators similarly is to humiliate their opponent by emasculating their men.

Government, paramilitary, and other opponents usually target women because of their ethnic, national, religious, racial, and/or political affiliation. But there is a gender component as well. The subservient cultural and social position of women throughout the world fosters the conditions in which women are subject to abuse and left without the resources and recourse to address harms and prevent future wrongs. Adding to this disadvantaged state, refugee women find themselves outside whatever familiar institutions exist in their native states, and often unable to communicate in their new environments.[33] Unaccompanied women and girls are particularly vulnerable to protection infringement as they are removed from the structures of their community that could shield them from being targets of abuse.[34] In addition, the reproductive role of women makes them less mobile and more susceptible to physical abuse.

The issue of rape in war was headline news after cases of systematic rape were reported in Bosnia in 1993, but throughout history soldiers have raped women as part of war.[35] Mass rapes of women have been documented in recent years in such diverse countries as Bosnia, Cambodia, Haiti, Peru, Somalia, and Uganda.[36] Ruth Seifert identifies the following characteristics of wartime rape:[37]

1. rape has been treated as part of the "rules of war" – it is a right mainly conceded to victors;

2. in military conflicts the abuse of women is part of male communication, a graphic demonstration of triumph over men who fail to protect "their" women;

3. wartime rape is also justified by acceptance of the notion that soldiers are "naturally" masculine and that masculinity is "naturally" violent and abusive;

4. rapes committed in war are aimed at destroying the adversary's culture;

5. orgies of rape originate in culturally ingrained hatred of women that is acted out in extreme situations.

Women are targeted for sexual abuse as the property of the enemy nation *and* as women.[38] In this sense, women are doubly dehumanized – as woman, as enemy. In one act of aggression, the collective spirit of women *and* of the nation is broken, leaving a reminder long after the troops depart.

Even after they make it to a "safe zone," women and girls are at risk of sexual assault. Often the perpetrators are the very forces that are supposed to protect them. Long-term inhabitants of refugee camps are often lured into prostitution rings or made to perform sexual acts in return for food or favours such as an asylum hearing. Human rights groups have documented cases of women refugees or migrants being raped or sexually assaulted by border guards or security forces.[39] Not surprisingly, the chief source of fear for displaced women and girls is gender-based violence. Although men also may be subjected to rape in wartime, for women the probability of such abuse is greater.

In addition to direct violence against themselves, women must perform their traditional role as caretaker in dealing with the violence committed against their loved ones, husbands, parents, and children. When men are attacked or imprisoned, women are frequently left alone to take care of the family and to work for the release of male family members. Conflict situations may also increase the levels of domestic violence against women. Domestic violence is defined as violence among members of a family or members of the same household. Regimes that exercise power by undermining self-esteem and self-expression usually encourage domination based on gender as well as on class and ethnic differences.[40] Although any person in a household could be the target of domestic violence, it is most frequently experienced by women.

Physical violence and severe forms of discrimination constitute human rights violations. In addition, uprooted populations face threats to social and economic rights, including the right to access to basic necessities such as food, water, shelter, blankets, and clothing. A report by the World Food Programme suggests that women and girls are worse off than men with respect to the denial of their social and economic rights. Women and girls often eat last and receive less food, and female-headed households receive less than male-headed households in terms of food allocation.[41]

Women usually have the burden of feeding and clothing their families. Moreover, humanitarian aid packages often do not provide for women's needs, such as gynaecological care, stockings, and cosmetics. Groups who work with refugee women argue that such items are not a luxury: if given the choice, women refugees may ask for them before other things. Despite improvements with respect to the provision of gender-specific aid packages, the prevailing understanding of "humanitarian essentials" may still exhibit an implicit gender bias.

For women, a particularly important right that is endangered in humanitarian crises is the right to health and to access to health care, including reproductive health services, mental health care, and maternal child care. Access to reproductive health care and contraception is crucial to a woman's well-being. However, such services are scarce or non-existent in most refugee camps. For example, members on a fact-finding mission to Sarajevo in October 1993 found that as "women of Sarajevo have been used to family planning programs and the Pill, but neither [were] available," a very high number of abortions were being performed in unsafe conditions by unqualified practitioners.[42] World Health Organization officials in Haiti successfully argued that family planning devices should be among the items excepted from the prohibition on imports established by international economic sanctions. After intense pressure by humanitarian staff and human rights advocates, the standard aid package has in most cases been updated to address the needs of women and girls. At the same time, advocates continue to press for improved recognition of the particular impact of displacement on the fundamental rights of females.

Access to remedies, and to asylum in particular, is influenced by gender-related factors. As explained more fully below, women who are persecuted because of their gender may have greater difficulty proving refugee status. In addition, women who are victims of military attack may have a hard time proving they are victims of persecution rather than random violence. Since some asylum officers still see rape and sexual violence as random offences, a soldier's rape of a woman, for example, may be discounted even though rape in war *is* accepted as a violation of established international humanitarian law. Asylum officers often discount women's experiences of conflict as being "not severe enough" to constitute persecution.

In sum, every stage of displacement – from the root cause of flight to the experience of flight, displacement, and resettlement – is gendered. Although women and men experience these stages of conflict differently, they do have an important commonality. In displacement, the socially constructed gender roles of both men and women are challenged in ways that profoundly affect their lives. Responsibility for addressing these problems rests not only at the state level but above the state, in trans-sovereign institutions, and below the state, with non-governmental organizations.

Trends in responses

Responsibility for responding to the problems described above has shifted from the old domain of the state to international governmental and non-governmental bodies. In both UN agencies and many non-governmental humanitarian organizations, mechanisms for improving the plight of refugee and displaced women have been put in place, guidelines have been established, gender positions created, and training programmes addressing gender concerns begun.[43]

Humanitarian organizations have begun to realize that involving women in programmatic activities is "not solely a matter of equity but, in a range of activities, a condition for achieving development and, as far as projects are concerned, a condition of their success also."[44] Many humanitarian organizations have taken steps to integrate gender throughout their programming. This entails at the initial stage the establishment of a policy on gender indicating goals and the creation of a gender strategy for achieving these goals. Gender strategies underscore the importance of men and women benefiting equally from assistance and recognize the different needs, interests, and capacities of men and women. "Given that women are usually in a disadvantaged position as compared to men of the same socio-economic level," the adoption of gender strategies "usually means giving explicit attention to women's needs, interests and perspectives. The ultimate objective is the advancement of women's status in society."[45] Drawing from the experiences of the gender and development movement, these strategies thus seek "to transform the position of women from one of subordination to one of equality, by recognizing the inessential and transitory nature of the assumptions which underpin that subordination."[46]

The movement to add gender policies has been accompanied by efforts to improve gender programmes within agencies and institutions. In general, there have been two conflicting responses: the mainstreaming of gender throughout all organizations and all programmes, versus the establishment of a gender focal point or gender unit within an organization. The latter concept is straightforward: each organization would have at least one central point tasked with addressing gender issues. The gender unit could offer technical assistance and expertise on gender issues to other parts of the organization. The mainstreaming concept is more complex. Mainstreaming emerged as an effort to increase the impact and effectiveness of development programmes in incorporating women and women's issues into development policies and programmes. Today, the concept is applied in the humanitarian field to refer to "achieving women's full participation with men in decision-making; getting women's issues centralized (not just near the center); putting women on a par with men in the process of initiating ... activities."[47]

Both the mainstreaming and focal point approaches have drawbacks. On the one hand, the mainstreaming approach risks submerging gender within the organization, so that the concerns are no longer identified and addressed. It may also result in words on paper but few changes in programming. On the other hand, the gender focal point approach risks marginalizing gender within the organization so that it is treated as something "special" that is not to be addressed at all unless within the specified unit. Where woman-specific programmes exist there is little guarantee that gender will be found in any other projects. The tension between these two approaches has yet to be fully mediated.

International policy changes and efforts to mainstream gender are accompanied by specific programmatic changes. Although the changes vary according to the mission, history, focus, and nature of the organization, they include following:[48]

- involving refugee women in the design and implementation of all programmes dealing with refugees;
- invoking practices to deal with all incidents of sexual violence and to respond to related protection and assistance issues;
- including information about refugee women, preferably written by and with refugee women, in all educational activities carried out in refugee programmes;
- including information about uprooted women in public media campaigns to combat the abuse of and discrimination against refugee women;
- improving the design of refugee camps to promote greater security according to the needs voiced by refugee women – such measures could include better lighting, security patrols, and special accommodation for single women, women heads of household, and unaccompanied minors;
- offering gender-sensitive and culturally appropriate counselling to women victims; this counselling should be conducted by trained, experienced counsellors, preferably from the refugees' culture and/or community;
- supporting the operation of SOS hotlines and "safe houses" for women refugees, staffed where possible by women refugees and/or women counsellors from the refugees' same culture and/or community;

- providing emergency resettlement to refugee women who may be particularly exposed to abuse;
- ensuring that refugee women are not forced to stay for long periods in closed camps or detention centres where they are more likely to be the victims of violence;
- employing female protection officers and female community social workers to work with all women, to provide safe places for women to talk to one another, and to provide remedies for women who are victims of violence;
- placing international staff who have received gender-sensitive training in border areas that refugee women must cross to enter countries of asylum as well as in reception centres, refugee camps, and settlements; and
- providing gender-sensitive training for host country border guards, police, military units, asylum officers, aid personnel, and others who come in contact with refugees and displaced persons.

Roadblocks to progress

Despite the dramatic change in the level of attention devoted to gender in humanitarian responses, four sets of roadblocks remain:
1. a gap between policies adopted at headquarters and their implementation in the field;
2. a continued failure to address the needs of uprooted populations who remain internally displaced;
3. the continued inability of those who suffer gender-based persecution to obtain asylum; and
4. the failure of gender programmes to address the position of men.

First, the gap between policies adopted at headquarters and implementation in the field of such measures remains a wide one. At both the governmental and non-governmental levels, programme mandates have been revised to require greater participation of local men and women in decision-making about programme conception and operation. However, field staff have a poor record when it comes to implementing participatory approaches. Their programme mandate may state that they are to draw on the skills of men and women within displaced populations. Yet aid agencies still tend to see women as vulnerable victims, not as survivors capable of shaping their own lives. The displaced populations served by these programmes complain that they rarely participate in programme planning and are at best marginally involved in programme operation. They also chastise aid agencies for creating a dependency relationship and infantalizing them.

Despite increased awareness about sexual violence in conflict situations and women's human rights, displaced women continue to raise grave protection concerns. As Judy Benjamin has noted, "[i]n general, agencies have been more willing to direct attention and resources to providing material assistance than to involving themselves with participation, protection and gender violence issues ... Agencies have not devoted adequate attention to reporting gender violence, documenting lessons learned, or establishing the effect of programs."[49] Benjamin speculates that this lack of attention may stem from the emergency mentality under which interventions for internally displaced persons operate.

Responses to emergencies tend to be ad hoc and highly dependent on political negotiations. Another explanation for the lack of attention to protection issues lies in the tendency of local aid staff to dismiss the treatment of sexual violence and other difficult issues as belonging in the realm of "culture" and thus beyond the scope of foreign assistance. A related explanation for shortcomings, Roberta Cohen has suggested, rests with the culturally ingrained insensitivity of many male staff members of UN agencies.[50]

Another tremendous roadblock to progress on gender issues is the general failure of humanitarian organizations to address the concerns of uprooted populations who remain within their country of origin. Most of the efforts to adopt gender-based programming are designed to reach only those who can fit the legal definition of refugee, and thus the needs of the vast majority of women imperilled by conflict remain unaddressed. Because internally displaced people remain within their country of origin, in most cases the very government that has caused their displacement has the primary responsibility for their protection, thus complicating access and the provision of protection and assistance. As Roberta Cohen has observed,

Often they are caught up in internal conflicts between their governments and opposing forces. Some of the highest mortality rates ever recorded during humanitarian emergencies have come from situations involving internally displaced persons. There is ... no one international organization with responsibility for providing protection and assistance to the internally displaced.[51]

Cases of human rights violations against internally displaced women have been well documented by Judy Benjamin and Khadija Fancy.[52] Burundi women refugees living in Tanzanian camps received far greater protection and assistance than displaced women living in Burundi. In the refugee camps, provision was made for health care services, food rations, skill training, and the education of children. In addition, UN protection officers monitored the grounds to ensure physical safety. In the camps for the displaced, by contrast, none of these services was available. and women had no mechanisms for reporting sexual violence and other forms of exploitation.

At first glance, it appears that great progress has been made in addressing gender-based catalysts for flight. Although attempts to add "woman" or "gender" to the refugee definition have been flatly unsuccessful, efforts to interpret the "political" or "other social group" grounds to include gender have been increasingly successful.

The main strategy of successful advocates has been to address the "public/private divide." Violations of women's rights that are viewed as occurring in the "private" sphere are shown to be forms of persecution just as violations of men's rights occurring in the "public" sphere are. In developing this strategy, advocates have placed particular emphasis upon the recognition of violence against women (such as wartime rape and particularly abusive "cultural practices") as persecution grounds under the 1951 Convention on the Status of Refugees.

The success of this strategy can be detected in changes in UN refugee policy. Bowing to pressure from advocates in 1985, the United Nations High Commissioner for Refugees (UNHCR) formally recognized that the 1951 Convention may encompass gender-based violence.[53] It issued a statement that states "are free to adopt the interpretation that women asylum seekers who face harsh or inhuman treatment due to their having trangressed the social mores of the society in which they live may be considered as a 'particular social group' within the meaning of [the 1951 Convention]." Six years later, the UNHCR issued its *Guidelines on the Protection of Refugee Women*, emphasizing the fact that gender-based persecution exists and should be recognized by "refugee-receiving" states as a basis for asylum.[54] Today, two states – Sweden and South Africa – have binding legislation recognizing gender-specific persecution as grounds for asylum, and Canada, the United States, the United Kingdom, Australia, New Zealand, and a number of European countries have adopted non-binding policies on gender persecution.

These changes, while promising, have in practice had only nominal impact on the expansion of the refugee definition. The number of applicants for asylum under these guidelines remains insignificant. In the United States, for example, a very small number of claims are from women seeking protection in part or wholly because of persecution on account of their "particular social group." US and most other country guidelines apply only to claims made at the port of entry to an asylum state and not to visa offices abroad. Because of disproportionately adverse social and economic constraints, women are far less likely than men to reach the port of entry of the industrial nations that have the guidelines. And, once at the port of entry, women face great hurdles in successfully articulating their claims to Western immigration officials, who have their own ethnocentric and essentialized view of female asylum applicants. Because asylum officials assume that female asylum applicants are poor, uneducated, and incapable of confronting their oppression, women who do not fit this mould (that is, most of the women who actually make it across borders) are viewed with suspicion. Heaven Crawley explains this result as the natural extension of the "depoliticization and decontextualization of women's experiences of persecution ... and [of] women being viewed as passive victims."[55]

The failure of legal and programmatic victories to have a deep impact on uprooted populations can also be explained by the changed nature of today's wars, which are most often internal conflicts, fought for the express purpose of displacing populations. There are more uprooted people than ever, but they are not receiving asylum. As I have explained in an earlier work, in the Cold War era Western countries accepted asylum seekers based on a Cold War calculus.[56] Today, however, refugees are often victims of violence or natural disasters, not of ideological persecution. With the political motivation for refugee acceptance diminished, Western countries seek to close their doors to asylum seekers. Thus,

while the number of asylum seekers has skyrocketed over the past ten years, fewer and fewer of the uprooted successfully navigate the asylum process. The number of asylum seekers in Europe, North America and Australia increased from 90,444 in 1983 to over 825,000 ten years later. Between 10 and 20 per cent of all asylum seekers in Europe are accepted, a decrease from 50 per cent in the mid-80s.[57]

Instead of granting asylum, Western countries seek to contain populations within their country of origin. When women refugees do reach Western countries, they are still unlikely to satisfy the Refugee Convention's persecution grounds. As Audrey Macklin explains:

to claim the legal status of a Convention Refugee ... a person must prove that she was fleeing persecution on the basis of "race, religion, nationality, membership in a particular social group or political opinion." Simply through adopting this legal definition, millions of women are already eliminated, not because the impetus for their flight was gender specific, but because war, starvation and environmental disasters "don't count" for purposes of the legal definition.[58]

For all of these reasons, the enhanced acceptance of gender-based persecution as grounds for refugee status has not helped many women.

A final shortcoming of the strategies undertaken to date to address the gender dimension of displacement concerns the treatment of men.

Examination of gender should consider the roles of both males and females within communities and their respective needs, interests, and skills. Although most gender programmes have language to this effect, the operational aspects of programmes tend to focus on women and to exclude men. This leads Judy El-Bushra to wonder, "If 'gender' implies a web of relationships between women and men, old and young, powerful and powerless, should not men figure, integrally and equally, in the analysis of these relationships?"[59]

Scott Turner has found that the recipients of aid can identify when programmes target women to the exclusion of men. The UNHCR then becomes the scapegoat: "[M]en's feeling of powerlessness is projected onto UNHCR and its policy of empowering women." He explains that "[t]he ideology of gender equality was perceived as a threat to their masculinity with UNHCR taking their place as husbands and fathers."[60] Instead of empowering women, Turner found that gender programmes targeting women had the paradoxical effect of providing upward mobility for young men who found jobs within aid organizations, thus changing further the relations both between genders and between generations.

The consequences, says El-Bushra, of excluding men are far-reaching:

Giving preference to women in assistance programmes may contribute to eroding men's role (as protectors, providers and decision makers, for example) and hence their social position and self-esteem but still not challenge the dominant gender ideology in which men's and women's roles are viewed as "natural."[61]

As a result of neglecting men, humanitarian programmes do not fulfil their promise of promoting transformative social change. "The situation of displacement is an opportunity for renegotiating gender relations."[62] In her study of young men in refugee camps, Cathrine Brun concludes that "there is no reason why young men should not participate mutually with young women in changing understandings of gender."[63] But, she cautions, "active participation assumes awareness and it may be that there needs to be more provision of appropriate education for men to help them understand the consequences of changes in gender ideology." Gender-based policies and programming integrating the concerns and skills of women and men are in their nascent stages.

Conclusion

States are still crucial actors in addressing gender concerns in displacement. However, considerable authority to set policies and strategies on this issue now rests with international governmental and non-governmental organizations. For them, recognizing gender issues in displacement means more than designing programmes that target women. Rather, to be fully successful, humanitarian agencies and organizations should integrate the resources and needs of both women and men in all aspects of programme planning and implementation. We must not overlook the different needs and skills that uprooted women and men bring to efforts to address their own problems of displacement, flight, resettlement, and other conflict-related issues.

Although the actors and agencies of the humanitarian community have made considerable progress in integrating a gender perspective into their work, they still have a long way to go before the policies are fully implemented. In particular, they should closely examine the frequent lack of connection between headquarters mandates and fieldwork, the continued failure to address gender-based protection issues fully and consistently, and the overall poor record at integrating local men and women into decision-making positions in programme design and implementation. In addition, they must adjust to the changed context of displacement, which increases the likelihood that displaced people will remain inside their country of origin and makes it less likely that Western countries will grant asylum to the few who do make it to their borders. They should design programmes with the understanding that, despite legal advances, displaced women are still particularly unlikely to gain asylum status and, thus, other protection measures will be necessary. Lastly, gender-based programming should remember men's gendered roles and recognize the full range of women's *and* men's needs and their potential contributions to society. In addressing all of these challenges, humanitarian actors should bear in mind that there is no "one size fits all" solution. Rather, approaches should be carefully tailored to local contexts and made flexible to adapt to changing conditions. The actors who will be called upon to develop these approaches will most likely be trans-sovereign in both their nature and approach.

Notes

1. Sippi Azerbaaijani-Moghdam, telephone interview with Julie Mertus, 28 November 2000.
2. Rosalyn Higgins, *American Society of International Law Annual Proceedings*, vol. 88, 1994, p. 71.
3. Jean Bethke Elshtain, "Sovereign God, Sovereign State," *Notre Dame Law Review*, vol. 66, 1991, p. 1377.
4. Iris M. Young, *Justice and the Politics of Difference*, Princeton, NJ: Princeton University Press, 1990, p. 259.
5. V. Spike Peterson, ed., *Gendered States: Feminist (Re)Visions of International Relations Theory*, Boulder, CO: Lynne Rienner, 1992.

6. Elshtain, "Sovereign God, Sovereign State"; Jean Bethke Elshtain, "Sovereignty, Identity, Sacrifice," *Social Research*, vol. 58, 1991.
7. Iris Marion Young, "Polity and Group Difference: A Critique of the Ideal of Universal Citizenship," in Cass Sunstein, ed., *Feminism and Political Theory*, Chicago: University of Chicago Press, 1990.
8. Hilary Charlesworth, Christine Chinkin, and Shelley Wright, "Feminist Approaches to International Law," *American Journal of International Law*, vol. 85, 1991.
9. Karen Knop, "Re/Statements: Feminism and State Sovereignty in International Law," *Transnational Law and Contemporary Problems*, Fall 1993, p. 293.
10. Christopher C. Joyner and George E. Little, "It's Not Nice to Fool Mother Nature: The Mystique of Feminist Approaches to International Environmental Law," *Boston University Law Journal*, Fall 1996, p. 244.
11. See, for example, Nel Noddings, "Caring," in Virgina Held, ed., *Justice and Care: Essential Readings in Feminist Ethics*, Boulder, CO: Westview Press, 1995; Carol Gilligan, *In a Different Voice: Psychological Theory and Women's Development*, Cambridge, MA: Harvard University Press, 1982; Sarah Ruddick, *Maternal Thinking: Towards a Politics of Peace*, Boston, MA: Beacon Press, 1995.
12. Isabelle R. Gunning, "Modernizing Customary International Law: The Challenge of Human Rights," *Virginia Journal of International Law*, vol. 31, 1991, p. 211.
13. See, for example, Eva Feder Kittay, *Love's Labor: Essays on Women, Equality, and Dependency*, New York: Routledge, 1999, pp. 186–188.
14. Robin West, *Caring for Justice*, New York: New York University Press, 1997, p. 72.
15. Kathleen B. Jones, "The Trouble with Authority," *Differences*, vol. 104, no. 11523, p. 3.
16. Karen Knop, "Re/Statements," p. 15.
17. Cynthia Enloe, *Maneuvers: The International Politics of Militarizing Women's Lives*, Berkeley, CA: University of California Press, 2000, pp. 289–294.
18. Spike Peterson and Anne Sisson Runyon, *Global Gender Issues*, Boulder, CO: Westview Press, 1999, p. 104.
19. Celina Romany, "State Responsibility Goes Private: A Feminist Critique of the Public/Private Distinction in International Human Rights Law," in Rebecca J. Cook, ed., *Human Rights of Women: National and International Perspectives*, Philadelphia, PA: University of Pennsylvania Press, 1994.
20. Carole Pateman, "Feminist Critiques of the Public/Private Dichotomy," in S. I. Benn and Gerald F. Gaus, eds., *Public and Private in Social Life*, London: St. Martin's Press, 1983, p. 281.
21. Gunning, "Modernizing Customary International Law," p. 211.
22. Karen Knop, "Borders of the Imagination: The State in Feminist International Law," *American Society of International Law Annual Proceedings (6–9 April)*, vol. 14, 1994, p. 17.
23. Roberta Cohen, *Refugee and Internally Displaced Women: A Development Perspective*, Washington DC: Brookings Institute, 1995.
24. Human Rights Watch, *Seeking Refuge, Finding Terror: The Widespread Rape of Somali Women Refugees in North Eastern Kenya*, A Human Rights Watch Short Report, 5, no. 13, October 1993; *Human Rights Watch Global Report on Women's Human Rights*, New York: Human Rights Watch, 1995.
25. Human Rights Watch, *Shattered Lives: Sexual Violence during the Rwandan Genocide and Its Aftermath*, New York: Human Rights Watch, 1996.
26. Eshila Maravanyika, *Some Issues of Protection and Participation of Refugee Women: The Case of Mozambican Refugee Women in Zimbabwean Camps*, The Hague: Institute of Social Studies, July 1995.
27. *Human Rights Watch Global Report on Women's Human Rights*.

28. Srilakshmi Guruaja, "Gender Dimensions of Displacement," *Forced Migration Review*, December 2000, at www.fmreview.org/fmr091.htm.
29. Judy El-Bushra, "Gender and Forced Migration: Editorial," *Forced Migration Review*, 9 December 2000, at www.fmreview.org/fmr091.htm, p. 3.
30. Scott Turner, "Vindicating Masculinity: The Fate of Promoting Gender Equality," *Forced Migration Review*, 9 December 2000, at www.fmreview.org/fmr091.htm.
31. Julie Dungan, "Assessing the Opportunity for Sexual Violence against Women and Children in Refugee Camps," *Journal of Humanitarian Assistance*, 22 August 2000.
32. Judy Benjamin and Khadija Fancy, "The Gender Dimensions of Internal Displacement: Concept Paper and Annotated Bibliography," submitted to the Office of Emergency Programmes, the United Nations Children's Fund (UNICEF), Women's Commission for Refugee Women and Children, November 1998, p. 18.
33. Teresa L. Peters, "International Refugee Law and the Treatment of Gender-Based Persecution: International Initiatives as a Model and Mandate for National Reform," *Transnational Law and Contemporary Problems*, vol. 6, no. 1, Spring 1996.
34. UNHCR, *Sexual Violence against Refugees: Guidelines Prevention and Response*, Sub-Committee of the Whole on International Protection, Geneva: UNHCR, 1995.
35. Kelly Dawn Askin, *War Crimes against Women: Prosecution in International Tribunals*, The Hague: Martinus Nijhoff, 1997.
36. UNHCR, "Meeting New Challenges: Evolving Approaches to the Protection of Women at Risk," Discussion Paper presented at the workshop, Toronto, 27–28 April 1998; UNCHR, "Rape and Abuse of Women in the Territory of the Former Yugoslavia. Report of the Secretary-General, Commission on Human Rights," UN Doc. E/CN.4/1995/4, 30 June 1993.
37. Ruth Seifert, *War and Rape: Analytical Approaches*, Geneva: Women's International League for Peace and Freedom, 1993.
38. Julie Mertus, "Women in the Service of National Identity," *Hastings Women's Law Journal*, vol. 5, no. 1, 1994, p. 5.
39. Amnesty International, *Human Rights Are Women's Rights*, London: Amnesty International, 1995.
40. Judy El-Bushra and Eugenia Piza Lopez, "The Gender of Armed Conflict," in Judy El-Bushra and Eugenia Piza Lopez, eds., *Development and Conflict: The Gender Dimension*, Oxford: Oxfam, 1994, pp. 18–28.
41. Eftihia Voutira, "Improving Social and Gender Planning in Emergency Operations," Report Commissioned by the World Food Programme, Refugee Studies Programme, Draft, December 1995.
42. Pippa Scott and Mary Anne Schwalbe, *A Living Wall: Former Yugoslavia: Zagreb, Slovonski Brod & Sarajevo*, New York: Women's Commission for Refugee Women and Children, 1993.
43. UNHCR, *UNHCR Guidelines on the Protection of Refugee Women*, Sub-Committee of the Whole on International Protection, Geneva: UNHCR, 1991; UNHCR, *Sexual Violence against Refugees*.
44. Robert Casson, *Does Aid Work?*, 2nd edn, Oxford: Clarendon Press, 1994, p. 92.
45. UN Development Fund for Women (UNIFEM), "Further Promotion and Encouragement of Human Rights and Fundamental Freedoms, Including the Question of the Programme and Methods of Work of the Commission, Alternative Approaches and Ways and Means within the United Nations System for Improving the Effective Enjoyment of Human Rights and Fundamental Freedoms," UN Doc. E/CN.4/1997/131, 1997, p. 5.
46. El-Bushra, "Gender and Forced Migration: Editorial," p. 1.
47. Mary Anderson, *Focusing on Women: UNIFEM's Experience in Mainstreaming*, New York: UNIFEM, 1993.

48. See League of Red Cross and Red Crescent Societies, "Working with Women in Emergency Relief and Rehabilitation Programmes," Field Studies Paper no. 2, May 1991.

49. Benjamin and Fancy, "The Gender Dimensions of Internal Displacement," p. 4.

50. Roberta Cohen, "'What's So Terrible About Rape?' and Other Attitudes at the United Nations," *SAIS Review*, Summer–Fall 2000, p. 75.

51. Cohen, *Refugee and Internally Displaced Women*, p. 1.

52. Benjamin and Fancy, "The Gender Dimensions of Internal Displacement."

53. UNHCR, *Executive Committee Conclusion No. 39: Refugee Women and International Protection*, Geneva: UNHCR, 1985.

54. UNHCR, *UNHCR Guidelines on the Protection of Refugee Women*.

55. Heaven Crawley, "Gender, Persecution and the Concept of Politics in the Asylum Determination Process," *Forced Migration Review*, 9 December 2000, at www.fmreview.org/fmr091.htm, p. 2.

56. Julie Mertus, "The State and the Post–Cold War Refugee Regime: New Models, New Questions," *International Journal of Refugee Law*, vol. 10, no. 3, 1998.

57. Ibid., p. 337.

58. Audrey Macklin, "Opening the Door to Women Refugees: A First Crack," in Wenona Giles, Helene Moussa, and Penny Van Esterik, eds., *Development and Diaspora: Gender and the Refugee Experience*, Dundas, ON: Artemis Enterprises, 1996, p. 119.

59. El-Bushra, "Gender and Forced Migration: Editorial," p. 1.

60. Turner, "Vindicating Masculinity," p. 2.

61. El-Bushra, "Gender and Forced Migration: Editorial," p. 1.

62. Ibid.

63. Cathrine Brun, "Making Young Displaced Men Visible," *Forced Migration Review*, 9 December 2000, at www.fmreview.org/fmr091.htm.

Part III

Actors and institutions

13

Securitizing sovereignty? States, refugees, and the regionalization of international law

Gregor Noll

The structural disadvantages of refugee law

At first sight, international law seems to uphold both state sovereignty and individual sovereignty. The existence and autonomy of a state are secured by the obligation on other states to respect its territorial integrity and the prohibition on intervening in other states' domestic affairs. At the individual level, internationally guaranteed human rights serve comparable functions: they secure a minimum of autonomy and even preserve an "exit" option, because each individual retains a right to leave any country, including his or her own.[1]

In the area of forced displacement, this ostensible harmony never existed in practice. Because the human right to emigration has not been matched by a corresponding right to immigration,[2] and international law recognizes the power of states to control the composition of their own population, refugees have regularly encountered difficulties in exercising their exit right. The "right to seek and enjoy asylum" laid down in Article 14 of the 1948 Universal Declaration of Human Rights[3] has largely remained a fictional privilege for refugees, mainly because it was designed to insulate states granting asylum from reproaches by countries of origin rather than to protect individuals. Moreover, Article 14 remains a norm without legally binding force, which limits its effects to the political and symbolic levels.[4]

The lack of entry rights is also reflected in the 1951 Convention on the

Status of Refugees, which is rightly regarded as the cornerstone of the modern refugee regime. Although it launched an abstract refugee definition and a basic norm of non-return (the so-called prohibition of *refoulement* in its Article 33), it fails to address the crucial question of access to an asylum state in an effective and unequivocal manner. To be protected by the Convention, the refugee needs to make contact with the territory of a potential asylum state. It could be described as the Achilles heel of the international refugee regime: states are at liberty to block access to their territory and thus avoid situations in which persons in need of protection could invoke the provisions of the 1951 Refugee Convention or of other protective norms of international human rights law.

The dynamics behind recent developments in refugee and migration law are an interplay between three factors: the number of refugees on state territory, the level of rights accorded to them, and the degree of solidarity between states in protecting them. Although there is a minimum level of rights in international law that states cannot undercut, international solidarity in refugee reception is largely absent, so host countries make every effort to reduce the number of refugees by systematically outlawing refugee migration and by blocking all possible avenues of access. Attempts to limit access can take many forms and affect the internal domain, the transit routes, and also the countries or regions of origin. A marked feature of these limitative dynamics is that they undercut both individual sovereignty and the sovereignty of other states. Let me provide some examples, all of which potentially affect the respect for international law.

- Destination states in the North are constantly redesigning their asylum systems in order to remove incentives for protection seekers (for example, by introducing voucher systems instead of cash benefits). They legislate new reasons to reject claims (an infamous example is return to so-called safe third countries, regardless of the availability of protection in such countries) and they attempt to make the return of rejected cases more efficient. This puts the protective provisions of international law under increasing pressure and challenges the principle of non-discrimination in a number of areas.

- Destination states in the North attempt to control the travel routes of protection seekers and to cut them off by administrative measures such as visa requirements, sanctions against carriers transporting aliens without documents, and externalized forms of border control (for example by placing immigration officers in third countries). Such policies affect the exercise of the human right to leave any country.

- As the examples of the US intervention in Haiti and the NATO intervention in the province of Kosovo showed, the North's attempts to control refugee migration can even involve military intervention, which may encroach upon the sovereignty of other states. But intervention may also take milder forms than the use of force. Transit states as well as countries of origin are increasingly coming under pressure to police their territory or their seaways in order to block refugee migration.

This dual strategy – limitations on individual sovereignty as well as on the sovereignty of other states – is the subject of this chapter. The analysis will proceed in three steps. First, I shall show that the language of "human security" is unhelpful and merely colludes in the losses for individual sovereignty that contemporary refugee policies entail. Second, I will depict the conflicts in international law that are a consequence of the dual strategy. To do so, I shall examine the whole gamut of responses ranging from outright rejection of protective obligations (*insulation*) via refugee reception (*palliation* of human rights violations) to enforcement action in the country of crisis (*intervention*). Isolation, palliation, and intervention raise different questions of international law, and the objective here is to demarcate the borderlines. Third, I will demonstrate that this dual strategy of limiting sovereignty is propelled by regional cooperation, and the examples of the European Union and the North Atlantic Treaty Organisation (NATO) will be used to illustrate this point. Lastly, I offer a concluding discussion on the significance of these developments.

Questioning the security concept

The developments following 11 September 2001 have abundantly demonstrated that the security concept is not a neutral one that applies to states, citizens, and aliens in roughly the same manner. On the contrary; states have been drawing heavily on the security concept to justify a broad array of measures, ranging from the slashing of rights that protect individuals in hastily drafted domestic counter-terrorist laws to armed action in internal and international conflicts. In this crude argumentative framework, the security of the individual citizen is equated with the security of the state. In the following, I shall attempt to disentangle the various dimensions of the security concept.

In international law, the concept of security traditionally denotes the security of states. A pertinent example is the law of the UN Charter, which allocates certain competencies to the Security Council in situations where "international peace and security" are, or may be, threatened. However, modern international law extends beyond the regulation of inter-state relationships, and the security demands of quite a different actor have increasingly won recognition: human rights law, refugee law, and humanitarian law are concerned with another dimension of security, namely that of the individual. This dimension of law attempts, firstly, to pacify the individual against the exercise of power by the state, and, secondly, even to oblige the state to take positive action for and to devote resources to a basic protection of the individuals subject to its power. The discourse on these individual-protective norms is complex and, at times, confusing for the outsider. For that reason, and perhaps also to match the dimension of "state security" with a convenient counterpart, this dimension has been labelled "human security."[5]

It is easy to conceive of situations in which both security concepts are in tension, with the fight against terrorism being the most obvious example.[6] Therefore, a number of legal disputes have flared up regarding central concepts in the legal regulation of security. In the European debate on refugee law, the issue of protection from non-state agents of persecution, the relationship between full-blown refugee status and the rudimentary offer of temporary protection, as well as the question of exclusion from refugee status, are probably most pertinent today. The permissibility of the use of force in the absence of Security Council authorization and the issue of proportionality are, on the other hand, dominating the discourse on interventionist approaches.[7]

Labels matter. The concept of "security" is not a neutral label, allowing us to shuttle back and forth between the interests of individuals threatened with a violation of their rights and those of communities or states. As already stated, "security" has predominantly collective connotations in the discourse of international law. The concept of security is closely related to the concepts of "emergency," "the exceptional," and the legitimacy of force. The "securitization" of migration and flight[8] entails a parallel militarization and a move away from civil society discourse. A further characteristic of the security concept is its trump function: invoking security concerns seemingly reduces the legal constraints put on actors and increases the leeway for discretion. Thus, "securitizing" the discourse on flight and protection means introducing a bias that ultimately works against the individual.

The usefulness of the security concept is questionable for other reasons as well. In the discourse on persecution, flight, and protection, the security concept is employed in an asymmetrical and ultimately paternalistic manner. At first sight, it appears attractive to denote the concerns of both individuals and states with one and the same concept, but this practice all too easily colludes in the enormous differences in power and autonomy between the two actors. States not only have the power to define and defend their own security interests; they also usurp the power to define the security interests of individuals (and, in certain cases, take measures to defend them). The individual, on the other hand, has little or no voice in the security discourse, and the autonomous power to defend individually defined security interests is extremely limited. Two examples will illustrate this point – one related to would-be refugees, and the other to the electorates of potential host states.

First, industrialized states increasingly underscore the need to promote human rights in refugee-sending countries as a means of addressing forced displacement.[9] At first sight, this seems to cater for the security interests of the very states promoting that policy, as well as those held by the potential victims of persecution and other threats. However, the same industrialized states are simultaneously barring flight routes by ever more sophisticated means. What would appear as a fair trade-off to some – interventionist policies are swapped for the population's capability to vote with its feet – is de facto a net loss for individual security. At least in the short- and medium-term perspectives, the reach and efficiency of interventionist human rights policies are severely limited, and the "exit" option is extremely valuable for the individual's survival. Seen from the perspective of a would-be refugee's individual autonomy, this is a gross restriction of choices. This curtailment of individual autonomy contradicts a core assumption of liberal market economies, which otherwise allocate great importance to the "invisible hand" of individualized decision-making. At bottom, this trade-off is an illiberal paternalism on the part of the industrialized states practising such policies.

Secondly, however, the paternalistic features of the security concept also have an internal dimension. Taking the example of the European Union, it can be observed that its *demos*, and thus the object of security concerns, remains undefined after all these years, while its boundaries are vigorously enforced. This means that the "high politics" task of defining the content of these boundaries is delegated to the technicians of border control and security management at the legislative, administrative, and enforcement level. Ultimately, this practice is paternalistic vis-à-vis the electorates of the states, in whose name boundary enforcement is taking place.

Finally, one should be aware of the fact that attempts to securitize the enjoyment of human rights imply a breaking up of traditional legal terminology in the human rights field. To wit, human rights language normally employs the concept of security to describe the limits of individual rights. For example, after setting out a number of provisions on permissible limitations, the 1969 American Convention on Human Rights (ACHR)[10] addresses the issue of personal responsibilities in Article 32(2): "The rights of each person are limited by the rights of others, by the security of all, and by the just demands of the general welfare, in a democratic society." Article 27(2) of the 1981 African Charter on Human and Peoples' Rights[11] enunciates an analogous opposition between individual rights and collective security.[12] These quoted norms provide a graphic illustration of the dichotomy of rights and security in the human rights law discourse. Combining the rights concept in an all-encompassing security concept risks the dilution of the precision already attained in legal language, and thereby of the individual interests one seeks to protect.

Any attempt to conceptualize state interests and the interests of protection seekers under the umbrella of "security" is doomed to be imprecise at best and collusive at worst. The "individual security" of the protection seeker is clearly subordinated to the "collective security" of states. Hence, taking into account the discursive presuppositions of international law, it is wiser to speak of the human rights of the individual rather than of his or her "human security." In chapter 5 of this volume, Astri Suhrke introduces the concept of "vulnerability" as a more precise alternative to "human security." In the discourse of international law, "vulnerability" is strongly linked to the situation of the individual (the protection of "vulnerable groups" has become a recurring topos in contemporary refugee law, which attempts to cater for the specific needs of children, traumatized persons, and women at risk). It is not burdened with the military heritage and the collectivist bias of the security concept.

In the following sections, I shall track the policies of potential host states to reduce their protective obligations vis-à-vis refugees, and single out possible conflicts with their obligations under international law.

Three policy options: Insulation, palliation, and intervention

Three approaches can be distinguished when exploring a state's choices when it observes the occurrence of human rights violations in another state. First, a bystander state can choose to insulate itself from the effects of refugee-inducing phenomena in third countries. In some cases, natural impediments – such as geographical distance – will prevent such violations affecting its interests. Remote states such as Iceland are naturally insulated, which contributes to relatively low numbers of asylum seekers.[13] This approach can be supported by deflection and deterrence. By way of example, the reinforcement of immigration control by EU member states since the late 1980s is a way of amplifying already existing natural impediments.[14] This approach may validly be termed *insulation*. It tends to keep would-be refugees within the borders of their state or in the region of origin. Hence, such policies exacerbate the security situation in the country of origin and its neighbouring countries, while insulating the states in the North from the effects of forced migration. In other words, the security of persons in need of protection is traded off against the security of Northern welfare societies. The loss is considerable – suffice it to recall the precarious situation of internally displaced persons (IDPs). Whereas refugees are protected by a rudimentary international legal regime with binding protective norms, no such regime exists for IDPs, who remain at the mercy of the benevolent implementation of political guidelines.[15]

The second approach is *palliation*. During the Cold War, refugee reception abroad was seen as a major palliative for human rights violations by other states. After the Hungarian uprising in 1956, West European states swiftly offered asylum to a relatively comprehensive outflow – not least because the political symbolism of asylum could be exploited. In recent decades, however, the institution of asylum has increasingly come under pressure. Faced with the magnitude of the refugee problem, both developing and industrialized countries restrict access to their territories and attempt to promote early return, sometimes without due regard to norms of international law. Moreover, mechanisms of migration control have confined the reception of refugees in the immediate crisis region, leading to an overburdening of neighbouring states and a concomitant reduction of palliative capacity. Finally, the terrorist incidents of 11 September 2001 have been used by key actors in the North to amplify a restrictionist rhetoric and to call for measures to close the perceived security loopholes of asylum systems. The outcome of these developments remains to be seen, but it is worth recalling that none of the hijackers involved in the crimes of September 11 had used the asylum channel to enter their host countries.

In certain cases, these developments have been supported by a greater willingness on the part of some actors to intervene in the flight-inducing conflict – be it by means of diplomacy, humanitarian assistance, or military action. This brings us to the third approach, namely that of *intervention*. Relevant examples are the interventions in northern Iraq, Haiti, Somalia, Rwanda, Bosnia, and the province of Kosovo. Again, the relationship of such military humanitarianism to the norms of international law is problematic. The most recent example is the Kosovo intervention, which lacked authorization by the Security Council and is therefore held by some to violate international law.[16]

Thus, it may be concluded that none of the three options – insulation, palliation, and prevention – remains unaffected by the ramifications of international law. In the following, I shall give a brief survey of relevant norms.

Insulation

As a matter of principle, two gradations of the insulative approach can be distinguished. First, a state may choose to remain completely passive vis-à-vis protection seekers, trusting natural impediments such as geographical distance to keep them away from its territory. Second, a state may actively seek to prevent protection seekers from reaching and remaining on its territory. Throughout the past two decades, industrialized states have devised ever more sophisticated means to do this, including interception on the high seas, visa requirements coupled with carrier sanctions, as well as externalized means of border control. Other measures purport to curtail the contact of protection seekers with state territory and to shift the responsibility to another state. These measures go under the label of "protection elsewhere." Its pivotal elements are safe-third-country arrangements in domestic law coupled with readmission agreements between states. Finally, destination states also attempt to prevent migration by demanding that countries of transit and countries of origin exercise greater control over migratory movements. These kinds of policies – which can lead industrialized democracies to cooperate with regimes that do not respect human rights – must not be confused with policies encouraging the implementation of human rights in sending countries.

Without doubt, insulation policies are the expression of a defensive response to flight. They represent security thinking writ large. Therefore, the whole array of insulative measures described above has been heavily criticized by refugee advocates. However, it is not easy to discern the legal components of this criticism; concrete and specific arguments on why and how such measures violate international law are rare.

To address this gap, two questions should be asked. First, does the mere passivity of bystander states violate international law? Second, do active insulation measures violate international law?

Mere passivity

Starting with the legal qualification of "mere passivity," it is hard to conceive viable and sufficiently precise arguments of illegality. To do that, it would be necessary to identify a strong positive obligation to assist persons in need of international protection outside state territory. This meets with considerable difficulties. To start with, many relevant norms are linked to a requirement of territorial presence. A central human rights instrument such as the International Covenant on Civil and Political Rights (ICCPR) is limited in its scope of application to the territory and jurisdiction of a specific contracting party.[17] Refugee law does not have much more to offer: explicit protections against *refoulement* in Article 33 of the European Convention on Human Rights (ECHR) and Article 3 of the 1984 Convention Against Torture (CAT) presuppose that the beneficiary is in touch with the territory of the potential host state.

Furthermore, general norms commanding states to promote human rights are usually too abstract to allow for the derivation of specific duties to assist beyond the obligations set out in human rights treaties. A pertinent example is Article 56 of the UN Charter, by which UN member states have pledged to take joint and separate action in cooperation with the United Nations for the achievement of the purposes set out in Article 55 of the UN Charter. However, it has been claimed that the purpose of promoting universal respect for human rights enunciated in Article 55(c) of the Charter is too unspecific to qualify as a legal norm and should rather be regarded as a programme for further action.[18] There is little or no chance of doing away with ambiguities in an interpretation process following Articles 31 and 32 of the Vienna Convention on the Law of Treaties (VTC),[19] and the wide diversity of state practice and states' *opinio juris* would make it extremely difficult to identify some form of consensus on the precise content of such a hypothetical norm. The lack of uniformity in both areas would also bring down any attempts to construct a duty to assist in customary international law.

Active insulation

It is easier to problematize policies of active insulation in relation to human rights obligations. Such policies have drawn heavy fire from the perspective of moral philosophy.[20] But may they also qualify as partly or wholly illegal under international law? Undoubtedly, the doctrine of the sovereign power of a state to determine its population is a relevant backdrop, seemingly suffocating all arguments in favour of outsiders' protection interests. Most certainly, instruments requiring the territorial presence of beneficiaries cannot be invoked in this context. However, instruments obliging states to consider human rights in the exercise of their jurisdiction open new avenues for refugee lawyers. Lamentably, these avenues have so far been discussed to only a very limited extent.[21]

Active insulation impedes efforts by protection seekers to make contact with state territory by preventing their arrival. One of the more striking examples in recent history was the Australian government's determination not to allow the asylum seekers aboard the Norwegian vessel *Tampa* to land on Australian territory, unless other states made assurances that they would accept the applicants.[22] Although this incident exposed the thrust of active insulation policies, it is more representative to look at situations in which the would-be applicant does not even get close to the territory of the potential state of refuge.

Let us therefore consider the legal position of a person in need of protection who applies for an entry visa at a diplomatic representation of the goal state in due course. Normally, a visa would be denied if the visa officer became aware of the purpose of the visa request – namely, to seek asylum upon entry into the goal state. Elsewhere, I have shown that an interpretation of Article 3 of the ECHR along the lines of Articles 31 and 32 of the VTC means that this article obliges states in certain situations to grant an entry visa through their diplomatic representations.[23] Such situations are characterized by a pressing need for protection by the state from which an entry visa is requested; reasonably, there would be no other options of protection accessible to the claimant. The goal state may be obliged to grant an entry visa because the processing of visa requests at embassies is within the jurisdiction of the sending state, and thus subject to the obligations flowing from the ECHR.

Why is that so? The ECHR requests in Article 1 that contracting parties "secure" the rights and freedoms enshrined in its Section I. This obligation is a positive one. Given a sufficiently large risk that a protection seeker would be subjected to treatment contrary to Article 3 of the ECHR if denied a visa, and thus denied the possibility of entering the state in question, the goal state is under an obligation to allow entry. This argument does not contend that visa requirements are illegal per se. Rather, it maintains that denying visas to a class of persons protected under positive obligations flowing from Article 3 of the ECHR is illegal. It should be noted that the above line of argument is applicable not only to Article 3 of the ECHR but in principle to all rights guaranteed by the ECHR and its protocols. The limitative element is the scope of the positive obligations under a specific right, which can be assessed only *in casu*.[24] It must be underscored that the granting of an entry visa is not equivalent to the grant of protection. The purpose of the entry visa is solely to avert the imminent risk and to allow the conduct of a proper determination procedure in a safe place – i.e. the goal country. Clearly, if no sufficient reasons for protection emerge during such determination procedures, the goal state is free to remove the applicant from its territory with due respect to other norms of international law.

Mutatis mutandis, the same line of argument could be invoked against other, individualized forms of insulation policies. Where migration liaison officers assist in the emigration procedures in third countries and thereby assist in the deflection of persons coming under the protective scope of Article 3 of the ECHR, this would engage the responsibility of an ECHR contracting party sending out the officers.

But the ECHR is not the only instrument whose scope is limited only by a requirement of the exercise of jurisdiction. The American Convention on Human Rights is constructed in the same fashion, and needs to be construed along the same lines. Article 1(1) spells out that states parties undertake "to ensure to all persons subject to their jurisdiction the free and full exercise of … rights and freedoms" recognized in the ACHR. Among these rights, we find a prohibition of torture and inhuman or degrading punishment or treatment (Article 5(2)).

The 1989 Convention on the Rights of the Child (CRC) provides a further example. Article 2(1) states that "States Parties shall respect and ensure the rights set forth in the present Convention to each child within their jurisdiction." Thus, there is no requirement that a child wishing to benefit from the positive obligations enshrined in the CRC be present on the territory of a state party from which these benefits are sought. To exemplify the source of such obligations, one may refer to Article 37 of the CRC, which contains a prohibition of torture and other forms of ill-treatment.

For children seeking an entry visa from the goal state's diplomatic representation located in a *transit* country, Article 22(1) of the CRC may also be of relevance.[25] This provision reads as follows:

States Parties shall take appropriate measures to ensure that a child who is seeking refugee status or who is considered a refugee in accordance with applicable international or domestic law and procedures shall, whether unaccompanied or accompanied by his or her parents or by any other person, receive appropriate protection and humanitarian assistance in the enjoyment of applicable rights set forth in the present Convention and in other international human rights or humanitarian instruments to which the said States are Parties.

Thus, the minor visa claimant would benefit from a state obligation to "take appropriate measures to ensure that a child ... receive appropriate protection and humanitarian assistance in the enjoyment of applicable rights." Among these rights, we find, for example, the protection from torture and ill-treatment in Article 37 of CRC, mentioned earlier. An appropriate measure to ensure freedom from torture or other forms of ill-treatment in an imminent case of non-protection from such risks in the transit country could be to grant an entry visa into the goal country.

It should be noted that both the United Kingdom and Singapore introduced reservations upon ratification, which may make the interpretation expounded above inapplicable to them.[26] Germany introduced a declaration upon ratification, which was intended to safeguard the area of immigration control from being affected by the CRC.[27] However, both Germany and the United Kingdom would still have obligations under the ECHR, which offers an analogous protection not just to children but to everyone.

These arguments on the basis of the ECHR, the ACHR, and the CRC show that indiscriminate insulation by potential goal states risks violating international law. To avoid such risks, states must provide for protection-related entry visas in a manner conforming to the positive obligations under the said instruments. Thus, although international law knows of no explicitly stated right to entry for non-nationals, there is an obligation based on human rights to grant provisional access to territory in exceptional situations.

To determine the precise extent of positive obligations, individual risks have to be weighed against the protective resources of the state. In the identification of protective resources, the protection demands of citizens and residents of the goal state shall also be taken into account. This is where so-called security interests enter into the conceptualization of positive obligations. This may baffle some who recall the non-derogable nature of the prohibition of torture and other forms of ill-treatment.[28] Non-derogability and absoluteness most certainly affect and delimit the negative obligations flowing from this prohibition, but they do not inform us about how far positive obligations extend. Thus, weighing and balancing remain a necessity when pondering the legality of active insulation policies, which, in turn, gives leeway to what have been termed security interests.

Palliation

Even before 11 September 2001, the institution of asylum appeared to be under siege, and this assessment has been confirmed ever since. States in the North attempt to limit their obligations under the 1951 Refugee Convention and other relevant instruments of international law by testing and proliferating a battery of restrictive measures. These are aimed at blocking access to territory or asylum procedure, cutting short the length of stay, and slashing the packages of rights to which protection seekers are entitled. In the South, refugee protection has seen a number of grave crises in the past decade, with massive *refoulement* incidents following the Rwandan genocide, and mounting problems with the militarization of refugee camps. The dynamics behind these phenomena are grounded in the absence of regional and international responsibility-sharing arrangements, which makes defection from protection obligations an all too rational choice for would-be host states.

But the "asylum crisis" should not obscure the fact that palliation is still practised to a very large extent. It can take the form of full-blown refugee status under the 1951 Convention or of minimalist protection from *refoulement* on a short-term basis.[29] Although large groups of persons are declared not to be refugees or otherwise entitled to protection, industrialized states refrain from actually returning them, given the unstable situation in their country of origin. Although these cases figure as rejectees in the asylum statistics, they are de facto protected, although in a very precarious manner. Moreover, the example of Kosovo has shown that palliation is still regarded as a standard component of states' dealings with massive human rights violations, although much of the physical protection was delegated to states in the immediate vicinity (the

Federal Republic of Yugoslavia, Macedonia, and Albania), some of which received considerable material assistance by more affluent states.

Restriction has triggered a counter-reaction by refugee advocates and therefore forced the legal discourse to move forward in the clarification of important borderline issues of refugee law. Because of the declining role of the 1951 Convention in practice, refugee advocates have increasingly relied on human rights law in the context of refugee protection. In the European context, the significance of the ECHR was constantly on the rise throughout the 1990s. If protection seekers seek the assistance of the European Court of Human Rights (ECtHR) when asserting their rights under Article 3 of ECHR, the Court almost routinely requests states to stay expulsion,[30] and has declared removal to contravene Article 3 of the ECHR in a number of landmark cases. By way of example, the ECtHR has taken a clear stand on an important issue of dispute, namely whether or not persons risking violations by non-state agents of persecution are entitled to protection, thus countering exclusionary interpretations by some European states. On a universal level, the CAT Committee has analogously challenged restrictionist readings of refugee law. Finally, the UN human rights machinery displayed greater willingness to deal with refugee-related questions during the 1990s.[31] Thus, refugee law and human rights law have come to overlap each other at a hitherto unprecedented level.

As we shall see below, this is reflected in regional developments. In the European Union, a common human-rights-related status reflecting the obligations flowing from the ECtHR and CAT is currently under deliberation.[32] Nonetheless, it would be inadequate to depict the current state of affairs as a newly won balance between restrictionist tendencies and the increasing impact of human rights law. Rather, the pendulum has swung in the opposite direction since 11 September 2001.

The sweeping rationale to fight terrorism incited states to redefine the asylum door as a security risk. In the absence of visible links between the asylum system and the terrorist acts that triggered counter-terrorism, this comes dangerously close to an official endorsement of xenophobic positions taken in domestic discourses.[33] UN Security Council Resolution 1373 of 28 September 2001[34] made an explicit linkage between asylum and terrorism by obliging states to

(f) Take appropriate measures in conformity with the relevant provisions of national and international law, including international standards of human rights, before granting refugee status, for the purpose of ensuring that the asylum seeker has not planned, facilitated or participated in the commission of terrorist acts;

and to

(g) Ensure, in conformity with international law, that refugee status is not abused by the perpetrators, organizers or facilitators of terrorist acts, and that claims of political motivation are not recognized as grounds for refusing requests for the extradition of alleged terrorists.

These obligations are legally binding, because the Council acted under Chapter VII of the UN Charter when adopting the Resolution.

True enough, they could be taken to represent a mere reiteration of existing obligations under Article 1F of the 1951 Refugee Convention, while underscoring that any repressive measure must be in conformity with human rights as well as international law at large. Taking into consideration that the international mobility of the terrorists of September 11 was based on migration channels other than asylum, it gives rise to concern that the Security Council chose to single out the asylum channel. In Europe, some states made extensive use of this linkage in their attempts to launch counter-terrorist legislation. By way of example, the German as well as the Danish draft laws were criticized for using terrorism as a pretext for clamping down on asylum.[35]

Although these moves exacerbate the opposition of host state community and asylum seekers in the political domain, it should be emphasized that the basic legal tenets of asylum remain untouched. It is reasonable to expect, though, that the interpretive battles fought over them will gain a new, and perhaps unprecedented, momentum. To exemplify, the European Commission has elaborated a "Working Document on the Relationship between Safeguarding Internal Security and Complying with International Protection Obligations and Instruments" on the initiative of the EU Council. Although this document generally strikes a tone of moderation and caution, it nevertheless suggests the abolition of the principle of "inclusion before exclusion," implying that asylum seekers can be excluded from refugee status before a full assessment of the facts speaking for their inclusion in such a status has taken place.[36] This implies a marked downgrading of the applicants' legal standing. One may safely assume that this will intensify the debate on the precise interpretation of the obligations flowing from the Geneva Convention and especially its Article 1F. This shift of position of the Commission is a reminder that even generally protection-minded actors are repositioning themselves in line with the restrictionist signals sent out by states in the North.

Intervention

After the dealignment of the bipolar structure in international relations after 1989, hitherto impracticable forms of interventionism again became an option for powerful states. Without purporting to reflect the complex motives of the intervening states or coalitions in their entirety here, it is remarkable that the prevention of massive human rights violations and of ensuing refugee outflows was increasingly brought to the fore as a justification for the use of military means.[37] In the relevant resolutions adopted by the Security Council, a remarkable linkage was struck between massive displacement and the existence of a threat to international peace and security as a precondition for UN-mandated intervention. In terms of *realpolitik*, however, states rarely put their military resources at the disposal of crisis prevention and resolution if their own security interests are not at stake. So, restating a truism, the "international peace and security" alluded to are congruent not with refugee interests but with those of the intervening states.

Earlier examples of this new interventionism manifested themselves within the framework of the UN Charter. The Security Council adopted clear mandates for interventions in Somalia, Rwanda, and Haiti.[38] Although all three cases involved a considerable degree of forced displacement, the prevention or mitigation of a refugee crisis was not invoked by the relevant resolutions to justify intervention.[39] The Security Council mandate for the intervention in East Timor reproduced the same pattern; although there was an important component of displacement in reality, the authorizing resolution did not invoke it.[40]

By contrast, a second category is not so clear-cut. The imposition of no-fly zones over Iraq to protect Kurds from persecution in the wake of the conflict between Iraq and Kuwait is a pertinent example. By virtue of a resolution not taken under Chapter VII, the Security Council mandated the Secretary-General, and not member states, to use all means at his disposal to address the needs of refugees.[41] The actual imposition of a no-fly zone by states participating in the "coalition of the able and the willing" ended the repression of Kurds in northern Iraq, but obviously lacked an express mandate to do so. Because Turkey had closed its borders to potential refugees, the palliative response was simply unavailable, and the choice was between passivity and intervention. The no-fly zones have been upheld ever since, which indicates that interventionist responses are not necessarily of shorter duration than palliative ones.

In the cases of Kosovo and Afghanistan, however, the Security Council was bypassed, and the intervening states violated the UN Charter in doing so. The Kosovo intervention was expressly justified by the human rights violations, which were driving Kosovars into neighbouring countries. To what extent military action by NATO contributed to, or even triggered, persecution and refugee outflows was intensely discussed during and after the intervention. At present, it is not possible to see an end to the international presence in the province of Kosovo, again indicating that interventionism cannot be reduced to military action in the narrow sense.

The intervention in Afghanistan adds another facet to the emerging picture. It drew on a counter-terrorist agenda, to which refugee interests were irrelevant, although persecution especially of women by the Taliban was named as a second-order justification for the action taken by the intervening powers. However, it was clear that the US and UK bombings caused flight and displacement in their own right. No international collaboration alleviated the considerable protective burdens of neighbouring countries, initially Iran and Pakistan, which promptly reacted by closing their borders. This stood in marked contrast to the Kosovo crisis: when Macedonia closed its borders, NATO states brought political pressure to bear on its government and international efforts were made to share the burdens of reception. As a result, the Macedonian government allowed refugees into its territory again.[42] In the case of Afghanistan, a comparable solution was not even debated in a serious manner, and the rhetoric of the intervening states concentrated mostly on post-conflict reconstruction.

The dynamics of regionalization

Universally valid norms of international law have a disadvantage. The price of consensus in a large constituency is abstraction, and such abstraction tends to empty universal norms of content and enforceability. One way out is a limitation of the constituency, that is, the number of states whose consensus is needed. This is what regionalization is all about. In the area of human rights, regionalization is routinely associated with progress – more detailed rights, more muscle in monitoring, and, it is hoped, a more coherent pattern of norm compliance in state practice. The linkage of regionalization to progress is not self-evident, however. Rather than specifying and strengthening universal obligations, the steps taken by a regional grouping may also dilute and undermine such obligations. The following subsection on the harmonized asylum and migration policy of the EU member states attempts to illustrate that point.

Apart from the risk of diluting universal norms further, regionalization poses other risks. One is the risk of fragmenting international law at large, which would ultimately break up into a myriad disconnected or even contradictory regional norm systems. Such fragmentation contains additional risks – for example, that of a false universalism, which mistakenly ascribes universal validity to regional norms. At the core of such risks is the preservation of the international legal axiom of sovereign equality. Where inequality among states and state groupings is on the rise, the state-centred model of international law will become obsolete and give way to an international law condoning empires. I shall attempt to illustrate the risk of false universalism by tracking recent developments in the mandate of NATO, which are closely connected to the issue of forced migration.

Palliation in the European Union

The European harmonization of migration and asylum law was never intended to be a comprehensive solution to the problems of refugee protection. It was conceived as a technical consequence of the abolition of internal borders.[43] Drawing on the language employed by member states, one could validly claim that the harmonization of asylum law among member states is a flanking measure in response to the dismantling of internal border control. To a significant degree, this heritage still haunts the contemporary *acquis communautaire*, and, as we shall see below, it affects the conceptualization of security in the primary law of the European Union.

The EU framework for the harmonization of asylum and migration policies was reworked by the 1997 Treaty of Amsterdam, which brought a major reshuffle of competencies, a binding timetable for future integration, the integration of the Schengen *acquis*, and a protocol downgrading the legal standing of protection seekers who happen to be EU citizens.[44] At first sight, the most striking change brought about by the Amsterdam Treaty is a wholesale transfer of asylum and immigration matters from the third to the first pillar, implying augmented supranational decision-making. Although the remaining intergovernmental elements have significantly reduced the impact of this transfer, new doors have been opened. The move to the first pillar makes available the powerful legislative tools of Article 251 of the Treaty on European Union (TEU) – that is, regulations, directives, and decisions – offering undisputed bindingness, justiciability, and, under certain preconditions, even direct effect. Henceforth, the Council may adopt legislation on a wide array of specified issues relating to asylum, external borders, and immigration, and not only on certain visa issues. Furthermore, scrutiny of adopted measures now comes under the ambit of the European Court of Justice (ECJ).

Technically, this has been achieved by inserting a new Title IV into the TEU. The portal provision of this title, Article 61, delimits the competencies of the Union under this title:

In order to establish progressively an area of freedom, security and justice, the Council shall adopt:

(a) within a period of five years after the entry into force of the Treaty of Amsterdam, measures aimed at ensuring the free movement of persons in accordance with Article 14, in conjunction with directly related flanking measures with respect to external border controls, asylum and immigration, in accordance with the provisions of Article 62(2) and (3) and Article 63(1)(a) and (2)(a), and measures to prevent and combat crime in accordance with the provisions of Article 31(e) of the Treaty on European Union;

(b) other measures in the fields of asylum, immigration and safeguarding the rights of nationals of third countries, in accordance with the provisions of Article 63.

The main ideas of the whole title are spelt out here. With the allusion to "an area of freedom, security and justice," a new telos is introduced. Looking at Article 61 of the TEU only, one might think that such security serves insiders and outsiders alike: whereas paragraph (a) caters for EU citizens and denizens, paragraph (b) apparently seeks to provide a legal framework for protection seekers and third-country nationals. Such a reading was seemingly confirmed by the European Council in its Tampere Conclusions, which frame the area of freedom, security and justice as one not per se limited to EU citizens.[45] However, a thorough look at the structure of Title IV suggests that it is not endorsing a universal security concept, but prioritizes the security of insiders over that of outsiders.

To support this contention, we have to involve the obligations that Title IV links to the competencies meted out in Article 61 of TEU. The Council is assigned to adopt the following measures within a period of five years after the entry into force of the Treaty of Amsterdam:

- measures on the crossing of internal borders;[46]
- measures on the crossing of the external borders of the member states, establishing standards and procedures to be followed by member states in carrying out checks on persons at such borders[47] as well as rules on visas for intended stays of no more than three months;[48]
- measures setting out the conditions under which nationals of third countries shall have the freedom to travel within the territory of the member states during a period of no more than three months;[49]
- criteria and mechanisms for determining which member state is responsible for considering an application for asylum submitted by a national of a third country in one of the member states;[50]
- minimum standards on the reception of asylum seekers in member states;[51]
- minimum standards with respect to the qualification of nationals of third countries as refugees;[52]
- minimum standards on procedures in member states for granting or withdrawing refugee status;[53]

- minimum standards for giving temporary protection to displaced persons from third countries who cannot return to their country of origin and for persons who otherwise need international protection;[54]
- measures on illegal immigration and illegal residence, including repatriation of illegal residents.[55]

For the sake of simplicity, I call these measures "the obligatory measures" in the following.

The temporal obligation is not merely a political one, but possesses legal character. If the Council fails to act, the member states and the other institutions of the Union may bring an action before the Court of Justice under Article 232 of the TEU.[56] However, the drafters could not agree to affix temporal obligations to all of the issues enumerated under Title IV. Strikingly, Article 63 of the TEU exempts three types of measures from the obligation to legislate within five years:

- measures promoting a balance of effort between member states in receiving and bearing the consequences of receiving refugees and displaced persons (burden-sharing);[57]
- measures on the conditions of entry and residence, and standards on procedures for the issue by member states of long-term visas and residence permits, including those for the purpose of family reunion (legal immigration);[58]
- measures defining the rights and conditions under which nationals of third countries who are legally resident in a member state may reside in other member states (mobility rights for legally present aliens).[59]

In doing so, the drafters created a hierarchy within the competencies of Article 63 of the TEU, dividing measures into an obligatory and a facultative group. Measures adopted earlier certainly set the parameters for those adopted later. For example, the exemption of burden-sharing from the list of obligatory measures is fatal for protection interests, because it makes restrictiveness in the drafting of the obligatory instruments rational state behaviour. Thus, control continues to enjoy a first mover's advantage over protection. This illustrates graphically whom the "area of freedom, security and justice" is intended to protect – namely the insiders. It may be validly concluded that the security concept of Title IV is a particularist one.

A further underpinning of this contention can be derived from Article 64 of the TEU, prescribing that Title IV "shall not affect the exercise of the responsibilities incumbent upon Member States with regard to the maintenance of law and order and the safeguarding of internal security." Through this provision, member states have reserved the right to take unilateral measures, should they consider the Union measures insufficient to uphold internal security.[60] This adds another particularist layer to the whole construction of Title IV. Member states' internal security is at the top, followed by Union security. Subordinated to both, we find the security of the protection seeker.

Interventionist self-empowerment: NATO and WEU

Interventionist approaches to forced migration have been increasingly discussed throughout the past decade, so it is appropriate to ask whether this debate has left traces in the mandate of relevant international organizations in the area of defence. In this section, I shall look into the developing mandates of the North Atlantic Treaty Organisation (NATO) and the Western European Union (WEU). In doing so, special attention will be paid to the relationship between the mandates of both organizations and the framework for interventionist measures provided in the UN Charter.

The traditional security concept of NATO has focused on attacks on the territorial integrity of its members. Averting such attacks by forcible means had a clear basis in the international law doctrine of collective self-defence.[61] After the dismantling of the Warsaw Pact and the military threats flowing from it, the need to define a new role for the organization became apparent. As we shall see in the following, member states of NATO have accorded the organization the legal capacity to act "out of area," with or without the mandate of the UN Security Council. Compared with the straightforward Cold War mandate, this raises questions about the legal basis in international law. The Security Council may indeed authorize regional organizations to take enforcement action under Article 53 of the UN Charter.[62] However, this article states unequivocally that "no enforcement action shall be taken under regional arrangements or by regional agencies without the authorization of the Security Council." Thus, at face value, there is no legal basis for out-of-area tasks assumed by NATO without the prior and explicit authorization of the Security Council.[63]

Is there a link between out-of-area activities, involving the use of force, and forced migration? The answer is to be sought in the 1999 Strategic Concept adopted by NATO members' heads of state. Although the Strategic Concept is not a treaty instrument, it nevertheless sheds light on the agreement of NATO members on how to construe the organization's mandate. Against that backdrop, its importance should not be underestimated.

Paragraph 10 of the 1999 Strategic Concept divides the tasks of NATO into two categories. One is "fundamental" and covers the dimensions of security, consultations, and deterrence. The second provides for the areas of crisis management and partnership with other actors and aims at enhancing the security and stability of the Euro-Atlantic area. The task of crisis management is described as follows: "[t]o stand ready, case-by-case and by consensus, in conformity with Article 7 of the Washington Treaty, to contribute to effective conflict prevention and to engage actively in crisis management, including crisis response operations."

Paragraph 31 of the 1999 Strategic Concept clarifies the meaning of the term "crisis response operations" and puts it into the context of international law:

In pursuit of its policy of preserving peace, preventing war, and enhancing security and stability and as set out in the fundamental security tasks, NATO will seek, in cooperation with other organisations, to prevent conflict, or, should a crisis arise, to contribute to its effective management, consistent with international law, including through the possibility of conducting non-Article 5 crisis response operations.

More specifically, paragraph 24 of the 1999 Strategic Concept provides the link between crisis response and forced migration. This paragraph starts by alluding to the traditional mandate of territorial defence, and then moves on to an extension of this mandate to cover other risks, including that of migratory movements:

Any armed attack on the territory of the Allies, from whatever direction, would be covered by Articles 5 and 6 of the Washington Treaty. However, Alliance security must also take account of the global context. Alliance security interests can be affected by other risks of a wider nature, including acts of terrorism, sabotage and organised crime, and by the disruption of the flow of vital resources. The uncontrolled movement of large numbers of people, particularly as a consequence of armed conflicts, can also pose problems for security and stability affecting the Alliance. Arrangements exist within the Alliance for consultation among the Allies under Article 4 of the Washington Treaty and, where appropriate, co-ordination of their efforts including their responses to risks of this kind.

The paragraph thus provides the link between migratory movements, consultations, and collective crisis response by NATO. It should be stressed that it is the uncontrolled movement of people, and not the causes behind it, that poses the security threat and thus the goal of crisis response. In spite of the Kosovo experience, no mention is made of massive human rights violations as a cause for flight movements. A careful reader cannot avoid the impression that NATO targets the symptom and not necessarily the disease.

Such crisis response activities are legally unproblematic, provided there is a clear mandate by the Security Council. However, the Strategic Concept does not make such an authorization a precondition for undertaking crisis response activities. In practice, the Alliance's willingness to take action outside or without a Security Council mandate was illustrated by its intervention in Bosnia–Herzegovina and in Kosovo.

The described developments within NATO have a parallel in those of the Western European Union. The WEU, founded in 1948, currently serves as an organizational framework for a common defence policy within the European Union.[64] In 1997, the WEU was given an explicit, treaty-based competence to deal with the so-called Petersberg tasks.[65] According to the Treaty on European Union, questions that may be dealt with in the framework of WEU "shall include humanitarian and rescue tasks, peacekeeping tasks and tasks of combat forces in crisis management, including peacemaking."[66] Strikingly, there is no geographical limitation restraining WEU member states in the pursuit of Petersberg tasks.[67]

The question remains whether the assumption of such tasks presupposes prior authorization by the Security Council. Article 11(1) of the TEU sets out that the Union's common foreign and security policy shall *inter alia* serve the following objectives:

– to safeguard the common values, fundamental interests, independence and integrity of the Union in conformity with the principles of the United Nations Charter; ...
– to preserve peace and strengthen international security, in accordance with the principles of the United Nations Charter, as well as the principles of the Helsinki Final Act and the objectives of the Paris Charter, including those on external borders.

On the other hand, Article 17(1) prescribes compatibility between NATO and WEU defence policies:

The policy of the Union in accordance with this Article shall not prejudice the specific character of the security and defence policy of certain Member States and shall respect the obligations of certain Member States, which see their common defence realised in the North Atlantic Treaty Organisation (NATO), under the North Atlantic Treaty and be compatible with the common security and defence policy established within that framework.

Thus, the WEU provides another regional mechanism, which has been explicitly mandated by its members to assume interventionist tasks. Although the terminology used in the NATO and WEU frameworks differs to some degree, there is a basic convergence: both organizations may act out of area invoking their members' security interests, and both may use force in doing so. In both cases, relevant texts allude to the UN Charter, but do not make a prior authorization of interventionist measures by the Security Council a precondition for action. This is, of course, a threat to the monopoly of the Security Council when it comes to authorizing international force beyond the realm of self-defence. In the current state of play, it is also a threat to the universality of international law.

Regionalizing security and outlawing refugee migration

There are strong indications that the three responses to flight – insulation, palliation, and intervention – are currently undergoing a process of regionalization. Although global regimes exist when it comes both to refugee protection and to the use of force in international law, these regimes risk being sidelined by regional arrangements, all of which draw heavily on an expanded security concept.

Regionalization is certainly not an evil in itself. It may provide badly needed detail and momentum to vague and under-resourced global arrangements. But it may also undermine global arrangements and thus contribute to the fragmentation of international law and world order. Simply, much depends on the question of whether or not regional arrangements are strictly subsidiary to global ones. There are strong indications that the necessary subsidiarity is lacking. This is apparent in all three areas, where developments within the European Union and NATO indicate a marked ambiguity towards the question of subsidiarity. Especially when it comes to the use of force, the spectre of a *ius imperium* resurfaces, evoking unhappy memories of Carl Schmitt's regionalized conception of international law.[68]

When it comes to forced migration in general, the particularist concept of community security is no longer pursued by each state separately. A movement towards increased inter-state cooperation can be traced, and the particularist perception of security has infested the discourses of migration control and defence. Parallel to this movement, we observe an increasing tendency to outlaw refugee migration. The remainder of these conclusions will take a look at various manifestations of this tendency.

Because visa requirements, carrier sanctions, and externalized border control have increasingly blocked protection seekers' access to countries of asylum, irregular channels of migration have become ever more important, often providing the sole avenue to safety. Irregular channels are problematic per se: they force protection seekers to accept the considerable risks of being smuggled, and they rely on a market mechanism according to which protection is available not for the most needy but rather for the most affluent. Industrialized states bear a moral responsibility for promoting and expanding the market for human smuggling by designing indiscriminate insulation policies. Had the same states opened alternative avenues to protection for those in need of it (for example by the device of humanitarian visas outlined above), interest in the services of human smugglers would have decreased proportionately, and the legitimacy of the fight against illegal migration would have been enhanced.

However, industrialized states have not been interested in a balanced approach. Rather, they have embarked on a wholesale criminalization of migration without documents. This criminalization is indiscriminate, because it does not distinguish between forced migration and other forms of migration. It associates assistance to protection seekers with human trafficking and the trading of illegal narcotic substances. This strategy works in two ways. First, it finds expression in a growing number of instruments addressing smuggling and trafficking, the UN Convention Against Transnational Organised Crime[69] being one of the most recent examples.[70] Second, criminalization influences the public perception of refugees. When all legal avenues to safe territories are blocked, the victims of human rights violations are transformed into law-breakers by virtue of their flight attempt. Moreover, there is a risk that states will abuse the discourse on smuggling as a way of diverting attention from the detrimental effects of their insulative policies. What remains is the image of refugees as the clients of criminals, with the concomitant guilt by association.

Beyond the measures against human smuggling and migration without documents, we find another dimension of the ongoing outlawing process. Because it is increasingly difficult to obtain formal protected status in any country, protection seekers are faced with deciding whether a formal application is worth while. The alternative is to rely on the informal networks at their disposal and to avoid all form of contact with the authorities, including the filing of a request for asylum. The disadvantage is that they lose access to the material and formal benefits linked to the seeking of asylum, but there are advantages as well, such as the avoidance of detention or forcible removal. There are good reasons to assume that this phenomenon is occurring on a significant scale in industrialized host states. To the extent that such underground migrants would be entitled to protection under international law, they represent the "outlaws" created by the ever more sophisticated restrictionism of asylum countries – disentitled, easy to exploit, and confirming the self-fulfilling prophecy of the bogus refugee.

Notes

1. See Article 12(2) of the International Covenant on Civil and Political Rights (ICCPR), 16 December 1966, 999 UNTS 171.

2. The construction of free movement rights has therefore been termed "asymmetrical." For a discussion, see G. Noll, *Negotiating Asylum. The EU acquis, Extraterritorial Protection and the Common Market of Deflection*, The Hague: Martinus Nijhoff, 2000, pp. 416–432.

3. Universal Declaration of Human Rights (UDHR), GA Res. 217 (III) of 10 December 1948.

4. Noll, *Negotiating Asylum*, pp. 357–362.

5. Human security "means, first, safety from such chronic threats as hunger, disease and repression. And second, it means protection from sudden and hurtful disruptions in the patterns of daily life – whether in homes, in jobs, or in communities" (United Nations Development Programme, *Human Development Report*, Oxford: Oxford University Press, 1994, p. 23). As any observer will note, this concept is too abstract to have an impact on the opposition between refugee interests and host community interests.

6. In fact, the UNDP concept of "human security" is of little help in such clashes, because it accommodates both individual and community (i.e. state) interests. Both interests can be formulated so as to fit into the definition quoted above. It is particularly enlightening to compare this definition with the concept of "societal security" developed by Ole Wæver, an exponent of the Copenhagen School. Wæver defines societal security as concerning "the ability of a society to persist in its essential character under changing conditions and possible or actual threats. More specifically, it is about the sustainability, within acceptable conditions for evolution, of traditional patterns of language, culture, association, and religious and national identity and custom" (O. Wæver, "Societal Security: The Concept," in O. Wæver et al., *Identity, Migration and the New Security Agenda in Europe*, London: Pinter, 1993, p. 23). Quite clearly the UNDP emphasis on "sudden disruptions" would be easy to colonize for the essentialist conception of security suggested by Wæver.

7. See, e.g., the discussion on the Kosovo intervention in the Editorial Comments by Louis Henkin, Ruth Wedgwood, Jonathan I. Charney, Christine M. Chinkin, Richard A. Falk, Thomas M. Frank, and W. Michael Reisman in *American Journal of International Law*, vol. 93, no. 4, October 1999, pp. 824–862. The present discussion on the legality of the US/UK intervention in Afghanistan also features an important component of proportionality in the context of self-defence.

8. For a good overview of EU policies in this regard, see Jef Huysmans, "The European Union and the Securitization of Migration," *Journal of Common Market Studies*, vol. 38, no. 5, pp. 751–777.

9. See the mandate of the EU High Level Working Group on Asylum and Migration, established by a Council Decision on 8 December 1998. See Council of the European Union, "Terms of Reference of the High Level Working Group on Asylum and Migration; Preparation of Action Plans for the Most Important Countries of Origin and Transit of Asylum Seekers and Migrants," 25 January 1999.

10. American Convention on Human Rights (ACHR), 22 November 1969, OAS Official Records, OEA/Ser.K/XVI/1.1.

11. African Charter on Human and Peoples' Rights, 26 June 1981, ILM no. 21, p. 59.

12. Article 29(3) of the same instrument lays down an individual duty "[n]ot to compromise the security of the State whose national or resident he is." This article turns on the specific relationship of loyalty between citizen and state, which brings it outside the scope of this text, which remains concerned with the relationship of non-citizens and potential host states.

13. In 2000, Iceland had 20 asylum applications (UN High Commissioner for Refugees, "Global Refugee Trends," Geneva, May 2001).

14. The control strategy has combined a coordinated visa list with more than 120 country

entries, a common set of instructions for consular officers in issuing visas, the imposition of sanctions to discourage carriers from bringing aliens without documents to the Union, and the posting of migration liaison officers abroad to render pre-departure control more efficient. For a full description of the legal instruments employed, see Noll, *Negotiating Asylum*, pp. 161–182.

15. See chapter 8 in this volume on internally displaced persons by Erin D. Mooney.

16. See, for example, Peter Hilpold, "Humanitarian Intervention: Is There a Need for a Legal Reappraisal?" *European Journal of International Law*, vol. 12, no. 3, 2001, pp. 437–468; Ann Orford, "Muscular Humanitarianism: Reading the Narratives of the New Interventionism," *European Journal of International Law*, vol. 10, no. 4, 1999, pp. 679–712; and Huysmans, "The European Union and the Securitization of Migration."

17. See, e.g., Article 2(1) of the ICCPR, requiring that the individual be "within [the contracting party's] territory and subject to its jurisdiction." The 1950 European Convention on Human Rights (ECHR) provides the exception to this rule. Its Article 2 delimits the scope of application to everyone within the jurisdiction of a contracting party, omitting the demand for presence in that party's territory. I shall return to the significance of this solution below.

18. K. J. Partsch, "Human Rights in General," in R. Wolfrum, ed., *United Nations: Law, Policies and Practice*, Dordrecht: Martinus Nijhoff, 1995, p. 606, n14, referring to the Advisory Opinion on Namibia, ICJ Reports 1971, 16 (57).

19. For a brief introduction to the methodology of interpretation with further references, see Noll, *Negotiating Asylum*, pp. 379–382. See also Anthony Aust, *Modern Treaty Law and Practice*, Cambridge: Cambridge University Press, 2000, pp. 184–206.

20. One of the most carefully argued approaches may be found in J. Carens, "The Philosopher and the Policymaker: Two Perspectives on the Ethics of Immigration with Special Attention to the Problem of Restricting Asylum," in K. Hailbronner, D. Martin, and H. Motomura, eds., *Immigration Admissions: The Search for Workable Policies in Germany and the United States*, Oxford: Berghahn Books, 1997, pp. 3–50.

21. Article 3 of the ECHR might impose obligations to grant admission in specific situations, including the obligation to issue an entry visa.

22. The *Tampa* incident took place during the last week of August and the first weeks of September 2001, and triggered diplomatic representations by Norway, the flag state of the *Tampa*, to the Australian government. The asylum seekers aboard the *Tampa* had been rescued at sea, evoking memories of the "boat people" from Indo-China in the late 1970s.

23. Noll, *Negotiating Asylum*, pp. 441–446.

24. Ibid., pp. 467–474.

25. A child seeking an entry visa at a diplomatic representation located in the country of origin would fall outside the scope of Article 22; because such a child is not outside its country of origin, it is not to be regarded as a refugee in the sense of Article 1 A.(2) GC.

26. The United Kingdom introduced the following reservation: "The United Kingdom reserves the right to apply such legislation, in so far as it relates to the entry into, stay in and departure from the United Kingdom of those who do not have the right under the law of the United Kingdom to enter and remain in the United Kingdom, and to the acquisition and possession of citizenship, as it may deem necessary from time to time."

Singapore introduced the following reservation: "Singapore is geographically one of the smallest independent countries in the world and one of the most densely populated. The Republic of Singapore accordingly reserves the right to apply such legislation and conditions concerning the entry into, stay in and departure from the Republic of Singapore of those who do not or who no longer have the right under the laws of the Republic of Singapore, to enter and remain in the Republic of Singapore, and to the acquisition and possession of citizenship, as it may deem necessary from time to time and in accordance with the laws of the Republic of Singapore."

Portugal and Sweden both objected to the reservations by the Republic of Singapore, considering that "reservations by which a State limits its responsibilities under the Convention by invoking general principles of national law may create doubts on the commitments of the reserving State to the object and purpose of the Convention and, moreover, contribute to undermining the basis of international law." It could, of course, be asked why analogous objections have not been presented against the reservation by the United Kingdom, whose reference to domestic law is no less sweeping than that utilized in Singapore's reservation.

27. Germany made the following declaration upon ratification: "Nothing in the Convention may be interpreted as implying that unlawful entry by an alien into the territory of the Federal Republic of Germany or his unlawful stay there is permitted; nor may any provision be interpreted to mean that it restricts the right of the Federal Republic of Germany to pass laws and regulations concerning the entry of aliens and the conditions of their stay or to make a distinction between nationals and aliens."

28. See, e.g., ECHR Article 15.

29. This is the fragile protection accorded to would-be victims of non-state agents of persecution claiming protection in Germany. The T.I. vs. the U.K. case before the European Court of Human Rights (ECtHR) offered some graphic insights into the precarious status accorded to this class of protection seekers in one of the most affluent economies of the industrialized world. ECtHR (Third Chamber), *Decision as to the Admissibility of Application No. 43844/98 by T.I. against the U.K.*, 7 March 2000 (unpublished).

30. The ECtHR is competent to make such a demand under Rule 39 of its Rules of Procedures. Contracting parties to the ECHR usually comply with that request, although there is no explicit legal obligation to do so.

31. For a good overview, see G. Loescher, "Refugees: A Global Human Rights and Security Crisis," in T. Dunne and N. Wheeler, *Human Rights in Global Politics*, Cambridge: Cambridge University Press, 1999, pp. 246–248.

32. This status has been termed "subsidiary protection" or "complementary protection." The European Commission has presented the draft of a binding instrument defining the beneficiaries and rights under this status. European Commission, "Proposal for a Council Directive Laying down Minimum Standards for the Qualification and Status of Third Country Nationals and Stateless Persons as Refugees, in Accordance with the 1951 Convention Relating to the Status of Refugees and the 1967 Protocol, or as Persons Who Otherwise Need International Protection," Brussels, 12 September 2001, COM 2001/510.

33. It should be noted, though, that some states explicitly stated that the action taken was not directed against Muslims or Islam generally, and distanced themselves from xenophobic tendencies. See, e.g., European Council, *Conclusions and Plan of Action of the Extraordinary European Council Meeting on 21 September 2001*, Brussels, 21 September 2001, SN 140/01.

34. UN Security Council Resolution 1373, 28 September 2001, S/Res/1373 (2001).

35. The German non-governmental organization Pro Asyl repeatedly voiced this criticism during the debate on the German draft law in autumn 2001 (see press releases of the period available at www.pro-asyl.de), and the Danish Centre for Human Rights emphasized that much of the change to Danish aliens law proposed in the counter-terrorist draft legislation presented in October 2001 was unrelated to the struggle against terrorism (see English summary of the "Statement by the Danish Centre for Human Rights on the Anti Terror Package," November 2001, available at www.humanrights.dk).

36. European Commission, "Working Document on the Relationship between Safeguard-

ing Internal Security and Complying with International Protection Obligations and Instruments," Brussels, 5 December 2001, COM (2001) 743 final, section 1.4.3.2.

37. For a critical assessment, see D. Chandler, "The Road to Military Humanitarianism: How the Human Rights NGOs Shaped a New Humanitarian Agenda," *Human Rights Quarterly*, vol. 23, no. 3, 2001, pp. 678–700.

38. See UN Security Council Resolution 794 (1992) of 3 December 1992 on Somalia, UN SC Resolution 929 (1994) of 22 June 1994 on Rwanda, and UN SC Resolution 940 (1994) of 31 July 1994 on Haiti.

39. For an analysis, see F. Harhoff, "Unauthorized Humanitarian Interventions – Armed Violence in the Name of Humanity?" *Nordic Journal of International Law*, vol. 70, nos 1–2, pp. 65–199, at pp. 90–92.

40. UN SC Resolution 1264 of 15 September 1999.

41. UN SC Resolution 688 of 5 April 1991.

42. See M. Barutciski and A. Suhrke, "Lessons from the Kosovo Refugee Crisis: Innovations in Protection and Burden-sharing," *Journal of Refugee Studies*, vol. 14, no. 2, 2001.

43. This understanding was already explicitly endorsed in the mid-1980s. See, e.g., the "Political Declaration of the Member States on the Free Movement of Persons," annexed to the Single European Act, OJ (1987) L 169/26.

44. "Protocol on Asylum for Nationals of Member States of the European Union," annexed to the Treaty on European Union and to the Treaty Establishing the European Community, 6 October 1997, Doc. no. CONF 4007/97, TA/P/en 24.

45. European Council, *Presidency Conclusions*, Tampere European Council, 15/16 October 1999, paras. 2 and 3. It should be recalled that the Conclusions are not legally binding, whereas the TEU is.

46. TEU Article 62(1).

47. TEU Article 62(2)(a).

48. TEU Article 62(2)(b).

49. TEU Article 62(3).

50. TEU Article 63(1)(a).

51. TEU Article 63(1)(b).

52. TEU Article 63(1)(c).

53. TEU Article 63(1)(d).

54. TEU Article 63(2)(a).

55. TEU Article 63(3)(b).

56. K. Hailbronner, "Die Neuregelung der Bereiche Freier Personenverkehr, Asylrecht und Einwanderung," in W. Hummer, ed., *Die Europäische Union nach dem Vertrag von Amsterdam*, Vienna: Manz, 1998, p. 182.

57. TEU Article 63(2)(b).

58. TEU Article 63(3)(a).

59. TEU Article 63(4).

60. For an argument that TEU Article 64(1) does not prejudice the powers of the ECJ under Title IV, see G. Noll and J. Vedsted-Hansen, "Non-Communitarians: Refugee and Asylum Policies," in P. Alston, ed., *The European Union and Human Rights*, Oxford: Oxford University Press, 1999, p. 374.

61. Compare Article 5 of the Washington Treaty and Article 51 of the UN Charter.

62. It is a moot point whether NATO is a regional organization in the technical sense or not.

63. On the legal framework of the use of force in the context of so-called humanitarian interventions, see Jens Elo Rytter, "Humanitarian Intervention without the Security Council: From San Francisco to Kosovo – and Beyond," *Nordic Journal of International Law*, vol. 71, nos 1–2, 2001, pp. 212–160.

64. Although they are EU member states, Austria, Denmark, Finland, Ireland, and Sweden are not full-fledged members of the WEU.

65. WEU foreign and defence ministers met in 1992 in Petersberg, Germany, and agreed on a listing of WEU tasks:

"Apart from contributing to the common defence in accordance with Article 5 of the Washington Treaty and Article V of the modified Brussels Treaty respectively, military units of the Member States, acting under the authority of WEU, could be employed for
– Humanitarian and rescue tasks;
– Peace-keeping tasks;
– Tasks of combat forces in crisis management, including peacemaking"

See Fabrizio Pagani, "A New Gear in the CSFP Machinery: Integration of the Peters-berg Tasks in the Treaty on European Union," *European Journal of International Law*, vol. 9, 1998, pp. 737–749.

66. TEU Article 17(2).

67. Pagani, "A New Gear in the CSFP Machinery," p. 741.

68. In the early 1940s, Schmitt developed a theory of international law based on the concept of *Grossraum* and drawing on the Monroe doctrine. In this theory, the right to intervene in other countries is reserved for the hegemon power in the region, and powers external to the region are barred from intervening. Historically of little surprise, his theory fitted well with the imperialist aspirations of the German government at the time. Lament-ably, international relations have not improved to a point making the *Grossraum* theory obsolete. Carl Schmitt, *Völkerrechtliche Grossraumordnung mit Interventionsverbot für raumfremde Mächte. Ein Beitrag zum Reichsbegriff im Völkerrecht*, Berlin: Duncker & Humblot, 1941.

69. Signed by some 120 states on 15 December 2000 in Palermo, Italy. A Protocol Against the Smuggling of Migrants by Land, Sea and Air has been adopted together with this instrument. Measures include criminalization of traffickers and smugglers with appro-priate penalties, protection of victims in receiving countries, and information-sharing between countries on trafficking methods. Increased border restrictions and the imple-mentation of carrier sanctions are recommended.

70. After lobbying by the UN High Commissioner for Refugees, legal safeguards for refu-gees were included in this instrument, thus at least acknowledging the possibly negative effects of anti-smuggling instruments on the legitimate human rights interests of refu-gees. On the ground, however, such safeguards are of little help when it comes to pre-serving flight routes for protection seekers with no documents.

14

A new Tower of Babel? Reappraising the architecture of refugee protection

William Maley

It is not an easy time to be helping refugees. Three wars in Europe and numerous crises of state disruption in the developing world made the last decade of the twentieth century a turbulent one. As usual, a major symptom of this turbulence was population displacement, both within and across the borders of states. Alas, this turbulence was not matched by an upsurge of generosity on the part of richer and safer states. Instead, political leaders in the West increasingly groped for reasons to vilify or disparage those for whom flight was the only option. Those who arrived in the West without visas were "illegal immigrants" or "queue jumpers," deserving of no mercy.[1] The 1951 Convention Relating to the Status of Refugees, it was hinted, was a "Cold War" document, inappropriate to an era of large-scale refugee movements. And the Office of the United Nations High Commissioner for Refugees (UNHCR) came under increasing pressure – its staff under fire,[2] its responsibilities stretched, its funding unequal to the challenge of those responsibilities. Its position was and is invidious: charged with protecting refugees, its donors more and more expect it instead to protect their borders.

In September 1999, Reuters News Agency carried a remarkable report from its bureau in the Pakistani capital of Islamabad. According to the dispatch, a spokesman for the UNHCR office in Pakistan urged Afghan refugees in Pakistan "not to approach its offices" for resettlement, stating that "UNHCR simply does not have the capacity to handle the increased volume of people demanding to be sent to the Western countries." The spokesman concluded that "we cannot cope with it, and our daily work on behalf of refugees has been seriously disrupted by this outpouring."[3] Although there was surely something quite startling about refugees being asked not to seek the help of a refugee relief organization lest they interfere with its work, the report from Reuters passed almost unnoticed in a world regularly preoccupied with horrors of which refugees are the principal victims. This was a pity, for it highlighted some longstanding challenges confronting those charged with managing humanitarian crises, and at the same time pointed to inadequacies in the institutional architecture for refugee protection. It is with these inadequacies, and with possible ways of addressing them, that this chapter is concerned.

The central challenges relate to two distinct but overlapping dimensions of refugee assistance. On the one hand, a refugee is a person who, as the 1951 Convention puts it, "owing to a well-founded fear of being persecuted for reasons of race, religion, nationality, membership in a particular social group, or political opinion, is outside the country of his nationality and is unable or, owing to such fear, is unwilling to avail himself of the protection of that country." To assist such persons, it is necessary that they be identified, and that an assessment be made of whether they fear persecution, whether their fears are well founded, and whether they fear persecution for a "Convention" reason. Those who are refugees must not be returned to face the persecution they fear. The focus of such refugee protection is the individual, and the concepts of asylum and non-*refoulement* lie at its core.[4] On the other hand, "refugees," in popular parlance, are rivers of humanity in need of sustenance, shelter, and care when events drive them en masse from their homes, whether they cross a border or not. To assist such persons, it is necessary to mobilize resources, often at high speed, so that they do not fall victim to starvation or disease. The focus of such refugee relief is the collective, and concepts of shelter, nutrition, and hygiene lie at its core.

In this chapter, I use the expression "refugee assistance" to embrace both these dimensions, and "protection" and "relief" when more precise delineation of the dimensions is required. Refugee protection and refugee relief both involve attention to human security, to the needs of people rather than of states as such. However, the kinds of response that they demand vary considerably, and so does the disposition of the international community to respond appropriately: relief is calculated to keep refugees at arm's length from Western populations. This is not, of course, a novel insight.[5] At the moment, however, the challenges of protection and relief are frequently not being met – as the dire situation of newly arrived Afghan refugees in Pakistan in 2001 made clear.[6] There is no shortage of actors in the field to provide aid to refugees. But too often they occupy a dysfunctional Tower of Babel, metaphorically speaking languages that their fellows cannot understand. And the refugees whom they aim to help are the immediate victims of their operational and organizational weaknesses. It is therefore worth while to explore how things might be done better.

The chapter is divided into five sections. In the first, I examine the ways in which refugee assistance has been shaped by the contours of the international system and by the characteristics of international organizations. The second discusses specific problems of refugee assistance, drawing for examples on developments from the post–Cold War period. The third turns to the past experience of proposals to reform the mechanisms for aiding the needy. The fourth offers suggestions for institutional reorganization to overcome some of the most troubling problems that beset the present regime for refugee protection. In a spirit of realism, the fifth identifies the more important obstacles to reform. A theme that runs through the chapter, and that it is important to highlight from the outset, is that *all* refugee assistance has political implications, and that to believe in a "pure" humanitarianism divorced from politics is profoundly naive. On the contrary, although certain organizational pathologies have adversely affected the provision of refugee assistance, the deeper threat to refugee relief *and* protection comes from the power of vested political interests. Too often, refugees can find that they have fled from the frying pan to the fire. I am not at all optimistic that things are likely to change for the better, but it is only through the utopian exercise of imagining other worlds that we can begin to see how a better world might be built.

The shaping of refugee assistance

The Westphalian order – contestable as that notion may be – was premised on a direct link between rulers and ruled. In such a system, boundaries between states were designed to create safe neighbourhoods by imposing limits on destructive intervention of the kind that led to the Thirty Years War. The "pure" Westphalian system, as Stephen Krasner has recently demonstrated in detail, was never fully realized.[7] Sovereignty is an *idea* of enormous potency, but it is increasingly under pressure both from processes of globalization that erode the capacities and autonomies of the state, and from cosmopolitan ideas that challenge the unfettered right of the state to treat its subjects as it wishes. In an ideal world, it has been argued, the state should function as a device for ensuring that general duties to our fellows are properly discharged.[8] Refugees are the victims of the failure of such a system of "assigned responsibility" to work effectively. It is a commonplace observation that ordinary people can become the targets of their fellows. The world is littered with states that fall far short of respecting elementary standards of humanity – totalitarian states, sultanistic states, genocidal states, or weak states in which the instrumentalities of government, even if they are so minded, seem powerless to prevent the predations of one social group upon another.[9] And although there is much ground for rejoicing in the so-called "third wave" of democratization, it is also the case that many new democracies remain unconsolidated, and some have resulted in the empowerment of *un*civil society, with devastating consequences.[10] In the light of these factors, the phenomenon of the refugee is most unlikely to disappear.

Mechanisms for refugee assistance developed almost hand in hand with international organizations more generally. This was in part because, until the twentieth century, large-scale movements of people recognized as refugees were rare. Given the relative weakness of passport controls and policing systems in the nineteenth century,[11] individual political exiles moved through Europe following some of that century's major revolutionary upheavals, but they did not remotely threaten the stability or well-being of their hosts. The major transnational organization to emerge from the nineteenth century, the Red Cross, was concerned more with the alleviation of suffering in war than with refugee relief per se. However, it was the President of the International Committee of the Red Cross (ICRC), Gustav Ador, who in 1921 appealed to the young League of Nations to take measures for the protection of the large numbers of refugees displaced by the Russian civil war, and triggered the appointment of Dr. Fridtjof Nansen as High Commissioner for Russian Refugees, a position he occupied until 1930.[12]

To trace the various forms that mechanisms for refugee assistance took in the 1930s and 1940s lies beyond the scope of this chapter.[13] But an outline of the contemporary mechanisms of refugee assistance does not. Assistance to refugees broadly comes from states and their citizens, from international organizations, and from non-governmental organizations (NGOs). States can provide assistance by offering an adjacent haven to which refugees flee. This can be burdensome, especially as states within disruptive neighbourhoods or failed states are often far from stable themselves: consider the cases of Rwanda and the Democratic Republic of Congo. States that do not themselves border regions of conflict can also provide assistance, either through orderly resettlement of refugees from countries of first asylum (as occurred for Indo-Chinese refugees from 1979, and from 1989 pursuant to the Comprehensive Plan of Action), or through funding relief programmes in countries of first asylum, or, if they are parties to the 1951 Convention, by granting protection to those refugees who reach their shores and benefit from the Convention's non-*refoulement* provisions. NGOs too play major roles in re-fugee relief. Wherever a significant refugee population is to be found, so are NGOs. Some concentrate on the delivery of emergency relief, some on programmes with a distinctly developmental flavour, and some see advocacy on behalf of their refugee clients as a significant element of their mandate. The International Committee of the Red Cross, often functioning alongside such NGOs, enjoys an ambiguous status because of the role of states in the governance of the Red Cross movement. Not purely an NGO, it is not purely an international organization either. Its core principles, most importantly neutrality and impartiality, prevent it from playing an advocacy role of the type adopted by NGOs such as Médecins sans Frontières, and on occasion this has led to agonizing sit-uations, such as that which arose during the Holocaust.[14] Nonetheless, in an environment more richly populated with NGOs than was the case during the Second World War, the Red Cross's approach can usefully complement that of more overtly political bodies.

It is with international organizations that the remainder of this chapter is concerned. There are a number of agencies that provide aid to refu-gees. An important one that is not part of the UN system is the Inter-national Organization for Migration (IOM), which, as the Provisional Intergovernmental Committee for the Movement of Migrants from Europe, had taken over the resettlement operations of the old Interna-tional Refugee Organization (IRO) from 1 February 1952, just a month before the IRO went into liquidation. It is now a fully fledged indepen-dent agency based in Geneva. The oldest UN refugee agency, often overlooked, is the United Nations Relief and Works Agency for Pales-tine Refugees in the Near East (UNRWA), which is distinctive in that it deals with refugees from one particular conflict. Other significant agencies with global responsibilities are the Rome-based World Food Programme, the New York-based United Nations Development Pro-gramme (UNDP), and the United Nations Children's Fund (UNICEF). The UN Office for the Coordination of Humanitarian Affairs (OCHA) has important coordination responsibilities. But the most important of all, and the main focus for reform proposals, is the UNHCR, which came into existence on 1 January 1951 as the result of a resolution of the United Nations General Assembly. The UNHCR is now a thoroughly entrenched element of the international landscape, with its own Execu-tive Committee drawn from important UN member states and a distin-guished current leader, former Dutch Prime Minister Ruud Lubbers.

The UNHCR, despite depending for its existence on recurring reso-lutions of the General Assembly, is for most practical purposes an inde-pendent agency. Its record of achievement is very considerable and its field staff often face extreme danger, as the murders of staff in West Timor in 2000 made clear. Unfortunately, it has also come to display a number of the weaknesses with which international organizations are afflicted. Barnett and Finnemore have argued that some of the sources of a bureaucracy's capacity may also be sources of pathology: those on which they focus are what they call "the irrationality of rationalization, universalism, normalization of deviance, organizational insulation, and cultural contestation."[15] Procedures develop lives of their own, they are applied in contexts in which they are inappropriate, what should be exceptions come to be treated as rules, organizations become insulated by norms of professions and by the absence of feedback loops, and different *Weltanschauungen* within an organization lead to dysfunctionality. To these problems, three other sources of pathology should be added. First is the problem of bureaucratic politics and bureaucratic interests. It is by now a trivial proposition that bureaucracies may be motivated by interests of their own[16] rather than by their ostensible purposes, and that different fragments of a bureaucracy may be similarly driven: "Where you stand depends on where you sit."[17] Second is cognitive dissonance or denial, in which unpalatable realities are screened out of consideration; Walkup has argued that this is a particular peril for those who enter relief organizations with high expectations that reality cannot sustain.[18] The third, of course, is global politics: international organizations with functional responsibilities are in a real sense dependent upon their key state supporters, which have the option to walk away from them. This is potentially costly from a political point of view if formal departure is required. It is relatively easy when no more than the withholding or reduction of funding is involved. The UNHCR has been touched by all these problems.[19]

Problems of refugee assistance

Count Ciano wrote in his diary that victory finds a hundred fathers but defeat is an orphan.[20] A parallel observation applies to humanitarian action: success tends to be systematically documented, whereas failure has to be pinned down with anecdotes. This is perhaps less the case now than it was a decade ago: the virtues of feedback are increasingly appreciated, and in any case, since vigilant media are to be found in most theatres of operations, bungles are hard to hide. Yet much that is disturbing emerges only through fragments of individual testimony. To focus on this is not to deny the achievements of the UNHCR and other such agencies in assisting very large numbers of refugees, but, given the fatal consequences that can result for individual refugees from inadequacies in the refugee protection regime, the regime must perform to an almost superhuman standard of excellence.[21]

The problems with which this system for refugee assistance is confronted are manifold. Refugees in some parts of the world live in unutterable squalor; refugees in need of resettlement are rejected in favour of those who seem cheap to resettle;[22] in some cases the route to refugee resettlement has been through bribery of those empowered to effect it.[23] All these problems point to a system under stress. The system's problems arise from the conjunction of at least five factors: an increase in the numbers of persons in need of assistance and an insecure funding base for the UNHCR; a growing reluctance on the part of wealthy states to accept refugees for whom voluntary repatriation or settlement in countries of first asylum do not constitute durable solutions; a magnification of pressures on the UNHCR to engage itself in roles that might at first glance appear to lie well beyond its direct responsibilities; a reluctance to address root causes of refugee flows when these relate to the behaviour of "sovereign" states; and incoherent political signalling as a result of conflicting international political and humanitarian agendas.

The data on refugee numbers are alarming. The total number of refugees at the end of the UNHCR's first year, on 31 December 1951, was 2,116,200. A quarter of a century later, on 31 December 1976, the figure was 3,757,700. From this point, the figure began to climb. It reached 10,194,900 at the end of 1981, 12,589,200 at the end of 1986, and 17,022,000 at the end of 1991. Through the 1990s, the figure fell: to 13,228,500 at the end of 1996, and to 12,148,000 at the end of 2000.[24] However, these figures do not tell the full story, since they exclude other "persons of concern to UNHCR," namely asylum seekers, returned refugees, and internally displaced persons and others of concern. At the end of 2000, the most recent point for which data are available, the total of refugees and these other persons was 21,126,010.[25] This figure is almost 50 per cent higher than it was a decade earlier. The largest single group of refugees consists of Afghans, of whom there are over 2.5 million. This group *on its own* outnumbers the *worldwide* total of refugees at the end of the UNHCR's first year. The next largest group of refugees originate from Iraq: over 500,000. It should also be noted that these figures exclude Palestinians registered with UNRWA, currently around 3.5 million. What is striking here is that these large concentrations are products of conflicts that have proved intractable. The Afghan state has collapsed and, even with the overthrow of the Taliban in late 2001, will take years to reconstruct and reinstitutionalize;[26] the Iraqi state is totalitarian, with no apparent prospects for peaceful internal reform; and the gulf dividing Israelis and Palestinians seems wider than ever with the emergence of the right-winger Ariel Sharon as Israel's prime minister and Israel's reoccupation of the West Bank in 2002 in response to suicide bombings by Palestinian militants. And, in dealing with these large and intractable problems, the UNHCR and UNRWA are heavily dependent upon voluntary contributions from UN member states.[27]

In addition, the willingness of wealthy countries to receive refugees has not kept up with the swelling numbers of those in need. Formal, permanent resettlement is practised by only a small number of states, most importantly the United States, Canada, Australia, Norway, New Zealand, Sweden, Finland, Denmark, and the Netherlands. However, the fall of the Iron Curtain broke down barriers that previously existed between Western Europe and the Eurasian mass and, as a result, European states were confronted in the 1990s with a large volume of asylum applications. The years 1992 and 1993 saw particularly large numbers of applications, but in the year 2000 the figures remained very substantial: 18,280 in Austria, 42,690 in Belgium, 38,590 in France, 78,760 in Germany, 18,000 in Italy, 43,890 in the Netherlands, 16,370 in Sweden, 17,660 in Switzerland, and 97,860 in the United Kingdom.[28] Yet, if annual numbers of applications have declined in a number of key states, the political climate in these countries has become steadily chillier.[29] The rise of the right in Austria is the most obvious manifestation of an anti-immigrant mood, but disturbing rhetoric has also emanated from sources as unlikely as Jack Straw, the United Kingdom's "New Labour" Home Secretary from 1997 to 2001, and currently the Foreign Secretary.[30] UN High Commissioner Lubbers has recently expressed in no uncertain terms his alarm at the spread of this rhetoric. In an article published on World Refugee Day (20 June), he warned:

Asylum seekers have become a campaign issue in various recent and upcoming election battles, with governments and Opposition parties vying to appear toughest on the "bogus" asylum seekers "flooding" into their countries. In some nations – Australia, Austria, Denmark, Italy and Britain, for example – individual politicians and media appear at times to be deliberately inflating the issue. Statistics are frequently manipulated, facts are taken out of context, and the character of asylum seekers as a group is often distorted in order to present them as a terrible threat – a threat their detractors can then pledge to crush. Politicians taking this line used to belong to small extremist parties. But nowadays the issue is able to steer the agenda of bigger parties ... Genuine refugees should not become victims yet again. Surely, there are other ways to win elections.[31]

Part of this rhetoric is driven by a fear that people-smuggling – a market response to the gap between the demand for resettlement and the supply of offshore resettlement places – is a threat to state sovereignty. Even in Australia, well protected from mass population movements by its status as an island continent, there has recently been a bizarre panic over the arrival by boat of Afghan and Iraqi refugees.[32] This culminated in the so-called "Tampa Affair" in August 2001, in which Australian commandos were used to seize and occupy a Norwegian vessel, the M.V. *Tampa*, whose Captain, Arne Rinnan, had rescued refugees and asylum seekers from a sinking boat off the Australian coast and brought them into Australian territorial waters.[33] Panicking governments of this ilk increasingly look to the UNHCR to accept a narrowing of the definition of "refugee," or to view the asylum seeker more sceptically, in order to relieve them of what they see as domestic political pressures.[34] The UNHCR at one level may be able to resist such pressures, if only because in the UN General Assembly, formally responsible for revisions to the 1951 Convention, there is unlikely to be a majority in favour of the exclusionist approaches of the developed states. On occasion, however, the UNHCR has buckled in the face of more specific pressures from such states, in a way that is worrying for those who look to the UNHCR to protect vulnerable individual refugees.[35]

At the same time that the UNHCR has had to cope with large numbers of refugees and frostier attitudes from the industrialized states, it has been under pressure to assume further major responsibilities, which have inevitably taxed its human resources. These responsibilities were in large measure a product of the crises that hit the United Nations in the early 1990s in the Balkans. In response to chronic problems of coordination of discordant UN family members, the United Nations sought new ways of managing humanitarian relief operations. In October 1991, the UN Secretary-General wrote to the UNHCR requesting that it coordinate humanitarian action in what was a rapidly deteriorating political situation. This was to become a massive and troubling commitment for the UNHCR. At one level, it performed extremely well,[36] especially when compared with the less-than-brilliant actions of some other elements of the United Nations system.[37] It also received (and deserved) credit because, as David Rieff puts it, "the UNHCR staffers told the truth unswervingly."[38] However, the UNHCR found itself deeply enmeshed in two types of politics.[39] One was the politics of the conflict itself, given that humanitarian aid and access to vulnerable populations were resources that combatants could aspire to control. This was awkward given that the Statute of the UNHCR, adopted by the General Assembly in Resolution 428 (v) of 14 December 1950, provides in Article 2 that "[t]he work of the High Commissioner shall be of an entirely non-political character."[40] This has always been something of a myth, but rarely has the UNHCR been as invidiously placed as it was during the Bosnian war. The other was the politics of the UN system, in which, irrespective of the wishes of the Secretary-General, the Security Council was positioned to adopt decisions about the mandate of the UN Protection Force (UNPROFOR) that could impact upon the way in which local actors would perceive the UNHCR as an element of the UN system. Dealing with militaries is always a tricky task for humanitarian agencies,[41] and this is so even if the militaries themselves are struggling with the hopeless task of keeping peace in the middle of a war.

What can make such exercises deeply problematical is the reticence that relevant actors – sometimes at the apex and sometimes at the base of the UN system – can show in speaking of root causes of refugee flows with any degree of candour. Rather, in order to relieve states of the burden of difficult political decisions and aid workers of the need to face unpalatable realities, myths are too often woven to create the impression that no more robust political action is required or that things are not as bad as they seem. Several examples come to mind.[42] One such myth was the depiction of the Bosnian conflict as purely a civil war in which equally unattractive and illegitimate forces battled for supremacy. Another such myth was the claim that the Indonesian military was a reliable and neutral source of security for East Timorese voters in the run-up to the August 1999 "popular consultation"; this was proved to be a myth in the most gruesome possible way.[43] A third such myth denied the fundamental role of Pakistan in operationalizing and orchestrating the activities of the anti-modernist Taliban movement in Afghanistan.[44] These myths can be integral elements of the denial strategies about which Walkup has written, but the consequences of the resultant political misdiagnoses can be severe for ordinary people.

The result can often be incoherent political signalling arising from the salience of such myths for some components of the UN system but not others. Consider the case of Afghanistan. For over two decades, Pakistan provided the principal base from which the UNHCR and other humanitarian agencies supplied relief not only to Afghan refugees in Pakistan, but to communities in Afghanistan via cross-border operations. Yet, in the period after the Soviet withdrawal from Afghanistan in February 1989, Pakistan was also the principal *meddler* in Afghanistan, with its support for the Taliban amounting to a creeping invasion. The respected observer Ahmed Rashid concluded that "[b]etween 1994 and 1999, an estimated 80,000 to 100,000 Pakistanis trained and fought in Afghanistan";[45] and in January 2000, the UN Special Rapporteur on Human Rights in Afghanistan stated that many refugees reported encountering "Urdu-speaking men in positions of authority during the fighting in the North as well as in Kabul and Kandahar."[46] After the United States' sharp turn against the Taliban following the bombing of its embassies in Kenya and Tanzania in August 1998 by associates of the Taliban-protected terrorist Osama bin Laden, the Security Council adopted two resolutions – Resolution 1267 and Resolution 1333 – which imposed sanctions against the Taliban and put Pakistan at grave risk of being identified as a sanctions-breaker. Through these measures, the Security Council sought to send an unambiguous message to the Taliban and their backers. However, the message was blurred by the eagerness of field staff to ensure a more felicitous working environment. In September 1999, the Secretary-General reported to the Security Council that he was "deeply distressed over reports indicating the involvement in the fighting, mainly on the side of the Taliban forces, of thousands of non-Afghan nationals, mostly students from religious schools and some as young as 14 years old."[47] He was then reportedly contradicted by the United Nations' Relief Coordinator in Islamabad, who, after one visit to Taliban front lines in the company of Taliban officials, commented: "Generally these types of statements are sound bites and taken by the press as catchy headlines,"[48] adding that he "regretted the Taliban believed Annan was personally responsible for the report which he himself had not actually written."[49]

From these examples, we can see how the humanitarian imperative can conflict with strategies for addressing the political foundations of refugee movements and other symptoms of socio-political crisis. It took the crisis following the 11 September 2001 terrorist attacks to ameliorate these immediate tensions. There is much wisdom in Paula Newberg's observations on this problem: "When the United Nations speaks, it must be able to do so with one voice, and certainly with one humanitarian voice – and that voice must belong to the Secretary-General. This is important in any emergency but is critical in failed states."[50]

Past reform proposals

In 2001, the UNHCR undertook a major series of Global Consultations on Refugee Protection, involving the 56 states appointed to the UNHCR's Executive Committee by the UN Economic and Social Council, and a number of other states, international organizations, NGOs, and academic specialists. Leading up to a December 2001 ministerial conference of all parties to the 1951 Convention and its 1967 Protocol, the consultations had an agenda-setting aim. However, it is questionable to what extent the actual architecture of the key institutions of refugee assistance will be altered as a result of this process. This reflects a fundamental problem of the present system of international organizations, namely the extreme difficulty not only of bringing about basic structural reform, but even of having it seriously and *sincerely* discussed outside the relaxed and speculative circles of academia. I will return to this in the final section of this chapter, where I note some of the obstacles that would stand in the way of the suggestions I put forward in the next section. The following remarks do two things: first, they note some key reform proposals from the past; second, they highlight the areas where reform of the key institutions of refugee assistance seems most required.

The UNHCR has been the subject of surprisingly little formal, external scrutiny. States on its Executive Committee have on occasion voiced (or leaked) concerns about its operations or finances, but on the whole even disgruntled states have not been prepared to devote significant resources to pressing for change.[51] Perhaps guided by the old proverb that a fish rots from the head down, when the UNHCR was in a moribund state in the late 1980s the response of its key backers was not to push for structural reform but quietly to push for a new High Commissioner. During the 1990s under High Commissioner Sadako Ogata, the UNHCR embarked on a programme of internal reform, but, as Goodwin-Gill has caustically pointed out, this was dominated by managerialism, and refugee protection hardly received a mention.[52]

It is in the wider UN system that some serious attempts at structural reconfiguration have been made, and they deserve mention as background to an identification of the area where the UNHCR most requires structural reform. These attempts all fundamentally relate to the problem of *coordination*. As is well known, at the birth of the UN system the United States successfully pushed for a sectoral approach, with a good deal of functional independence for the United Nations' Specialised Agencies. This has been a problem ever since, with devices such as the Administrative Committee on Coordination proving ineffectual in procuring the smooth functioning of a diversified system.[53] In 1991, the General Assembly endorsed the appointment of a high-level Emergency Relief Coordinator, and in due course that position came into being: the current Emergency Relief Coordinator, and Under-Secretary-General for Humanitarian Affairs, is Kenzo Oshima. The UN Office for the Coordination of Humanitarian Affairs (OCHA), established in 1998, enjoys ready access to the Security Council – reflecting the increased role of that body in areas that previously would have seemed the purview of the Economic and Social Council – but it lacks a large field staff, and faces the problems that have confronted all its predecessors in imposing order on the system's discrete components. In a pessimistic analysis, James Ingram, writing from years of experience in the system as Executive Director of the World Food Programme (WFP), has argued that the United Nations is limited by the structure of the system, by personalities, by donor policies, and by UN management culture.[54] These problems continue to dog OCHA.[55] The "lead agency" approach does not offer a solution to these problems, because conflict between mandates, and between ultimately autonomous agencies, can persist. Something more fundamental is required.

Reform of the institutions of refugee assistance requires attention to at least four different levels of relationship.

1. The relationship between UN refugee assistance agencies and the wider UN system. This, of course, cannot be readily divorced from issues of UN systemic reform. It is necessary to have agencies to discharge both the function of protecting individual refugees and the function of providing emergency or long-term relief to needy refugee populations.

2. The relationship between UN refugee assistance agencies and NGOs. The UNHCR has sought to build a framework for this through the Partnership in Action Process, but some NGOs regard this with a degree of cynicism, as do some UNHCR staff. Competition between agencies is not necessarily unhealthy, but it can easily take a very unhealthy direction. Any structural reform needs to take into account the importance of this relationship.

3. The relationship between UN refugee assistance agencies and UN member states, whether as donors, as hosts to refugees, or as potential threats to refugees. Assistance agencies have to be capable of managing relations with both states that are supportive and states that are unspeakable.

4. The relationship between UN refugee assistance agencies and refugees themselves. The agencies must cater to refugees' core needs without creating a cycle of dependency that will be costly for the world community and ultimately destructive of refugee welfare.[56]

Reform thus has a paradoxical character. On the one hand, it needs to improve *coordination*, which to some degree involves breaking down the autonomy of elements of the UN system which have stood in the way of coherent responses to emergency situations. On the other hand, it needs to improve individual *protection*, which requires enhancing the autonomy of elements of the system in the face of pressures that self-interested states might wish to apply. Within the present structure of the system, to achieve these goals simultaneously would be virtually impossible. With different structures, however, they could be attained. The next section explores how.

Suggestions for reform

Ingram, after criticizing the viability of the "lead agency" designation, proposed an alternative: "A more realistic option might be to create a new UN agency dedicated to managing operations at the onset of sudden disasters. The existing agencies would carry out operations at a later stage, after the situation has settled down, much in the way that ICRC sometimes looks to WFP to take over feeding responsibilities after the initial crisis has been surmounted." However, he noted also that "there has been great reluctance to consider solutions that could lead to the creation of new agencies."[57] It is in the context of these observations that new ways of addressing the problem identified by Ingram can be considered. Specifically, much could be gained from separating altogether the UNHCR's emergency relief functions from its refugee protection role. This would leave the UNHCR free to focus, as it should, on refugee protection; while refugee relief would fall in the first instance to a new agency, which might go by the name of the United Nations Refugee and Disaster Organization (UNRDO).

Refugee protection is in need of revival; too often, political refugees are immersed in the wider river of displaced humanity and their individual needs are overlooked. Although lip-service is paid to third-country resettlement as the only durable solution for certain refugees, in practice it can be almost impossible to access it. In Pakistan, it proved exceedingly difficult for even longstanding and prominent anti-Taliban activists – that is, those most at risk in Pakistan as well as Afghanistan – to secure a proper interview with a protection officer; and an interview with a locally employed Pakistani was not a fruitful or appealing substitute.[58] This is a reflection not on the individual occupants of protection officer positions, but rather on the dominance of the world-view that defined the Afghan refugee phenomenon simply in terms of emergency relief ("our daily work on behalf of refugees").

To address this problem, the UNHCR needs to rediscover its core functions. Yet, as long as new relief burdens are piled upon it, this is most unlikely to occur. More drastic surgery is required. The Department of International Protection should be at the heart of the UNHCR, complemented by key staff from regional bureaus and a revitalized Centre for Documentation and Research. This resource centre has historically trodden a very fine line: on the one hand, the UNHCR as a "non-political" body seeks to avoid supplying analyses that UN member states may find unpalatable, but, on the other, attempts at analysis that avoid tough language can be quite misleading in their depiction of events, as the notorious reticence of the United Nations in properly labelling the Rwandan genocide makes clear.[59] The UNHCR can and should make use of scholarly analysis by independent consultants, whose work can be authoritative but at the same time can carry a disclaimer to the effect that it does not necessarily reflect the views of the UNHCR. Some such analyses have been circulated in digital form through "Writenet." A UNHCR refocused on protection could work more closely with an enhanced Office of the United Nations High Commissioner for Human Rights,[60] and especially the Special Rapporteurs appointed by the High Commissioner for Human Rights, than is currently the case. This is not to say that the UNHCR should simply be a lawyers' cabal; on the contrary, such an organization would depend upon a dynamic interaction between staff with legal skills and staff expert in the politics of particular countries or regions. A refocused UNHCR of this sort should be funded from the core UN budget and should report directly to the General Assembly.

This refocusing of the UNHCR's concerns would leave relief tasks to be taken up by a UNRDO. Such an organization would need to absorb chunks of both the UNHCR and OCHA.[61] This would have two advantages. On the one hand, the UNRDO would have field staff, some of them former employees or partners of the UNHCR, on whom it could rely, overcoming the problem faced by the old UN Disaster Relief Organization, and subsequently the Secretariat's Department of Humanitarian Affairs and then OCHA, of having to rely on the cooperation of other agencies' field staffs without having the authority to compel it. On the other hand, such an agency would have direct access to the top levels of the UN system, in particular the Secretary-General and the representatives of the permanent members of the Security Council. An organization of this sort, with a wider focus than the UNHCR enjoys, would be able to address the problems not only of those who have crossed an international border, but also of internally displaced persons (IDPs), who at least formally lie outside the UNHCR's original mandate. This is not to deny that on occasion the UNHCR's narrow mandate has some advantages. For example, when Pakistan pressured the UNHCR to undertake activities inside Afghanistan as a way of preventing refugee outflows, its motive was almost certainly political[62] rather than humanitarian: to drive UN agencies into dialogue with its Taliban allies, whom the Security Council was seeking to isolate. The UNHCR was able to cite its formal mandate in order to avoid drinking from this poisoned chalice. However, in many circumstances, the distinction from a humanitarian point of view between refugees and IDPs is entirely artificial, and provides no rational basis for a divided institutional structure.

Would it be confusing to have two UN agencies with ostensible responsibilities for refugees? In my view no. The worlds of refugees are themselves messy and complex, and we should heed Aristotle's warning against expecting more parsimony and precision than the real world permits. It is not what agencies are called that is most important, but what they do. Would there be overlap between the objects of these two bodies? Inevitably, and also between their objects and those of non-UN bodies such as NGOs and the IOM. Very often they would be dealing with the same persons. The key point, however, is that they would be dealing with different *needs* of these persons, and institutional separation would offer a better guard against the "triage" mentality that treats protection for a few as ultimately less important than relief for the many. This is particularly important when one is talking about repatriation. Here, the danger is that a "relief" agency with global responsibilities may have direct economic incentives to procure the "voluntary" repatriation of a group of refugees as quickly as possible, in order to liberate scarce resources for use elsewhere. In order to facilitate repatriation, the severity of conditions in refugees' homelands may be unconsciously (or even consciously) downplayed, at the expense of those with ongoing protection needs.[63] The UNHCR is formally the guardian of the refugees' interests, but one of the great questions of politics is who will guard the guardians themselves? One classic response points to the guardian's virtue, but virtue in this day and age is an elusive commodity. A more compelling answer, as Montesquieu realized, is separation of powers. The "accountability" of the UNHCR to its Executive Committee does not meet this need, since the Committee's members have interests of their own, which need not extend to effective refugee protection. However, if a UNRDO were formally responsible for managing repatriation, a refocused UNHCR could be charged with monitoring and even vetoing repatriation if refugees seemed at risk.

What refugees cannot be asked to sacrifice is an agency with principles of protection at its heart. Crude utilitarianism too often threatens core UN principles, as occurred, for example, in 1998, when a senior UN official signed a Memorandum of Understanding with a Taliban official that stated, *inter alia*, that "women's access to health and education will need to be gradual."[64] Refugees often know this as well as anyone. Such a willingness to compromise principles for some perceived greater immediate good is best combated in the long run by an organizational *culture* of protection,[65] in which there is widespread consensus within the organization as to values and objectives. This would replace the Tower of Babel with a more harmonious edifice. A culture of this sort helps shape an organization that is organic rather than mechanistic in its operations, and insulated from some of the grosser pathologies I noted earlier. However, a culture of this sort is unlikely to take hold in an organization with widely diverse and potentially conflicting priorities. An organization with a culture of protection is better positioned than the present UNHCR to act fearlessly to shame those states that violate their commitments under international refugee law and other relevant international instruments of which refugees may also be beneficiaries, such as the Convention Against Torture and the International Covenant on Civil and Political Rights.

These proposals do not offer a magic solution to the UNHCR's current problems. There is no magic solution. Institutional reforms typically have unintended as well as intended consequences, and may at best be able to do no more than ameliorate destructive tendencies driven by powerful exogenous forces. Like all UN agencies, a new UNHCR could expect to be buffeted by the ferocious bureaucratic and inter-agency politics of the UN system. It could be perverted, undermined, or marginalized. It could be starved of resources and its staff could be intimidated, or much worse. But the protection mandate of the UNHCR as it currently operates is equally threatened. And one must begin somewhere.

Obstacles to reform

Proposals such as these may have a certain rationality, but this provides no guarantee that they will appeal to anyone who matters. It seems appropriate, therefore, to conclude with some reflections on the obstacles that would stand in the way of their implementation. Some of these are obstacles to UN reform more generally, whereas others relate to these proposals in particular. As will be seen, they arise from the first three spheres of relationship in which UN refugee assistance agencies are entangled: with the wider UN system, with NGOs, and with member states. Sad to say, refugees are usually impotent observers of organizational change, even though their insights and experiences may be a source of striking illumination.

In 1969, Sir Robert Jackson, one of the most dynamic and accomplished organizers ever to work for the United Nations,[66] produced a memorable report on the UN Development System. The whole report merits careful reading even today, but Jackson's characterization of the likely sources of resistance to reform remains of particular interest. Craftily set out in the form of a draft letter to an unnamed head of state in a developing country, it pointed to three particular areas of difficulty. The first was that officials, although admitting the need for reform, would be "so heavily committed to the present operation that they could not physically find time to introduce a major reorganization." The second was that agencies "have learnt to safeguard and increase their powers, to preserve their independence, and to resist change." The third was that change would be resisted "in the Cabinets of individual Member States" where "Departmental Ministers have advocated policies in the governing bodies of the particular Agency which concerned them ... which were in direct conflict with his government's policies toward the UN system as a whole."[67] All these problems are a continuing barrier to reform of the UN system, and the last is of particular concern in the refugee area, where home secretaries and immigration ministers with agendas of exclusion rather than protection are likely to speak with loud voices.

A particular problem with the idea of a UNRDO is that it could be seen as a potentially predatory bureaucracy, more empowered than the present UNHCR to trespass on the mandates of other UN specialized, development, or humanitarian agencies. At least some such agencies would therefore likely attempt to strangle a UNRDO in its cradle. Such things have happened before: the Office of the United Nations Co-ordinator for Humanitarian and Economic Assistance Programmes Relating to Afghanistan, set up in 1988 after the signing of the Geneva Accords and initially headed by Sadruddin Aga Khan, who had served as High Commissioner for Refugees between 1965 and 1977, was squashed almost flat between viciously competing agencies in the early years of its existence.[68] To guard against such infanticide, a UNRDO would need vigilant *parents*, in this case the Secretary-General and the General Assembly. However, it would be important also to guard against resistance to such a body by NGOs, which often have the ear of powerful figures in the governments of the countries in which they are head-quartered. As at present, it is vital that relations between key UN agencies, NGOs, and bodies such as the ICRC be cooperative relations based on trust rather than antagonistic relations resulting from UN attempts to enforce conformity.

The most troubling obstacle to reform, however, arises from the political interests of states, many of which benefit from the emphases of the present system and use selective visa requirements to exclude those who are likely to seek protection.[69] As Chimni has noted, although "the major donor states have always exercised 'undue influence' on the organization ... UNHCR's financial dependence is today being used to preempt it from protesting too hard the erosion of basic protection principles."[70] Of course, not all states are equally well placed to block reform. The United States currently provides over a quarter of the UNHCR's approved budget (initially set at US$955.5 million for 2000–2001,[71] but later cut to US$825 million in the light of reduced donor contributions) and is markedly the largest country of resettlement, typically making over 85,000 places available for refugee resettlement. US approval for any reforms is therefore vital. By contrast, although Australia remains a significant country of resettlement, with some 4,000 places made available for refugees each year, its contribution to the UNHCR's budget in 2002 was less than the total of *private* donations to the UNHCR, and per head of population was much lower than that of the Scandinavian countries. It therefore carries less weight than the volume of its rhetoric might lead one to expect.[72] However, the drift of opinion among industrialized states is notably away from robust commitment to protection, and the Global Consultations process may prove to have done little to invigorate it.

That said, there are important developing countries that, as a result of

propinquity alone, are unlikely to be able to isolate themselves from refugee flows from trouble spots, and they do not have much incentive to
assist the rich industrialized countries in building walls through which
they will admit only the cream of the world's refugee population. In this
divergence of interest there may be some hope. It is also the case that
states' perceptions of their interests may change over time. For example,
at some point, Australia may come to realize that the successful implementation of a "Fortress Europe" policy is hardly in Australia's interests,
since it would divert towards Oceania a large number of those currently
moving westward from the Middle East and South Asia.[73] What may
ultimately help the cause of *fundamental* reform is that the "reforms" on
offer from so many industrialized states are either band-aids with no
pretence of producing more than fleeting, stop-gap "solutions" to the
problem of forced migration, or examples of "balloon squeezing," that is,
measures that reduce a problem in one area in a way that leads to an
exacerbation of the same problem elsewhere. Again, such approaches do
not offer durable solutions to global problems.

In his address to the Executive Committee of the UNHCR in October
2000, UN Secretary-General Annan did not mince his words, and those
words provide an appropriate note on which to close. He observed that
the UNHCR has become a "massive relief agency" but with "neither
sovereign authority nor regular budget." His text then assumed a harsh
tone, at odds with his gentle mode of delivery, and, as an indictment of
the approach to refugees of all too many states, it deserves to be quoted
in full:[74]

Too often, when donor governments decide which of your activities to fund, there
is flagrant political arrière-pensée. Your humanitarian work is used, or rather
abused, as a substitute for political action to address the root causes of mass displacement.

You have become part of a "containment strategy," by which this world's more
fortunate and powerful countries seek to keep the problems of the poorer at
arm's length.

How else can one explain the disparity between the relatively generous funding
for relief efforts in countries close to the frontiers of the prosperous world, and
the much more parsimonious effort made for those who suffer in remoter parts of
the world such as Asia or Africa?

And how else can one explain the contrast between the generosity which poor
countries are expected to show, when hundreds of thousands of refugees pour
across their frontiers, and the precautions taken to ensure that as few asylum
seekers as possible ever reach the shores of rich countries?

As a diagnosis of our current woes, this could hardly be bettered. And,
although perhaps it was not so intended, it also stands out as a cry for a

reappraisal of the adequacy of the institutional architecture for the protection of refugees. But it remains to be seen whether anyone is listening.

Notes

1. See Peter Mares, *Borderline: Australia's Treatment of Refugees and Asylum Seekers*, Sydney: University of New South Wales Press, 2001, p. 24.
2. See, for example, John Martinkus, *A Dirty Little War*, Sydney: Random House Australia, 2001, pp. 415–416.
3. *Reuters*, 20 September 1999.
4. This narrow concept of "protection" has been challenged in recent years, notably by the UNHCR; see Ruud Lubbers, "My Focus Is Protection – Safeguarding and Nurturing It," *Refugees*, vol. 1, no. 122, 2001, pp. 16–17, at p. 17; and Howard Adelman, "From Refugees to Forced Migration: The UNHCR and Human Security," *International Migration Review*, vol. 35, no. 1, Spring 2001, pp. 7–32. However, given the dangers that *refoulement* can pose for those with a well-founded fear of persecution, it is important not to lose sight of "protection" in this more limited sense, as can easily happen if everything done to help the indigent is defined as protection.
5. See, for example, Shelly Pitterman, "International Responses to Refugee Situations: The United Nations High Commissioner for Refugees," in Elizabeth G. Ferris, ed., *Refugees and World Politics*, New York: Praeger, 1985, pp. 43–81, at pp. 44–47; Guy S. Goodwin-Gill, "Refugee Identity and Protection's Fading Prospects," in Frances Nicholson and Patrick Twomey, eds., *Refugee Rights and Realities: Evolving International Concepts and Regimes*, Cambridge: Cambridge University Press, 1999, pp. 220–249.
6. See Ewen MacAskill, "Pakistan Keeps Annan from 'World's Worst' Camp," *The Guardian*, 13 March 2001; Rory McCarthy, "Wrapped in Plastic, the Rejected Wait to Die: The Guardian Gains Access to the Afghans' Grim Refugee Camp Which the Pakistani Authorities Kept from the Eyes of the UN Secretary General," *The Guardian*, 16 March 2001.
7. See Stephen D. Krasner, *Sovereignty: Organized Hypocrisy*, Princeton, NJ: Princeton University Press, 1999.
8. See Robert E. Goodin, "What Is So Special about Our Fellow Countrymen?" *Ethics*, vol. 98, no. 4, July 1988, pp. 663–686.
9. On these categories, see Juan J. Linz, *Totalitarian and Authoritarian Regimes*, Boulder, CO: Lynne Rienner, 2000; H. E. Chehabi and Juan J. Linz, eds., *Sultanistic Regimes*, Baltimore, MD: Johns Hopkins University Press, 1998; Leo Kuper, *Genocide*, New Haven, CT: Yale University Press, 1981; Leo Kuper, *The Prevention of Genocide*, New Haven, CT: Yale University Press, 1985; Joel S. Migdal, *Strong Societies and Weak States: State–Society Relations and State Capabilities in the Third World*, Princeton, NJ: Princeton University Press, 1988.
10. On democratic consolidation, see Andreas Schedler, "What Is Democratic Consolidation?" *Journal of Democracy*, vol. 9, no. 2, April 1998, pp. 91–107; Larry P. Diamond, *Developing Democracy: Toward Consolidation*, Baltimore, MD: Johns Hopkins University Press, 1999. On uncivil society, see Jack L. Snyder, *From Voting to Violence: Democratization and Nationalist Conflict*, New York: W. W. Norton, 2000.
11. See John Torpey, *The Invention of the Passport: Surveillance, Citizenship and the State*, Cambridge: Cambridge University Press, 2000.
12. See Claudena M. Skran, *Refugees in Inter-War Europe: The Emergence of a Regime*, Oxford: Oxford University Press, 1995, pp. 84–85.

13. For a brief survey, see William Maley, "Refugees and Forced Migration as a Security Problem," in William T. Tow, Ramesh Thakur, and In-Taek Hyun, eds., *Asia's Emerging Regional Order: Reconciling Traditional and Human Security*, Tokyo: United Nations University Press, 2000, pp. 142–156, at pp. 147–150; and for a detailed overview, see Gil Loescher, *Beyond Charity: International Cooperation and the Global Refugee Crisis*, New York: Oxford University Press, 1993, pp. 32–54.

14. See Jean-Claude Favez, *The Red Cross and the Holocaust*, Cambridge: Cambridge University Press, 1999.

15. Michael N. Barnett and Martha Finnemore, "The Politics, Power, and Pathologies of International Organizations," *International Organization*, vol. 53, no. 4, Autumn 1999, pp. 699–732, at p. 719.

16. William A. Niskanen, *Bureaucracy and Representative Government*, Chicago: Aldine Atherton, 1971.

17. Graham T. Allison, *Essence of Decision: Explaining the Cuban Missile Crisis*, Boston, MA: Little, Brown, 1971, p. 176.

18. Mark Walkup, "Policy Dysfunction in Humanitarian Organizations: The Role of Coping Strategies, Institutions, and Organizational Culture," *Journal of Refugee Studies*, vol. 10, no. 1, March 1997, pp. 37–60.

19. See Gil Loescher, *The UNHCR and World Politics: A Perilous Path*, Oxford: Oxford University Press, 2001.

20. Malcolm Muggeridge, ed., *Ciano's Diary 1939–1943*, London: Heinemann, 1947, p. 502.

21. I recall my despair on hearing a senior Australian bureaucrat speak complacently of "isolated cases of *refoulement*" of Afghan refugees from Pakistan during the rule of the Taliban. *Refoulement* is never "isolated" for the refugee being "refouled."

22. For example, Australia's Special Humanitarian Programme requires that an applicant for resettlement have a "proposer" in Australia, on whom a substantial burden of the refugee's resettlement costs is likely to fall.

23. See, for example, Mark Riley, "UN Staff Accused over Refugee Bribes," *Sydney Morning Herald*, 22 February 2001.

24. UNHCR, *The State of the World's Refugees: Fifty Years of Humanitarian Action*, Oxford: Oxford University Press, 2000, p. 310; UNHCR, *2000 Global Refugee Trends: Analysis of the 2000 Provisional UNHCR Population Statistics*, Geneva: UNHCR, May 2001.

25. UNHCR, *2000 Global Refugee Trends*.

26. See William Maley, "The Reconstruction of Afghanistan," in Ken Booth and Tim Dunne, eds., *Worlds in Collision: Terror and the Future of Global Order*, London: Palgrave Macmillan, 2002, pp. 184–193; William Maley, *The Afghanistan Wars*, London: Palgrave Macmillan, 2002, chap. 11.

27. See Raimo Vayrynen, "Funding Dilemmas in Refugee Assistance: Political Interests and Institutional Reforms in the UNHCR," *International Migration Review*, vol. 35, no. 1, Spring 2001, pp. 143–167.

28. UNHCR, *Asylum Applications Submitted in Europe, 2000*, Geneva: UNHCR, 25 January 2001, p. 2.

29. See Amnesty International, *Refugees: Human Rights Have No Borders*, London: Amnesty International, 1997.

30. See Randall Hansen and Desmond King, "Illiberalism and the New Politics of Asylum: Liberalism's Dark Side," *Political Quarterly*, vol. 71, no. 4, October–December 2000, pp. 396–403. More detailed discussion can be found in Danièle Joly, *Haven or Hell? Asylum Policies and Refugees in Europe*, London: Macmillan, 1996; Liza Schuster, "A Comparative Analysis of the Asylum Policy of Seven European Governments," *Journal of Refugee Studies*, vol. 13, no. 1, 2000, pp. 118–132.

31. Ruud Lubbers, "Don't Kick Refugees Just to Score Points: Politicians Who Demonise Asylum Seekers Are Playing with People's Lives," *The Australian*, 20 June 2001.

32. See William Maley, "Security, People-Smuggling, and Australia's New Afghan Refugees," *Australian Journal of International Affairs*, vol. 55, no. 3, 2001, pp. 351–370.

33. Captain Rinnan, his crew, and the shipping line for which they worked subsequently received the Nansen Award from the UNHCR. For a more detailed discussion of this incident, see Jean-Pierre Fonteyne, "'Illegal Refugees' or Illegal Policy?" in William Maley, Alan Dupont, Jean-Pierre Fonteyne, Greg Fry, James Jupp, and Thuy Do, *Refugees and the Myth of the Borderless World*, Canberra: The Australian National University, Department of International Relations, Research School of Pacific and Asian Studies, Keynotes no. 2, 2002, pp. 16–22.

34. Some scholars have advocated comprehensive policy changes based on temporary protection: see James Hathaway, ed., *Reconceiving International Refugee Law*, The Hague: Martinus Nijhoff, 1997. However, these run the danger of being pillaged by states in ways that leave refugees in limbo, deprived of benefits that make the comprehensive packages coherent.

35. For example, in 1995 the then Australian government took umbrage at a presentation to an Australian parliamentary committee by a UNHCR official based in Canberra that implicitly raised doubts about the appropriateness of a piece of legislation put forward by the government, namely the Migration Legislation Amendment Bill (No. 4) 1995. The presentation, which I witnessed, was simply a straightforward statement of the UNHCR's views. Within a short space of time, the official was withdrawn by the UNHCR from his position, and was left without a substantive position upon his return to Geneva. Neither the Australian government nor the UNHCR seemed to be much influenced by the spirit of Article 100 of the Charter of the United Nations, which provides *inter alia* that UN staff shall not "receive instructions from any government," and that each UN member "undertakes to respect the exclusively international character of the responsibilities of the Secretary-General and the staff and not to seek to influence them in the discharge of their responsibilities."

36. Thomas G. Weiss and Amir Pasic, "Reinventing UNHCR: Enterprising Humanitarians in the Former Yugoslavia, 1991–1995," *Global Governance*, vol. 3, no. 1, January–April 1997, pp. 41–57.

37. See William Maley, "The United Nations and Ethnic Conflict Management: Lessons from the Disintegration of Yugoslavia," *Nationalities Papers*, vol. 25, no. 3, September 1997, pp. 559–573.

38. David Rieff, *Slaughterhouse: Bosnia and the Failure of the West*, New York: Touchstone, 1996, p. 206.

39. For more detailed discussion, see S. Alex Cunliffe and Michael Pugh, "UNHCR as Leader in Humanitarian Assistance: A Triumph of Politics over Law?" in Nicholson and Twomey, eds, *Refugee Rights and Realities*, pp. 175–199.

40. UNHCR, *Statute of the Office of the United Nations High Commissioner for Refugees*, Geneva: UNHCR, 1996, p. 8.

41. See Thomas G. Weiss, *Military–Civilian Interactions: Intervening in Humanitarian Crises*, Lanham, MD: Rowman & Littlefield, 1999.

42. For a more detailed discussion, see Fiona Terry, *Condemned to Repeat? The Paradox of Humanitarian Action*, Ithaca, NY: Cornell University Press, 2002. This is by no means a recent phenomenon; for an egregious earlier example relating to the Khmer Rouge, see Linda Mason and Roger Brown, *Rice, Rivalry and Politics: Managing Cambodian Relief*, Notre Dame, IN: University of Notre Dame Press, 1983, pp. 138–139.

43. See William Maley, "The UN and East Timor," *Pacifica Review*, vol. 12, no. 1, February 2000, pp. 63–76.

44. See William Maley, "Introduction: Interpreting the Taliban," in William Maley, ed., *Fundamentalism Reborn? Afghanistan and the Taliban*, New York: New York University Press, 1998, pp. 1–28.

45. Ahmed Rashid, "The Taliban: Exporting Extremism," *Foreign Affairs*, vol. 78, no. 6, November–December 1999, pp. 22–35, at p. 27.

46. UN Special Rapporteur on Human Rights, *Report on the Situation of Human Rights in Afghanistan Submitted by Mr. Kamal Hossain, Special Rapporteur, in Accordance with Commission Resolution 1999/9*, Geneva: United Nations, Economic and Social Council, Commission on Human Rights, E/CN.4/2000/33, 10 January 2000, para. 46.

47. UN Secretary-General, *The Situation in Afghanistan and Its Implications for International Peace and Security: Report of the Secretary-General*, New York: United Nations, S/1999/994, 21 September 1999, para. 40.

48. *Reuters*, 1 December 1999.

49. *Agence France-Presse*, 2 December 1999.

50. Paula R. Newberg, *Politics at the Heart: The Architecture of Humanitarian Assistance to Afghanistan*, Washington DC: International Migration Policy Program, Carnegie Endowment for International Peace, Working Paper No. 2, July 1999, p. 26.

51. This contrasts with the case of UNESCO under Director-General M'Bow, whose political agenda so offended the United States that Washington was prepared to mount a sustained campaign against both M'Bow and the way in which the organization was operating.

52. Goodwin-Gill, "Refugee Identity and Protection's Fading Prospects," pp. 235–237.

53. See Douglas Williams, *The Specialized Agencies and the United Nations: The System in Crisis*, London: Hurst, 1987, pp. 108–110.

54. James Ingram, "The Future Architecture for International Humanitarian Assistance," in Thomas G. Weiss and Larry Minear, eds., *Humanitarianism across Borders: Sustaining Civilians in Times of War*, Boulder, CO: Lynne Rienner, 1993, pp. 171–193, at pp. 175–179.

55. That said, OCHA has persisted with efforts to improve the quality of coordination. See, for example, *Final Report: OCHA/PFP Ministerial Conference on Regional Cooperation and Coordination in Crisis Management for Europe and the NIS*, Geneva: Office for the Coordination of Humanitarian Affairs, 2000.

56. A case can be made that UNRWA has fallen into this trap; see Nitza Nachmias, "The Case of UNRWA: Five Decades of Humanitarian Aid," in Eric A. Belgrad and Nitza Nachmias, eds., *The Politics of International Humanitarian Aid Operations*, Westport, CT: Praeger, 1997, pp. 69–87, at p. 84. However, UNRWA's role has been so important in sustaining core beliefs relating to Palestinian refugee identity that any attempt to wind it up or reallocate its functions could risk an explosion from the population it exists to serve. I am indebted to Dr. Robert Bowker, formerly of UNRWA, for his observations on this point.

57. Ingram, "The Future Architecture for International Humanitarian Assistance," p. 183.

58. For an elaboration of this point with examples, see Maley, "Security, People-Smuggling, and Australia's New Afghan Refugees." I have witnessed from afar both the assassination and the *refoulement* of Afghan acquaintances in Pakistan.

59. Nicholas J. Wheeler, *Saving Strangers: Humanitarian Intervention in International Society*, Oxford: Oxford University Press, 2000, pp. 220–221. On the Rwandan genocide, see Roméo Dallaire, "The End of Innocence: Rwanda 1994," in Jonathan Moore, ed., *Hard Choices: Moral Dilemmas in Humanitarian Intervention*, Lanham, MD: Rowman & Littlefield, 1998, pp. 71–86; Human Rights Watch, *Leave None to Tell the Tale: Genocide in Rwanda*, New York: Human Rights Watch, 1999; *Report of the Independent Inquiry into the Actions of the United Nations during the 1994 Genocide in Rwanda*, New York: United Nations, 15 December 1999; OAU, *International Panel of Eminent Personalities*

to Investigate the 1994 Genocide in Rwanda and the Surrounding Events: Special Report, Addis Ababa: Organization of African Unity, 7 July 2000.

60. Enhancing this Office is an important recommendation of the Brahimi Report. See *Report of the Panel on United Nations Peace Operations*, New York: United Nations, A/55/305–S/2000/809, 21 August 2000, paras. 244–245.

61. The UNHCR's contribution would likely consist more of meat than of fat, given that at 31 December 1999 its headquarters staff totalled only 691, and its total staff only 4,902; see *UNHCR Global Report 1999*, Geneva: UNHCR, 2000, p. 58.

62. Paula Newberg, "No Money, No Space, No Patience – The New Refugee Welcome," *Los Angeles Times*, 25 February 2001, while noting the burden that Pakistan has long carried, points out that "the Government of Pakistan provides more substantial support to war in Afghanistan than to refugees."

63. I recall my sense of disquiet at UNHCR-funded group repatriations to zones of northern Afghanistan in which only an optimist would have asserted that durable stability had returned. This repatriation was certainly not "forced," but nor was it exactly "spontaneous." For some discussion of this model, see Rupert Colville, "The Biggest Caseload in the World," *Refugees*, vol. 108, no. 2, 1997, pp. 3–9, at p. 9.

64. For the text of the Memorandum of Understanding, see "Memorandum of Understanding between the Islamic Emirate of Afghanistan and the United Nations 13 May 1998," *International Journal of Refugee Law*, vol. 10, no. 3, July 1998, pp. 586–592. I discuss this episode in more detail in William Maley, *The Foreign Policy of the Taliban*, New York: Council on Foreign Relations, 2000, pp. 23–24.

65. I agree very much on this point with Guy Goodwin-Gill, "Editorial: The International Protection of Refugees: What Future?" *International Journal of Refugee Law*, vol. 12, no. 1, 2000, pp. 1–6, at p. 6.

66. Jackson was once memorably described as "a racing engine in a family automobile"; see Brian Urquhart, *A Life in Peace and War*, New York: W. W. Norton, 1987, p. 116. After the production of the 1969 Capacity Study, he played major roles in refugee relief during the Bangladesh crisis and on the Thai–Cambodian border; see William Shawcross, *The Quality of Mercy: Cambodia, Holocaust and Modern Conscience*, New York: Simon & Schuster, 1984, pp. 219–221.

67. Robert Jackson, *A Study of the Capacity of the United Nations Development System*, Geneva: United Nations, 1969, pp. iv–v.

68. See William Maley, "Reconstructing Afghanistan: Opportunities and Challenges," in Geoff Harris, ed., *Recovery from Armed Conflict in Developing Countries: An Economic and Political Analysis*, London: Routledge, 1999, pp. 225–257, at pp. 238–239.

69. See John Morrison, *The Trafficking and Smuggling of Refugees: The End Game in European Asylum Policy?* Geneva: UNHCR, Evaluation and Policy Unit, July 2000, para. 3.2.1.

70. B. S. Chimni, "Globalization, Humanitarianism and the Erosion of Refugee Protection," *Journal of Refugee Studies*, vol. 13, no. 3, September 2000, pp. 243–263, at p. 256.

71. *UNHCR Financial Overview 2000 (in US$ m.) 30 November 2000*, Geneva: UNHCR, 2000.

72. Some such rhetoric is undoubtedly intended for domestic political consumption; see Maley, "Security, People-Smuggling, and Australia's New Afghan Refugees."

73. Wiser heads in the Australian Department of Foreign Affairs and Trade are already aware of this, but in the Department of Immigration and Multicultural Affairs, perhaps not so notable for a sophisticated view of global political complexities, such harsh realities are yet to be grasped. Here again we see the problem of political coordination *within* states that Sir Robert Jackson, himself an Australian, highlighted so effectively.

74. *Press Release: United Nations Secretary-General Addresses Executive Committee of UNHCR*, Geneva: UNHCR, 2 October 2000, pp. 2–3.

15

Distance makes the heart grow fonder: Media images of refugees and asylum seekers

Peter Mares

This chapter looks at the way the media in the developed world portray refugees and asylum seekers. It is written from the perspective of a journalist working in Australia but with a view to providing some insight into the way the media function in a broader context. I argue that, in general terms, the level of concern and empathy expressed in the media for the plight of refugees and asylum seekers is in inverse relation to their proximity to the place where any given report appears. Viewed from a distance, displaced people are often portrayed as helpless victims of circumstance, deserving of compassion and assistance. This imagery changes dramatically when refugees and asylum seekers make their way to the developed world to seek protection under the 1951 Convention Relating to the Status of Refugees. Refugees and asylum seekers who display this level of agency suddenly shed the veneer of innocence and become a threat to the order and security of the receiving state. They are transformed from passive objects of compassion into untrustworthy actors who provoke a sense of fear. Without absolving journalists and editors of responsibility for the manifest inadequacies in media coverage of refugee issues, I argue that this results in part from what is, at best, a lack of political courage among authority figures in developed nations, and, at worst, cynical political expediency. However, I also argue that humanitarian agencies are themselves at times responsible for promoting unrealistic and unsustainable images of refugees that ill prepare developed nation audiences for coping with the complexity of the unauthorized movement of people in the contemporary world. Finally, although there is no simple relationship between media reporting and political action on refugee issues, I propose some strategies for refugee advocacy groups who wish to promote more constructive media coverage.

Shaping perceptions

On 23 June 2001, the Saturday edition of Brisbane's *Courier Mail* newspaper led its front page with the headline "Typhoid Found in Refugee Centres."[1] The story was branded "EXCLUSIVE" and revealed that Australian authorities had found "almost 1000 cases of illegal immigrants carrying infectious diseases such as typhoid, tuberculosis and hepatitis B and C" in the past 18 months. The overall message of the *Courier Mail* article was to warn of the danger posed by the outsider, the foreigner who arrives uninvited. This was made explicit in the wording of the poster promoting that day's edition of the *Courier Mail* outside the newsagent (which was arguably read by more people than the newspaper article itself). It stated bluntly, "Detainees bring deadly diseases." The article and the banner headline served to justify Australia's harsh policy of mandatory detention for all non-citizens who arrive in the country without valid travel documents, including those who seek protection under the provisions of the 1951 Geneva Convention on Refugees.[2]

The facts of the *Courier Mail* story were as follows. Since 1 January 2000, federal immigration department officials had notified various state health authorities of 973 instances of infectious diseases in Australia's six immigration detention centres. The vast majority of the people identified with health problems would have been asylum seekers. Most would have come originally from the Middle East and would have arrived in Australia via Indonesia, undertaking the last stage of the journey by boat. In all, authorities had identified 10 cases of typhoid, a disease "eradicated decades ago in Australia," as the paper breathlessly informed us. In fact this information, which formed the basis of the front-page headline, was neither new nor exclusive. The immigration minister had spoken about the discovery of typhoid in the detention centres more than four months earlier, and had used it then to convey exactly the same message of risk, hitting back at critics who called for asylum seekers to be released more swiftly from detention.[3] Health authorities had also confirmed eight cases of active tuberculosis, requiring immediate treatment. However, the vast bulk of the "infectious diseases" identified amongst the detainees in fact posed very little immediate risk to the general community. There were around 700 notifications of inactive TB infection requiring follow-up by chest clinics. This is hardly surprising, given that around one-third of the world's population (including about one-third of all Australians over the age of 50) are latent carriers of TB. Few of these people fall sick with the disease and are most likely to do so only if their overall health is severely compromised by other factors, such as poor nutrition. Another 200 notifications were made for cases of hepatitis B or C, which are transmissible only by the exchange of blood or other bodily fluids and not by general human contact. There were also a handful of notifications of sexually transmitted diseases and four cases of HIV. At no point did the *Courier Mail* attempt to clarify the actual risk of infection to the general community from these notified diseases.

In a different context, a story about the discovery of infectious diseases in a "refugee centre" would invoke the sympathy of the audience, and might involve an implied or explicit call for humanitarian assistance by international agencies and Western governments. However, although an affliction.can be cause for compassion in one instance (as in reporting of the Kosovo crisis in 1999 or the fate of displaced Afghans in late 2001, of which more below), in another it can be used to invoke feelings of fear. In this case, the editorial intention of the article was not to express concern for the well-being of the detainees but to warn of the grave threat that these uninvited visitors posed to Australian society. The message of threat was reinforced by quotes in the article from both sides of politics. "Any Australian Government would fail if it let people possibly carrying infectious diseases out into the general community before all health checks," said the Immigration Minister Philip Ruddock from the conservative Liberal Party. His opposite number in the Labour Party, Con Sciaca, declared that "it was absolutely necessary" to carry out health checks to "protect the wider community." The editorial intent of the article was further reinforced by a commentary piece published in the same edition and written by the same author.[4] Of course, it is both logical and sensible to check the health status of people who arrive in Australia in an unauthorized and unregulated manner but, once these checks are done and appropriate action taken, any risk to the wider community is removed and the justification for continued detention disappears.

Setting the terms of the debate – the role of political leadership

The perhaps unintended but nevertheless pernicious implication in the *Courier Mail* story – that (all) "refugees" carry "infectious diseases" – is further reinforced by the writer's confused terminology. The discrepancy between the words used in the headline ("refugee centres") and those used in the body of the text ("illegal immigrants") is telling. Such confusion, or conflation, of terminology is not uncommon. Even on the non-commercial Australian Broadcasting Corporation, which is meant to uphold the highest standards of journalism in Australia, news stories sometimes use the term "illegal immigrant" in the first sentence (e.g. "A boat load of 123 suspected illegal immigrants has been discovered off the coast of Western Australian today"), to be followed by the term "asylum seekers" in the next (e.g. "It is expected that the asylum seekers will be taken to Pt Hedland detention centres"). The failure to distinguish between asylum seekers, refugees, and unauthorized migrants means that all are implied to be untrustworthy and illegitimate and ultimately results in patently nonsensical constructions such as "illegal asylum seekers" and even "illegal refugees," terms that have appeared with surprising frequency in recent media reports.

Political leaders must shoulder considerable responsibility for this confusion. It is inevitable that journalists will report or broadcast the words of government ministers and parliamentarians; indeed they would be derelict in their duty if they did not do so. When a politician refers to asylum seekers as "illegals" or as "queue jumpers" who are "stealing places" from the "most vulnerable" refugees, then this language is dispersed through the media and swiftly becomes common currency. The notion of the queue jumper is powerful because it offends our sense of fair play. This simple image of someone shoving their way to the front of an otherwise orderly line reassures the audience that a tough approach to asylum seekers is justified. Those who push their way into the developed world are seen as undeserving because they lack the virtue of patience. Their perceived failure to obey the rules of common courtesy reinforces the sense of "otherness," increasing the perception that such people do not belong in this society. As Corlett argues, a "more appropriate metaphor to that of a 'refugee queue' might be that of a 'refugee heap' out of which very few are plucked for resettlement" in third countries.[5] The 1951 Convention makes no distinction between refugees who have money and those who do not, and it should be obvious that rich and poor can be persecuted alike. Nevertheless, journalists who wish to counteract the simplistic "queue jumper" image can find themselves bogged down in complex and detailed argument about the nature of global refugee flows and the definition of a refugee.

As Corlett argues in the Australian context, when increasing numbers of asylum seekers began arriving on Australia's coast without authorization from mid-1999 onwards, politicians "inflamed hostile community sentiments for their own political purposes." Although official reaction was in part a reflection of community attitudes and concerns, the government failed to offer "constructive responses" to ill-founded fears.

"What was missing was a national leadership that took seriously the nation's concerns but which also posited productive responses."[6] Kaye reaches a similar conclusion in analysing media references to asylum seekers and refugees in the United Kingdom. Although newspaper reports frequently used pejorative terms such as "phoney" and "bogus," he found that the writer rarely initiated the use of the expression:

In the majority of cases the usage was a report or a quotation of the use by someone else – most commonly a UK politician or government official. This would suggest ... that newspapers are largely accepting the agenda as defined by politicians and government officials, and framing the news accordingly.[7]

As Pickering notes, reporting on the unauthorized arrival of asylum seekers across national boundaries "often elides the vocabulary of war with that of crime":

Metaphors of war justify the need to repel whatever is hostile and threatening. "Immigration controls" become matters of "national security"; a "national emergency" requires "full deployment" of the armed forces on a "prime defence mission" to "detect incursions."[8]

In times of war or crisis, the need for firm and decisive action can override concern for individual rights. However, by any objective measure Australia is not confronted by such a situation. Although onshore applications for asylum in Australia jumped by 50 per cent in the financial year 1999/2000, the total of 12,713 applications was still relatively small. Roughly one-third of those applicants arrived in the country without a valid visa (either by boat or by air) and the Migration Act required that these "unlawful non-citizens" (in the official terminology of immigration authorities) be held in detention until a positive decision was made to grant them protection, or until they were removed from Australia. Two-thirds of all asylum seekers arrived in Australia lawfully (i.e. with a valid visitor visa) and applied for asylum after clearing immigration controls. These people live in the community and are able to apply for work permits. Although these "lawful non-citizens" outnumbered detained (i.e. "unlawful") asylum seekers by a ratio of two to one, and although they were (statistically) much less likely to be recognized as refugees under the Convention, their presence was not a matter of public concern and rarely received media coverage. In other words, as Pickering notes, the scale of the refugee "problem" confronting Australia in no way justifies the alarmist language employed by politicians and the media:

The need for "blunt warnings" to deter "queue jumpers" has very little to do with sending messages to international communities and everything to do with sending messages to domestic communities and justifying expansionist penal policies.[9]

Evidence of the way in which the asylum seeker/refugee issue is exploited for short-term political gain is not hard to come by. In July 2001, several months out from a federal election, candidates from the conservative Liberal Party in Australia had produced leaflets warning that the opposition Labor Party was "soft on illegal immigrants." The "illegal immigrants" referred to in the pamphlets were in fact refugees.[10] They had initially arrived in Australia without authorization and were detained. However, after being assessed through Australia's rigorous refugee determination system, they were found to face a risk of persecution if returned to their homeland; they were released from detention and permitted to reside in Australia on three-year "temporary protection visas."[11]

The demonization of refugees and asylum seekers for political gain reached its apotheosis during the campaign for the Australian federal election that was held on 10 November 2001. Rather than focusing on traditional domestic issues such as taxation levels or spending on health and education, the election campaign was fought on issues of national security and border protection. The international backdrop to the campaign was the US-led military offensive in Afghanistan (for which Australia volunteered troops) following the 11 September 2001 terror attacks in New York and Washington. Within 48 hours of the September 11 attacks, Australia's defence minister, Peter Reith, made an explicit link between terrorism and asylum seekers, warning that the unauthorized arrival of boats on Australian territory "can be a pipeline for terrorists to come in and use your country as a staging post for terrorist activities."[12] The irony that Afghan asylum seekers were fleeing the very same "terror" regime that Australia was helping to fight did not appear to concern him. Neither did it worry Australia's "shock-jocks," the prime-time millionaire talkback hosts who dominate the airwaves on commercial radio. On September 12, Alan Jones, the top-rating breakfast host on radio 2UE in Sydney, declared that the terror attacks had been carried out by "sleepers" – terrorists who had been living quietly in the United States for years. Turning to the Australian context, he then posed the following rhetorical question: "How many of these Afghan boat people are 'sleepers'?"[13] Prime Minister John Howard revived the theme just a few days before polling day, telling Brisbane's *Courier Mail* newspaper that "[y]ou don't know who is coming [on the boats] and you don't know whether they do have terrorist links or not."[14] However, his conservative Liberal/National coalition was not alone in making the link. Addressing parliament just before the election was called, the immigration spokesman for the opposition Labor Party stirred similar fears, albeit in a less direct manner:

We know, of course, about what happened in the United States only last week. People become far more aware of the matters involved in illegal immigration and the integrity of border issues when they see the sorts of unspeakable horrors which occurred in the United States.[15]

The campaign for Australia's 2001 federal election also followed in the wake of the so-called Tampa affair, when the Australian government used the navy to prevent a Norwegian container ship, the M.V. *Tampa*, from landing 434 asylum seekers at the Australian Indian Ocean territory of Christmas Island. On 26 August 2001, the M.V. *Tampa* rescued the asylum seekers from their sinking wooden ferry after being alerted to their plight by the Australian search and rescue organization. However, the Australian government insisted that the captain return the asylum seekers to a port in Indonesia, rather than the closer port of Christmas Island. The captain of the M.V. *Tampa* maintained that it was not safe for him to transport so many passengers back to Indonesia, and the Australian government countered with an order that his vessel must not enter the 12-mile exclusion zone around Christmas Island. After a standoff lasting several days, the captain of the *Tampa* defied the ban and steamed towards Christmas Island, arguing that his rescued passengers required medical treatment. Australian authorities responded by sending élite SAS troops to board his vessel.

The Tampa affair marked a fundamental turning point in Australia's refugee policy. Prime Minister John Howard declared that asylum seekers rescued by the M.V. *Tampa* would not set foot on the Australian mainland, and instead naval vessels were used to transport them to Nauru and New Zealand. Australia then adopted the same approach to all subsequent vessels attempting to carry asylum seekers to its territory from Indonesia. The vessels were boarded by Australian naval personnel and told that they must return to Indonesia. In some cases warning shots were fired over the bows. If boats persisted in entering Australia's exclusion zone, then they were boarded at sea and the asylum seekers were transferred to detention centres in Nauru or, subsequently, Papua New Guinea.

Amidst the fears and uncertainties unleashed by the September 11 terror attacks, the tough line on the "boat people" proved enormously popular with voters. As the *Australian* newspaper commented, it represented "one of the Government's chief claims to national leadership" and was the "main preoccupation" of the election campaign.[16] The government used the rhetoric of "border security" at every available opportunity, often demonizing vulnerable people in the process. For example, on 7 October 2001, in the first full week of the election campaign, Immigration Minister Philip Ruddock announced that a group of asylum seekers trying to reach Australia had thrown children overboard "in a clearly planned and premeditated" attempt to force their way into Australia.[17] The story made immediate headlines and two days later, on October 9, Prime Minister John Howard declared on radio, "I certainly don't want people of that type in Australia, I really don't." On October 10, Defence Minister Peter Reith released photographs of children in the sea wearing life jackets, which he presented as documentary proof of what had happened. He told ABC radio 774 in Melbourne that "[w]e have a number of people, obviously RAN [Royal Australian Navy] people, who were there who reported the children were thrown into the water." Yet serious doubts had emerged about the veracity of the original reports, and, in fact, the "evidence" on which the immigration minister, the defence minister and the prime minister had based their public statements was third-hand gossip, which they made no attempt to check. After the election, it was revealed that the photographic "evidence" of children in the water was from a separate incident, the following day, when the children were rescued after their boat sank. Military officers and senior public servants were aware that the reports of children being thrown overboard were untrue and that the photographs did not depict such an event. They had tried to correct the public "mistake" of their political masters before the election. However, the three relevant ministers – the prime minister and the ministers for defence and immigration – claim this advice never reached them. (At one point the defence minister even blamed a bad phone line for his failure to understand this information when it was delivered to him directly by the acting commander of the Australian Defence Force.) By the time the story was corrected, the election was over and the government had been returned to office. No apology was made to the asylum seekers for the way in which they had been so publicly wronged.

Binary logic: Citizens versus non-citizens

Said has noted that "the insidious form of binary oppositions" has "infected" the public domain.[18] Pickering identifies the binary logic that dominates media reporting on asylum seekers and refugees. She gives the examples of bogus/genuine or legal/illegal to describe the ways in which asylum seekers are constructed as "a deviant population in relation to the integrity of the nation state, race and disease."[19]

I would add citizen/non-citizen (the bureaucratic pairing used in the official terminology of Australia's immigration officials) to Pickering's binary oppositions in order to underline the way in which the moral panic directed at the boat people and refugees on talkback lines and in letters to the editor is driven by notions of entitlement. Citizens are entitled to have their rights protected and to enjoy the full protection of the law. The rights of non-citizens are restricted; they can be detained indefinitely without trial and are accused of abusing the system if they seek to use the courts to advance their claim to refugee status. Citizens pay taxes and are therefore entitled to government services. Non-citizens have no such entitlements and are seen as competitors for scarce public goods such as health and education. As Thomas writes,

[Displaced people] are not an acknowledged part of any society, and therefore, cannot claim even the basic right to life itself because they are not citizens of a legitimate "nation." Furthermore, their position is weakened by the sometimes "real" sometimes "imagined" impact that their presence has on the livelihood of "legitimate" nationals inhabiting those areas close to a refugee camp.[20]

Notions of entitlement came to the fore when the federal government began releasing from detention those Afghan and Iraqi "boat people" who arrived in Australia in the latter half of 1999, and who had subsequently been recognized as refugees under the Convention. The *Today Tonight* programme on the commercial Channel 7 TV station broadcast a story on the arrival of the first such group to be sent to the southern city of Adelaide. The men had been held for several months in remote detention centres in the far north-west of Australia. They arrived in Adelaide after a bus trip spanning three days and nights and were taken to a suburban office of the state welfare agency Centrelink for initial processing. The Centrelink office had opened early, at 7 a.m., to allow the refugees' business to be conducted privately and without disruption to other clients. But to Channel 7 this was evidence of a "covert conspiracy."[21] In tones of righteous indignation, and with backing music evoking shadowy intrigue, *Today Tonight* described how a bus had been "laid on" to "secretly" bring 30 "illegals" halfway across the country "to be granted visas, benefits and Medicare entitlements, all behind the locked doors of an Adelaide Centrelink office." The report even claimed, completely erroneously, that the refugees were being given A$2,500 to "fight any attempt to remove them" from Australia. *Today Tonight* also called on an "outspoken" senator (well known for his opposition to immigration) for an opinion. He declared that the refugees were "criminals ...

with no right to stay here," and mischievously (if bizarrely) implied that they were receiving preferential treatment because they were Muslims. It was left to Immigration Minister Philip Ruddock to add some balance to the story, by pointing out that people are released from detention only if "they clearly meet the Refugee Convention definition." This did not cut much ice with *Today Tonight*, which referred to Australia's obligations under the 1951 Refugee Convention as "the UN loophole."

As people without entitlement, refugee non-citizens are acceptable only in a certain guise – as the passive and grateful recipients of the generosity that we, as citizens, might choose to bestow. The media are comfortable with images of refugees and asylum seekers as helpless and bedraggled. In the schema of binary opposition, politicians contrast the "queue jumper" with the stereotyped image of refugees "waiting patiently" in squalid refugee camps. These deserving refugees are portrayed as passive. We (the entitled citizens) can choose to bestow our generosity on them (the unentitled non-citizens), or we can choose to withhold it. In other words, they are subject to our control. By contrast, "boat people" arriving on Australia's shores display a disagreeable degree of self-will. They are willing to take action to address their situation, arrive uninvited, and are consequently perceived and represented as a threat.

The experience of the "safe haven" refugees is illustrative here. The Australian government created the safe haven visa in 1999 to offer temporary sanctuary to people fleeing the war in Kosovo. Special legislation was rushed through parliament with regulations that initially allowed for only one kind of visa – subclass 448 (Kosovar safe haven (temporary)) visa.[22] The legislation offered the Kosovars entry into Australia, but prevented them from applying to reside in the country on any other grounds, including as refugees under the Convention. The safe haven visas can be extended, shortened, or cancelled by the minister for immigration, but there is no right to appeal such a decision before any court or tribunal. In short, the safe haven legislation was designed to circumscribe the extent of Australia's generosity towards the Kosovars by extinguishing their legal rights.[23]

Prime Minister John Howard and his wife were on hand personally to welcome the first Kosovars to arrive in Australia. But when one Kosovar family later led a protest about conditions at the Singleton camp, 230 kilometres north-west of Sydney, they were portrayed as ingrates. With an invalid grandmother to care for, the family objected to the lack of privacy in shared facilities and to the fact that bathroom and toilet facilities were hundreds of metres away from the wooden huts where they were to sleep. Government officials described the complaints as "totally unreasonable" and suggested that they could send the family back to

Kosovo if they were dissatisfied with Australia. As David Brearly commented in *The Australian*, the charity on offer to the refugees was conditional: "A beggar's gratitude is the prescribed response; anything less renders the whole deal suspect."[24]

Nevertheless, the safe haven experience proved that an openhearted response to refugees is possible. Many Australians got to know the Kosovars and remarkable links were established with the refugees, particularly in country towns, defying the image of rural Australia as a place antagonistic to new immigrants. Tasmanian author Richard Flanagan described the response of his home state to the Brighton refugees (so named because of the place they were housed) in moving terms:

It might be expected that Tasmanians would ignore, or even show hostility to the government-sponsored refugees, since the island is routinely portrayed as red-necked and reactionary. Yet when one beleaguered community looked into the eyes of another worse off, it perhaps saw something familiar.... The Brighton Kosovars were flooded with offers of help and gestures of friendship. Business provided free clothes, free food, free meals, free tours. Cinemas offered free weekly tickets.... The Hobart newspaper, the *Mercury*, ran articles in Albanian. A commercial television news broadcast began with an introduction in Albanian. Far from being outcast, the Kosovars were taken in.[25]

When it came time for the Kosovars to leave Australia, many were understandably reluctant to return to their devastated homeland. They found vocal supporters amongst the Australian population, including state premiers in South Australia and Tasmania, who argued that the refugees should be allowed to settle permanently.

Good and bad refugees

So why were the media, and the general public, so much more sympathetic to the Kosovar "safe haven" refugees than to the "boat people" refugees who were arriving in Australia at around the same time? Why were the Kosovars portrayed as "good" refugees and Afghans and Iraqis as "bad"? As indicated above, I argue this had in part to do with the level of agency displayed by the refugees themselves and the degree of control exerted by Australian authorities. The more passive and under control the refugees appeared, the more sympathetic the response. Clearly it was also influenced by official attitudes toward the refugees; government leaders welcomed the Kosovars but remained hostile to onshore asylum seekers. At another level, detailed and very immediate reporting of the Kosovo conflict had given Australians some understanding of why people had been forced to seek refuge outside their home country. The media presented the war as a contained narrative with a clear aggressor (Serbia/Milosevic) and obvious victims (the Kosovars). By comparison, the tragedy of Afghanistan, when it was reported at all, was portrayed as a long-running saga with no obvious beginning or end point. The country was generally presented as an intractable site of conflict, in which individual actors could not easily be identified or ascribed with motives. Even after 11 September 2001, when the barbarity of the Taliban regime received more detailed coverage – in particular the oppression of women – sympathy for Afghans themselves was constrained by the identification of their country as enemy territory and the home of terrorists. Similarly, although coverage of Iraq tended to portray Saddam Hussein as the arch-villain (the equivalent of Milosevic), one enduring legacy of the Gulf War is that sympathy for people suffering under his regime is tempered by the identification of the country as a whole as an aggressor and an enemy.

Australia was not the only developed nation where Kosovo refugees were "popular" whereas refugees from elsewhere remained "unpopular." Gibney identifies a number of reasons for this.[26] The first is regionality. The proximity of the Kosovo crisis required countries in Western Europe to develop a more organized and coherent response to the refugee outflow. Established measures simply to block the movement of refugees (such as visa restrictions and carrier sanctions) were unlikely to succeed. As a consequence, rather than risk the spontaneous, large-scale movement of refugees spilling across the continent, it was in the political and economic interest of states in Western Europe to develop an alternative and more ordered response to the outflow. This required the support of domestic populations. In other words, host governments had an interest in convincing their citizens that the Kosovars should be welcomed. Secondly, Gibney notes that "the situation in Kosovo also threatened to detract from the prestige of those organisations charged with protecting European security." The NATO alliance had used the language of "humanitarian values" to intervene in Kosovo in the first place.[27] In this sense, developed states were "implicated" in Kosovo, just as, for example, the United States, Australia, Canada, and France had been implicated in the Vietnam War, and consequently displayed a degree of responsibility and compassion to refugees who fled after the communist victory in 1975. Finally, Gibney identifies the issue of "relatedness" (which others have more bluntly described as "race"). He argues that the response to the Kosovars was sympathetic because they were European – "people sharing a common civilization and culture."

Whereas African refugees remain "alien" and "enigmatic" to European audiences, here were "forced migrants who looked and dressed like them ... and who, through the use of articulate and well-educated translators, could express their suffering in terms that resonated with Western audiences."[28]

Media and policy

The Kosovo case provides some insight into the relationship between media reporting and policy formation. Some writers tend to posit a simple relationship between media coverage and government action. For example, Arnot argues in relation to Somalia that television reporting drove both the US intervention in Somalia in 1992 and the ignominious withdrawal of US forces some months later. The marines arrived "after a veritable media blitz" of images of starving children denied food by armed warlords, but were soon forced to retreat again because, in "the most horrendous example of 'pack' journalism," the media drew the simple conclusion that US forces "don't belong in Somalia."[29] A more dispassionate weighing of the evidence suggests that the case is not nearly so clear-cut. Mermin shows that the interest of US television networks in Somalia in fact coincided with the concern about the situation in the country voiced by influential actors in Washington:

In other words if the television inspired American intervention in Somalia, it did so under the influence of governmental actors – a number of Senators, a House committee, a presidential candidate, and figures within the Bush administration – who made considerable efforts to publicize events in Somalia, interpret them as constituting a crisis, and encourage a U.S. response.[30]

Mermin shows that coverage of Somalia on US television networks "was in proportion to the interest Somalia had sparked in Washington."[31] Neuman points out that, if "TV pictures alone compelled Bush to intervene in Somalia, then they should also have had a similar impact in the Sudan, where the starvation was equally devastating, the pictures equally horrific, and, at first equally in evidence on CNN." Equally, she argues that the US withdrawal from Somalia (under a different president) was not the inevitable result of television reporting:

If Clinton had wanted to use political capital to explain to the American public why the United States was in Somalia, if he had used the bully pulpit of high office to make a case that the United States had an obligation to stay, he could have countered the weight of those pictures from Mogadishu. By choosing not to expend his political capital for a cause not of his own choosing, the legacy of an earlier administration, Clinton allowed the pictures to dominate. It is not inevitable, or even desirable, that leaders cede this power to television.[32]

Mermin and Neuman do not deny that the media exert an influence on policy formation, nor do they present journalists as simple tools in the hands of politicians. Rather, they argue that the relationship between media reporting and government decision-making is more complex and textured than simple models of action/reaction would suggest.

In an attempt to reach a more accurate understanding of the interplay between media and government, Robinson seeks to identify the conditions under which reporting can have a decisive impact on policy.[33] Under his model, media influence is greatest in situations in which there is "policy uncertainty" and in which there is "critically framed media coverage that empathizes with suffering people":

In this situation, policy-makers, uncertain of what to do and without a clearly defined policy line with which to counter critical media coverage, can be forced to intervene during a humanitarian crisis due to media-driven public pressure or the fear of *potential* negative public reaction to government inaction.[34]

This model certainly accords with events surrounding the Australian government's decision to offer temporary "safe haven" to refugees from Kosovo in 1999. Australia had never previously confronted the difficult questions posed by the Kosovo crisis – whether or not it should participate in an international effort to provide short-term sanctuary to those fleeing an immediate crisis – and initially the federal government was reluctant to act. On Easter Sunday, 4 April 1999, the minister for immigration, Philip Ruddock, flatly declared that "flying planeloads of refugees into Australia would not be an appropriate response" to the Kosovo crisis.[35] The United Nations High Commissioner for Refugees (UNHCR) had not asked Canberra for assistance and the minister was holding fast to established policy: that Australia offers places for the permanent resettlement of refugees rather than for "temporary outcomes."[36] The media chastised the government for being mean and hardhearted. Talkback lines ran hot with criticism. Over the Easter break, senior government ministers were even pressed to act by members of their own families; after watching distressing television footage from the Balkans, children asked their politician parents why Australia was doing so little to help.[37]

When cabinet convened on the Tuesday after Easter, it was clear that something had to be done. Mr Ruddock took a rough briefing paper to the meeting, canvassing a range of options. One option was to offer permanent resettlement to a large number of Kosovars by "borrowing" places from the future annual refugee resettlement intake.[38] This posed two problems. First, refugees from other regions would be unfairly squeezed out. Secondly, permanent resettlement could play into the hands of the Serb leader, Slobodan Milosevic, by inadvertently supporting his ethnic cleansing in Kosovo. On the other hand, providing short-term refuge for the Kosovars presented its own difficulties. There was no legislative basis for the measure and no established procedures for dealing with such an intake. It would put a huge strain on the bureaucracy and it would be very costly. The cabinet debate was protracted and passionate, but, in the end, temporary refuge appeared to be the only option and Australia offered to provide "safe haven" for 4,000 Kosovar refugees.

In this case the conditions of Robinson's model appear to be satisfied. In the absence of clear policy on an issue, cabinet deliberations were influenced by a barrage of media criticism that portrayed the government as hard-hearted in the face of human suffering. In this sense, the policy outcome was a "victory" for the media and for those ethnic community organizations and refugee advocacy groups that had lobbied hard for government action. In terms of public policy, however, it was not necessarily the best possible outcome. Australia spent at least A$100 million on the Kosovar safe haven programme in 1999, or a minimum of A$25,000 per refugee. In the same year, Iran received less than US$20 worth of UNHCR assistance for each one of the almost 2 million Afghan and Iraqi refugees living within its borders.[39] It can be persuasively argued that Australia's "safe haven" money might have been better spent supporting refugee camps in Macedonia and other front-line states in the Balkans, or indeed in other trouble spots around the world.

The limits of media influence on the Kosovar issue became apparent when it was time for the safe haven refugees to return home. This time, the first of the two conditions in Robinson's policy–media interaction model was absent: there was no uncertainty in government policy. From the outset the Australian government had stated firmly that the "safe haven" programme would be temporary and that refugees would be returned once the conflict was over. Again, the media were generally very critical of the government, arguing that the refugees should be given more time and that no one should be pressured to return before they felt ready to do so. But, apart from offering concessions to a small number of people suffering serious illnesses or displaying severe psychological problems arising from their experiences of trauma, the government was unwavering in its determination to remove the Kosovars. Those who resisted were placed in immigration detention alongside asylum seekers who had arrived in the country without authorization.[40]

Conclusion: The limits of influence and the responsibility of advocates

From the above discussion it becomes apparent that media reporting can shape public perceptions of refugees and asylum seekers. Compassionate and sympathetic coverage can help to promote public understanding and encourage generous assistance to refugees and others in need. Negative reporting can generate and intensify feelings of fear. Without absolving journalists and editors of responsibility for the tone and style of their reporting, it must be recognized that political actors play an important role in setting the terms of the debate. The media can influence public policy on refugee issues, encouraging a humanitarian response to people in need, but are more likely to do so when government policy is uncertain.

What lessons can be drawn from this for refugee advocates wishing to use the media to influence government action? First, it should be recognized that the media are not monolithic: at the same time and in the same "market" different outlets will take different approaches to a story. For example, on the same weekend that the *Courier Mail* ran the front-page typhoid story discussed above, *The Sunday Age* newspaper in Melbourne carried a full-page spread sympathetically detailing the stories and personal experiences of Afghan and Iraqi refugees who had made it to Australia.[41]

Secondly, it must be recognized that the media are as much a source of entertainment as they are a source of news and information. Although the philosophical starting point of many journalists is that they work to serve the public interest, there is a commercial motive at the base of most (although not all) media enterprises that does influence editorial policy. It can, and often does, encourage a tabloid approach to issues – dumbing down, over-simplification, stereotyping, and sensationalism. For example, it is not unusual for a newspaper to run an inaccurate but attention-grabbing picture even though it has no real connection with the story. Photographer Howard Davies recalls that a UK broadsheet used one of his pictures of a Vietnamese refugee in a Hong Kong camp to accompany an article about the poor living conditions of Filipino maids. He recounts how another editor, viewing his pictures from Somalia, asked "for a few prints for the 'famine file'."[42]

One response to these problems is to train refugee workers in media skills, to increase their chances of delivering appropriate messages, rather than feeding into pre-existing and often narrow media perceptions of the story.[43] If refugee advocates understand the way in which the media work – the pressure of tight deadlines, the hunger for a new angle, the need for ready quotes and picture opportunities – then they can exert greater influence over what finally gets published and broadcast. A complementary approach is to seek meetings with senior editors in an attempt to influence the overall shape and direction of editorial policy. Elizabeth Ferris, Executive Secretary for International Relations at the World Council of Churches, claims some success in this regard:

Some of the best cases I've seen have been when representatives of churches and other non-government organisations have met with editorial boards or with groups of correspondents or have organised sessions where they can really talk in some depth about issues which the media are covering.[44]

Ferris argues that such a dialogue can help to reduce the sometimes adversarial relationship that exists between advocates and the media. She notes that, within the non-government sector, opinion is divided on how best to handle the media. Some refugee workers argue that there is a need to work more closely with journalists "to show them the situations, to get the kind of coverage that will engender an outpouring of humanitarian response." Others are more cautious and emphasize the need to educate the media "on the causes and complexities of the situation to encourage more responsible kinds of reporting."[45]

At the heart of the issue is the double-edged response that media reporting on refugee issues can invite: compassion and pressure for the protection "of" refugees on the one hand, and fear and the desire for protection "from" refugees on the other.

When relief agencies take journalists to sites of conflict, they often do so with the aim of raising cash to fund their operations. But this noble intention can go astray. If the outcome is a report that shows a situation of despair and desperation, it can engender "compassion fatigue." Alternatively, it might result in short-term gain – donations – but long-term damage. Greer has described how, in Ethiopia in 1984, "photographers searching for the most harrowing pictures stuck their cameras in the faces of children who were actually breathing their last, and won prizes for doing it":

In the images that were flashed around the world the children had no names or, worse, made up names. They were no longer people but emblems designed and redesigned to stimulate the charitable impulse.[46]

Greer refers to this type of reporting as "the pornography of charity." Vaux makes a related point when he argues that aid agencies (including, presumably, refugee agencies) sometimes lack introspection:

In order to express concern for other people, we have to believe that they are good. In effect aid agencies have preserved the concept of the "deserving poor." The idea is that poor people deserve help because they are innocent victims.[47]

As noted above, the media have an inherent tendency to cast events in binary terms – to look for "goodies" and "baddies," "victims" and "perpetrators," the "innocent" and the "guilty." This does little to encourage the development of a sophisticated understanding of complex situations or to promote the development of nuanced policy responses. But, as Ferris notes, this approach is often encouraged by relief agencies themselves:

It's very effective ... in fund-raising to show images of children, who are suffering, who are hungry, with the unspoken and often spoken message that by contributing money you can ease the situation of this child. And yet what partners in many regions want to be portrayed is not just the suffering, although that is there as well, but also the fact that people can take charge of their future, that they do have resources that they can bring, that they are strong.[48]

If relief agencies persist in encouraging representations of refugees as passive innocents, as "smiling and very grateful and quiet,"[49] then audiences in the developed world will continue to be disconcerted when they discover that real world refugees do not fit that stereotype. To portray refugees as passive innocents sheltering in squalid camps is to fulfil one half of Said's "insidious" binary opposition. On the flip side of that coin is the stereotype of the queue jumper. As Ferris argues, perhaps it is time to portray refugees as survivors rather than victims:

Even in some of these most desperate situations you find incredible stories of hope. You find stories of ... people hiding members of a persecuted ethnic group, or people risking unpopular decisions of standing up for others.... [Refugees] are strong people, these are determined, resilient people who can escape from unbearable situations and often times carry their children through weeks of walking through the bush to reach safety ... [T]o look at the way in which we present the people that we are trying to help, is an important part of a response with integrity to desperate situations.[50]

Notes

1. Michael McKinnon, "Typhoid Found in Refugee Centres," *Courier Mail* (Brisbane), 23 June 2001.
2. For a detailed critique of Australia's policies, see Peter Mares, *Borderline: Australia's Treatment of Refugees and Asylum Seekers*, Sydney: University of New South Wales Press, 2001.
3. Chips Mackinolty, "Detention Curbs Disease Risk, Says Ruddock," *The Age* (Melbourne), 2 February 2001.
4. Michael McKinnon, "Why the Fences Won't Come down," *Courier Mail* (Brisbane), 23 June 2001.

5. David Corlett, "Politics, Symbolism and the Asylum Seeker Issue," *University of New South Wales Law Journal*, vol. 23, no. 3, 2000, p. 18.
6. Ibid., p. 31.
7. Ron Kaye, "Redefining the Refugee: The UK Media Portrayal of Asylum Seekers," in Khalid Koser and Helma Lutz, *The New Migration in Europe: Social Constructions and Social Realities*, London: Macmillan, 1998, p. 173.
8. Sharon Pickering, "The Hard Press of Asylum," *Forced Migration Review*, no. 8, December 2000, p. 32.
9. Ibid., p. 32.
10. Andrew Clennell, "Refugees Used to Fuel Campaigns," *Sydney Morning Herald*, 31 July 2001.
11. Prior to October 1999, people assessed as refugees in Australia were granted permanent residency. After that date, however, the federal government introduced a system of three-year "temporary protection visas" for refugees who had originally arrived in Australia without a valid visa. These temporary protection visas (TPVs) are not to be confused with the temporary "safe haven" visas discussed below, which were granted to displaced people from Kosovo and East Timor in 1999.
12. *Australian Associated Press*, 13 September 2001.
13. For discussion of this issue, see Gerard Henderson, "Unleashing a 'Sleeper' Issue: Ethnic Suspicion," *The Age*, 18 September 2001.
14. See Dennis Atkins, "PM Links Terror to Asylum Seekers," *Herald Sun* (Melbourne), 7 November 2001. For a defence of Howard's statement, see Tim Blair, "Beware of Terrorists in Refugee Clothing," *The Australian*, 8 November 2001.
15. *Hansard*, Australian House of Representatives, 19 September 2001.
16. "Boat Children Overboard," *The Australian*, 8 October 2001.
17. "Boat People 'Threw Children Overboard,'" *The Age*, 8 October 2001.
18. Edward Said, "The Case for Intellectuals," Alfred Deakin Lecture published in *The Age*, 21 May 2001.
19. Sharon Pickering, "Common Sense and Original Deviancy: News Discourses and Asylum Seekers in Australia," paper presented to the conference on The "Integrity of Our Shores": Asylum Seekers and Refugees in Australia, United Theological College, North Parramatta, 20 October 2000, p. 1.
20. Pradip N. Thomas, "Refugees and Their Right to Communication," in Pradip Thomas, *Refugees and Their Right to Communicate: Perspective from South East Asia*, London: World Association for Christian Communication, 2001, p. 52.
21. *Today Tonight*, Channel 7, 3 April 2000.
22. The "safe haven" visa was later extended to allow Australia to offer sanctuary to people from other regions. A detailed discussion of the safe haven experience in Australia can be found in Mares, *Borderline*.
23. Michael Head, "The Kosovar and Timorese 'Safe Haven' Refugees: A Test for Democratic Rights," *Alternative Law Journal*, vol. 4, no. 6, December 1999.
24. David Brearly, "From Wretches to Whingers," *The Australian*, 19 June 1999.
25. Richard Flanagan, "Our Keith – Why Can't He Stay?" *The Age*, 22 July 2000.
26. Matthew J. Gibney, "Kosovo and Beyond: Popular and Unpopular Refugees," *Forced Migration Review*, no. 5, August 1999.
27. Ibid., p. 29.
28. Ibid., p. 30.
29. Bob Arnot, "Waiting for the Cameras: Journalism and Humanitarian Crises," *World Refugee Survey 1995*, Washington DC: US Committee for Refugees, 1995, at www.refugees.org/world/articles/journalism_wrs95.htm.
30. Jonathan Mermin, "Television News and American Intervention in Somalia: The

Myth of a Media-Driven Foreign Policy," *Political Science Quarterly*, vol. 112, no. 3, 1997, p. 386.

31. Ibid., p. 389.
32. Johanna Neuman, *Lights, Camera, War: Is Media Technology Driving International Politics?* New York: St. Martin's Press, 1996, p. 21.
33. Piers Robinson, "The Policy–Media Interaction Model: Measuring Media Power during Humanitarian Crisis," *Journal of Peace Research*, vol. 37, no. 5, 2000.
34. Ibid., p. 614, emphasis in original.
35. Michelle Grattan, "Backflip So Quick Details Are Yet to Be Settled," *Sydney Morning Herald*, 7 April 1999.
36. John Zubrzycki, "Ruddock Vetoes Asylum," *The Australian*, 6 April 1999.
37. Dennis Shanahan, "Anyone Who Had a Heart," *The Australian*, 10 April 1999.
38. In addition to the "onshore" processing of refugee applications by those who arrive uninvited on its shores, Australia offers permanent resettlement to a number of refugees and other displaced people identified by the UNHCR or sponsored by relatives already in need. The size of this "offshore" or "humanitarian programme" is determined each year by government. However, in recent years the government has reduced the number of "offshore" visas by the number of "onshore" visas issued in a given year.
39. As of 31 December 2000, there were 1,482,000 Afghan and 387,000 Iraqi refugees and/or asylum seekers sheltering in Iran. *World Refugee Survey 2001*, Washington DC: US Committee for Refugees, p. 3.
40. For a more detailed treatment of the safe haven experience, see Mares, *Borderline*, p. 162 ff.
41. Larry Schwartz, "Invisible Journeys: Tales from the Human Pipeline," *The Sunday Age*, 24 June 2001.
42. Howard Davies, "Accountability in the Media," *Forced Migration Review*, no. 9, April 2001, p. 37.
43. See, for example, Melissa Phillips, "Working with the Media: Notes for Refugee Advocates," *Forced Migration Review*, no. 8, December 2000.
44. Elizabeth Ferris, interview with the author, Melbourne, 5 July 2001.
45. Ibid.
46. Germaine Greer, "We Are Big Brother," *The Australian (Media Section)*, 12 July 2001, p. 8 (reprinted from the *Observer*).
47. Tony Vaux, *The Selfish Altruist*, London: Earthscan, 2001 (excerpt published in *The Australian Financial Review*, "Review" section, 22 June 2001, p. 9).
48. Elizabeth Ferris, interview with the author.
49. Ibid.
50. Ibid.

16

Changing roles of NGOs in refugee assistance

Mark Raper

Humanitarian crises provoke the engagement of three "benign forces":[1] international organizations, governments, and non-governmental organizations (NGOs). Each of these actors has an important role in giving refuge, protection, and assistance to forcibly displaced populations. For ordinary citizens in liberal democracies, NGOs offer the most effective avenue for interpreting and addressing the needs of the millions whose plight is so vividly communicated to them by the media, or who increasingly knock on the doors of the "rich" countries, seeking asylum. Apart from the particular expertise that each NGO brings to this effort, their effectiveness is based on their independence (which often enables them to gain early access to affected populations), their flexibility and mobility, their capacity to collaborate with many other actors, and, of course, their credibility.

This chapter identifies, from an NGO practitioner's perspective, the changing roles of the private sector in the humanitarian field, the relationships between NGOs, governments, and international organizations (which are mandated by governments), and the practical, professional, and even ethical challenges posed to NGOs by the new contexts.

Describing non-governmental organizations

With each new humanitarian crisis, a plethora of new organizations attempts to respond to the human drama. Some subsequently close down when the crisis subsides, whereas others refine and redefine their roles in response to subsequent challenges. The number of NGOs, the resources they command, and their public profiles continue to grow. Moreover, as human security challenges state security as the guiding principle in public policy, NGOs have increasingly significant roles in providing protection as well as material assistance, in bringing brutal realities to international audiences, and in campaigning against human rights abuses. There is a trend for policy makers to take NGOs into account more seriously both in the formulation of public policy and also in the management of responses to complex emergencies.

Despite the complexity of modern emergencies, improved communications enable NGOs to respond in ways that are at once more comprehensive, coordinated, and focused. When Jody Williams, who together with the International Campaign to Ban Landmines was awarded the Nobel Peace Prize in 1997, was asked how she managed to organize over 1,000 NGOs across six continents, despite the opposition of most governments, she replied: "e-mail." Globalization's preferred tool gives significant new leverage to non-governmental organizations, enhancing their capacities for information, coordination, and flexibility.

Some examples

Some NGOs are immense, some are tiny. Some are founded as an ad hoc response to the latest crisis and are subsequently disbanded; others are centuries old. The international NGOs, with their headquarters in Western countries, have access to the media, to powerful governments, to strong funding bases, and often to influential publics. Local or indigenous NGOs have an important role and yet, since they do not command comparable resources, are often quite overlooked in the humanitarian emergencies.

The International Committee of the Red Cross (ICRC), now with over 10,000 personnel, is one of the most important actors outside the UN system. Founded in 1863, it originated as an initiative to assist wounded soldiers left lying unattended on the battlefield of Solferino in northern Italy. Because of the neutrality built into its mandate, and since governments have a role in its governance, it maintains an identity apart from the NGO world, while remaining open to assist NGOs in many instances.

Save the Children Fund and Caritas are both initiatives that followed the First World War. The International Rescue Committee was founded in 1933 at the request of Albert Einstein, it claims, in order to assist the opponents of Hitler, and so was quite active attending to the people displaced in Europe by the Second World War. The Irish agency Concern and the originally French and now international Médecins sans Frontières (MSF) both arose out of responses to the civil war over Biafra in

Nigeria in the late 1960s. Oxfam describes itself as a "development, relief and campaigning organisation" and, together with another 10 national organizations, has built a worldwide movement aiming "to build a just and safer world." The American Refugee Committee was begun by a small group of concerned people who first helped with the resettlement of Indo-Chinese refugees in the United States in 1978, subsequently sent a medical team to the camps in Thailand, and several years later had field teams in a number of countries. The Jesuit Refugee Service, with which I worked for 20 years, grew from the response of a Catholic religious order to the Vietnamese boat people crisis, and led to a worldwide organization that opened its first field offices simultaneously in 1981 in the Horn of Africa and in South-East Asia, and is now present in over 60 countries. Its mission is to "accompany, serve and defend the rights of forcibly displaced people," and it draws support from a social base comprising thousands of communities and institutions around the world.

The largest single association of agencies working under the same identity and set of guiding principles is the Catholic Church's Caritas federation, which comprises 154 national relief, development, and social work agencies, present in 198 countries and territories throughout the world. This federation commands more personnel, a greater budget, and a broader public involvement than any agency of the United Nations.

Challenges to local NGOs

Although local NGOs may have been on the scene and working away in difficult conditions for a long time, in times of emergencies they are often pushed aside by the international NGOs, which come in with superior technical capacity and material means but rarely with a profound knowledge of a local situation. Worse, local NGOs are often "cannibalized" and their personnel recruited to work in the visiting agencies. Even though these local agencies are the ones that will pick up the pieces again once the crisis is over and the international agencies depart, they have often been consumed and destroyed in the time of the crisis. It should be said that some international NGOs are disposed to assist local NGOs once this problem is exposed. The outsiders are able to support and develop local networks, introducing information technology and other technical support, as well as training in management or in human rights investigation and reporting. And of course through these partnerships the international bodies receive a lot. Good local NGOs are embedded in the religious and cultural institutions of civil society and the information they may command and their insights into local cultures and needs are often far superior to those of the international NGOs.

Facing new challenges

In the 1960s and 1970s, the preoccupation of many NGOs was with the growing disparity between the rich and the poor in the world, and their activities were often neatly divided between the fields of "development" and "relief." Development was regarded as a more thorough and long-term task, whereas relief was often criticized as being a "band-aid" and not going to the "root causes." The failure of those "development decades," the growth of poverty, and the increasingly uneven access to and control over resources – among other causes – have led to new patterns of conflict and indeed to new patterns of forced migration, and thus to new needs for both assistance and protection of basic rights. As a consequence, many of the NGOs that formerly gave a priority to the long-term task of promoting human development have now chosen to respond to the urgent needs of forcibly displaced people. For one thing, they would not long remain credible to their supporters if they were not seen to be involved in the urgent humanitarian disasters that now occur with depressing regularity and that impinge forcefully on the consciousness of their constituents.

Post–Cold War humanitarianism

As new patterns of interrelationship between states have become manifest since the end of the Cold War, so the forces that displace people within and outside of their countries have evolved. With quite rare exceptions, wars today are internal. There is also a significant rise in the size of the civilian populations who are displaced within their own countries by these conflicts. In today's conflicts, the growing number of non-state actors makes it quite difficult to distinguish between civilians and soldiers, bringing a new ethical dilemma to those who intervene with assistance. When an NGO chooses to assist combatants, it risks becoming a party to the conflict. When civilians and combatants are indistinguishable, the risks are greater. For precisely these reasons, governments and international agencies may not venture in to assist, whereas NGOs are more likely to be present.

A common strategy of today's warfare is to target civilians as the cheapest and easiest surrogate for the enemy. In mobilizing for this type of warfare, differences of ethnicity, religion, or territory are exploited. In practice, these differences amount to extraordinarily superficial features, such as the colour of skin, the shape of a nose, a way of dressing or of cooking food. But one result is the proliferation of refugees and of war wounded. Moreover, possibly because the wars are internal or possibly because the protection offered to refugees outside their country of origin is in many cases insignificant, most are not crossing frontiers and remain as internally displaced persons. For this reason, they may be temporarily outside the brief or reach of an international organization whose mandate forbids them to cross borders at will. But they are accessible by NGOs, which work with fewer or different restraints.

Both NGOs and international organizations struggle to understand the new forces at work. The rhetoric of humanitarianism and of the pursuit of human rights can be manipulated in the service of national or regional security, giving NGOs new reasons for caution. The appeal to humanitarian arguments in order to justify even a military intervention is made with significant selectivity. For many governments, the humanitarian argument carries such valuable political weight that they are reluctant to leave humanitarian initiatives to the humanitarian agencies.

Kosovo was a glaring example. Ironically, even though the use of force creates refugees, and in the case of Kosovo it most certainly did, the argument used in favour of force was that it would prevent refugee movements. Moreover, in the Kosovo crisis the military moved into the humanitarian field and, rather than complementing or reinforcing the agencies mandated by the international community for these services, they often displaced them, claiming from these actions a legitimacy and visibility that belied their true role. The risk for the NGOs in these situations is not so much that they will be excluded from service, but rather that they too will be used by governments to displace the "neutral" roles of international organizations. NGOs often carry national flags and many depend on large funding by governments, thus presenting a profile by which governments may demonstrate their readiness to support humanitarian initiatives.

The real crisis for the United Nations High Commissioner for Refugees (UNHCR)

Because it is the major intergovernmental agency at work with refugees, any challenge to the UNHCR's identity obviously affects the NGOs that work with forcibly displaced persons. In the perspective of some governments, the agency has become so large and dependent on donors that financial management has been more an issue to them than core functions. There have been criticisms of the UNHCR by its donor governments and cuts to its budget and numbers of personnel. These have been demoralizing for its professional staff and diminish its capacity to maintain an effective field presence and network of information. Yet the real crisis for the UNHCR lies not in the cuts to its budget, serious as these are. The crisis is that the very governments that are signatories to the

1951 Convention Relating to the Status of Refugees are today under-mining both its meaning and its effectiveness through uneven ratification, divergent interpretations, or sheer disregard of its implications.

The word "partnership" is often used to describe the relationship between the UNHCR and the NGOs that work with refugees. Ironically, as the pool of funds that the UNHCR disburses to NGOs is diminishing, so the appeal to the practice of partnership is increasing, since the UNHCR now has a far greater need of the NGOs in order to accomplish its traditional tasks. Yet some governments are tending to seek out non-government partners and financing them directly to implement programmes, seeing them as cheaper, more flexible, and perhaps more malleable than the intergovernmental bodies.

Realizing that the international system of refugee protection is in a state of disarray and could possibly face "fragmentation, or worse disintegration," the UNHCR's Executive Committee, meeting in 2000, endorsed the need to engage in Global Consultations aimed at revitalizing "the international protection regime and to discuss measures to ensure that international protection needs are properly recognised and met, while due account is also taken of the legitimate concerns of States, host communities and the international community generally."[2] NGOs are included at the edges of these discussions, which is correct since states have primary obligations and they mandate specific responsibilities to their multilateral agencies, such as the UNHCR. Nonetheless, NGOs exercise significant roles in ensuring that those who need protection do get it, and all must work together to ensure that responsibilities are met.

Advocacy and protection

At the time of their formation, many NGOs were limited by public attitudes and in some cases by legislation which restricted their engagement in politics, but most now include advocacy or campaigning in their core activities, along with their regular tasks of providing relief assistance, promoting human development, public education, and, of course, raising funds. Through the NGOs, ordinary citizens can become powerful advocates to influence governments. Ironically, although the NGOs work more closely with international organizations, it is less easy to influence their policies. These bodies are neither democratic nor accountable to anyone except the governments that mandate them. In recent years, international NGO campaigns have had significant success on such themes as the ban on land mines, opposing the recruitment of children for armed conflict, and a campaign to cancel the international debt carried by poor countries.

Until recently it was rare that a relief agency would take advocacy as an integral part of its mission. Médecins sans Frontières (MSF) was an early exception. MSF traces its origins to the Biafran war, in which the media were used to great effect as a weapon by parties to the conflict, in particular through the attention given to humanitarian suffering. Several French doctors recruited to work with the ICRC complained then that they could not speak about what they saw because of the agency's strict guidelines on neutrality. So they founded MSF, whose website now says: "when medical assistance is not enough to save lives, MSF will speak out against human rights abuses;" in another place it goes further: "MSF will address the human rights violations our volunteers witness while giving medical attention."[3] Advocacy was from the beginning integrated as a normal component of the agency's tasks and it has a triage approach to emergencies, generally keeping clear of long-term development projects.

Protection roles of NGOs among refugees and internally displaced people

Nowadays many more NGOs have missions that commit them to offer protection to people at risk. The presence of NGO personnel, particularly international personnel, among forcibly displaced populations is one of the means of protecting them. When US citizens lived in communities in El Salvador, for example, or accompanied indigenous communities returning home to Guatemala from exile in Mexico, the military were less likely to harass and disrupt the communities, given such witnesses.

In times of conflict, the role of "accompaniment" takes a higher priority than technical services such as education or health care, though these will continue if possible. The presence of expatriate civilian companions can have further beneficial consequences as a preventive measure, for example protecting refugees from violence, rape, or forced recruitment. Accompaniment enhances human dignity by demonstrating what the people's human rights are. It may enable them to practise their religion. It may also help them to explain and give testimony concerning the abuse of rights that they have already experienced or do now suffer. Companions from outside can advocate for them, helping them to express their needs and fears to authorities or to an international audience.

Other preventive strategies to protect the rights of forcibly displaced people concern, for example, the planning of settlements: the location, design, and staffing of facilities such as toilets, water sources, markets, schools, and health services. Particular attention must be given to ensure that women are not isolated or exposed to dangers. Minimum standards for these basic services have been elaborated in many places and assist in making settlements safe.

Accompaniment may sometimes deter human rights abuses, but, when NGOs are confronted by an offence or when they observe a pattern of violations, they need strategies for action. Apart from preventive measures, the principal options open to NGOs include monitoring and reporting. Sometimes they might do this by offering solidarity and accompaniment to local or refugee-run organizations, enabling them to speak with their own voices. Or they will make the report themselves. In other cases they will seek the support of a specialist human rights agency. Given that the primary role of many NGOs is normally a specialist service such as health care, food distribution, or sanitation, they need to have clearly developed protocols for monitoring and reporting on human rights abuses, so that they can continue efficiently what they came to do.

Monitoring human rights violations

Human rights violations are not uncommon in refugee situations. After all, refugees are themselves human rights abuse made manifest. All NGO field personnel should be trained to notice and to report these facts within their agencies. Sometimes the NGO worker observes patterns of individual abuses, such as theft, rape, or domestic violence. Sometimes there is an institutional disorder, such as the diversion of food supplies, the presence of armed elements in camps, or the location of a camp near to a conflicted border. Normally there should be a forum within the agency and among the group of NGOs working in that settlement or in that region or country where these events can be reported and discussed and the appropriate courses of action decided. But since refugee situations are notoriously insecure, and since NGO personnel are normally without significant protection, they need to be circumspect when choosing how to document and report on abuses. A judgement has to be made whether to report to the United Nations officials or to local authorities; whether to local government, to military or rebel authorities, or at national level. NGOs have sometimes found that the local UNHCR protection officer may be working so closely with local authorities that the problem is safest reported to the UNHCR's national representative to follow up discretely, or even in Geneva, and then handed back down the line anonymously. In the cases where none of these avenues is safe or effective, NGOs may withdraw completely, using the occasion of their withdrawal for an exposé.

Collaboration between service agencies and human rights agencies

Another option for field NGOs is to collaborate with international human rights agencies. Such cooperation enables information about the violations to be made public anonymously, without threatening the continued NGO presence with the refugees. Moreover, since the human rights agencies are specifically prepared for this task, they are more effective in putting pressure on governments, non-state actors, and the United Nations to respect human rights norms. The field NGO can provide the human rights NGO with credible information that will reinforce its public education about refugees' rights and contribute to the prevention of root causes of refugee movements.

For over a decade, the Jesuit Refugee Service has maintained such a partnership with Human Rights Watch (HRW), assisting HRW to develop its capacity to give a priority to the human rights of refugees. Through this partnership, HRW at various times engaged personnel who systematically focused on refugee human rights in Asia, the Americas, and Africa. The two agencies also collaborated in several investigations.

Although the agencies can, with relative ease, share an overarching goal of human rights for refugees, it stands to reason that there is a marked contrast at field levels between the operational goals, methodology, and timetables of each. Whereas a field NGO is concerned with serving and healing individual survivors or groups of clients, the human rights NGO is focused on collecting and analysing data in order to build a case, which, if well argued, can ultimately lead to a change of policy. The human rights NGO workers cannot stay behind to heal the traumatized people whom they have interviewed.

The major human rights organizations welcome this type of collaboration. They are also particularly good at encouraging local NGOs in their roles. "Our goal is to strengthen a group's power to pursue solutions locally and then to reinforce those solutions within international arenas," said Michael Posner, Executive Director of the Lawyers' Committee for Human Rights. Posner says, speaking particularly but not exclusively of local human rights organizations:

[A]s the NGO community has become larger and more sophisticated, they have had better access at the national and international levels. Part of their strength lies in their ability to testify – to provide powerful, real-life accounts of human rights abuses. As a result of their view from the frontlines, their information has become a central part of decision-making on issues such as aid, trade and a whole range of diplomatic questions.[4]

The United Nations High Commissioner for Human Rights can supply only modest support for field and local NGOs. Although a strong regime of international human rights and humanitarian law is desirable, it is not yet universally effective. In so far as they are close to the victims, NGOs have access to sound information and they are strongly motivated to advocate a better and stronger international human rights regime.

Diverse situations in which NGOs serve forcibly displaced persons

The diversity and flexibility among the NGOs can be an advantage, given the quite varied causes of forced displacement and the value of exploring all strategies to meet different problems. Generally NGOs claim allegiance to a "mission" rather than to a "mandate."[5] This already gives them greater flexibility than is available, say, to international organizations, whose clearly defined mandates form part of international law and cannot be radically adapted to suit changing needs without a major revision by the member governments. Whereas the United Nations is an organization set up to preserve the integrity of nation-states, some NGOs have no such allegiances and will regularly cross national borders if they have a humanitarian reason for doing so.

Nor are the NGOs restricted to a mandate definition of who is a refugee, as in the Convention Relating to the Status of Refugees of 1951, which attempts to be quite precise and refers to individuals who have left their country for fear of persecution. By contrast, for example, Catholic Church NGOs are guided by an official church document that uses a much broader term, "de facto refugee," as a guide for its agencies. It applies the expression "de facto refugee" to

all persons persecuted because of race, religion, membership in social or political groups; to the victims of armed conflicts, erroneous economic policy or natural disasters; and for humanitarian reasons to internally displaced persons, that is civilians who are forcibly uprooted from their homes by the same type of violence as refugees but who do not cross national frontiers.[6]

The use of this term acknowledges that today's forcibly displaced are often victims of the same conflicts that create refugees. Forcibly displaced people not only are found in camps, but also include the internally displaced, asylum seekers and homeless foreigners in urban settings, those imprisoned in immigration detention centres, and stateless persons.

NGOs are found serving all of these. NGOs will defend the refugee regime and use the UNHCR Convention as an important tool. However, they are not normally proscribed by these limits, unless they enter a contract with an international organization in which they accept to operate within its mandate.

Access in times of emergency – refugee camps

Providing services to refugees in camps requires planning. At least four bodies need to collaborate in the planning and delivery of services: the international community, usually represented by UNHCR; the host country, sometimes represented by security forces; the service providers, which are usually NGOs; and the refugees. Formal agreements usually involve only the first three. The refugees are often left out in planning phases, although they have an essential role in managing a camp. Refugee committees are appointed, or chosen in either democratic or traditional ways. Sometimes resistance or militia leaders in the background direct actions and dictate positions taken by the refugees, but remain hidden (as was the case with the Guatemalans in Mexico or the Rwandans in Kivu in 1994 to 1996).

The cuts in funding to the UNHCR are having drastic effects on field programmes for refugees in camps. The result is to put in question the link that the UNHCR has for a long time maintained with some validity, namely that humanitarian assistance can be a means for providing protection. When funding is not available, there are several possible courses of action for the UNHCR: programmes may be cut completely, services in the camps may be diminished, or responsibility for services may be given over to another agency. When services are cut, this may lead ultimately to political decisions by host countries to send refugees back home. It may not always be bad that the situation is forced to a conclusion, as in the case of the Eritreans in the Sudan, some of whom had been there since the 1980s. Yet it is alarming when people are forced to return just because programmes are cut (for example, the Sierra Leoneans in Guinea and Liberia in 2000 and 2001), or are simply abandoned in a difficult situation (for example, the East Timorese in West Timor in the same years). In those cases, some NGOs remained without even the logistical or communications support from the UNHCR on which they had relied when the programmes were initiated. Increasingly the UNHCR has asked NGOs to remain present in camps and to offer services yet to seek most of their own funding. Some NGOs have commented that this leads to competitiveness within a group that is normally collaborative: the UNHCR is in effect urging NGOs to bid against one another for the right to be present in a camp.

Access to internally displaced persons

Working with internally displaced persons presents quite different sets of challenges from working in refugee camps, even if the services provided – health care, shelter, food distribution, education – are similar. The main problem facing humanitarian organizations in conflict situations is how to reach internally displaced people. Serving the internally displaced is more precarious than accompanying refugees, because too often the conflict is still ongoing, or their own government is their attacker, or people are constantly on the move, or armed groups exist within the displaced populations. Agencies are present on sufferance of the state or of the de facto authorities. It makes a big difference whether or not a peace agreement has already been reached and is being honoured. Fighting may make access impossible, or terrain or meteorological conditions do not allow the passage of relief goods, or convoys are looted. Difficulties in gaining access are frequently man-made and intentional. These impediments can lead to disastrous consequences, as events in Somalia, Bosnia, or southern Sudan have shown.

No international organization is assigned the task of protecting internally displaced persons. So, in each case, collaboration among the NGOs and the international organizations still has to be worked out on an ad hoc basis. The international humanitarian system is less able and often less willing to intervene when victims of conflict remain contained within the conflict-affected countries. This severely reduces the scope for responding to their needs. Nonetheless, *Guiding Principles* have been elaborated that help a lot in these situations.[7]

When security risks are too high, the international agencies are obliged to withdraw. Yet, if conditions are unsafe for the agency workers, then *a fortiori* they are insecure for the displaced people themselves. Even if UN personnel must withdraw, it may still be possible for NGOs to remain, since they may be perceived as independent, they may be better integrated with the local population, or their services may be appreciated by the local militias or other authorities. Sometimes NGOs can remain not because they are perceived as independent, but because they are not neutral or they appear to be supporting a particular faction of the conflict. In fact neutrality is rarely possible. But an NGO needs to be very aware both of the position it actually takes as well as the positions its members are perceived to take in regard to the parties to a conflict.

Return, reintegration, and reconstruction

Returning refugees are often accompanied by NGOs, both in the preparation phase and during their return and reintegration. The return requires a lot of preparation, especially in information and instruction concerning the rights of the returnees. On return they are no longer refugees, but many become displaced again and still in need of protection. Post-conflict returns, and the rehabilitation and reconstruction that accompany the transition from war to peace, require time, expertise, political will, solid financial support, and considerable human resourcefulness. Since many of these returns are now precipitous and hastened by governments before conditions in the home country are ripe, there is a need for NGOs to remain and to continue to accompany populations that have returned home.

After any conflict, successful reintegration and rehabilitation are long and arduous processes. Legal and education systems need to be rebuilt, and housing and employment provided. After war, orphans and widows abound. The deepest work of all, reconciliation and peace-building, takes decades, and starts to take root only when the grief begins to ease. Often international resources are most readily available at the height of emergencies but, when long-term development assistance is needed, the people are left to themselves. The United Nations has a big responsibility in designing the return phase and in assigning tasks to NGOs, particularly in fostering the development of local NGOs and civil society for long-term services. In the reconstruction phase, NGOs have a big responsibility to respect the local governments, which may still be in a fragile state. Roads, clinics, and schools built by the NGOs may be the future responsibility of the local authorities to staff and maintain, so they should be jointly planned.

Refugees and asylum seekers in urban settings

Not all refugees live in camps or settlements. Many live in urban areas or in villages, dispersed among the local populations. Asylum seekers can be found in every capital of the world, from Moscow to Maputo, from Nairobi to New Delhi. Many have not yet gone through refugee status determination procedures and so may have no legal status within the country of refuge. Some may be recognized as refugees by the UNHCR but may be only barely tolerated by the host government, thus making them vulnerable to harassment and extortion by police and other authorities. In African cities, for example, this relatively invisible group mingles with the numerous rural poor and survives in the same ways, through finding illegal work, through the mutual support of ethnic communities, through support of NGOs, or through a mixture of all of these. Because of the irregular status of many of this population of urban foreigners, the NGOs work in a grey area, supporting persons who are not approved by the state. This may require both discretion and courage.

Care for asylum seekers in Western countries

The number of people entering and claiming asylum in Western countries has risen dramatically in recent years. A great number of new NGOs respond to the new needs, and international NGOs also find themselves called on to work in their countries of origin. States have mounted various responses. First, they attempt to reduce the numbers of refugees who actually reach their frontiers, through a great range of deterrents and non-entrée measures. Secondly, they develop their status determination procedures. Occasionally, the developments make the procedures more efficient and speedy. But generally they are made restrictive and cumbersome. NGOs are present, where possible, at each stage, offering material support to the new arrivals as well as legal counsel. Yet, in many instances, they are excluded from contact in the early stages after arrival. NGOs also lobby for assistance for the source countries, in an effort to improve conditions in the countries of origin and to remove the reasons for flight.

A recent study of the situation of irregular migrants in Europe[8] revealed that "de facto refugees form a substantial proportion of irregular entrants and residents in European countries." Among the range of factors explaining this, the study identifies "distrust of state asylum determination procedures, reluctance to be detained, and fears about return." Moreover, "restrictive measures force legitimate refugees into illegal activities to enter the state in the first place." This "illegal refugee" phenomenon leads to a privatizing of assistance, since the burden of housing, welfare, and health care is put on relatives, ethnic communities, and NGOs.

Imprisoned immigrants

Many individuals who cross borders illegally are placed in immigration prisons or detention centres, where their human and legal needs are great. This occurs both in rich countries such as Australia, the United States, or Germany and in developing world locations such as Thailand or Zambia. A proportion of these migrants have an arguable claim to asylum as refugees. Their detention is at once a symptom of the breakdown in the international system protecting refugees and an indication of many countries' failure to "manage" migration. In Western countries, punitive measures such as detention are used to cultivate electoral support or because constructive responses to the presence of foreigners are too elusive. For NGOs in some countries, there is a conflict between publicly protesting against the inadequacies and even injustices of the detention system, and working quietly to assist those who are detained.

Often, if an individual or an agency takes the former course they are barred access to the facility. For detainees, stress exacerbates any pre-existing social, psychological, spiritual, and medical problems, once again placing the onus on community groups and NGOs to assist.

The demand for increased professionalism

As the range and complexity of NGOs' tasks grow, as well as the amount of funds that they control, there is a demand for increased professionalism among NGOs. This applies both to the standards by which needs are measured or by which services are established and evaluated, and to the professional competence of the personnel engaged by NGOs.

Professional formation

Over the past 10 years, professional formation programmes have blossomed. Masters-level formation is available at the Refugee Studies Centre at Oxford University, the Centre for the Study of International Migration at Georgetown University, at Deusto University in Bilbao, Spain, and at a dozen other universities, including quite a number in Africa, where refugee studies programmes are often linked with law departments. Many serious NGOs profit from these links to university centres to promote better training and also to have more solid research data and investigation skills on which to base programme planning, monitoring, and evaluation.

Setting standards

A number of major international NGOs have argued that, given the right of aid recipients to quality care, certain principles and standards should also be set. They established the Sphere Project to do precisely this, publishing a draft document outlining a Humanitarian Charter and Minimum Standards in the late 1990s.[9] This set standards for the care sectors of water supply, sanitation, nutrition, food aid, shelter and site management, and health services. A subsequent edition added standards regarding gender and protection.

Several humanitarian organizations – predominantly French NGOs[10] – have distanced themselves from the Sphere initiative. Of course they are not opposed to minimum standards, but they object when these become rules rather than tools of reflection. "Putting the respect for principles above all else stifles the search for innovative ways with which to best access people in need," argue Médecins sans Frontières.[11] They claim that, by concentrating on high technical standards, these standards distract from the crucial issues confronting humanitarian organizations, namely protection against *refoulement* or attack, and they do not assist the agencies to confront ethical dilemmas, such as how one can remain silent when witnessing diversion of humanitarian aid or human rights abuses. Another objection raised against the Sphere standards project is that agencies risk losing their independence when governments set adherence to standards as a condition for receiving funding.

Apart from the NGO-led Sphere Project initiative, there have been some other important standards-setting efforts, which are relevant to NGOs as well as to international organizations. The UNHCR's *Handbook on Procedures and Criteria for Determining Refugee Status* has been a bible not only for UNHCR officials but also for governments, and is a useful document for NGOs. The *Guidelines on the Protection of Refugee Women and Refugee Children*, also produced by UNHCR, provides an important human rights framework for the care and protection of refugee women and children. The *Guiding Principles on Internal Displacement*, prepared by the Representative of the UN Secretary-General on Internally Displaced Persons, does not help an agency in knowing how to get access to the displaced in the complex and dangerous situations in which they are to be found. Nonetheless it is a useful first step since it outlines responsibilities.

Professional associations also exist, principally for the purpose of coordination of activities. There are important national bodies, such as Interaction in the United States and the Australian Council for Overseas Aid (ACFOA) in Australia. In Europe, the European Council on Refugees and Exiles (ECRE) groups the myriad agencies active with asylum seekers who reach Europe, but it also includes some NGOs working in countries of origin. National refugee councils also exist in many countries and they too provide a focal point for the dialogue between national NGOs and the government. These associations often also reach agreement, both formally and informally, on certain codes of conduct and ways of working.

Conclusion

The world is paradoxically both more intimately interconnected and more painfully divided than ever before. The means of travel and communication are more sophisticated and more available, yet great numbers of people are being excluded from communities and made refugees or forced migrants. NGOs arise precisely because of these divisions, and they are aided by the means of communication that a globalized world makes available. NGOs generally rise out of and draw their material strength and motivation from interest groups that view the world from an ethical perspective. Their success often comes from their flexibility and capacity to innovate in response to needs, as well as from their ability to form alliances among themselves but also with other interest groups such as ethnic associations, workers, students, and religious groups. In serving forcibly displaced people, their roles differ from those of governments and international organizations, yet they provide a needed complement to them. While acknowledging the painful factors that give rise to the NGOs, we can give thanks that they are growing, acknowledge their focus on the human and ethical aspects, and rejoice in the initiatives for service and cooperation that they represent.

Notes

1. William Shawcross, *Deliver Us From Evil*, London: Bloomsbury, 2000, p. 12.
2. UNHCR, *Global Consultations – Agenda for Protection*, at www.unhcr.ch.
3. Médecins Sans Frontières website, at www.msf.org.
4. Interview with Michael Posner, *Advisor*, Newsletter of the Lawyers' Committee for Human Rights, vol. 5, no. 2, Spring 2001.
5. MSF draws this distinction. These NGOs are free to select the means that will help them achieve their mission, whereas the mandates under which international organizations work limit their choices of means.
6. *Refugees: A Challenge to Solidarity*, Vatican City, 1992.
7. *Guiding Principles on Internal Displacement*, 1998, available from the UN's Office for the Coordination of Humanitarian Affairs (OCHA). English, French, and Spanish versions are posted on the website of OCHA at www.unhchr.com.
8. Matthew J. Gibney, "Outside the Protection of the Law: The Situation of Irregular Migrants in Europe," RSC Working Paper no. 6, December 2000 – a synthesis report commissioned by the Jesuit Refugee Service Europe and produced by the Refugee Studies Centre, Oxford.
9. See the Sphere Project website at www.sphereproject.org.
10. Fiona Terry, "The Limits and Risks of Regulation Mechanisms for Humanitarian Action," *Humanitarian Exchange*, no. 17, October 2000.
11. Ibid.

Contributors

B. S. Chimni is Professor of International Law at the School of International Studies, Jawaharlal Nehru University, New Delhi. He has been a Fulbright Visiting Scholar at the Harvard Law School (1995–1996) and a Law Fellow at the Centre for Refugee Studies, University of York, Canada (1993). He was a member of the Academic Advisory Committee of the Office of the United Nations High Commissioner for Refugees from 1997 to 2000. His most recent publication is *International Refugee Law: A Reader* (Sage, 2000). He is on the international advisory boards of several national and international journals, including the *Indian Journal of International Law, International Studies*, the *Journal of Refugee Studies, Georgetown Immigration Law Journal*, and the *Refugee Survey Quarterly*.

Patricia Weiss Fagen is a Senior Associate at the Institute for the Study of International Migration (ISIM), Georgetown University, USA. Until recently she was an official of the United Nations High Commissioner for Refugees, serving as Public Information Officer in Washington DC and Chief of Mission in El Salvador. She has also held senior secondments or positions at the United Nations Research Institute for Social Development and at the World Bank. Before entering UNHCR, Dr. Fagen was a professor of history at San Jose State University, California. Among her publications are *Exiles and Citizens. Spanish Republicans in Mexico* (University of Texas Press, 1973); *Central Americans in Mexico and the United States* (with Sergio Aguayo, Centre for Immigration Policy and Refugee

Assistance, 1989); *Fear at the Edge: State Terror and Resistance in Latin America* (co-edited, Georgetown University Press, 1992); and "El Salvador: Lessons in Peace Consolidation," in Tom Farer, ed., *Beyond Sovereignty: Defending Democracy in the Americas* (Johns Hopkins University Press, 1996). Dr. Fagen received her Ph.D. in history from Stanford University.

Mervyn Frost studied law and political philosophy at the University of Stellenbosch, South Africa, before going up to Oxford on a Rhodes Scholarship. Prior to taking up a Chair of International Relations at the University of Kent at Canterbury, UK, he was Professor of Politics and Head of Department at the University of Natal in Durban, South Africa. He was president of the South African Political Science Association from 1992 to 1994. For the past 20 years he has been an active scholar in the field of normative international relations theory. His major publications are: *Towards a Normative Theory of International Relations* (Cambridge University Press, 1986), *Ethics in International Relations* (Cambridge University Press, 1996), and *Constituting Human Rights: Global Civil Society and the Society of Democratic States* (Routledge, 2002). He has published articles on ethics in international relations in the journals *Political Studies, Review of International Studies, Millennium: Journal of International Studies,* the *Cambridge Review of International Affairs, Paradigms,* and *Politikon.*

Khalid Koser is Lecturer in Human Geography at University College London and a member of the

Migration Research Unit. He is co-editor of *New Approaches to Migration* (Routledge, 2002), *The End of the Refugee Cycle?* (Berghahn, 1999), and *The New Migration in Europe* (Macmillan, 1998).

Gil Loescher is Senior Fellow for Migration, Forced displacement and International Security at the International Institute for Strategic Studies (IISS), in London. For 25 years he was Professor of International Relations at the University of Notre Dame, USA. He has been a consultant for the United Nations High Commissioner for Refugees, the European Council on Refugees and Exiles in London, the Ford Foundation, and the US government, among others, and has held visiting research appointments at Princeton University, Oxford University, the London School of Economics, and the IISS in London. For several years, he chaired the Academic Advisory Committee of the UNHCR's report *The State of the World's Refugees* and served as an adviser to the UNHCR to establish a policy research unit in Geneva. His most recent book is *The UNHCR and World Politics: A Perilous Path* (Oxford University Press, 2001). His other major publications include: *Beyond Charity: International Cooperation and the Global Refugee Problem* (A Twentieth Century Fund book, Oxford University Press, 1996); *Calculated Kindness: Refugees and America's Half-Open Door* (Free Press, 1986); *Refugee Movements and International Security* (International Institute for Strategic Studies, 1992); *Refugees and*

International Relations (edited, Oxford University Press, 1990); and *The Moral Nation: Humanitarianism and US Foreign Policy* (University of Notre Dame Press, 1990), as well as other books and articles. He holds a Ph.D. in international relations from the London School of Economics and Political Science.

William Maley is Professor and Foundation Director of the Asia-Pacific College of Diplomacy at the Australian National University, having taught for many years in the School of Politics, University College, University of New South Wales. He has served as a Visiting Professor at the Russian Diplomatic Academy, a Visiting Fellow at the Centre for the Study of Public Policy at the University of Strathclyde, UK, and a Visiting Research Fellow in the Refugee Studies Programme at Oxford University. He is also a Barrister of the High Court of Australia, Chair of the Refugee Council of Australia, and a member of the Australian Committee of the Council for Security Cooperation in the Asia Pacific. Dr. Maley is author of *The Afghanistan Wars* (Palgrave Macmillan, 2002); co-author of *The Theory of Politics: An Australian Perspective* (Longman Cheshire, 1990), *Regime Change in Afghanistan: Foreign Intervention and the Politics of Legitimacy* (Westview Press, 1991), *Political Order in Post-Communist Afghanistan* (Lynne Rienner, 1992), and *The Australian Political System* (Longman Australia, 1st edn 1995, 2nd edn 1998). He edited *Dealing with Mines: Strategies for Peace-keepers, Aid Agencies and the International Community* (Australian Defence Studies Centre, 1994),

Shelters from the Storm: Developments in International Humanitarian Law (Australian Defence Studies Centre, 1995), and *Fundamentalism Reborn? Afghanistan and the Taliban* (New York University Press, 1st edn 1998, 2nd edn 2001); and co-edited *The Soviet Withdrawal from Afghanistan* (Cambridge University Press, 1989), *The Transition from Socialism: State and Civil Society in the USSR* (Longman, 1991), and *Russia in Search of Its Future* (Cambridge University Press, 1995).

Peter Mares is a journalist with the Radio Australia and Radio National networks of the Australian Broadcasting Corporation. He has reported on Asian and Pacific affairs for the ABC for more than 14 years and has a long-standing interest in refugee issues. He is the author of *Borderline: Australia's Treatment of Refugees and Asylum Seekers* (University of New South Wales Press, 2001) and is a visiting fellow at the Institute for Social Research at Swinburne University of Technology in Melbourne.

Julie Mertus is a Senior Fellow at the US Institute of Peace and an Assistant Professor in the Department of International Peace and Conflict Resolution, American University, School of International Service. She is the author of *War's Offensive on Women: The Humanitarian Challenge in Bosnia, Kosovo and Afghanistan* (Kumarian Press, 2000), *Kosovo: How Myths and Truths Started a War* (University of California Press, 1999), and *Local Action/Global Change: Learning about the Human Rights of Women and Girls* (UNIFEM, 1999).

Erin D. Mooney has been engaged with the issue of internal displacement both as a scholar and as a practitioner for the past decade. Currently based at the School of Advanced International Studies (SAIS) of Johns Hopkins University in Washington DC, she is the Deputy Director of the Brookings Institution–SAIS Project on Internal Displacement and a Special Adviser to the Representative of the United Nations Secretary-General on Internally Displaced Persons. From 1995 to 2001, she worked for the Office of the United Nations High Commissioner for Human Rights in Geneva, serving as a focal point for issues of forced migration and as the Special Assistant to the Representative of the Secretary-General on Internally Displaced Persons. Her Master's and Ph.D. at the University of Cambridge examined international protection responses to deliberate displacement. She has held Visiting Fellowships at the Ecole Normale Supérieure in Paris and the European Centre for Minority Issues in Flensburg, Germany. Has published widely on issues of forced migration, human rights, and humanitarian action, and has also taught on these subjects at the University of Cambridge, Oxford University, and York University (Toronto) and at workshops in various countries of internal displacement.

Edward Newman is an Academic Officer in the Peace and Governance Programme of the United Nations University. He was educated in the United Kingdom at the University of Keele and the University of Kent, where he received a Ph.D.

in international relations. He has taught as a lecturer at Shumei University and Aoyama Gakuin University, both in Japan. He is also a founding executive editor of the journal *International Relations of the Asia Pacific*, published by Oxford University Press. Recent publications include *Recovering from Civil Conflict: Reconciliation, Peace, and Development* (co-edited, Frank Cass, 2002), *Democracy in Latin America: (Re)Constructing Political Society* (co-edited, United Nations University Press, 2001), *The United Nations and Human Security* (co-edited, Palgrave, 2001), *The UN Secretary-General from the Cold War to the New Era: A Global Peace and Security Mandate?* (Macmillan, 1998), *The Changing Nature of Democracy* (co-edited, United Nations University Press, 1998), and *New Millennium, New Perspectives: The United Nations, Security and Governance* (co-edited, United Nations University Press, 2000).

Gregor Noll (LL.D.) is an Assistant Professor of International Law at the Faculty of Law, Lund University, Sweden, and the editor-in-chief of the *Nordic Journal of International Law*. He has served as the research director at the Danish Centre for Human Rights, Copenhagen, and has taught international law, human rights law, and refugee law at graduate and postgraduate level in a variety of contexts. In 2000, he published his doctoral thesis on the compliance of the asylum *acquis* with norms of international law (*Negotiating Asylum*, Martinus Nijhoff Publishers). He also co-edited a volume on the effects of EU enlargement on asylum and migration policies (*New Asylum Countries?*, Kluwer Law International, 2002) and directed two studies on the externalized processing of asylum claims by states in the North (commissioned by the UNHCR and the EU Commission, respectively). In addition, he has published a number of articles on the issues of gender and persecution, democracy theory and refugee law, burden-sharing, the return of rejected asylum seekers, and the Dublin Convention.

Mark Raper is currently director of Uniya, the Jesuit Social Justice Centre, Sydney, Australia. Uniya is the administrative base of the Jesuit Refugee Service (JRS) in Australia. In 2000, Fr. Raper stood down after 10 years in service as the Rome-based International Director of the Jesuit Refugee Service. In 2000–2001, he was the holder of the Visiting Jesuit Chair in the School of Foreign Service at Georgetown University, USA. As International Director of JRS, Fr. Raper oversaw assistance to refugees and forcibly displaced people in some 60 countries. During the 1980s, as JRS's first regional director for Asia Pacific, he set up programmes in all of the camps for Cambodian, Lao, and Vietnamese refugees. In 2001 he was given the Order of Australia (AM) in recognition of his service to refugees and displaced people around the world for the previous 20 years.

Susanne Schmeidl is a Senior Research Analyst at the Swiss Peace Foundation (SPF). She received her Diploma in social work from the Evangelische Stiftungsfachhoch-

schule für Sozialpädagogik and her M.A. and Ph.D. in sociology from The Ohio State University, USA (1989 and 1995). She worked at the Centre for Refugee Studies (York University, Canada) as a post-doctoral researcher (1995–1996), coordinator of the Prevention/Early Warning Unit (1996–1997), and coordinator of the interim secretariat of the Forum on Early Warning and Early Response (1996–1997), and as a consultant for the Food and Statistics Unit of the UN High Commissioner for Refugees (Geneva, 1997). She has been active with the International Studies Association, serving in several positions, including chair (2000–2001) for the Ethnicity, Nationalism and Migration Section and the Peace Studies Section. Dr. Schmeidl joined the SPF in 1998 as a senior research analyst for FAST (Early Recognition of Tension and Fact Finding) and the team leader for South Asia. She has also worked as a consultant and resource person for the Inter Governmental Agency for Development and with the United Nations Development Programme in Romania to assist in setting up conflict early warning and response mechanisms in the Horn of Africa and South Eastern Europe.

Joanne van Selm is a Senior Policy Analyst at the Migration Policy Institute, Washington DC. She is also a Senior Researcher at the University of Amsterdam's Institute of Migration and Ethnic Studies. Dr. van Selm has published widely on temporary protection, European asylum policy, and other refugee- and migration-related topics. Her publications include: *Refugee*

Protection in Europe: Lessons of the Yugoslav Crisis (Kluwer Law International, 1997) and the edited volume, *Kosovo's Refugees in the European Union* (Continuum, 2000), as well as numerous articles and book chapters. Most recently, she has authored chapters on the perceptions of Kosovar refugees for *Kosovo: Perceptions of War and Its Aftermath* (Continuum, 2002) and on the EU's High Level Working Group on Migration and Asylum for a volume on the external impacts of EU immigration policy integration. She is also co-editor of the *Journal of Refugee Studies* and a member of the executive board of the International Association for the Study of Forced Migration. She holds an M.A. and Ph.D. in international relations from the University of Kent at Canterbury, UK.

Astri Suhrke is a Senior Research Fellow at the Chr. Michelsen Institute in Norway where she works on conflict, human security, refugees, and humanitarian assistance. She was a participant in the multi-donor evaluation of international assistance in the Rwanda emergency, and has written widely on the politics of humanitarian policies. Her most recent book is *Eroding Local Capacity.*

International Humanitarian Action in Africa, co-edited with Monica Kathina Juma (Nordic Africa Institute, 2003). Dr. Suhrke is a member of the Advisory Council on Humanitarian Affairs of the Norwegian Ministry of Foreign Affairs, and has a Ph.D. in international relations.

Gary G. Troeller is the United Nations High Commissioner for Refugees Regional Representative for the Baltic and Nordic Countries, Stockholm. Prior to his current assignment, he held senior posts with the UNHCR in Japan, Canada, Somalia, and Turkey and in the agency's HQ in Geneva. Before joining the UNHCR, he worked for the Battelle Institute, Frankfurt and Geneva; Chase Manhattan Bank, Frankfurt; and United Press International Brussels. He holds a Ph.D. in international relations from Cambridge Uni-versity and has been a Research Associate at St. Antony's College, Oxford University. Dr. Troeller has been a visiting professor in international relations at Japanese, Korean, and US universities, and he has authored, edited, and con-tributed to several books and written a number of articles for policy and academic journals and the media.

Index

Catalogue Request

Name: _____

Address: _____

Tel: _____

Fax: _____

E-mail: _____

To receive a catalogue of UNU Press publications kindly photocopy this form and send or fax it back to us with your details. You can also e-mail us this information. Please put "Mailing List" in the subject line.

United Nations University Press

53-70, Jingumae 5-chome
Shibuya-ku, Tokyo 150-8925, Japan
Tel: +81-3-3499-2811 Fax: +81-3-3406-7345
E-mail: sales@hq.unu.edu http://www.unu.edu